Jeep CJ
Rebuilder's Manual
1972 – 1986
by Moses Ludel

**Mechanical Restoration
Unit Repair and Overhaul
Performance Upgrades**

**for Jeep CJ-5, CJ-6, CJ-7
and CJ-8/Scrambler**

B BentleyPublishers™
.com

Table Of Contents

Disassembling Your Jeep, see Chapter 1

Engine Rebuilding, see Chapter 2

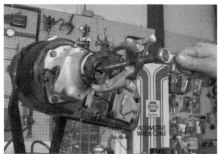

Transmission and Clutch, see Chapter 3

Transfer Case, see Chapter 4

Axle Rebuilding and Upgrades,
see Chapter 5

Electrical and Ignition System Upgrades, see Chapter 8

Fuel and Exhaust Systems, see Chapter 9

Accessories and Safety Equipment, see Chapter 10

Bentley Publishers, a division of Robert Bentley, Inc.
1734 Massachusetts Avenue
Cambridge, MA 02138 USA   Information that makes
800-423-4595 / 617-547-4170   the difference®

Bentley Publishers™
.com

Technical contact information
We value your feedback. Technical comments and suggestions are helpful to us. Please post your comments to our technical discussion forums:
www.BentleyPublishers.com/tech
From time to time, updates may be made to this book. A listing of updates can be found on the web at
www.BentleyPublishers.com/updates

Copies of this book may be purchased from most automotive accessories and parts dealers specializing in Jeep Vehicles, from selected booksellers, or directly from the publisher.

The publisher encourages comments from readers of this book. These communications have been and will be carefully considered in preparation of this and other books. Please contact Bentley Publishers at the address listed on the top of this page or e-mail us through our website.

This book was published by BentleyPublishers. Jeep/DaimlerChrysler does not vouch for the accuracy of the technical specifications and procedures described in this book.

Library of Congress Cataloging-in-Publication Data

Ludel, Moses .
Jeep CJ rebuilder's manual, 1972-1986 : mechanical restoration, unit repair and overhaul, performance upgrades for Jeep CJ-5, CJ-6, CJ-7, and CJ-8/Scrambler / by Moses Ludel. --1st ed.
    p. cm.
  ISBN 0-8376-0151-7 (pbk. : alk. paper)
  1. Jeep automobile--Maintenance and repair. 2. Antique and classic cars--Conservation and restoration. I. Title.

TL215.J4L8298 2003
  629.28' 722--dc22   2003018531

Bentley Stock No. GJR2

Editorial closing 04/03

11 10 09 08 07 06 10 9 8 7 6 5 4 3

The paper used in this publication is acid free and meets the requirements of the National Standard for Information Sciences-Permanence of Paper for Printed Library Materials. ∞

Front Cover: Photo by Jon Richard, 1974 Jeep CJ-5 Renegade provided by Eric Peltonen.
All other photography in this book is by Moses Ludel.

Introduction

Author's note: In the fall of 1992, the first edition of my **Jeep Owner's Bible** *reached the Jeep community. Support for the original book encouraged me to update material, include new Jeep vehicles and share aftermarket product developments. I wish to thank those readers who purchased and liked the first edition. Your enthusiasm inspired my line-by-line edit and revision of material, which appears in the newer edition.*

Whether your preference is a restored CJ-2A or a hybridized CJ-7, the manuals provide the information to fully rebuild the vehicle. Your safety and satisfaction with Jeep product were the primary aim in presenting the material.

My firsthand exposure to the CJ Jeep began with my parent's sparkling new, Spruce Green 1964 CJ-5. I earned my driver's license behind the Jeep's big steering wheel, and in the following years, we racked up thousands of dirt road miles with that cloth-topped, four-cylinder model.

I now have nearly forty years of Jeep experience, yet the distinctive drone of an F- or L-head 134 four-banger, or the low-range whine of Spicer's Model 18 transfer case, continues to grab my attention. As a journey-level mechanic, I have rebuilt, restored and upgraded a variety of CJ Jeep models, including an AMC -built 1981 CJ-5 that served as a step-by-step, serialized project in **OFF-ROAD Magazine**. There is no part of any 1946-86 CJ model that I do not know intimately.

For the 1972-86 Jeep CJ owner, this book will provide the details necessary to disassemble, rebuild and reassemble each of the vital components found in these models. Whether your aim is mechanical restoration, including gear and axle unit overhaul and repair procedures, or practical performance improvements, you will find the information you need.

Many CJ owners intend a stock-type restoration, and for that purpose, I offer details on properly rebuilding original equipment components. Additionally, this book describes the variety of upgrades that I find essential when making a Jeep CJ more versatile and safe---both on- and off-pavement.

The prototype vehicle for most of the mechanical work depicted within this book is a 1986 CJ-7, originally equipped with a four-cylinder engine and four-speed manual transmission. I disassembled and rebuilt the Jeep under the close scrutiny of my strobe lights and cameras. For this ambitious undertaking, I contracted the construction of a suitable shop, a facility that offers sufficient tooling and a garage-like studio backdrop.

The '86 CJ-7 provides an optimal prototype for the book's subject coverage. This last year CJ model featured many factory advances, yet the majority of its unit repair and rebuilding procedures apply equally well to the very first, 1972 AMC/Jeep CJs. Where technical differences between the various 1972-86 models occur, I draw attention to those details and offer coverage of the earlier sub-assemblies.

True to AMC/Jeep engineering and service standards, I painstakingly rebuilt major sub-assemblies of this vehicle. To satisfy builders of other AMC-era CJ models, I accessed and photographed the rebuilding of components not found in the '86 CJ-7, including the Spicer 20 transfer case and Dana/Spicer 44 rear axle.

Unlike the many hybridized Jeep vehicles, this '86 model still boasted its original engine and appearance items, which left me with a crucial choice: Should my buildup reuse the stock, original components? Or should I promote the proven modifications that affect safety, reliability and better backcountry performance?

For my standards, some modifications were essential. However, I also recognize the importance of sharing all aspects of original equipment repairs and sub-assembly overhaul. As you will discover, I elected to serve both the OEM restorer and those intent on building a more versatile and rugged trail runner and highway use vehicle. I believe CJ owners will appreciate and value the changes depicted.

The concept for providing step-by-step photos came from enthusiasts sharing that the typical technical manual does not supply an adequate number of illustrations or explanations. Such books, we know, rely largely on impassive words, with a limited number of photos or drawings.

Accepting the huge task of staging tightly sequenced photos, I set out to photograph each crucial step of a CJ Jeep buildup. Performing both the mechanical work and photo chores stretched my customary six-to-twelve month mechanical project into a three-year endeavor. In the end, I believe the result justifies the effort, as the builder can, at his or her own pace, use this book to rebuild a 1972-86 Jeep CJ from the bare frame up.

In the interest of those whose ambitions fall short of a bare-frame buildup, I have broken the book into sub-assembly chapters. Should your goal be a basic tune-up, an axle or transfer case overhaul, installation of a locking differential, or an entire mechanical restoration, the appropriate section offers necessary details. Whether your workplace is a well-lit garage or a lantern's light at a remote campsite, the table-of-contents and index will point the way.

Evolution of the '72-'86 AMC/Jeep CJs

In model years 1966-69, the Jeep CJ-5 and CJ-6 enjoyed brisk sales. The optional 'Dauntless'/Buick 225 V-6 had provided impressive performance in these lightweight chassis. American Motors Corporation (AMC) purchased Kaiser's Jeep Corporation in 1970 and continued to offer the classic F-head four and Buick V-6 engines through the 1971 models. 1972, however, would prove a significant change year for the popular CJ-5 and CJ-6 models.

AMC's involvement with Kaiser dated to the mid-'sixties. Kaiser had utilized the 232 AMC inline six as a standard powerplant, and the 327 AMC V-8 became an optional engine choice for J-trucks and full-size Wagoneers. Owners discovered the ruggedness and reliability of these engines. With the acquisition of Jeep Corporation, AMC made full use of its seven-main bearing 232 and 258 sixes and the evolved 304 and 360 V-8 engines.

Note: Kaiser's use of Buick's 225 V-6 and 350 V-8 engines was phased out by AMC after the 1971 model year. The 225 served in CJs, while J-trucks and Wagoneers offered the Buick 350 V-8 option.

The 304 and 360 V-8s were modern, lighter weight engines that had replaced the earlier 327 AMC design. Rugged inline 258 sixes provided more torque and horsepower than their counterpart 232 design, making the 258 flexible enough for J-truck use. Matched to these engine offerings were a variety of advances in geartrain and axle components.

1972 marked the launch of the first true AMC CJs, and this is where the ***Jeep CJ Rebuilder's Manual: 1972-86*** begins. The significant changes to the chassis, engine and geartrain abruptly ended the Willys/Kaiser Jeep era. Best of all, despite these technical advances, AMC did not compromise the legendary off-road capability of the CJ models.

Note: There were carryover Kaiser-engineered vehicles, 134 F-head four-cylinder powered models, available through 1973. Owners of these rare models should refer to the **Jeep CJ Rebuilder's Manual: 1946-71** for information on the F-head engine and other carryover components.

The lengthened wheelbase enabled installation of the 232 and 258 inline six-cylinder engines. A factory V-8 option, the durable AMC 304, offered the performance many buyers expected by 1972.

To meet the added weight and handling demands, Saginaw re-circulating ball-and-nut steering came on line, available in manual type or optional power-assisted version, a first for CJs. These gears remain the most reliable steering available for light truck use. Gone were the primitive Ross cam-and-lever and worm-and-roller manual steering gears. (Cam-and-lever steering dates to the WWII MBs!)

The Dana/Spicer open knuckle Model 30 front axle first appears in these 1972 CJs. This was timely, as the tighter turning radius of the open knuckle axle offers backcountry nimbleness even with the 3-inch longer wheelbases.

A rugged Dana/Spicer '44' rear axle assembly with one-piece, flanged axle shafts lines up directly behind a through-drive Spicer 20 transfer case. That, too, was a first for CJ Jeep models. 11"x2" brakes at each wheel were a milestone. Like the 304 V-8 option, these hefty brakes were the best performance offering to date for CJ models, rivaling the aftermarket brakes that owners often retrofitted to the earlier Willys/Kaiser CJs and their military counterpart models.

Overall, the new 1972 Jeep CJ-5 and CJ-6 (84" and 104" wheelbases, respectively) were better handling, more modern vehicles. Without compromising the traditional light truck ruggedness of CJs, these AMC offerings were an immediate success.

The model years 1972-86 presented a variety of changes and upgrades. Notably, the boxing of the frame rails with the 1976 CJ models was significant. '76-up frames offer more stamina than the open-section frames of '75 and earlier models.

During the 1977 model year, front disc brakes first appear on the CJ models. Disc front, drum rear brakes have distinct advantages, especially for stream fording and wet weather driving. The CJ-7, introduced in 1976, featured a 94" wheelbase that offers improvements in on-highway handling and overall vehicle stability. This optimal wheelbase length continues through the CJ, YJ/Wrangler and TJ/Wrangler eras! While some enthusiasts hold to the 84" wheelbase CJ-5 for tight-access backcountry rock crawling, the CJ-7 and 104" wheelbase CJ-8/Scrambler offer the kind of dual-purpose, on- and off-highway vehicles that many owners prefer.

The longer wheelbase CJ-7 allowed the first use of an automatic transmission in a factory CJ model. CJ-7s with Warner's chain drive 'Quadra-Trac' full-time four-wheel drive transfer case system feature General Motors' failsafe THM400 transmission. (This rugged transmission has served well in 'Class A' motorhomes!) Later, with the introduction of the Dana 300 transfer case in 1980, the durable Chrysler '909' and '999' automatic transmissions make the option list for CJ-7s and the '81-'86 CJ-8 chassis.

Component Overview

Dana 300 transfer cases feature helically cut, constant mesh gears for quieter, more reliable operation. These units also feature a lower ratio in low range (2.61:1 versus 2.03:1 in the Spicer Model 20 units). Iron cases and through-drive designs, both the Dana 300 and Spicer 20 transfer case units deliver exceptional service. The Dana 300 offers the kind of low range crawl ratios popular with seasoned backcountry users.

Few of the manual transmissions of the 1972-86 AMC/Jeep era stand out as optimal for off-pavement or severe duty use. While the three-speed all-synchromesh units (T14A, T15A or T150) of the '72-'79 models work well enough, their first gear ratios do not support extreme rock crawling, especially behind the Spicer 20 transfer case with its 2.03:1 low range ratio. Later ('80-up) T-4, SR-4, and T-5 transmissions have frailties, too, primarily their passenger car stamina and ratios. The T-176 holds favor with many owners, and this is a reasonably stout four-speed design.

As for ruggedness and utility, the T-18 Warner four-speed ranks high. Derived from the T-98 unit, this is a true truck transmission with a non-synchromesh compound first gear. A fresh T-18 holds up behind engines in excess of 300 horsepower. The 4.02:1 factory "close ratio" first gear is not the most desirable setup, however, and many T-18 changeovers involve the common Ford truck version that features a 6.32:1 first gear ratio. This swap requires an aftermarket retrofit kit yet still proves cost effective as a means for achieving a low crawl ratio.

So, Where Are We Going?

In building a CJ Jeep, few builders leave out the prospect of making changes to improve their vehicle. The Jeep CJ is unique in this regard, ranking among the most personalized vehicles in the world. Aside from the rare and historically significant Jeep models, few Jeep CJs remain in their original assembly line

form for long. This is especially true of AMC-era vehicles.

I took this into account when constructing the 1986 CJ-7 prototype for this book. The CJ-7 was nearly stock when I began, featuring the original AMC 2.5L four-cylinder engine and a Warner T-4 transmission. The engine had labored severely, trying to accommodate the owner's recreational interests by hauling a canoe, lugging an aftermarket hardtop around and attempting to pull 31"x10.50"x15" aftermarket tires with tall 3.54:1 axle ratios. Add to this a considerable number of stop-and-go Los Angeles freeway miles, and the 2.5L engine did okay. It lasted to 109,000 miles before losing oil pressure due to sludge buildup and a severe overheat.

Was it wise to simply rebuild the four-cylinder engine? Some might say, "Yes!" I drew on my years of interacting with Jeep CJ owners and their expectations. Opting for a 4.2L 258 six-cylinder engine, my buildup began. As you will see within this book, that staid four-cylinder, California emissions-equipped CJ-7 Jeep, a one-owner vehicle, was ready for improvements!

I tailored this vehicle buildup to meet the typical trail runner's needs. Painstakingly, I rebuilt the Jeep with many genuine Mopar parts, including the Mopar Performance EFI/MPI Conversion Kit to enhance the vehicle's versatility and performance. My careful selection of aftermarket components rounds out the finished Jeep, a CJ-7 now ready for another lifetime of hard work and play!

Note: **Chapter 9** includes the Mopar Performance EFI/MPI conversion and also my blueprint overhaul of an OEM Carter 'BBD' carburetor. A Mopar rebuild kit helped make a success of that carburetor overhaul.

Your plans may focus on basic restoration or state-of-the-art upgrades that turn a CJ Jeep into the ultimate backcountry access vehicle. Either approach requires professional level standards---at the shop, your home or, if necessary, alongside a remote trail. Work like axle and geartrain rebuilding can be expensive, or in the most awkward case, you could be so far from a quality service outlet that money is of no value. Within this book, you will find the information needed to rebuild these components for safe and reliable service.

I believe a determined owner can master these skills and properly build a gear system, axle or any other component of a CJ Jeep. Whether you do so in your garage or fifty miles from nowhere on a primitive trail, this book provides the vital steps needed to disassemble, inspect and rebuild the crucial components of your Jeep vehicle.

If you intend to access remote backcountry, I highly recommend that you keep this manual in your onboard toolbox. On the trail, far from home and civilization, the information contained here could very well save a life. On a cliff-hanging switchback in low-range four-wheel drive, the reliability of your Jeep's mechanical and safety components proves just as critical as your driving prowess.

The Jeep Mechanic

Considering the remoteness of backcountry travel, a Jeep mechanic must be innovative and resourceful. Throughout this book, I share ways that you can simplify tasks through the use of readily available devices. In some instances, original factory-recommended tools no longer exist or prove too expensive for occasional use. Here, I offer numerous suggestions on how you can attain professional results with inexpensive alternatives and even homemade tools.

Within this book, you will find references to parts sources. I maintain high standards when it comes to restorative work on my Jeep vehicles. Fortunately, at the time of this printing, many Genuine Mopar parts from DaimlerChrysler/Jeep Corporation are still available for the AMC-era CJs. The commonality of AMC parts and ample production numbers for these vehicles offer assurance that price competitive factory and aftermarket parts will be available for years to come.

Rugged simplicity is a hallmark of all Jeep CJ models, and for that reason, popular parts sources will continue to provide components for these utility vehicles. Consider the parts sources described within the book. Your Jeep vehicle deserves OEM or equivalent quality parts. Save yourself extra work. Buy the best parts available.

In presenting the *Jeep CJ Rebuilder's Manual: 1972-86*, I trust that your emerging skills as a Jeep mechanic will create the kind of safe, reliable vehicles that my family has enjoyed for four decades. When you head for the outback to discover your Jeep's spirit, please join us in driving safely and promoting Tread Lightly!

Chapter 1

Disassembling Your Jeep

1

A Place to Start

Depending upon your Jeep's condition, a rebuild can be as simple as a powertrain renewal or as complex as complete disassembly of the vehicle. If your Jeep CJ has years of trail use and wear, a frame-off rebuild might well be in order.

The disassembly process is relatively fast and straightforward, as the photo-steps in this chapter indicate. Deceptively, the teardown to sub-assembly level may take no more than a couple of weekends, especially with the use of air tools. Many Jeep restorers then discover that the reconditioning of parts, metal and paint finishing, unit repair/overhaul and re-assembly of the vehicle may take months, sometimes even years, of detailed work.

In the rush to complete the disassembly, parts and hardware can get mixed. Months after disassembling a Jeep, few builders can remember the precise attachment point for each nut and bolt. To avoid trouble, separate and label hardware in plastic jugs or coffee cans. *If necessary, loosely install hardware in its original location.*

Before stripping your CJ to the bare frame, carefully evaluate whether your Jeep needs this degree of work. If so, designate a large, unobstructed area for laying out parts. Start your project by thoroughly steam cleaning the entire vehicle.

> *CAUTION—*
> * *Before fiddling with wires or the fuel tank, the battery must be disconnected or, better yet, removed from the vehicle.*
> * *Handle the battery carefully. If the battery is worn out, dispose of it at a recycling outlet.*
> * *Before disassembling a Jeep, drain all fluids from the cooling system, axles, engine, transmission and transfer case.*
> * *Avoid exposure to the coolant and lubricants. Wear latex gloves.*
> * *Dispose of drained oil, coolant and brake fluid in an environmentally safe manner.*

 Fig. 1-1

View from the rear undercarriage: An '86 CJ-7 at 109,000 miles of moderate trail and freeway driving. This is a one-owner, 2.5L four-cylinder model with an aftermarket hardtop.

◁ **Fig. 1-2**

Through-drive '80-'86 Dana 300 transfer case sets much like the '72-'79 Spicer 20. Broad skid plate serves as an engine mounting crossmember. Original catalytic converter hints of a stone stock vehicle, a great starting point. This vehicle has never been apart!

◁ **Fig. 1-3**

Years of debris, grit and oil make access to hardware difficult. Unless you want a grimy shop or garage, steam clean the undercarriage before disassembling your Jeep. Make the job appealing, and avoid handling greasy, oily parts!

> **CAUTION—**
> * Identify the transmission, transfer case and axle housing drain plugs. (Later differentials have no drain plug and require removal of the inspection covers for draining.) Aged gear oil is foul smelling and very difficult to clean up. Use suitable drain pans and avoid spills. Wear latex mechanic's gloves. Allow oil to drain completely. This will make disassembly and clean-up much easier. Spare the rags!
> * When steam cleaning your Jeep, avoid or pass gently over areas like the electrical connectors, electrical tape or soft items like the glovebox and seats. Keep water out of the gear systems.

◁ **Fig. 1-4**

This is the typical view of a late-'77 to'86 CJ front end with "open knuckle" Dana 30 axle and disc brakes. '72 to early-'77 looks much the same but with drum brakes. Saginaw manual steering gear is a radical improvement over earlier Willys/Kaiser cam-and-lever and worm-and-roller gears.

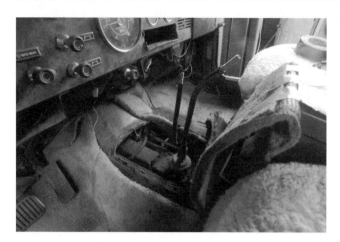

 Fig. 1-5

Carpet needs replacement on this vehicle. Remove the shift knobs and rubber boots, then the floorpan insert. If you intend to reuse carpet or mat, loosen the carpet carefully and lift it over the levers. I opted for carefully cutting the worn out carpet, which will be replaced.

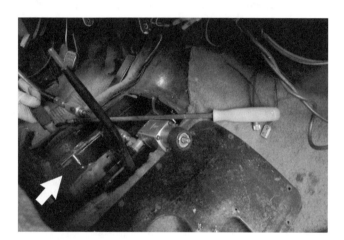

Fig. 1-6

T-4's transmission shifter with top plate (**ARROW**) comes out next. Unless you intend to disassemble and clean the transmission, *make certain you do not drop debris into the open cavity of the transmission.*

Fig. 1-7

After thirty years of rolling around on creepers, I built a shop with a hoist to accommodate the *Jeep CJ Rebuilder's Manual* projects. Here, I use a 2-ton capacity tripod safety stand to support the transfer case/transmission while removing the skid plate crossmember. Working from this position is very much appreciated.

1

 Fig. 1-8

Most mechanics remove the two driveshafts first. I wanted to present this view, which also gave easier access to the forward U-joint flange and transfer case shift linkage. Note the relationship of the transfer case and transmission.

CAUTION—

If you remove the driveshafts last, support the transfer case securely before attempting to loosen the drivelines! When removing driveshafts, keep track of U-joint straps, bolts or U-bolts and nuts. Place hardware in its original location or label the pieces. You may need to carefully pry the joints loose from the yoke flanges. When doing so, do not pry against the delicate U-joint seals or any machined surfaces on the yoke. Keep U-joint bearing caps in place, and secure them with duct tape.

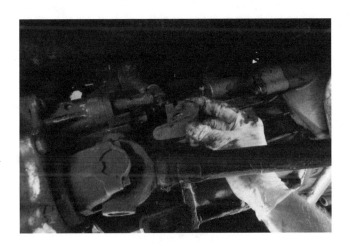

◀ **Fig. 1-9**

Here, I remove the shifter linkage. Two tiny cotter pins, two pivot pins, and this piece comes out. A bit more steam cleaning might have helped.

◀ **Fig. 1-10**

Large pin clip secures shifter pivot shaft. Hold the shaft with an open-ended wrench while removing the acorn (wheel type) nut. Shift lever is now free, and parts can be eased from the chassis.

 Fig. 1-11

Use a hex-head (six-point) socket to remove the U-joint strap bolts. These bolts can be tough to loosen, and you don't want a rounded head or broken socket! Slide the joints away from their yoke flanges.

◄ **Fig. 1-12**

Here, I carefully strap the transfer case and transmission to my ½-ton transmission jack. This is a precaution that I do not overlook. The jack makes this work easy and reduces risk of damage or physical injury. If you don't have a jack, consider renting one.

◄ **Fig. 1-13**

Clutch slave cylinder out of the way, unbolt the transmission from the bellhousing. The jack will support the weight and keep the transmission input gear and front bearing retainer from becoming damaged.

CAUTION—

When handling bellhousing (clutch housing) and clutch parts, keep track of hardware and note lengths of bolts.

Warning: Hazardous Clutch and Brake Materials

When servicing or working around clutch or brake parts, beware of clutch lining material and dust. The AMC-era Jeep CJs have asbestos content in these friction materials. Do not use air tools around asbestos-content dust! The OEM Jeep clutch lining contains asbestos fibers, and these slough off into the housing as the clutch wears.

When removing the bellhousing and clutch cover, use hand tools to reduce the dust hazard. Loosen clutch cover bolts a slight amount at a time to relieve pressure evenly. This will prevent warpage of springs and the clutch cover.

AUTHOR'S TIP!

I wear an asbestos-rated dust respirator when working around the bellhousing, clutch and flywheel! Soaking this area with a soapy water solution helps contain the dust. Always protect yourself from exposure to asbestos fibers and dust. Soak up and dispose of asbestos residue with extreme care. This applies to clutch, brake and some engine gaskets found on CJ Jeep vehicles.

Holding asbestos in an aqueous solution is one method of containment. Once the liquid dries, however, asbestos returns to being a dust hazard. Follow O.S.H.A. and E.P.A. hazardous waste guidelines when handling asbestos products. Shops use special aqueous solution brake and clutch parts washers to reduce risk of asbestos exposure.

Wherever possible, use recommended non-asbestos replacement linings for brakes shoes, pads, a clutch disc or the engine's cylinder head or exhaust system gaskets. As of this writing, asbestos brake and clutch materials are still in the marketplace. Specify non-asbestos materials when buying replacement parts, and read the labels carefully.

1

◁ Fig. 1-14

The engine mounts are well enough balanced that the exhaust system easily holds the block near level. There is no risk of damaging parts here.

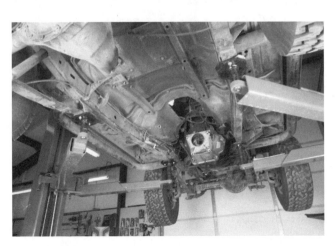

◁ Fig. 1-15

This view depicts the transmission and transfer case removed from the vehicle with plenty of space and room to maneuver. This is the appealing aspect of Jeep work! If a clutch job were underway here, you would unbolt the bellhousing next, exposing the clutch assembly.

 Fig. 1-16

Loosen the radiator hoses, and remove the radiator. Disconnect wires, battery cables, fuel hoses and anything else tying the engine into the engine bay. Hook up and lightly tension the engine hoist before loosening the exhaust system and motor mounts. When all is clear and free, carefully lift the engine from the chassis.

 Fig. 1-17

Tilt and lift the engine over the radiator core support and grille. If you have an Oberg cable tilt or equivalent, this task can be simplified. The Oberg unit makes steep angles possible and protects sheet metal from damage. Always lift slowly and methodically.

Front Clip and Body Tub Removal

For the early CJs covered in *Jeep CJ Rebuilder's Manual: 1946-1971*, I opted to strip the 1955 CJ-5 to its bare frame. Fewer '72-'86 CJs require such an approach. For most AMC/Jeep CJs, the focus is axle, powertrain and chassis work. The '86 CJ-7 had rust-free sheet metal and did not require body removal from the frame. The body removal shown in the following section involves my '55 CJ-5 and is representative of steps common for all tub-off-the-frame CJ projects. I have included this information for builders needing to remove their Jeep's body tub.

◁ **Fig. 1-18**

First step in disassembly is hood removal. Author's friend Brent demonstrates use of a coffee can for hardware. If necessary, label the can and hardware, or loosely re-install hardware in original locations.

◁ **Fig. 1-19**

Following hood removal, Brent loosens and detaches upper and lower radiator hoses. Strategy is to remove front "clip" (grille/fenders) as an assembly. On a CJ, this can include the grille, radiator, fenders and related parts.

◁ **Fig. 1-20**

At center base of grille, detach the front core support bolt and hardware. Body parts will still rest on cushion mount.

1

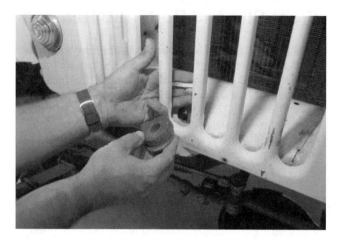

 Fig. 1-21

Keep cushions and washers with the mounting bolt for re-assembly.

Fig. 1-22

Upper core support rods detach readily. Mark location of nuts on rods before loosening. This will ease adjustment of the core support/front clip when you re-assemble the body.

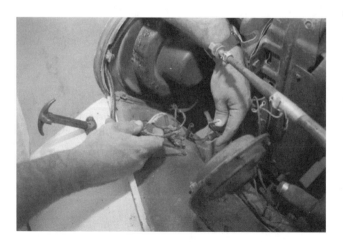

Fig. 1-23

Follow wires to fender junctions. Identify wires that will stay with the chassis and those that come loose with the front clip. Note cloth wire deterioration of early 6-volt wiring. This CJ needs a re-wiring job! Many AMC/Jeep CJs also need wiring attention.

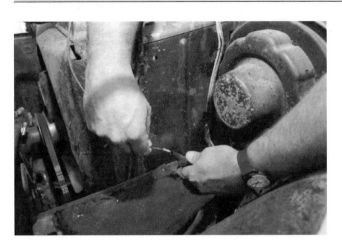

Fig. 1-24

All wire disconnect points are not at junction blocks. Look for individual wire connectors between the body and frame. Visualize any wire that will not remain with the front clip. Mark wires with masking tape and felt-tip pen notations, using a numbering system for re-assembly later.

Fig. 1-25

After loosening the fender-to-body tub attaching bolts, Brent carefully rolls the front clip forward, making certain that parts are ready for removal. The pieces of the front clip remain intact.

Fig. 1-26

Two adults can lift the front clip assembly free of the frame. If too awkward, consider using an engine hoist or chain fall. Use of nylon straps will help protect paint and trim.

 Fig. 1-27

Remaining core support hardware is here. Note steel sleeve that fits through elongated frame slot on this earlier model CJ. Remember to keep related hardware together!

Fig. 1-28

Brent scans open engine area. Front clip set aside, access to engine and body tub is relatively easy now.

Fig. 1-29

As with other wiring, identify frame harnesses and body tub attachments. Here, headlight dimmer switch attaches to tub while wiring runs along frame. Using firewall opening in this application, detach dimmer switch from floorboard, keeping wiring intact.

 Fig. 1-30

Here, another wire bundle travels from the frame to body tub. If wires will be reused, masking tape and a numbering system can help identify matches. Time spent labeling wires will save considerable energy later!

NOTE—

Electricians use adhesive numbers to mark and label wiring at junctions. When disassembling wire harnesses, consider such a tagging method. See an electrical supply for numbering kits. Most AMC/Jeep CJ wiring is topside of the tub floor, by design more resistant to damage.

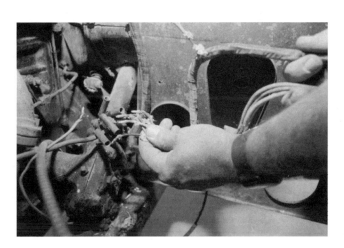

◀ **Fig. 1-31**

This harness disconnects with multiple wire connectors. Note poor condition of vintage cloth-wrapped wire. Later CJs' plastic wiring is better, with convolution tubing as a protective barrier. Still, you should inspect wiring carefully and be prepared for a re-wiring job if your electrical system looks like this!

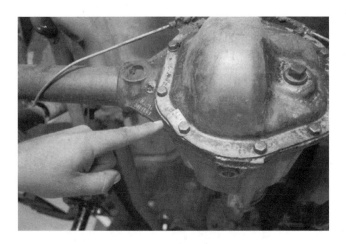

◀ **Fig. 1-32**

Tags like axle ratio (ring/pinion tooth count) should be noted and preserved. 5.38:1 ratio is OEM on this '55 CJ-5. Note the aftermarket brake pipe wrapped improperly around left axle tube! This inherited mess will be remedied during restoration phase.

CAUTION—

*I avoid a frame-off restoration if possible. With my '55 CJ-5 project, the tub removal was not as difficult or busy as the '72-'86 CJs. If you must remove the body tub, do so with extreme care. Cleanliness is essential when loosening the brake master cylinder and clutch cylinder pipes. (See **Chapter 7** for details.) Cap off tubes and cylinders to prevent contamination. Remove the steering shaft and any other hardware linking the body and frame. This includes the fuel filler neck and any hoses or wiring that span the frame and body. Note that I did not remove the front clip or tub when rebuilding the '86 CJ-7.*

 Fig. 1-33

Remove all body cushion bolts and carefully lift the tub from the drivable chassis. Here, the hefty chassis hoist served nicely! You may find a come-along and nylon straps will do, perhaps using an old swing set as an A-frame. Note that on this vintage Jeep, the solid steering column and gear were detached from the chassis before lifting the body free.

Fig. 1-34

Term "drivable chassis" is clear. Install the steering gear, a fuel tank, pedals and linkages, and this Jeep could conceivably move along. The relationship of parts is evident here. Notably, the vintage Willys/Kaiser CJs were simpler than the more modern AMC/Jeep models.

Fig. 1-35

Willys/Kaiser era CJs boasted a busy array of shift levers. The four sticks shown account for the transmission, transfer case (2 levers) and an aftermarket Warn overdrive lever.

NOTE—

*On this vintage CJ, the three-speed T-90 transmission coupled to the two-speed Model 18 transfer case and a two-speed (25%) overdrive offers 12 forward speeds and four reverse speeds! The Model 18's use of a PTO outlet and side-drive design provides for the novel use of overdrive. The AMC Jeep CJs do not have a provision for the transfer case mounted Warn/Saturn overdrive. In the 1980s, the lighter duty T-5 transmission provided a fifth gear overdrive option for many CJs. AMC-era CJ owners often opt for an upgrade 'World Class' T-5 retrofit or even the NV3550 and NV4500 five-speed type transmissions. See **Chapter 3** for further details.)*

◀ **Fig. 1-36**

Early Jeep has a solid steering shaft that rises from the gear. Your '72-'86 model has a more modern shaft design with provision for uncoupling the shaft when either removing the steering column or lifting the body from the frame. The steering gear can remain attached to the chassis.

◀ **Fig. 1-37**

Willys/Kaiser and AMC CJs were assembled in similar fashion. The body went on last, after the engine, axles, wheel, and geartrain systems were in place. Recall that the earliest versions of these vehicles were built for wartime service. Endearing quality is ease of service access and simplicity. Two of us had the complete body off the chassis in mere hours. This process is somewhat more involved with AMC-era CJs.

Disassembly of the Chassis

NOTE—

Your hand tool set will expand during the buildup of your Jeep. You will discover, for example, that to do this kind of work properly, you cannot use a pickle fork or pry bar to remove a reusable steering joint! The resulting damage will render the joint useless. Two-jaw or specialty tie-rod pullers make the best tools for this task...Loosening tapered studs of any kind requires a puller or appropriate force. One method for loosening steering joint studs is to hold a heavy steel hammer on one side of the steering arm's rounded end; with a similar hammer, apply a sharp blow to the opposing side. Essentially, you are squeezing the area where the stud seats in the arm. This effect will usually pop the stud loose. Use extreme care not to damage parts in the process. Wear safety goggles! If excessive force is required, use a suitable puller.

WARNING—

Do not attempt to drive ball studs loose with a hammer atop the stud! Pickle forks damage rubber or dust seals. Use of proper tools prevents damage to reusable, expensive parts.

CAUTION—

Wear eye protection when using punches, hammers and pullers. Parts under pressure can sometimes shear or scatter debris.

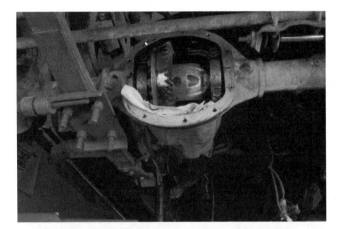

◄ **Fig. 1-38**

Transfer case/transmission assembly and the engine/clutch assembly are now set aside safely for further teardown and service. *(See unit service sections of this book for details.)* Front axle drained for removal and service, I wipe up all remaining gear lube with disposable rags. This is the '86 CJ's original 3.54:1 ring-and-pinion gearset. Save all axle, transmission and transfer case identification tags!

◄ **Fig. 1-39**

Cotter pins and castellated nuts are common attachment hardware for Jeep steering linkage. To disconnect the steering linkage system, begin with removal of cotter pins and each castellated nut. I separate tie-rod joints with a two-jaw tie-rod end puller.

1

 Fig. 1-40

If you intend to remove the axle assemblies, you will need to detach the shock absorbers, U-bolts and spring plates. *Leave spring U-bolts and nuts in place until you have the axle strapped to a suitable jack!* Safely support the axle assembly before removing the shackle U-bolts and springs.

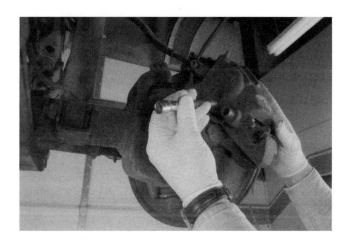

Fig. 1-41

Either disconnect the brake hose from the wheel cylinder or disc caliper, or remove the caliper with the hose attached. Leaving the hose attached to the caliper eliminates risk of debris getting into the system. Here, I elected to remove the caliper and hang it carefully out of the way with mechanic's wire.

CAUTION—

Do not let a brake caliper or backing plate hang loosely with the hose attached! Tie the assembly to the chassis in a way that will prevent pressure on the brake hoses and pipes. Mechanic's wire works well for this task.

WARNING—

*If you loosen a brake hose or pipe, make certain that no debris gets into the system! Always use a flarenut wrench on brake tube fittings! Cap off ends of hoses and pipes to prevent contamination and loss of brake fluid. Rubber vacuum caps or the plastic caps from hose fittings work well for this chore. (For details on brake work, see **Chapter 7**.) If brake fluid is very dirty, flush brake pipes with denatured alcohol before you install or re-attach the brake cylinders. (Air-dry pipes thoroughly before refilling the system with brake fluid.) Inspect pipes for kinks, deterioration, weakened seams and flare end damage.*

 Fig. 1-42

Gently pry the brake pads apart. There is a special spreader available for this task. This time, the caliper slid easily, and light pressure with a small pry bar was sufficient. *To prevent damage, do not pry against lining or disc piston!*

Fig. 1-43

On '86 CJ, I gently pry springs away from caliper and pads. Do not stretch or distort these springs.

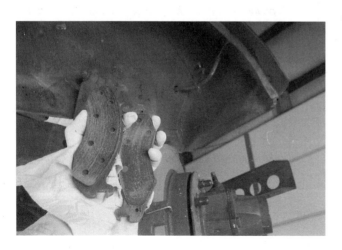

Fig. 1-44

Caliper removed and pads out, inspect the lining. If wear is evident, replace the pads before reinstalling the caliper.

 Fig. 1-45

Caliper is hung with hose relieved of any pressure. Perform same procedure on other end of the axle. Make certain that there is no risk of the axle moving while you are disassembling these parts.

> **CAUTION—**
>
> *Be certain to relieve spring tension before loosening or removing the shackles, springs or U-bolt! Springs should be fully suspended and unloaded. Jack is in place but not exerting force on the axle housing. If the jack is under pressure, you are at risk of the axle or spring unloading its tension when the U-bolt nuts come free.*

Fig. 1-46

Here, I have the Dana 30 front axle fully supported and strapped to my transmission jack. There is no weight bearing on the leaf spring as I loosen the front shackle and carefully allow the spring to swing out from under the axle housing. The axle is now free, and the springs can be safely detached from the chassis.

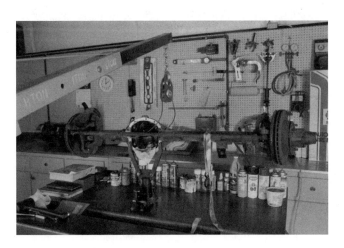

Fig. 1-47

Next place for the front axle assembly is on my workbench. I use Mark Williams Enterprises' "Bench Mule" for unit repair work. This highly versatile apparatus will support the axle assembly and permit easy rotation and tilting during overhaul procedure. *(See **Chapter 5** for details.)* This is a must item for the one-person shop!

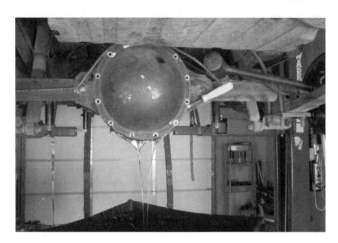

 Fig. 1-48

Rear axle oil drains into drain pan/tank. Model 20 AMC axle, used from '76-'86, is a rugged, readily serviceable unit. Its ring gear diameter of 8.875" is actually larger than the Dana/Spicer 44's 8.75".

◁ **Fig. 1-49**

Disconnecting the rear brake hose at the frame allows removal of the axle assembly with the brake backing plates and all piping in place. Note my use of a flarenut wrench for the pipe nut. I remove the retainer clip with a screwdriver.

CAUTION—

*Cap or tape the hose end to keep debris out of brake components. Before assembling hydraulic cylinders, you should flush and clean the brake system with denatured alcohol, then air-dry all parts thoroughly. (Refer to **Chapter 7** for further details.)*

◁ **Fig. 1-50**

Parking brake cables disconnect easily at the cable guide. The brake hose is taped or capped to prevent contaminants from entering the system. (Brake pipe at frame has been capped.) Spring plate/shock mounts have been unbolted. This axle is resting on the springs and ready to come out as a complete unit.

1

Fig. 1-51
Again, the hoist and transmission jack make my day! I supported the axle housing while carefully lowering the springs. I am able to safely perform this work alone without risk of injury. Note that the axle is complete, brake drum to drum.

Fig. 1-52
Entire powertrain and both axle assemblies are now free from the Jeep. The only wear items remaining on the vehicle would be the manual steering gear and column, brake and clutch master cylinders, clutch and brake pedals, gas tank, hoses, electrical switches and devices, wiring, seats, carpet and body mount cushions.

At this stage, the Jeep is ready for detailed inspection, unit repairs, subassembly rebuilding, plus useful upgrades and modifications. For this one-owner, four-cylinder CJ-7 at 109,000 miles, I elected not to remove the body tub or strip out the OEM wiring. An '86 Jeep from the Western region of the United States, the CJ-7 was free of rust perforation and in near-stock condition.

NOTE—
Many owners, especially from the Midwest and East Coast regions of the United States, will elect to replace or remove the body tub. For that reason, I have shared the body tub removal details from the '55 CJ-5 buildup found in **Jeep CJ Rebuilder's Manual: 1946-1971**.

Mechanical sub-assemblies safely detached, I backed my car-hauling trailer beneath the chassis. With 5-ton stands placed at appropriate frame points, I lowered the body/frame assembly onto the four-legged stands. Then I very carefully pulled the trailer out of my shop. The trailer on level and the Jeep body covered and protected with clean tarps, I left the CJ-7 outside the shop until I was ready to reassemble the vehicle.

CAUTION—
Use 5-ton capacity stands if you want to safely leave your Jeep on stands. Always use at least a 2-1/2-ton-rated floor jack for any lifting. If you or your Jeep club can afford a transmission jack, get one! If not, consider renting a transmission jack for tasks like removing the transfer case, transmission and axles. While your CJ Jeep may come apart quickly, reassembly could take months, or even years!

Chapter 2

Engine Rebuilding

Jeep Engines

The AMC-era CJs feature proven automotive engines. The seven-main bearing 232 and 258 cubic inch (4.2L) inline sixes came directly from the AMC car lines yet served exceptionally well in both Jeep and International-Harvester light trucks. The 304 V-8 was also an AMC passenger car design. These overhead valve engine types have wide popularity among engine rebuilding shops and the parts aftermarket.

GM's 'Iron Duke' four, a 2.5L/151 cubic inch Pontiac design, was a popular CJ "base" engine used from 1980 to early-1983. The Iron Duke helped AMC meet strict emission and fuel-efficiency standards during that period. AMC's own 2.5L four came on line in 1983, a pushrod five-main bearing design patterned off the AMC inline sixes.

These engines enjoy wide popularity and coverage in common workshop manuals, and you will find details on engine building and service data readily available. For that reason, I offer fundamental engine building suggestions but refer builders to readily accessible repair manuals for further details. Here, you will find my step-by recommendations for building an AMC inline six. The principles shared also hold true for the AMC four and even the 304 V-8.

NOTE—
The three-main bearing, F-head 134 four-cylinder engine from the Willys/Kaiser era is found in a small number of 1972-73 CJs. These carryover models are scarce and not considered AMC-era designs. If you have such an engine, **Jeep CJ Rebuilder's Manual 1946-1971** *addresses the F-134 engine in depth.*

AUTHOR'S TIP!
If you need detailed rebuilding or racing tips for the AMC/Jeep engine designs, an excellent resource is Mopar's own book, **Jeep Engines** *(part number P4529529), available through Mopar Performance and Jeep dealerships. I refer to* **Jeep Engines** *for OEM specifications, performance tips and all-out racing data. The book covers the 232/258 sixes, the later 4.0L six, the AMC fours, and the 360 (5.9L) V-8 (similar in design and construction to the 304 and 401 engines). A 350-page book,* **Jeep Engines** *includes high performance parts recommendations, engineering-based insights, and a thorough compilation of factory workshop manual data on these engines. A great read for the serious Jeep engine builder!*

Choosing the Right Engine Type

A worn engine presents an excellent opportunity for tailoring your Jeep to your needs and driving environment. You can select the engine that best meets your objectives. Drawing on my experience, I will share my view of the AMC/Jeep and Iron Duke engines, focusing on their suitability to different driving needs:

Four Cylinder Engines

Shortly after the purchase of Jeep Corporation from Kaiser in 1971, AMC phased out the use of the F-head 134 four cylinder in favor of its own six cylinder motors. It wasn't until 1980 that AMC offered a four cylinder engine again in the 151 Iron Duke.

NOTE—

Early Willys and Kaiser-era four-cylinder CJs were very light in curb weight, they had exceptionally low-geared axles, and highway use was not a primary consideration. When AMC offered the 151 Iron Duke as the base engine in 1980, I was suspect, and for good reason!

Although the Iron Duke is a very reliable engine, the gross weight of an '80s-era CJ-7 or CJ-8/Scrambler is over bearing for an emissions equipped four-banger. If you drive primarily off-pavement, Pontiac's 'Iron Duke' 151 or the AMC 150 four might be adequate for a stripped CJ. Adequate, that is, if the Jeep has a soft-top, no trailer towing is planned, no canoe will be on the roof, and the tire diameter remains near stock. If a four is the plan, keep the cargo light!

◁ **Fig. 2-1**
AMC 2.5L four is a very busy engine. Emission controls on this '86 CJ version serve California demands. Peak torque and horsepower arrive at a relatively high rpm, not very useful off-pavement. Any fuel efficiency is lost in overwork. The 258 inline six makes a practical replacement. This heroic four-banger was worn out at 109,000 miles.

Inline Six Cylinder Engines

AMC 232, 258 and later 4.0L engines are exceptionally reliable. Seven crankshaft main bearings and a fundamental pushrod 'OHV' design make these engines durable and very easy to service. Any of these engines will deliver long service and provide useful torque for off-pavement use. Since the 232 has become a scarcer engine to find and offers less performance, the nearly identical 258 would make the optimal bolt-in replacement for an OEM 232 six in a '70s CJ.

The 258 inline six is *my* CJ engine of choice for all-around use. Unless you need "high performance" for competition or other niche uses, the 258 is flexible enough to give most V-8s a good run, especially off-pavement. On-highway fuel mileage is reasonable (certainly better than most V-8s!), and power is very flexible and adequate for a vehicle of the CJ's curb weight and GVWR. The 258 can run for 140,000 or more miles with just routine maintenance. (Rebuilt and run on quality, 100% synthetic or equivalent oil, a 258 could serve dutifully for well over 200,000 miles.)

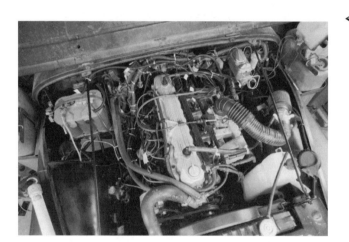

Fig. 2-2

A 258 six with Mopar EFI/MPI conversion kit is the best of all worlds! A bolt-on 50 horsepower gain gives this stump-puller undaunted performance while improving fuel efficiency. Off- and on-pavement, this is an excellent performer. EFI is useful, but if that's not within your budget, you can opt for carburetion, stock or aftermarket, as a cost-effective alternative.

Those seeking EFI/MPI might consider the engine swap involving a '91-up Wrangler or XJ/ZJ Cherokee 4.0L, however, the 258 offers more impressive low-end torque for back-country driving. I would opt for a freshened 258 and give real consideration to Mopar's EFI/MPI retrofit kit, which I detail in the "Fuel System" chapter.

NOTE—

There is a growing interest in retrofitting the 258's long-stroke crankshaft into the 4.0L engine block. This provides an even larger displacement six than the 258, delivering optimal torque and horsepower if that's your goal. HESCO at Birmingham, Alabama, has done a good deal of work with the 258 (4.2L)/4.0L hybrid. HESCO has developed close ties with Mopar Performance around enhancements for the 4.0L and 4.2L sixes.

2

The V-8 Engines

When AMC introduced the 304 V-8 in 1972, heads turned! This was unprecedented horsepower and torque for a CJ Jeep. Light and nimble, the CJ-5 or CJ-6 equipped with the V-8 was actually *overpowered* in some instances. Off-pavement, in particular, the V-8 proved largely unnecessary, as the low-range gearing did not require any more torque than the sixes produced!

 Fig. 2-3

This tuned 304 V-8 powers a '72 CJ-5 with plenty of back-country gear. The owner enjoys the muscle and added power for a variety of engine-driven accessories. He also pulls a light cargo trailer. The shorter CJ-5 does not offer the CJ-7's more stable highway handling, yet the CJ-5's 84-inch wheelbase proves exceptionally versatile on trails like the Rubicon!

> *CAUTION—*
>
> *Also be aware that the handling of a higher center-of-gravity, 84-inch wheelbase CJ-5 with V-8 muscle requires an experienced driver. Torque steer in this wheelbase length, especially with locking axles, can be a handful! Be sure you're ready for the challenges. When I step into my '55 CJ-5, its even shorter 81-inch wheelbase is always in mind.*

 The modern 'OHV' 304, 360, 390 and 401 AMC V-8s are all good designs, relatively light in weight, easy to service, very reliable, and they will fit in a '72-'86 CJ. AMC stretched and widened the engine bay in '72 to provide space for the inline sixes and 304 V-8. These bays provide room for swapping a variety of other V-8 types into this chassis.

Shown is a late 360 AMC/Jeep V-8 with Motorcraft 2150 two-barrel carburetor, a popular replacement engine fo r'72-up CJs.

I like the AMC V-8s and horsepower. Such muscle may be justified for highway use, trailer pulling and hefty cargo, although the decreased fuel efficiency will run up the gasoline tab.

So, do you need exceptional muscle? If so, and if an AMC engine is your preference, I would opt for the 5.9L/360 V-8 or even the 401. My camshaft of choice would be a grind like Competition Cams' mild 252 type. This provides bottom end (low speed) torque much like an inline six, great mid-range power for the street or even hill climb competition, and peak horsepower at a reasonable 4200-4400 rpm. (This camshaft will continue running strongly to 5000 rpm). The cam's strong manifold vacuum will be welcome at high altitudes in the Far West.

If you have an alternative small-block or even a big-block V-8 preference, it will likely fit the AMC/Jeep CJ chassis. Every popular domestic V-8 has been swapped into the CJ Jeep chassis. The AMC engine types require the correct motor mounts and frame brackets, while non-Jeep engine swaps will require aftermarket adapters or custom fabricated frame mounts.

I support owners' rights to personalize their Jeep in any way deemed sensible and appropriate to the vehicle's intended use, however, I would caution that very hefty V-8s can upset the weight distribution of the vehicle. Even the AMC V-8 CJs are noticeably more front-heavy than the six- and four-cylinder models. This can be damaging to the frame, drive system and vehicle handling.

CAUTION—

'72-'75 CJ frames do not fare well under severe duty. The frame is susceptible to cracking at the area just rearward of the front spring anchor brackets. This is the end-point for the front frame boxed section. A high-horsepower V-8 will put even more load on the frame.

If you quest after raw horsepower, keep the engine weight in check. Use aftermarket aluminum components wherever practical and tubular steel exhaust headers. Bolster the front suspension and make certain the frame will withstand the added power.

NOTE—

High horsepower no longer means high pollution levels. Modern EFI V-8 engines can offer high horsepower with very low emission levels. Consider a high-tech engine swap, and you may find that more power also yields a cleaner tailpipe.

Typical Jeep Engine Rebuild

AMC/Jeep engine designs are modern and familiar to builders. If you have built a modern pushrod engine, you can rebuild an AMC engine. For that reason, this section covers the fundamentals of a quality engine rebuild with focus on the common AMC 4.2L/258 six. These principles apply to the AMC fours and V-8s.

NOTE—

*The AMC engines have wide coverage in trade shop manuals and automotive industry service data. Like me, you may find that Mopar's **Jeep Engines** book provides a valuable builder's guide, or perhaps you have access to an OEM Jeep workshop book. Libraries, used bookstores, Jeep websites and swap meets offer workshop manuals and **Mitchell** or **Motors** shop manuals that cover your engine. These engines are very common.*

The current trend toward the use of "crate motors" or remanufactured engines encourages many to simply find a quality source for a remanufactured engine. A high quality source for remanufactured 4.2L six, 5.9L V-8 and 2.5L AMC four engines is your local Jeep/Mopar dealer. These warranted "Genuine Mopar" engines have been thoroughly cleaned, inspected, re-machined and assembled to like-new tolerances, using new and reconditioned parts.

 Fig. 2-4

This is a Genuine Mopar 4.2L/258 remanufactured engine. Available through Mopar/Jeep dealerships and offering a factory warranty, these like-new engines require only the transfer of peripheral parts from your old engine. Considering the cost of parts and machine shop sublet labor, the remanufactured engine is cost effective in today's market. Consider this option.

There are also local and regional shops that can perform the machine work and assemble your engine. Or, you may elect to sublet the necessary machine work and assemble the engine yourself. Shop around first. Currently, it is often less expensive to purchase a completely rebuilt and assembled "exchange" engine than to rebuild your original powerplant. A quality "reman" engine can save time and put your Jeep back on the trail much sooner.

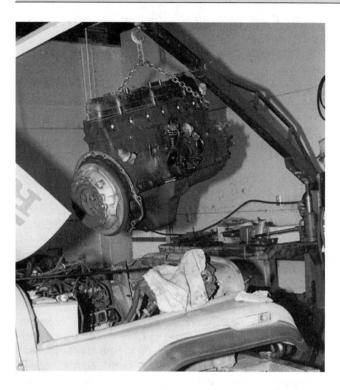

◄ **Fig. 2-5**

Here is the "long-block" engine coming out of a CJ engine bay. Removal of clutch and flywheel assembly, oil pressure sender, oil and coolant fittings, valve cover, distributor, oil pan, thermostat housing and the timing cover will have this engine assembly ready for either teardown or exchange with a reman "crate" engine.

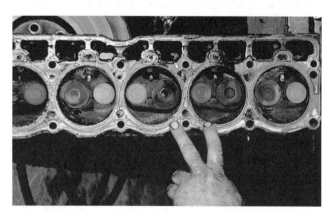

◄ **Fig. 2-6**

When troubleshooting this high-mileage 258, two adjacent cylinders showed low compression, the others were below normal. Teardown indicated a warped head and general piston/cylinder wall wear. This worn fitted block and cylinder head could have been exchanged for a quality reman engine.

◄ **Fig. 2-7**

As the engine comes apart, a piston reveals skirt scoring, sludge and wear. Bearings were worn as expected. Engine consumed a quart of oil each 250 miles.

2

◀ Fig. 2-8

Sloppy timing chain is common, in some instances bad enough to cause grating on the timing cover. Resulting late valve timing lowers manifold vacuum at idle and low speeds. This is common wear on high-mileage AMC engines.

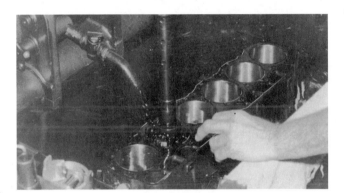

◀ Fig. 2-9

Boring bar creates a new cylinder surface. This is essential for proper fit-up between new oversized pistons and rings. Reman engines undergo this operation, so will the engine you choose to rebuild yourself. This is a 258 six, similar to the boring operation for any AMC engine.

◀ Fig. 2-10

Here, the 258's crankshaft undergoes regrinding. 0.010" is the first undersize, which this crankshaft will tolerate. Catching the engine rebuild in time, you will likely need only the 0.010" grind. Other common under-sizes are 0.020" and 0.030". In rare instances, a measurably round crankshaft may tolerate a simple polishing and proper refitting (using Plastigage) of new bearings.

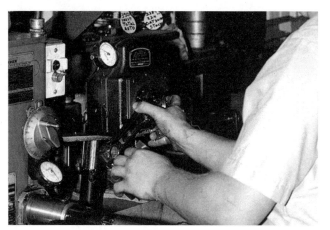

 Fig. 2-11

Seasoned connecting rods require a check for straightness and correct bore diameters. Like the block and cylinder head, rods require a Magnaflux test for cracks and stresses. Rods properly reconditioned and fitted with new bolts can offer like-new performance.

 Fig. 2-12

All castings require hot tanking. The block and cylinder head castings are ready for machining once they have been thoroughly tanked. Here, scale, rust, oil sludge, and deposits get eaten away, a vital step in rebuilding engines.

 Fig. 2-13

On this rebuild, the clean cylinder head receives new iron valve guide inserts. Depending upon valve stem material, either cast iron or silicone bronze liners will restore valve fit, oil control and proper valve seal. Consult your machinist when matching guide material and valves. Hard steel exhaust valve seats and stainless steel exhaust valves require compatible valve guides.

2

Fig. 2-14

Cutting three-angle valve seats is common practice for centering the seat and assuring proper seat width. This head will move to the cylinder head surfacing machine for truing the head deck. A straight head surface will seal properly and offer uniform compression.

Fig. 2-15

Original valves with proper stem diameters and adequate head margins can often be re-machined for service. If questionable, discard the valve. Concentrate on quality exhaust valves and hard exhaust seat inserts. Use of heavy-duty valves and springs is a longevity measure if you plan to keep your Jeep!

Fig. 2-16

On AMC engines, the valve stem height is critical. Non-adjustable rocker arms mean that clearance at hydraulic lifters is controlled by the stem height. Machinist will need to take the amount of cylinder head surfacing (milling) into account as well. Lifter clearance should be confirmed during assembly.

◄ Fig. 2-17

Rod small end requires heat to expand piston pin bore during assembly of rod/piston. Rod end heated, the fitted pin will slide easily through the bore. This machine eliminates risk of damaging piston and rod during fit-up.

◄ Fig. 2-18

Here, machinist checks rod/piston alignment. The piston in place and rod held on center, the piston is gauged to be square with the rod bore. If rod is square with piston and the cylinder bore is 90-degrees from a true crankshaft centerline, this engine will be true to tolerance and running freely!

◄ Fig. 2-19

First block assembly step is the cam bearing installation. Bearings must align properly with oil feed holes. Cam bearings help control oil pressure, and this means that cam journals and bearings must have proper clearance.

 Fig. 2-20

Use extreme care when installing the camshaft. Do not nick or gall bearings. Feed the camshaft through the block gently. Cam plug at rear of block is not installed yet. Heavy-duty valve springs *(shown)* match the new lobe profile demands of an aftermarket Clifford Performance 264 grind camshaft.

NOTE—

264 grind delivers more mid-range and high speed power. For maximum low speed torque, a Competition Cams 252 grind works well. Stock replacement camshaft is adequate for most uses.

2

CJ and Wrangler Blocks and Oil Filters

The 1972-86 CJ inline sixes have machining in the block for an oil check valve. By contrast, the '87-'90 Wrangler/YJ 258 blocks do not have this provision. The OEM oil filter diameter for the '86 and earlier engines is small enough to clear the motor mounts. Wranglers use a different type of motor mount and a larger diameter oil filter.

When selecting an engine block for your CJ, consider these distinctions. Although there are subtle differences in the later Wrangler engines (including the use of an improved, cast aluminum valve cover), you may be better off with the earlier block.

Fig. 2-21 Here is a critical AMC engine feature: an oil check valve at the filter connector. '72-'86 Jeep engines use this check valve. Later Jeep engines eliminate this valve and require an oil filter with built-in check valve.

NOTE—

Aftermarket aluminum valve covers can resolve the oil seepage problems common to AMC's stamped steel and plastic valve covers. You do not need to change the cylinder head to gain from an improved, cast aluminum valve cover.

NOTE—

AMC-built Jeep engines use an anti-drain back valve in the filter. If your engine requires the check valve, a new spring and valve is recommended at overhaul.

Fig. 2-22 Be careful! The 258 blocks built from 1987-90 have no provision for the spring and check valve. These engines use an anti-drain back oil filter that also has a built-in check valve. The Wrangler motor mounts are different and allow for a bigger diameter oil filter. If you cannot use this diameter filter, you will not have a check valve.

CJ and Wrangler Blocks and Oil Filters (continued)

Fig. 2-23 Here, I did a trial fit-up of a 1986 CJ oil filter connector with a modified check valve retainer. (I ground off the locating shoulder as you see in Fig. 2-22.) Note the OEM oil filter #J3242397 has a small diameter and does not offer a built-in check valve. The retainer's oil opening reveals a block orifice that is too small to receive the '86 and earlier check valve. *Upon review of this test fit-up, I was not satisfied with the retainer having no shoulder to locate it in the block hole. I discarded this approach.*

Fig. 2-24 My final compromise was to use a split-ring lock washer that matched the thickness of the OEM check valve retainer. In addition to using the Grade 8 lockwasher, I added Loctite 271 to the connector's threads, doubly assuring that the oil filter connector will stay in place and seal. All of this left me with no motor mount clearance for the larger diameter Wrangler oil filter!

WARNING—

Always make certain the oil filter is correct for your engine type! 258 blocks were produced from 1987-90 without provision for the oil check valve in the block. These YJ Wrangler blocks required an oil filter with both an anti-drain back valve and a check valve. (This holds true for late 5.9L V-8s as well.) If you end up with such a YJ block for your '72-'86 Jeep CJ, you may not have clearance for the later style YJ oil filter. If the smaller diameter OEM style CJ filter must be used, you have the anti-drain back valve but no check valve in the filter. Change such a filter at proper intervals, or you will risk damage to the engine! You also need the correct oil filter connector fitting to properly fit the filter to the later block. Frankly, you're better off finding a 1986 or earlier block for your buildup! (See Figure 2-25.)

Fig. 2-25 These pieces don't fit! Block is '87-'90 Wrangler YJ type with a casting design that does not provide for the oil check valve. Here, I have turned the '86 and earlier check valve retainer upside down to illustrate the block orifice diameter difference. On '86 and earlier AMC engines, the spring and check valve would fit in the orifice, the retainer would be fitted with its shoulder facing downward to locate the retainer in the block. This is not possible with the '87-up block castings.

Fig. 2-26

With block area spotlessly clean, main bearing half-shells now fit into the block saddles. Apply special engine assembly lube liberally to bearing surfaces. Make certain your hands are clean! The engine is open and contaminants could damage bearing surfaces. Set caps squarely in their proper locations, and torque main cap bolts into place.

2

Fig. 2-27

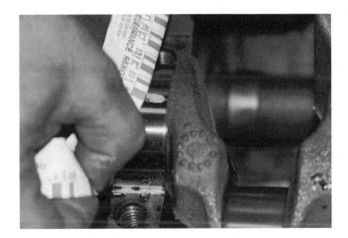

Plastigage is a simple means for confirming bearing-to-journal clearances. Whether you rebuild your engine completely (including fresh machine work) or simply replace bearings on an in-chassis repair job, Plastigage checks are cheap insurance. Clean all surfaces before torquing the rod or main caps to specification. Read Plastigage carefully.

Fig. 2-28

A sleeve or large impact socket serves here as a driver for installing the crankshaft sprocket. I like to support the flywheel end of crankshaft with a block of wood against a firm surface. This will prevent hammer force from driving the crankshaft against the thrust main bearing. Seat the new sprocket.

 Fig. 2-29

Here, timing marks align to specification. Take your time, as this is a crucial step. Make sure that a centerline drawn through the crankshaft and camshaft clearly places these dots in alignment! High performance tuners will want to use a degree wheel to verify camshaft timing.

Fig. 2-30

Install new rings according to instructions furnished with the ring set. Stagger the rings properly. Note that ring compressor binds rings firmly and rests squarely against the block deck as plastic handle taps piston into place. Always place plastic caps on rod bolts, and make sure rod clears the crankshaft journal.

AUTHOR'S TIP!

When installing rods, I turn the crankshaft rod journal downward, away from the block. "030" on piston crowns in Fig. 2-30 indicates the most common oversize for reman engine re-boring: 0.030". Pistons are available in 0.010", 0.020", 0.030", 0.040" and 0.060" oversize. Make certain the pistons face in the correct direction, with "Front" or an arrow facing toward the engine's front. This should aim the rod's oil squirt hole properly. The machine shop must install the rods in the correct direction, or the oil squirt holes will not lubricate the engine correctly.

Fig. 2-31

Journal down, rod/piston slides into position. Oil the cylinder walls to enable movement of the assembly. Protect the rod journals. Square up the rods as you install each rod bearing shell. Install new OEM rod nuts.

Fig. 2-32

New brass freeze plugs are common to the engine rebuilding industry. They resist corrosion. Use quality replacement parts when rebuilding your Jeep engine.

Fig. 2-33

Lube the base of lifters and lifter bores before installing the hydraulic lifters. *Never soak or pump the lifters full of oil before installing them! This could cause a valve(s) to hit piston crowns when you first crank the engine over.*

Fig. 2-34

The rebuilt cylinder head completes the long block assembly. Both the fitted block and cylinder head are now thoroughly reconditioned to offer like-new service.

 Fig. 2-35

A high-volume oil pump is good insurance. The AMC fours and sixes offer this option, the V-8s have limitations by design (the timing cover being part of the oil pump assembly). Again, this is good insurance and a low-cost upgrade at the time of engine rebuilding.

NOTE—

Always examine the AMC V-8 oil pump housing for wear and scoring. If damage or excess wear is evident, replace the timing cover!

 Fig. 2-36

Pushrods in place, install the rocker arm pivots. Valve stem heights correct, there is no need for valve adjust. Tighten the rocker arm pivots to specification. Prime the lubrication system after the valvetrain is in place. This will fill the lifters without unseating the valves.

CAUTION—

Be certain to prime the oiling system before attempting to crank the engine over! Make certain that the valvetrain is in place before priming the lubrication system.

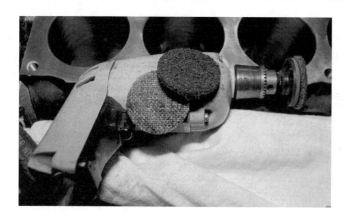

 Fig. 2-37

If you do an in-chassis overhaul ("ring-and-valve job"), far short of the engine reman or rebuild, you will find these Scotchbrite pads very useful. With care, you can remove gasket material from the block deck. Clean all debris away to avoid contaminating the crankshaft and other vital parts.

WARNING—

Older engine gaskets contain asbestos! Wear a suitable respirator when working around asbestos materials. Do not air blow or vacuum asbestos. When working around gaskets, do not scrape or wire brush the dry gasket material. A commercial parts washing cabinet, commercial hot tank or saturating the gasket material with a liquid gasket remover can reduce risk of exposure to asbestos. If asbestos might become airborne, use an appropriate, asbestos-rated respirator to prevent breathing asbestos fibers. Use hazardous waste precautions when disposing of old gaskets. Be aware that the typical shop vacuum filter will not trap asbestos particles, and in fact, will likely spread asbestos particles into the air! As of this writing, automotive service equipment and accepted methods for working around asbestos lining and materials focus on saturating and containing the material in a liquid, aqueous solution. You can find such equipment in the automotive brake repair industry. If you do any amount of this work, consider such equipment an investment in your health.

Fig. 2-38

Engine balancing is one way to extend an engine's life and improve performance. When rebuilding your engine, consider balancing the crankshaft assembly, including pulley/damper, flywheel and clutch cover.

Fig. 2-39

In addition to spin balancing the crankshaft and clutch assemblies, the matching of piston/rod weight can prove of additional benefit during rebuilding. The inline sixes are very smooth by design, yet any engine can benefit from these extra steps.

Assembling a Crate/ Remanufactured Engine

Ordering a remanufactured long-block assembly is convenient and often more practical than rebuilding your old engine. This trend continues to grow, as reman shops compete on price and availability of popular engines, often becoming the least expensive and quickest way to get your Jeep back together.

If you are now considering whether to exchange your Jeep's long block for a remanufactured/rebuilt assembly, review these steps. A quality engine, rebuilt properly and to OEM specification, could prove practical.

◄ **Fig. 2-40**

This out-of-the-crate Genuine Mopar 258 remanufactured long block is a smart alternative, available through Jeep dealers! Note that outer tin and covers do not come with the long-block. These and other peripheral parts transfer over from your old engine. *Clean all of your transfer parts thoroughly!*

◄ **Fig. 2-41**

New oil pump comes with the reman engine. Coat the gasket lightly with gasket sealant. Torque the pump bolts to specification. Be certain to prime oiling system before cranking the engine over.

◄ **Fig. 2-42**

Flat edge of an open-ended wrench is handy for tapping the oil screen pickup tube into the oil pump. Do not damage tube! Apply a thin film of sealant to outer surface of tube before installation.

◄ **Fig. 2-43**

Apply Loctite 242 to bolt threads as added assurance that the oil pump and screen will remain safely in place. Torque the hardware to specification.

◄ **Fig. 2-44**

Carefully align the timing cover gasket. I use Permatex 'High Tack' to hold gaskets like this in place. This is a quality sealer, too.

NOTE—

Note that the oil slinger is in place on crankshaft snout. Do not forget to install the oil slinger!

◄ **Fig. 2-45**

Use care to get a good seal and proper alignment of the timing cover seal. I used a depth gauge to measure the gap between the crankshaft and seal. If the pulley is even slightly off-center, the timing cover seal can seep oil. Torque timing cover bolts uniformly to specification.

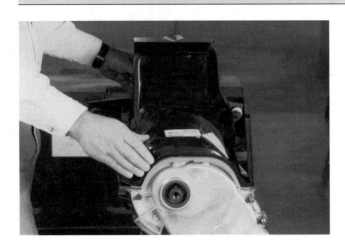

◀ **Fig. 2-46**

Set the new pan gasket in place and center up the oil pan. The new pan gasket is a one-piece design with updated oil sealing ability. This state-of-the-art gasket should maintain a leak-free oil pan.

◀ **Fig. 2-47**

Tighten oil pan bolts in sequence and stages. Do not over-tighten. Use an inch-pound torque wrench for accuracy on smaller hardware. All rubber, one-piece gasket does not re-quire sealant.

◀ **Fig. 2-48**

This step is often overlooked: brushing sealant on the end of the crankshaft pulley hub. I do this to assure a proper seal between the oil slinger face and the pulley hub. Note the light coating of sealant on inside face of hub. These measures re-duce risk of any oil leaks.

 Fig. 2-49

Coat the timing cover seal lip with grease before installing the pulley. This will provide initial lubrication for the seal and help extend the seal's service life.

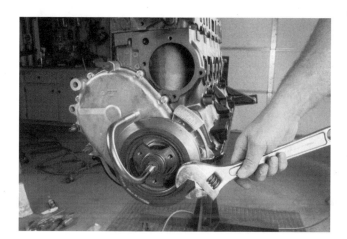

◄ **Fig. 2-50**

This spring U-bolt and old castellated nut provided the necessary tooling to safely pull the crankshaft pulley onto the crankshaft snout. To avoid stressing the thrust main bearings, I avoid hammering pulleys onto crankshafts. If you prefer, a length of threaded Grade 5 rod stock with a suitable nut and washer will also serve well here.

◄ **Fig. 2-51**

Once enough crankshaft thread is available, I use an old pulley bolt and air gun to set the pulley into position. This is an OEM Grade 5 type pulley bolt, which I will replace with a longer Grade 8 variety available from Mopar.

 Fig. 2-52

Always use Loctite 242 on the pulley bolt during final installation. Make certain the bolt matches the pulley type, and torque bolt to specification. The various Jeep pulleys require specific length and grade damper bolts. I install a new OEM washer with the correct bolt.

◄ **Fig. 2-53**

Place Loctite Threadlocker on oil filter connector threads. Torque the filter connector to specification. This long-block is a 1987-90 YJ 258 type that does not provide for the oil check valve and retainer. CJ blocks use a check valve, spring and a retainer that fits between the oil filter connector and block. *(See comments and illustrations Figs. 2-21 to 2-24.)*

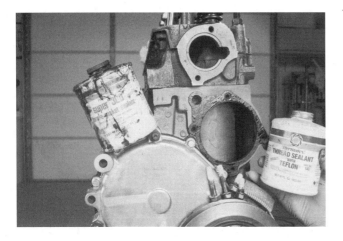

◄ **Fig. 2-54**

Sealant is important on water pump gaskets and pump bolts. 'Super 300' makes an excellent seal on the gasket. Teflon on bolts that reach to the coolant is practical. Take the time to use sealant and assure that your Jeep will be trouble-free on the most remote trails.

 Fig. 2-55

Torque water pump bolts in a cross pattern and to specification. The water pump, fan clutch and fan are safety items. Use new, properly graded lockwashers on the bolts. Recheck the torque after parts set for a few minutes.

◀ **Fig. 2-56**

Here, a Genuine Mopar rebuilt water pump and iron thermostat housing complete the cooling items. A new thermostat, installed carefully and facing in the right direction, will safeguard your rebuilt engine. Install the thermostat housing's gasket with Super 300 or equivalent sealant lightly coating each side of gasket.

◀ **Fig. 2-57**

Static timing the engine is important. Verify that the timing mark for TDC ("0"-degree advance) is lined up. I turn the crankshaft in its direction of normal rotation and slowly bring the mark up. This keeps any slack out of the timing chain to assure accurate alignment. If I pass the mark, I rotate the crankshaft fully through its cycles to the next time TDC is aligned for #1 cylinder to fire.

 Fig. 2-58

Watch the #1 cylinder's intake and exhaust valves as you rotate the crankshaft. The intake valve should open, and just as it closes, watch for the timing notch on the crankshaft damper to come up. Slowly bring the line to TDC on the timing tab. This is #1 cylinder up to fire, the spot to index the ignition distributor for #1 cylinder.

Fig. 2-59

Fill the crankcase with fresh oil, make sure the oil filter is snugly in place, and prime the oiling system. You can do this by rotating the oil pump's drive, using either a drive tool or improvised tooling. Rotate the pump until oil is liberally flowing at the rocker arms. With #1 cylinder lined up to fire, install the distributor and index the rotor to #1 spark wire. (Always install a new distributor gasket!)

AUTHOR'S TIP!

If you need to prime the oil system and have an old, worn distributor around, remove its drive gear and clean the housing and shaft thoroughly. Index the distributor shaft with the oil pump's drive slot, and clamp the distributor in place. Take a ½-inch, low-speed reversible drill and couple the chuck where the rotor normally sets on the driveshaft. While pushing downward to keep the distributor shaft engaged in the oil pump drive, rotate the oil pump shaft in the direction the pump normally turns. Run the drill until oil flows through the pushrods and into the rocker arms.

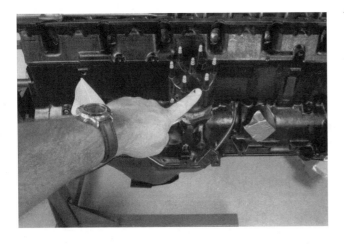

Fig. 2-60

Here, #1 cylinder is marked on the distributor cap. With #1 cylinder up to fire (both valves closed) and the damper's timing notch indexed to TDC, carefully line up the rotor with #1 spark plug wire in the cap. The oil pump drive slot can be rotated with a large screwdriver to line the pump drive with the distributor shaft key. Center up the distributor housing to #1 cylinder's firing position, and tighten the clamp. If you follow these steps, the engine will fire readily and merely need a slight timing adjustment with a timing light.

AUTHOR'S TIP!

For static timing a breaker point ignition, the points should just be cracking open with #1 cylinder aligned to fire. Clamp the housing at this position. You can come close with electronic ignitions by indexing the distributor housing so that #1 cylinder's reluctor arm aligns with the sensor (pickup). This will get the engine started, at which stage you can set the timing precisely with a timing light.

Fig. 2-61
The exhaust manifold and intake manifold share hardware. Here, I have installed the exhaust manifold and new gasket, dressing bolt and stud threads with Permatex Anti-Seize. There is nothing more frustrating than trying to remove seized or scorched exhaust manifold bolts. Anti-Seize helps prevent bolt seizure and prolongs hardware life.

2

AMC/Jeep V-8 Engine Oiling Notes

The Jeep 304/360/401 V-8s share several components and design features with the AMC inline sixes and fours. This helps the Jeep mechanic considerably, as familiarity with one engine type proves useful for working on the others.

In rebuilding the 304 and other AMC V-8s, one area of concern is the oiling system. For those unfamiliar with the external oil pump's features, the oil pump housing is actually a cavity in the aluminum timing cover.

It is not uncommon for the V-8 oil pump to loose efficiency. The drive gears for the oil pump wear over time, as does the aluminum cover plate surface. The cover casting is part of the oil filter mount. In rare instances, the upper end of the oil pump gears will wear into the timing cover, and this requires replacement of the entire timing cover.

Oil pump service is necessary when the oil pressure drops below 37 PSI at 1600 rpm and beneath 13 PSI at a 600 rpm idle. From my experience, these are definitely minimal pressures for these engines. Before condemning the oil pump or bearings, however, be certain that the oil pressure sender is accurate, as a defective oil pressure sender is fairly common on AMC engines.

Once you know the oil pressure is low, remove the oil filter stand (pump cover). Inspect the gears for excessive backlash and clearance between the outer ends of the gears and the widest points of the housing. Compare these specifications with those given in the factory or trade workshop manual covering your engine. If you suspect worn pump gears, this is a simple and inexpensive fix. A worn pump housing requires replacement of the entire timing cover.

One procedure I perform on the V-8 pump cover is to "mill" the machined surface. Using a flat piece of steel or auto safety glass as a backup, I wet sand the flat surface of the pump cover. Beginning with wet 400 grit, move to 600 or finer grit, using circular motions to remove all score lines and roughness. Once polished with the wet 600-grit, clean and air blow every cavity of the cover, with the pressure valve removed, and make certain that all parts are free of contaminants before assembling the pieces.

You need to either prime this oiling system or pack the oil pump cavity with petroleum jelly. If you fail to do this, it will take considerable time to pick up oil pressure, and damage to the engine bearings will likely occur. Always use a new pump cover gasket (furnished with the gear set), and torque bolts carefully to specification (typically 55 *inch*-pounds for ¼-20 threaded bolts). I usually go to 60 or so *inch*-pounds for safety sake, re-checking the bolt torque after the engine has warmed up completely.

The remaining service on these engines is very similar to other popular domestic pushrod V-8s and sixes. If you follow the factory procedures when rebuilding a 304/360/401 AMC V-8, the result will be a highly reliable and responsive powerplant.

Engine Peripherals and Accessories

There are a variety of intake systems and engine-driven accessories found on Jeep CJ engines. In the 'Carburetion and Aftermarket EFI' section of this book, you will find a step-by-step procedure for installing the Mopar EFI/MPI Kit. In that section, I continue installation of the OEM hardware and electrical components on the Mopar crate engine depicted within this chapter.

For installation details on the flywheel, the clutch assembly and transmissions, see **Chapter 3** of this book. There, I outline the kind of upgrade components that can enhance your Jeep CJ's performance and reliability. In **Chapter 10**, you will find the options and aftermarket add-on upgrades that many backcountry travelers want.

Keep That New Engine Cool!

Rebuilding an engine to like-new performance restores lost horsepower. The cooling system must meet the regained horsepower's demands. For proper engine performance and reliability, the BTUs (thermal units of heat), which directly correlate to horsepower output, must be able to dissipate effectively.

You want a thoroughly clean radiator to match the clean engine block and head(s). You also need a radiator that can handle the horsepower produced. Simply put, the more horsepower, the more heat.

NOTE—
*In Chapter 9 of my **Jeep Owner's Bible**, I discuss cooling dynamics at length. Engine swaps and any increase in horsepower output will place a higher load on the cooling system. While a worn engine may have worked okay with a sluggish radiator, a frisky rebuilt engine could overtax the cooling system!*

Have your local radiator shop clean the radiator and confirm its condition and capacity. Share with these experts the horsepower output of your engine and where you expect to drive the Jeep. If necessary, replace your radiator's core with a new or custom-built, properly sized unit.

Cooling also requires an adequate fan for proper airflow through the radiator. I heartily recommend the use of an engine-driven mechanical fan, as electric fans will not serve well in summer heat, heavy pulling, or rock-crawling situations. If you wish to reduce horsepower drain, a fan clutch drive unit is practical for engines that can be fitted with both a fan and clutch.

In addition to the right radiator and fan, use the correct thermostat. Removing the thermostat in summer is a mistake, as the factory-calibrated coolant flow rate will change, and the engine temperature will be uncontrolled. Automotive cooling systems require a certain amount of flow restriction, which the thermostat provides.

During the Willys and Kaiser L- and F-head era, 160-degree Fahrenheit thermostats were commonly installed for hot climate summer use. Sometimes you can get away with a lower temperature thermostat, although engine performance is best with a 180- or even 195-degree Fahrenheit type.

Fuel combustion is poor below 180-degree F settings, and for that reason, I prefer a 180-degree F thermostat for all-season use. This reduces carbon buildup, helps offset cold-weather balkiness, and shortens the warm-up periods.

CAUTION—

The 50-State legal Mopar EFI conversion kit comes with a 195-degree thermostat. This is required for the computer and engine management functions to work properly. On later Jeep emission engines, the thermostat is closely involved with combustion requirements. A colder thermostat could actually raise the levels of hydrocarbons and carbon monoxide. Use the recommended thermostat in any emission controlled engine.

◁ **Fig. 2-62**

Replacement 4.2L radiator sourced from Jeep/Mopar Performance is an air conditioning model application. The addition of a Mopar EFI/MPI Conversion Kit raised the engine's horsepower and demanded additional cooling. MPI kit comes with a 195-degree F thermostat.

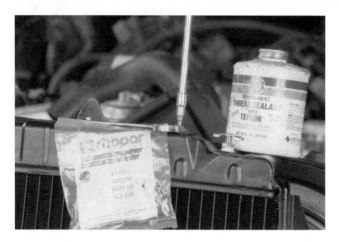

◀ **Fig. 2-63**

This Mopar radiator fits automatic and manual transmission applications. The '86 CJ had a 2.5L four and neither air conditioning nor an automatic transmission. This was the optimal radiator upgrade choice. The added flow and surface area provide ample cooling for the modified 4.2L engine.

◀ **Fig. 2-64**

New Mopar fan clutch and engine-driven fan will provide the kind of airflow needed for off-pavement driving. Electric fans do not have the CFM draw of mechanically driven fans. I avoid electric fans for off-pavement or severe duty usage. My choice is a quality OEM or aftermarket replacement fan.

◀ **Fig. 2-65**

Don't overlook the fan shroud! Here, a new Mopar molded plastic shroud helps direct air flow through the entire radiator core surface. Shrouds capture air from all corners of the core and assure maximum CFM flow.

 Fig. 2-66

Assembled cooling system reveals my use of Mopar's OEM-type molded coolant hoses and gear clamps. Avoid the use of "universal" flexible radiator hoses. Flex hoses can stress the inlet and outlet necks of the radiator. Note use of heavy-duty radiator, new fan clutch and mechanical fan.

AUTHOR'S TIP!
Even with engine swaps, you can find molded hoses by size, shape and bends. Talk to your parts retailer. Avoid the use of universal flex hoses.

Fig. 2-67

Permatex "High Tack" provides a quality seal on the inner ends of radiator hoses. Lightly coat the hose in the area that fits over the radiator inlet/outlet, water pump inlet and thermostat housing neck. Gear-type hose clamps match OEM type and hold up well in service. Torque the clamps securely. After the engine has run several miles, shut it off and allow a complete cool-down. Re-check the torque on each clamp.

Fig. 2-68

Watch for step-size heater hoses. Jeep coolant fittings often vary in size. OEM molded heater hoses accommodate these mismatched hose end sizes. If these hoses are not available from Jeep or the aftermarket, NAPA and other retailers offer universal lengths of bulk heater hose with step-up ends. Seek these hoses when fittings are not the same size at each end.

 Fig. 2-69

The use of High Tack or other suitable sealant at heater hose ends is advised. Take time to assure a pressure-tight, leak-resistant seal. Note that I use quality OEM Mopar clamps. Route hoses away from sharp edges or surfaces that might chafe the hose material in service.

The V-8 Water Pump Challenge

For those CJ owners who like power and power options, there is always the AMC 360 or 401 V-8 engine swap. These gutsy, reliable engines are, for the most part, easy to service. The spark plugs are readily accessible, the distributor is right at the front---even the oil pump is within easy reach, outside the crankcase and mounted at the base of the timing cover. If you like an engine with a lot of power options, however, you also need to know that one service item is not very easy to reach: *the water pump.*

Our '87 Grand Wagoneer's original water pump lasted 134,000 miles before giving up. This is a good deal of use, as the engine has power everything, including power steering and air conditioning. The V-belt load on the water pump bearings is heavy, yet the pump worked unflinchingly for a very long time.

I set aside a weekend morning to change the water pump. Thinking in terms of a two-hour job, I thought for sure that my air tools and hoist would make haste of this chore. Was *I* in for a surprise!

In and of itself, the water pump is relatively easy to change. Once one loosens all of the drive accessories at the front of the engine, the water pump is accessible. At that point, the pump assembly takes only twenty minutes to replace. Carefully removing and reinstalling all of the items necessary to expose the water pump housing, however, took me three hours and forty minutes!

Many Jeep builders want a muscle engine and a lot of accessory items as well. Miles from home, on a rocky trail like the Rubicon, would anyone look forward to changing the water pump on an AMC V-8 with a full complement of power accessories? Our CJs, by design, are light utility trucks. The operative word is "utility." I prefer to keep mine that way.

8:45 a.m. in the morning: From the bottom side, you can see the water pump. Fifteen minutes into the job, the coolant is drained, and I'm looking at four drive belts that need loosening.

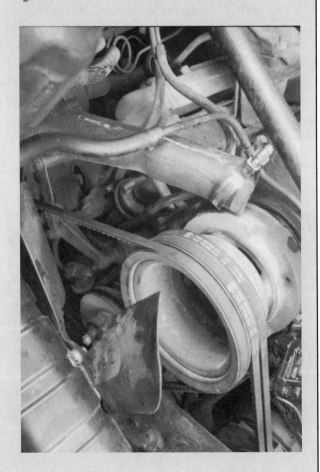

2

The V-8 Water Pump Challenge (continued)

9:30 a.m.: All belts loose, the fan and fan clutch removed, I'm starting to see the amount of items attached to the water pump…If only there wasn't an air conditioning compressor and brackets, the power steering pump assembly, the smog pump, and four drive belts in the way…And remember, I'm the fortunate fellow with the vehicle hoist and air tools, not the one rolling around in the dirt alongside the trail!

NOTE—

For those curious about the external oil pump, that's the pump at the left with oil filter attached. I changed the oil pump gears and primed the oil system in less time than it's taking me to figure out the best way to tackle this water pump removal!

11:30 a.m.: The new water pump is in place. Be assured that I painstakingly coated each side of the thin gasket with Super 300, coating the cleaned bolt threads, too. I wire brushed the pump mounting surface with a drill motor, vacuumed away all debris, and very patiently installed the pump, checking the gasket alignment all the way around with a mirror and using a torque wrench to assure proper fit-up! I rechecked torque carefully while installing the brackets.

NOTE—

This would be the last job on Earth you would want to have "come back" (not be done properly or suffer from a defective new pump). You definitely want Genuine Mopar quality, a new water pump that will last another 134,000 miles…Note that the power steering pump is still detached, the myriad A/C and other brackets and braces are back in place…

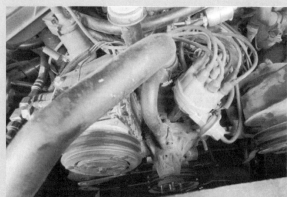

9:40 a.m.: I'm top side and beginning to realize how many power accessories share bolts and mounting brackets with the water pump…

12 p.m.: The fan and fan clutch can now go back in place…*This* is Jeep quality, a seven-blade, heavy-duty fan and clutch unit. Kaiser, AMC and Chrysler Corporation made the full-size Jeep Wagoneer a virtual icon of durability. For dependability, quality and engineering integrity, the '72-'91 AMC-built Wagoneer/Grand Wagoneer is hard to beat.

The V-8 Water Pump Challenge (continued)

12:15 p.m.: Air tools still ringing, the fan and fan clutch are in place, the belts and brackets now line up.

12:30 p.m.: Back in business. All parts torqued in place, four belts tensioned properly, it's time to fill the cooling system and check for leaks.

I'd rather rebuild a differential or change out ring-and-pinion gears than do another water pump replacement on a late Grand Wagoneer! In fact, on this very engine, I changed the rear main bearing seal, the timing cover/damper seal, *and* the oil pump gears in less time than it took to replace this water pump.

Do you want this degree of complication on your trail running CJ? Give that big V-8 with a York air compressor, power steering pump, smog pump and four V-belts some thought.

NOTE—

If you want an AMC V-8, keep power options to a minimum. These are truly great engines, but the 360 and 401 with power accessories look awfully busy for a CJ. V-8 engines with modern serpentine drive belt systems provide ready service access at the front of the engine. Mopar/Jeep's late version of the 5.9L/360 'LA' V-8 might be a consideration if you can navigate the MPI wiring needs, sensor hook-ups and PCM requirements.

Monitoring and Protecting the New Engine

As you complete the assembly of your new engine, think about the break-in period and watching the engine's vital signs. Run-in can be aided by "cycling" and other techniques. Whether you drive the vehicle or use a dynamometer for break-in, be sure to read the gauges continually.

Initial startup through warm-up is a critical period. The engine must pick up oil pressure immediately. The temperature should climb steadily to thermostat setting and then stabilize there. In order to assure that this is happening, the oil and temp gauges must be accurate and reliable.

2

Gauges are not decorative. They serve a critical purpose. From the first start in cold weather to the hours of grueling pulls through desert rock piles, the gauges provide vital information. Gauges monitor the engine's condition and stress loads.

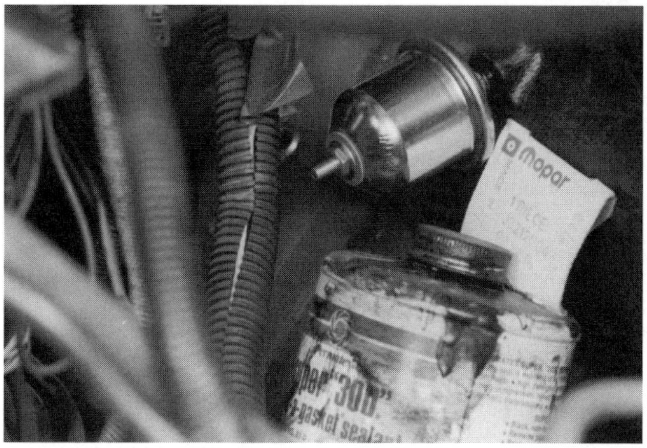

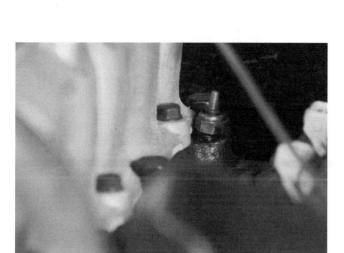

◀ **Fig. 2-70**

A new oil pressure sender is a must item. Jeep engine oil senders have small orifices and become unreliable at high mileage. Your rebuilt engine needs accurate monitoring! A new Mopar sender proves cheap insurance.

◀ **Fig. 2-71**

The temperature sender helps monitor coolant heat. I always install a new temp sender in a rebuilt engine. Use Permatex "Super 300" or equivalent sealant on the threads of oil and temp senders. A thin film of sealant, starting at the first thread, will seal well. Torque the sender to specification, and re-check torque at the first oil change.

◀ **Fig. 2-72**

I prefer OEM replacement oil filters. This Mopar filter meets the engine's oil system requirements. Aftermarket filters may fit but not meet exacting OEM specifications. OEM filters have the correct micron filtration and burst strength, anti-drain back protection, a by-pass provision if required, and correct pressure drop across the filter at normal engine oil pressures.

Chapter 3

Transmission and Clutch

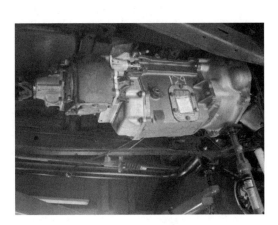

3

Rebuilding the Transmission

The AMC-era CJs carry on the tradition of Jeep 'Universal' versatility and utility. A transfer case divides power between front and rear axles and also provides a low-range ratio for crawling and severe loads. The transmission, transfer case and two driving axles deliver the exceptional tractability that only a 4-wheel-drive vehicle offers.

Addressing this complex geartrain, the true Jeep mechanic is a master at gear system rebuilding. Rebuilding a manual transmission is ground school for transfer case and axle work. For the AMC-era CJs, I have purposely focused on the Borg-Warner T-18 heavy duty four-speed commonly offered from 1972-1979.

NOTE—

The several Borg-Warner three-, four- and five-speed light duty gearboxes (T-14A, T-15A, T-150, T176/177, T-4 and T-5) used in various model years between 1972 and 1986 are thoroughly covered in general trade manuals, factory workshop manuals and parts catalogs. I selected the T-18 as a rebuild prototype for two reasons: 1) the T-18 is my "best pick" for CJ factory option transmissions, and 2) the T-18 requires the kind of rebuild procedures and concerns that are relevant to all other Jeep manual transmissions. Automatic transmissions like the G.M. THM400 ('76-'79 era Quadra-Trac models) and Chrysler 904/999 (1980-86) are beyond the scope of this book and typically sublet to automatic transmission shops for rebuilding.

The T-18, similar to the earlier Borg-Warner T-98A offering, was Jeep's heavy-duty transmission option. A gearbox popularized in the postwar and '50s American trucks from ½-ton to 2-ton capacity, the T-98A became a mid-'50s addition to the Jeep truck gearing options. Lightweight CJs, quite remarkably, became candidates for the rugged T-98, and in 1972, this transmission continued as an option in its T-18 form.

While the T-98A featured a compound low (1st) gear ratio of 6.39:1, the T-18 offered in the AMC-era CJs has a 4.02:1 1st gear ratio. Although this is not as low as the T-98, the 4.02:1 ratio is ample reduction for most backcountry performance. For the builder seeking a transmission with more stamina and a low first gear ratio, a T-18 transmission can be retrofitted in place of a CJ's light duty three-speed transmission.

NOTE—

The retrofit of an OEM Jeep CJ T-18 in place of a three-speed or light duty (T-176 or T-4) four-speed has become a costly proposition. The less expensive conversion method is to secure a common Ford-type T-18 transmission and use an Advance Adapters retrofit kit. This method also can benefit from Ford's lower 6.32:1 1st gear ratio, a highly desirable approach for off-pavement rock crawling.

Parts still abound for the AMC-era Jeep CJ transmissions. Your Jeep dealer or 4WD Hardware, Inc., and a variety of other aftermarket sources can supply every required piece for renewing a 1972-86 Jeep transmission.

Your rebuild may be light, requiring the minimal essentials like a small parts kit, brass blocking/synchronizer rings, new bearings, seals and gaskets. If the synchronizer assembly or hard parts (gears, shafts or countershaft and idler shaft) need replacement, cost will be considerably higher. When rebuilding a three-speed transmission gets too expensive, consider the option of swapping a more durable and versatile four-speed or five-speed truck type transmission into your Jeep. *(See later section in this chapter for details on the NV 3550 and NV4500 five-speed transplants.)*

3

Separating the Transmission from the Transfer Case

If you do not yet have the transmission free of the transfer case, refer to **Chapter 1** and review these steps:

1) On models so equipped, remove the control/shift housing assembly from the top of the transmission. Single-rod shifter transmissions simply require removal of the cane at this point.

2) Manual transmission '72-'79 CJs use a through-drive Spicer 20 transfer case. '80-'86 CJs use the through-drive Dana 300 unit. In both installation and transfer case can be readily separated by simply unbolting the transfer case. This makes for a far simpler removal strategy than the earlier side-drive Model 18 transfer case fit-up.

NOTE—
1941-71 Model 18 side-drive units use a gear behind an indexing retainer. The gear is attached with a lock nut at the end of the transmission main shaft. Disassembly involves additional work when separating the transmission and transfer case. The nut and gear must be loosened before separating the units.

3) Unbolt the transfer case from the transmission case. Carefully separate the units. Do not pry against machined surfaces or aluminum castings. The units should separate readily. If not, make sure all bolts and nuts have been detached!

T-18 Four-Speed Rebuild

Some CJ owners are fortunate enough to have the factory T-18 transmission or a retrofitted T-18 four-speed transmission in their Jeep. Due to the overwhelming stamina of this transmission in a lightweight CJ, rebuilding the unit is a rare need. Many builders, however, retrofit recycled (used) T-18 units into the CJ chassis, and most recycled or high mileage transmissions need attention.

CAUTION—
The transmission sub-assemblies require careful identification for replacing parts. Do not allow parts to get separated. Inspect for wear, heat discoloration/scoring, and proper clearances. These steps are critical, or your transmission rebuild job will be futile. Considering the large effort to access the transmission and the cost of replacement parts, you will surely want the unit to work properly.

NOTE—
For many years, Advance Adapters has offered a T-18 transmission-to-Model 18 transfer case retrofit kit. The typical retrofit gearbox is a common Ford two-wheel drive truck transmission with 6.32:1 compound first gear ratio.

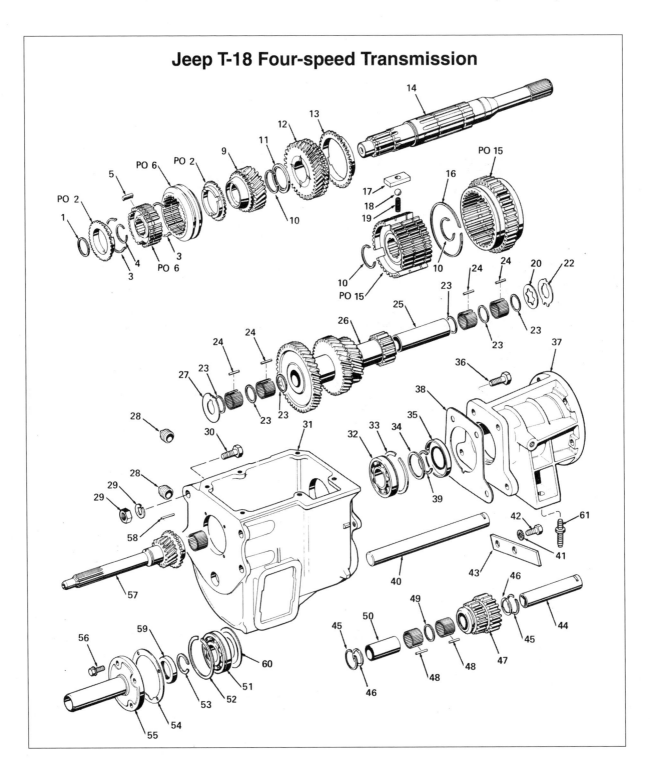

Jeep T-18 Four-speed Transmission

MANUAL TRANSMISSION

Key No.	Description	No. Req'd	Key No.	Description	No. Req'd
	TRANSMISSION ASSEMBLY (T18)	1	31	CASE, Transmission	1
1	SPACER, Pilot Bearing Roller	1	32	BEARING, Rear Ball	1
2	RING SET, 3rd and 4th Synchro.	1	33	RING, Bearing Lock (Front or Rear)	1
3	SPRING, 3rd and 4th Synchro.	2	34	WASHER, Mainshaft Thrust	1
4	SNAP RING, 3rd and 4th Synchro.	1	35	SEAL, Adapter Oil	1
5	PLATE, 3rd and 4th Synchro.	3	36	BOLT, 3/8-16 x 1-1/4	4
6	CLUTCH ASSEMBLY, 3rd and 4th Synchro.	1	37	ADAPTER, Transmission To Transfer Case	1
9	GEAR, 3rd Speed	1	38	GASKET, Adapter To Transmission	1
10	SNAP RING, Mainshaft	3	39	SNAP RING, Rear Bearing	1
11	WASHER, 2nd Gear Thrust	1	40	COUNTERSHAFT	1
12	GEAR, 2nd Speed	1	41	WASHER, Lock	1
13	RING, (a) 1st and 2nd Synchro.	1	42	BOLT, 3/8	1
	RING (b) 1st and 2nd Synchro.	1	43	LOCKPLATE	1
14	MAINSHAFT, Splined	1	44	SHAFT, Reverse Idler	1
15	CLUTCH ASSEMBLY, (a) 1st and 2nd Synchro.	1	45	SNAP RING	2
	CLUTCH ASSEMBLY, (b) 1st and 2nd (Less blocker ring)	1	46	WASHER, Thrust	1
			47	GEAR, Reverse Idler	1
	CLUTCH ASSEMBLY, (b) 1st and 2nd (With blocker ring)	1	48	ROLLER, Reverse Idler Bearing	74
			49	SPACER, Bearing	1
16	RING, (a) 1st and 2nd Plate Retaining	1	50	SLEEVE, Shaft	1
	RING (b) 1st and 2nd Plate Retaining	1	51	BEARING, Clutch Shaft	1
17	PLATE, (a) 1st and 2nd Synchro.	3	52	SNAP RING	1
	PLATE (b) 1st and 2nd Synchro	3	53	SNAP RING, Clutch Shaft	
18	BALL, 1st and 2nd Synchro.	3		(.117-.119 Thick)	AR
19	SPRING, 1st and 2nd Synchro.	3		(.120-.122 Thick)	AR
20	WASHER	1		(.123-.125 Thick)	AR
22	WASHER	1		(.127-.129 Thick)	AR
23	SPACER, Countershaft Bearing	6	54	GASKET, Front Bearing Cap	1
24	ROLLER, Countershaft Bearing	88	55	CAP, Front Bearing	1
25	SPACER, Countershaft Bearing	1	56	BOLT, 5/16-18 x 3/4	4
26	GEAR, Countershaft	1	57	SHAFT, Clutch (Input)	1
27	WASHER, Countershaft Thrust (Front)	1	58	ROLLER, Spline Shaft Pilot	22
28	PLUG, Pipe	2	59	SEAL, Front Bearing Oil	1
29	WASHER, Lock 7/16" (Upper)	2	60	BAFFLE, Oil	1
	WASHER, Lock 9/16" (Lower)	2	61	STUD, Mounting	1
	NUT, Hexagon 7/16" (Upper)	2			
	NUT, Hexagon 9/16" (Lower)	2			
30	BOLT, Hexagon 7/16" (Upper)	2			
	BOLT, Hexagon 9/16" (Lower)	2			

(a) Units built prior to August 22, 1983.
(b) Units built after August 22, 1983.

◀ Fig. 3-1

In neutral, with all gear oil drained and the shift cane removed, the overhaul begins. Loosen the control housing bolts and place them in a properly marked container. Grading and sizing of bolts is crucial to the proper function of a transmission. Early on, get in the habit of separating and carefully storing bolts.

 Fig. 3-2

Lift the shift control housing from the case. Note that the shift forks slide easily from the synchronizer clutch sleeves. On this version, the reverse fork remains attached to the case. (The upper end of the reverse shift fork (**ARROW**) is seen above the deck of the transmission case.) On very late versions, the reverse shift fork comes out with the control housing.

Fig. 3-3

The front bearing cap/retainer comes off next. Four bolts secure the retainer to the front of the transmission case. Note that an oil passage determines the location of the retainer. Gently scribing parts before teardown will assure proper reassembly. If the transmission has been disassembled before, follow these illustrations and comments closely.

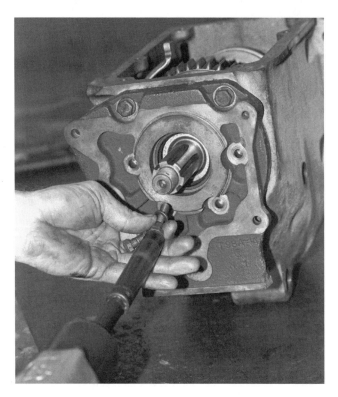

Fig. 3-4

The rear retainer plate serves the same role as a 4x4's adapter to the transfer case. Removal accesses the rear mainshaft and bearing.

 Fig. 3-5

Here, the 1st/2nd clutch sleeve is gently tapped forward with a weighted plastic hammer. The rear mainshaft bearing is accessible once the sleeve is out of the way.

 Fig. 3-6

Wearing safety goggles, use a long and blunt-ended punch to drive the rear bearing loose from the mainshaft. Extreme care must be taken to avoid damage to the mainshaft, transmission case or ball bearing (especially if the bearing may be reusable).

 Fig. 3-7

The clutch shaft and bearing can be easily accessed once the rear mainshaft bearing has been removed. Although a special puller will aid in the clutch shaft removal, the method shared here works well. Note that the chisel is simply used as a pry lever, with the hammer tapping the chisel end gently toward the case. Take care not to damage the gearcase.

 Fig. 3-8

Once the bearing has moved free of the case, the mainshaft and gear assemblies become accessible. If a special puller is available, the front (clutch shaft) bearing snap ring slot permits easy loosening of the bearing. An oil slinger/spacer fits between the bearing and clutch gear. Do not damage the oil slinger.

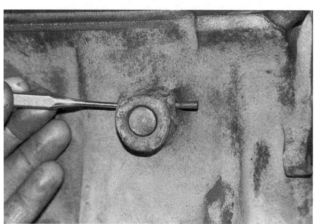

◀ **Fig. 3-9**

Remove tapered pin and then remove the support/pivot for the reverse shift fork. Note that the O-ring seal prevents gear oil from leaking out the case side. The inner groove is where the tapered pin seats. When the transmission is overhauled, replacement of this O-ring is cheap insurance. Silicone sealant assures a positive seal and easy installation.

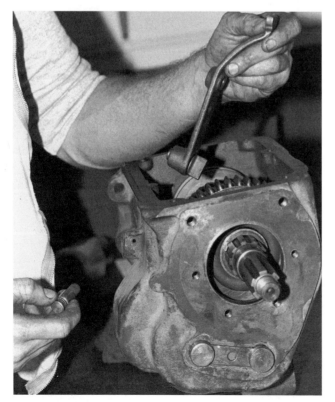

◀ **Fig. 3-10**

Now the reverse shift fork may be removed. This is the last obstacle before removing the mainshaft and its geartrain sub-assemblies.

Fig. 3-11

Lift the mainshaft from the case. Note that all pieces remain together.

Fig. 3-12

Knock out the rear shaft lockplate to access both the reverse gear/idler shaft and the countershaft.

◀ **Fig. 3-13**

The countershaft supports the countergear (cluster gear). Two sets of uncaged needle bearings fit in the ends of the countergear. With safety goggles and a blunt punch, the countershaft is tapped rearward from the case. Remove the reverse idler shaft in similar fashion. Now the teardown is complete.

◀ **Fig. 3-14**

The disassembled transmission lies on the workbench. (Note specialty pullers and drivers at rear.) Clean all parts thoroughly and inspect closely. Check bearings for roughness and all shafts for nicks or wear. Gear teeth and shafts require close attention. If you heard noises before teardown, find their source now. Replace gears in paired sets. To replace bearings, use proper pullers and a suitable press. If your shop does not include these tools, take the sub-assemblies to a transmission shop or machine shop.

◀ **Fig. 3-15**

Reassembly begins with loading the needle bearings into each end of the countergear. With a clean and lubricated countershaft (use fresh chassis or lighter wheel bearing grease), install the full set of needle rollers. Note that the grease and Keystone effect hold the bearings in place. Keystone principle assures that if all bearings are evenly in place, they will not fall inward. The only exception is when the bearing bore is worn to an oversized diameter. During your disassembly, pay close attention to the placement of bearing washer(s). Various applications of the T-98/T-18 have different bearing washer layouts. (Some versions require only one washer per countershaft end.)

3

 Fig. 3-16

Continue with the reverse idler gear and outer thrust washer.

Fig. 3-17

With all the needle rollers in place, the reverse idler shaft is carefully inserted through the gear. Note that slot at end of reverse idler shaft must face toward countershaft.

Fig. 3-18

New thrust washers, snap rings (always measure and match the thickness of the original snap rings) and other hardware are supplied in a small parts kit. Here, a thrust washer is placed at each end of the countergear. A film of grease holds the thrust washer in place. Note the locating tang engaging the notch in the case. (Force should not be required during assembly and installation of the countergear.)

Fig. 3-19

The countergear, with needle rollers and thrust washers in place, is lowered into the transmission case. Once the countergear occupies the space between the thrust washers, the bearings and washers will stay in place. Do not install the countershaft at this point.

Fig. 3-20

This snap-ring begins the mainshaft geartrain assembly. Sequence of assembly is important.

Fig. 3-21

Second gear and the second gear thrust washer are the first parts to be placed on the mainshaft.

3

 Fig. 3-22

1st/2nd gear clutch hub is a tricky mechanism to assemble. Three shifting plates, stiff springs and poppet balls must each be pressed into the hub at the same time. Four hands are a good idea here! Be careful not to stretch or bind the springs during assembly and watch for pinched fingers! Use of goggles is advised. This is the proper configuration for placing the poppet balls into position and sliding the 1st/2nd clutch sleeve over the hub.

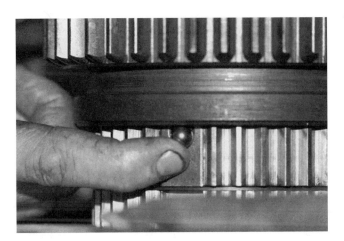

Fig. 3-23

Here's the trick. This poppet ball, and two others like it, must seat in the hub as the sleeve moves into place. Be very careful here.

Fig. 3-24

This is the correct configuration for the hub, three plates and the outer sleeve. Note the machined gear tooth ends on the outer sleeve and the direction in which the hub faces.

◄ **Fig. 3-25**

Look closely at both the outer gear tooth ends and the hub configuration. This is the proper relationship of parts. The rounded teeth on the 1st gear sleeve denotes the non-synchromesh design of compound low gear in these transmissions.

◄ **Fig. 3-26**

With the brass synchronizer ring in place, the 1st/2nd gear assembly slides down the mainshaft splines.

◄ **Fig. 3-27**

This is the mainshaft taking shape. Here, the 1st/2nd gear assembly has moved as far as possible without persuasion.

 Fig. 3-28

A little help from this driver tool will seat the hub. Stay aware of the brass synchronizer ring position as the hub is driven into place.

 Fig. 3-29

This snap ring is the lock for the 1st/2nd gear assembly. Always install new snap rings of proper thickness. Tolerances are found in an OEM level shop manual for the year and application of your transmission. Experience dictates the use of this style snap ring tool.

Fig. 3-30

The second speed gear easily fits into place. Note the use of grease on all friction surfaces of the gears. This is a precaution to prevent scoring or damage during initial run-in.

◀ **Fig. 3-31**

The completed mainshaft assembly is the major part of a T-98/T-18 overhaul. At this point, the 3rd and 4th gear synchronizer assembly is all that remains.

◀ **Fig. 3-32**

A detail of the assembled 3rd and 4th gear synchronizer. A hub, three plates, and two retaining rings fit inside the outer clutch sleeve. Note that the spring end is not inside the plate. When properly installed, the spring will place equal pressure on all three plates. The opposite spring captures all three plates in the same manner.

◀ **Fig. 3-33**

Note direction of the hub flange. The raised center of the hub faces forward. This snap ring completes the assembly of the mainshaft. All that remains is fitup of forward synchronizer ring. If this ring falls off as mainshaft assembly is laid into the case, no problem. Simply hold it in place as you install the clutch shaft.

3

◀ **Fig. 3-34**

Mainshaft pilot bearing roller spacer must be installed before clutch shaft is fitted. Grease again holds the piece in place.

◀ **Fig. 3-35**

Drop the rear end of mainshaft assembly through the bearing bore at the rear of the case. The mainshaft assembly rests atop the loose countergear at this stage.

◀ **Fig. 3-36**

Here the pilot needle rollers fit snugly in the bore of the clutch shaft. Keystone effect is apparent, with the complete circle of rollers creating outward pressure. This holds the rollers in place and serves as a reminder that the full set is present. Recall that the thrust washer rests on the nose end of the mainshaft.

◄ **Fig. 3-37**

With the brass synchromesh ring in place, the clutch shaft is carefully pushed into position. This operation is tricky, as the pilot needle rollers must stay in their bore. Also, the brass synchronizer ring must fit up properly with the three plates.

◄ **Fig. 3-38**

With the front bearing installed, you can now slide the rear bearing into place. The bearing is an interference fit on the mainshaft and requires some light encouragement to install. With its outer snap ring in place, the rear bearing is tapped forward. Front bearing retainer/cap is not in position at this point. It's necessary to watch the clutch gear. If the clutch shaft shows a tendency to move forward, place the pilot end of the shaft against a firm wood post. Drive the rear bearing until its outer snap ring seats against the rear of the case. Note that the inner collar of the bearing is the only area where force is applied.

> **CAUTION—**
> *For any tapping, use a suitable driver tool and plastic hammer to protect bearing from damage. Do not beat on outer bearing race, as this could damage bearings.*

◄ **Fig. 3-39**

Here the rear bearing is seated. Note that on this application, no snap ring is required on the mainshaft. (Outer snap ring is still used.) When the U-joint yoke is installed, the bearing will be squeezed between a shoulder on the mainshaft and the yoke. (An OEM shop manual for the year and application of the transmission will have details on whether the snap ring is required. If a retrofit assembly, see instructions with the adapter kit.)

Fig. 3-40

Now that the mainshaft/clutch shaft assembly is completely installed, the transmission case may be turned over. The countergear, floating in the bottom of the case, will easily align now with the countershaft bore.

Fig. 3-41

Using care, fit the countershaft through the thrust washer, roller/needle bearing assembly, the countergear, the opposite roller/needle bearing assembly, the opposite thrust washer, and the opposite end of the case. Before seating the countershaft in the case, be certain that the notched end faces the reverse idler shaft. Then tap the lock plate into place. This will align the two shafts.

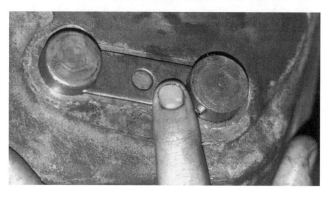

 Fig. 3-42

You can now feed the reverse shifting fork carefully into the case. It may be necessary to move the 1st/2nd gear clutch sleeve slightly to ease installation. Don't move the sleeve too far!

Fig. 3-43

The reverse fork pivot pin taps into place. A new O-ring and film of silicone sealant around the O-ring groove complete the effort. Then insert the tapered lock pin to secure the reverse fork pivot pin. Tap the small end of the taper into the hole and set the pin firmly with your hammer.

> **WARNING—**
> Wear safety goggles when driving the tapered lock pin. This steel is very hard and could splinter or chip!

Fig. 3-44

Install a new seal in the bore of the front bearing retainer/cap. Be certain to index the oil return passage (**ARROW**) with the case oil hole. A new gasket, coated with a thin film of Permatex Ultra Black (or its equivalent) is good assurance of leak proof service. Protect the new seal with a thin coat of grease on its lip. Make sure that sealant is used evenly and sparingly. The retainer fits easily over the clutch shaft. Sealant on threads of front retainer/cap bolts is a wise precaution. Torque these bolts to a maximum of 15 lb-ft or as specified.

3

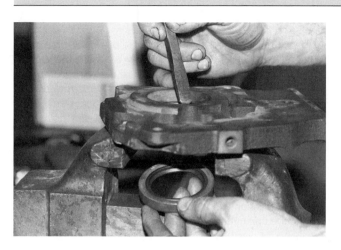

 Fig. 3-45

If required, the mainshaft rear retainer seal is easy to replace. This is good insurance. Apply a thin film of sealant to the outer rim of a new seal, and use a seal driver or suitable technique to drive in the seal. As with the front bearing retainer seal, these parts should be handled carefully to ensure a permanent repair.

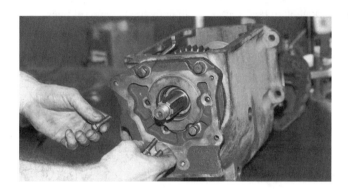

Fig. 3-46

Coat this new paper gasket with a film of Ultra Black or equivalent. Adapter plate bolts, clean and coated lightly with sealant, are tightened evenly. Final torque setting is a maximum of 35 lb-ft (3/8" threads) or 50 lb-ft (1/2" threads).

Fig. 3-47

With drain plug installed, pour oil onto gears and bearings through the P.T.O. or control housing opening. The finished assembly is easy to view through the PTO outlet. Install cover plate with a new, sealant coated gasket. Coat bolt threads lightly with sealant and torque to specification. (Most applications call for 35 lb-ft, but verify the figure in the shop manual covering your transmission application. If you use a PTO drive mechanism, always apply the higher torque setting).

◀ **Fig. 3-48**

The control housing is the last item. Before installing a gasket and bolts, make certain that the forks align with the synchronizer clutch sleeves. This measure is easy but highly important. The reverse slot in the shift mechanism must also be in alignment before the cover falls into place. Use a light coat of sealant on each side of a new gasket and the bolt threads to prevent nuisance oil leaks.

You now have a thoroughly rebuilt T-18 transmission assembly! Most builders install the control housing after the transmission is in the vehicle. If you do so, carefully cover the transmission top hole to prevent contaminants from entering the unit during installation.

Fig. 3-49

Exploded view of T-18 transmission provides a detailed sense for parts nomenclature and layout. The transmission illustrated is a common Ford 2WD truck variety, the design most often recommended for conversions and retrofits. (Courtesy of Ford Motor Company.)

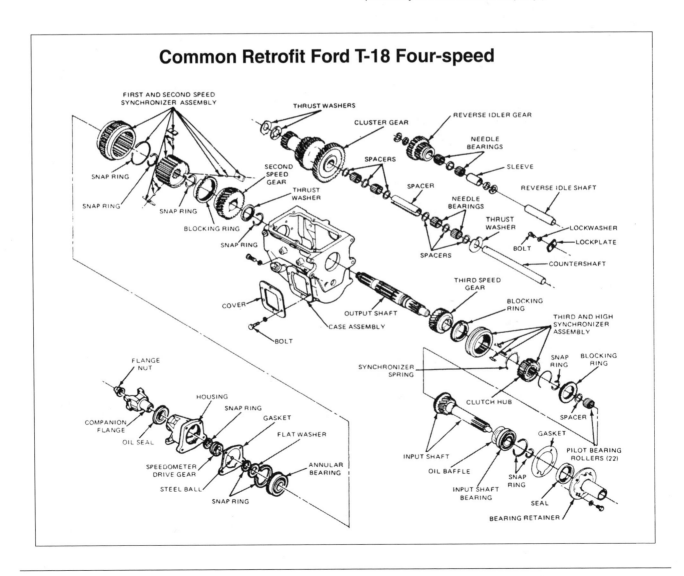

Common Retrofit Ford T-18 Four-speed

Retrofitting a T-18 Four-Speed

Any CJ, whether stock or with a retrofit engine, can benefit from a four-speed truck transmission. Jeep's own choice of the T-98A and T-18 was well conceived. The T-18 is a rugged box that has less bulk and length than most popular truck four-speed transmissions.

On the trail, where gearing makes all the difference, the 6.32:1 compound low gear ratio of the Ford-version Warner T-18 can *double* the 1st gear reduction and crawl ratio when compared to the typical three-speed gearbox! The AMC-era CJ's T-14A three-speed, by contrast, has a first gear ratio of 3.1:1. Even the 4.02:1 1st gear ratio of the Jeep-version T-18 is a noticeable improvement over the three-speed transmission ratios.

For retrofitting the T-18, there are two options: 1) Find an OEM Jeep T-18 four-speed and factory adapter pieces from a salvage yard, or 2) seek adapters from an aftermarket source like Advance Adapters, and find a recycled Ford truck gearbox. The OEM Jeep approach was once viable, when more CJs and J-trucks were available in recycling yards. Today, the practical approach is Advance Adapters' Ford version T-18 to AMC/Jeep CJ conversion.

Novak Enterprises and Advance Adapters

The pioneers in the Jeep engine/transmission adapter business were Novak Enterprises and Advance Adapters. Lloyd Novak, whose passing left a profound void in the Jeep community, was an exceptional metallurgist and machinist. Lloyd's adapter kit for the T-18 retrofit became widely used and sought by many builders. Lloyd will always be remembered and valued for his contribution to Jeep owners and the 4WD community.

Advance Adapters has become the leader in the development of high quality conversion and retrofit kits to serve Jeep and other 4WD enthusiasts. I highly recommend a copy of Advance Adapters' catalog/instruction booklet for the Jeep CJs. Today, Advance Adapters is the optimal source for Jeep engine, transmission and steering upgrade adapters. Advance Adapters also builds retrofit 'Atlas' transfer cases for extreme backcountry use.

 Fig. 3-50

This retrofit T-18/T-98 transmission is rebuilt and ready. Final touch is polishing face and shaft to remove surface rust and irregularities, also to provide a smooth surface for the adapter's lip seal. Protect the front bearing from polishing dust.

 Fig. 3-51

For this earlier Jeep application, Advance Adapters machines a front spacer plate to simulate what Kaiser/Jeep did years ago. An input shaft of correct length is crucial.

NOTE—

Correct depth of the bell housing or an adapter's thickness will provide the proper "stack height" between the flywheel, clutch and mounting face of the transmission. Release arm and bearing must locate correctly as well. To assure a leak-proof assembly, seal and secure these bolt threads with Loctite 242.

 Fig. 3-52

Modern assemblies use RTV-type sealant in place of gaskets. For proper parts fit and sealing, make certain you follow instructions furnished with the adapter kit. In some applications, a selective thickness gasket is needed for proper clearance and mate-up of parts.

 Fig. 3-53

For Willys-Kaiser era Jeep, the three-speed T-90 bearing retainer fits neatly to front adapter. Proper sealant and torquing bolts evenly to 15 lb-ft will wrap up the job. This is the way Kaiser/Jeep did it! Essentially, the Kaiser-built CJs with T-98A option looked like an aftermarket retrofit. 1972-79 CJs use a T-18 pattern bellhousing and the correct length input shaft to attain proper stack height.

NOTE—

Consult Advanced Adapters' catalog when selecting the proper bellhousing and T-18 input shaft. T-18 units were built with a variety of input shaft lengths.

 Fig. 3-54

This kit uses a cut (paper) gasket. Leakage between transmission and transfer case is common on Jeep models that use paper gaskets. Gasket, needed here for proper spacing, benefits from a thin, even coat of RTV sealant on each side.

NOTE—

Permatex Ultra/RTV sealants expand in the presence of lubricants. This assures a flexible, snug seal. The use of RTV sealant with a paper gasket offers a better seal than the older, less pliant gasket sealants that do not have this ability.

3

Fig. 3-55

Adapter's stud is fitted to case using Loctite Threadlocker. Double-nut the stud, and install it like a bolt. Once stud is secured snugly, loosen nuts and remove them.

Fig. 3-56

Making a cut gasket the old-fashioned way. A ball-peen hammer and edge of flange serve as a cutting tool. Note that bolt holes serve to align gasket. This piece is a factory adapter from a four-speed I-H Scout.

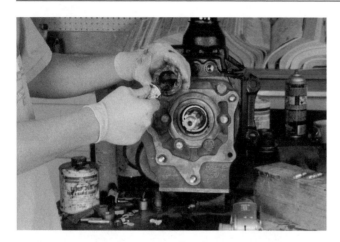

 Fig. 3-57

Bearing spacer fits between output bearing and drive gear on this I-H Scout adapter plate. To prevent oil from wicking past the spacer, I coat the ends of spacer with RTV sealant. Envision where oil might migrate. This arrangement, with sealant placed on the drive gear's splines, will seal the transmission from the transfer case.

Output Shaft Seal and Oil Transfer

Jeep CJs often operate on steep angles. For this reason, a number of Jeep transmission applications require an oil passage between the transfer case and the transmission as a means for stabilizing oil levels once the vehicle returns to flat terrain.

The T-90/Model 18 assemblies, beginning with CJ-2A Serial Number 24196, have two matching 7/16" oil passageways and no oil seal between the transmission and transfer case. Spicer's 20 transfer case found in manual transmission '72-'79 models is similar to the Model 18. Know what your transmission/transfer case setup requires, and be certain to accommodate the design.

When retrofitting a T-18 or other transmission types, follow the directions provided by Advance Adapters. Pay close attention to the proper method for installing gaskets and seals. If in doubt, call the technical phone line at Advance Adapters.

Builders using the 1980-86 Dana 300 transfer case benefit from a fully sealed transfer case. The input bearing retainer has a seal, its lip facing inward toward the transfer case. This seal keeps transfer case oil from moving forward. Similarly, the transmission seals in a manner that prevents transmission oil from migrating into the transfer case. This engineering eliminates the issue of oil transfer between cases.

On any automatic transmission model, ATF (transmission fluid) cannot mix with transfer case gear lubricant. All Jeep models with automatic transmissions require thorough fluid separation between the transmission and transfer case. *This also applies to retrofit automatic transmissions.*

 Fig. 3-58

In some Advance Adapters retrofit kits, like this one-off T-19 transmission unit, a sealed type output bearing is provided. The bearing requires no lubrication, and the sealed faces of the bearing help prevent transfer case oil from migrating into the transmission---and vice versa.

85

Fig. 3-59

Unlike this installation, the adapter plate seal may require that its lip edge face in the opposite direction, *rearward,* to keep transfer case oil from seeping into the transmission. Know which way the seal lip should face before installing the seal! Read the instructions supplied with the kit.

CAUTION—

The Jeep factory transfer case adapter plate seal has its lip edge facing rearward on the earlier Model 18 applications. If you have a stock four-speed CJ or a conversion, make certain that the rear adapter plate seal lip faces in the correct direction! Consult with Advance Adapters or a factory workshop and parts manual covering your specific transfer case and transmission application. The seal lip must face in the correct direction to prevent oil leaks and the transfer of oil from one gear unit to the other.

3

Fig. 3-60

This is a one-off T-19 transmission conversion. Once the sealant-coated gasket, adapter plate and lip seal have been fitted in place, there is no passageway for oil to migrate between the transmission and transfer case.

Fig. 3-61

This arrangement could seal the transmission completely. If, however, the lip of the adapter plate seal faces forward, transfer case oil could squeeze past the seal when the vehicle is on a steep down-slope. To prevent this, the seal would have its lip edge facing rearward.

 Fig. 3-62

Torquing 3/8" stud-size hardware to spec (35 lb-ft with sealant on threads and lockwashers in place), the spacer is visible, inserted through the lip seal. Grease on seal lip will reduce risk of damage during initial operation. Coat mating face of drive gear with RTV sealant, and apply sealant to splines between the output shaft and gear.

Fig. 3-63

Adapter plate from Advance Adapters mates T-98/T-18 transmission to early Jeep T-90 bellhousing. This example illustrates how the input shaft of the transmission must be of correct length for use with this spacer and the stock 134 four-cylinder bellhousing. These principles also apply to AMC-era CJ transmission retrofits.

Fig. 3-64

T-90 bearing retainer indexes (centers) the transmission properly in the bellhousing. Indexing of any manual transmission is essential for proper clutch and transmission input bearing function.

NOTE—

Fig. 3-52 shows machined shoulder used to index adapter to backside of bearing retainer. Backside of adapter fits snugly around shoulder of front bearing and snap ring.

 Fig. 3-65

Adapter plate bolted to bellhousing, the assembly looks like a stock T-90 from front view of bellhousing. Input shaft extends precisely the right length to properly engage clutch splines and pilot bearing. This dimension is crucial.

3

Ultimate Manual Transmission Retrofits

The retrofit of heavy-duty truck transmissions into CJs has gone on for decades. In some instances, the transmission was a tagalong item, tied with a V-8 transplant. Most swaps involve the need for lower overall gearing or a transmission with greater stamina than the OEM unit.

AMC-era use of the T-18 transmission was a step in that direction. The 4.02:1 first gear (compound low) ratio, however, does not match that of the NP435 (6.69:1), Ford T-18 (6.32:1), GM's SM465 Muncie (6.54:1), the SM420's exceptional 7.05:1, or the NV4500 in its 6.34:1 and later 5.61:1 versions. The trend toward lower "crawl ratios" for backcountry travel has popularized the use of truck transmissions.

 Fig. 3-66

Here's a swap I performed on an '81 CJ. Iron NP435 four-speed *(top)* offers 6.69:1 compound first gear ratio. Note how this transmission dwarfs the aluminum-cased T-4 that this CJ-5 sported as OEM equipment. A six-cylinder T-176 bellhousing and Advanced Adapters kit simplified this swap, which also benefited from a factory hydraulic clutch linkage system.

The simplest way to double the overall reduction or crawl ratio is the installation of a truck transmission with compound low gear. The Spicer 20 transfer case has a 2.03:1 low range ratio. Even the T-18 with 4.02:1 first gear ratio does not offer a very low crawl ratio. The builder installing a 6.32:1 Ford version T-18 immediately creates a 59% increase in gear reduction. If the original transmission was a T-14 or 15 three-speed, the reduction gain is over 100%!

◀ **Fig. 3-67**

This layout offers a sense for the Jeep OEM versus truck retrofit transmissions. Left-to-right counter gears: Jeep T-18, T-90, T-14 (first Jeep all synchromesh three-speed), T-5 overdrive type and massive GM 465 Muncie four-speed truck transmission. The NV4500 five-speed counter gear would dwarf the 465 Muncie's gear!

◀ **Fig. 3-68**

The optimal T-18 retrofit is a Ford two-wheel drive version. This gearbox is popular in '66-up Ford trucks. The 6.32:1 compound low gear version is advantageous. This gearbox is readily available in recycling yards.

◀ **Fig. 3-69**

An Advance Adapters conversion kit will typically include an adapter to the transfer case and a new output/mainshaft. Original Ford tail housing (*left*), mainshaft and U-joint yoke will not be reused. OEM Ford mainshaft is at lower left, replaced by a new shaft included in the kit.

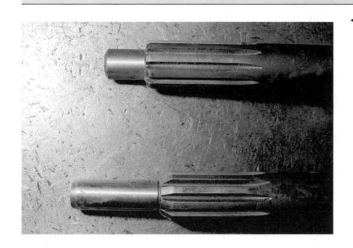

 Fig. 3-70

Input gear and pilot bearing engagement length in T-18 conversions is important! Some kits include a long pilot bearing for Jeep six- and V-8 engines. The pilot bearing supports the nose end of the input/clutch gear. Here, MIT enhances the effect with a long-nose conversion on the Ford input gear.

NOTE—

Finding a stock input/clutch gear for an original AMC/Jeep T-18 application can be expensive and difficult. You must disassemble the transmission to change the input/clutch gear and mainshaft. This involves the steps of a transmission overhaul (described earlier in this chapter).

From 1980 forward, the OEM Jeep CJ transmissions lose stamina. The T-176/177, T-4, SR-4 and T-5 Borg-Warner transmissions have nowhere near the stamina of a heavy-duty truck gearbox. (Of these stock light-duty transmissions, the T-176/177 is likely the strongest.) These transmissions also have taller first gear ratios that minimize backcountry crawl ratios.

There are also some lighter-duty transmission solutions for improved stamina. The late Wrangler TJ's NV 3550 transmission offers a torque rating capable of handling V-8 muscle. This is a transmission offered through Advance Adapters and others. The NV 3550 gearbox offers overdrive, however, it does not offer the ultra-low first gear ratio that hardcore rock crawlers want.

The truck four-speed transmissions do not offer overdrive. These transmissions, the ones I have installed and recommended for many years, provide exceptional backcountry benefit but no highway fuel efficiency gains. Notably, those replacing an OEM T-5 transmission with a truck four-speed will actually *lose* the advantage of overdrive.

Again, the builders of Spicer 20-equipped models have the disadvantage of a taller low range ratio (2.03:1). Unless a Dana 300 (2.61:1) or Atlas transfer case conversion is planned, you may very well need a truck transmission with compound low gear.

 Fig. 3-71

Muncie SM420 four-speed, popularized in '48-'67 G.M. trucks, is the granddaddy of compound 1st gear transmissions. The common version boasts a 7.05:1 ratio, which can make an unaltered Spicer 20 or a Dana 300 equipped Jeep well suited for any trail.

NOTE—

Considering the SM420? A 68.6:1 crawl ratio is possible with the Dana 300 and 3.73 axle gearing. The same axle ratio with a Spicer 20 transfer case provides a 53.4:1 crawl ratio. Also, there are now aftermarket gearset kits to lower the low-range ratio in these two transfer cases. Such a kit would provide even more reduction.

Transmission Choices and Rear Drive-shaft Issues

It is impractical to install an exceptionally long transmission into a CJ-5 with an 84-inch wheelbase! The OEM rear drive-shaft is short, and a longer transmission/transfer case assembly makes the rear driveshaft even shorter. An excessively short driveline, especially a shaft sloped by a suspension lift kit, is at risk of failure.

If you have a CJ-5 with an inline six that takes up the length of the engine bay, a longer transmission is problematic: The rear driveshaft length would be too short. Even a V-8 presents trouble: Moving a V-8 forward to increase rear drive-shaft length creates a weight shift to the front, which is not desirable. Moving a V-8 forward would also entail relocating the front motor mounts plus concern for fan, radiator, suspension and oil pan clearance.

I do not recommend the NV4500 for CJ-5s with an inline six. For these chassis, the T-18 and SM420 Muncie are the best choices, although neither of these units offers overdrive or synchromesh on compound 1st gear.

NOTE—

I did get away with a beefy NP435 four-speed and an in-line six in the '81 CJ-5, however, that's the limit. The rear driveshaft was short!

CJ-7 and CJ-8/Scramblers are far more tolerant of the longer transmission swaps. Keep this in mind with lengthy automatic transmission swaps as well. Advance Adapters' catalogs provide data on the lengths of various transmissions and adapters. *(For further details on driveshaft construction and issues, see the next section, "The 'NV4500' Transplant.")*

The 'NV4500' Transplant

The most formidable transmission swap for CJ Jeep vehicles is the New Venture 4500 series five-speed. This is a transmission designed for extreme loads in the range of 14,500 pounds gross vehicle combination weight (GVCW) and higher, serving various GM and Dodge light/medium duty truck applications. The iron-cased gearbox offers five forward speeds, each with synchromesh, including the compound low gear. In later Dodge versions, even reverse has synchromesh. A highly versatile 27% overdrive provides fuel economy on the highway. This is the ultimate heavy-duty truck transmission.

4WD enthusiasts immediately latched onto the NV4500 as a swap unit. The output readily works with Advance Adapters' conversion kit for the Dana 300 transfer case. The input gear can be either Dodge or GM type, depending upon the gearbox selected and which Advance Adapters kit you choose. This long gearbox pushes the transfer case rearward and requires a change in the rear motor mount, which the kit supplies. Modifications to the crossmember/skid plate are also required.

Despite its massive size, top-to-bottom and front-to-rear, the NV4500 will fit '72-'75 CJ-6s, all CJ-7s and CJ-8s with either six-cylinder or V-8 engines. (The CJ-8 was not available with an OEM V-8, although many CJ-8s have been retrofitted with V-8 engines.) If your four-wheeling requires a transmission with this kind of stamina, obviously a lifetime transmission, here's the NV4500 swap!

 Fig. 3-72

This Advance Adapters bellhousing mates the Dodge version of the NV4500 to a Jeep V-8 or inline six-cylinder engine. Iron release fork, boot, pivot stud and hydraulic slave cylinder are all available from Advance Adapters. Slave release rod is modified for use with this release arm. I apply Loctite 242 to pivot stud threads. A modified front bearing retainer, a GM-type input gear and an adapter pilot bearing round out the engine-to-transmission mate-up.

NOTE—

A stock dimension clutch, the recommended release bearing and a stock Jeep flywheel will work with this swap. Notably, I opted for a Centerforce clutch and the new Mopar flywheel depicted in the clutch section of this chapter. I matched the stamina of the clutch assembly and flywheel to the long-life NV4500 transmission.

3

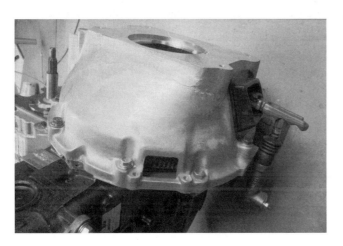

Fig. 3-73

Advance Adapters bellhousing mates 4.2L six to NV4500 transmission. Hydraulic clutch linkage is a reliable alternative to OEM Jeep mechanical linkage. Jeep V-8s use this bellhousing, too. Note the slot for flywheel pickup that enables use of this bellhousing with Jeep 4.0L EFI/MPI engine. *(See clutch section of this chapter for details on the flywheel, pilot bearing, clutch assembly and release mechanism.)*

Fig. 3-74

Fresh Mopar rebuilt engine mates to Advance Adapters' full bellhousing. Advance Adapters has set stack height (flywheel/pilot bearing through clutch) for a GM type input gear. Adapter kit's release arm is made of iron, a quality alternative. Note use of factory "shim" (spacer plate) between engine block and bellhousing.

 Fig. 3-75

New Mopar/Dodge NV4500 was the transmission of choice, available through Dodge Truck /Mopar dealers. A later version, this rugged, regular-duty unit features synchromesh on all forward gears and reverse. Advance Adapters installation kit called for a new GM input shaft (foreground) and custom front bearing retainer. The machined bearing retainer accepts the correct release bearing for this retrofit application.

Fig. 3-76

Dodge input/clutch gear on left was easily removed from front of transmission by wiggling the shaft gently while pulling it forward. Shorter GM gear is correct for this retrofit kit. Note pilot nose diameter difference and clutch splines. When removing the gear, use care not to lose any parts or dislodge the pieces at the forward synchronizer.

Fig. 3-77

For those curious just how the regular duty NV4500 rates 14,500 pounds GVCW, take a look at these gears! Unrivaled stamina for a light/medium duty truck transmission is obvious. Keep the front synchronizer and bearing pieces in place while changing the input gear.

 Fig. 3-78

Use '518' Gasket Eliminator, an anaerobic sealant. Coat the front bearing retainer evenly. Install the input gear carefully. Make certain that all pieces, including the caged and thrust bearings, reside in their places. Do not force parts together! I coat the input gear seal with light grease to protect it during run-in.

3

◀ **Fig. 3-79**

New GM input gear and Advance Adapters' modified bearing retainer now replace the OEM Dodge pieces. I put '518' sealant on retainer bolt threads and torqued the bolts to specification. Tighten bolts in cross. Come up to torque setting in stages. The transmission is now ready for installation.

◀ **Fig. 3-80**

I could not find the factory cover for this slot (found only on 4.2L engines built from 1987-90) nor was the 4.0L sensor pickup needed here. Instead, I fabricated this piece from light steel plate, using my cutting torch, grinder, drill press and MIG welder to produce an "OEM" look. I applied a bead of RTV sealant between the plate and housing surface. This opening must be sealed from trail debris and moisture.

 Fig. 3-81

Big enough? NV4500 is hefty enough to require an engine hoist to lift it onto my transmission jack! This is an iron-cased, massive gear size transmission. Complete with Mopar's factory rear adapter, unit is now ready to install.

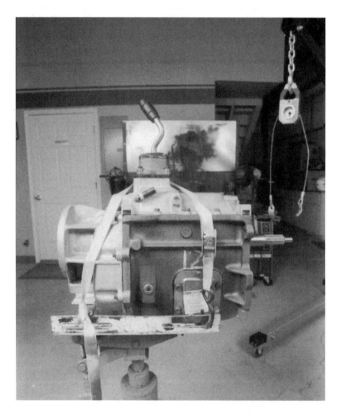

Fig. 3-82

My transmission jack is rated ½-ton capacity. I'm glad in this case! I use straps to secure the unit on the jack. Platform has tilts in four directions to align a transmission without muscling it around. This kind of equipment makes heavy work appealing. Tooling is a sound investment!

 Fig. 3-83

Engine weight at bellhousing is minimal. I support the engine in this manner to prevent stress to motor mounts. Note relationship of throwout bearing, release arm and hydraulic clutch slave cylinder. Quality machining on Advance Adapters' bellhousing is evident, the precise cuts and finishing match the Dodge or GM NV4500 factory pieces!

 Fig. 3-84

I really appreciate the versatility of this transmission jack! Without stressing a single part, I effortlessly tilted and angled this massive transmission as the input gear slid gently through the clutch hub.

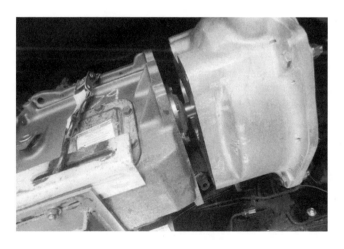

Fig. 3-85

I had carefully aligned the clutch disc during assembly, which enabled immediate engagement of the input gear's nose and the pilot bearing. In minutes, I had the transmission face-to-face with the bellhousing. At no point was there any weight stressing the clutch hub or pilot bearing.

Fig. 3-86

Once the mating bolts were securely tightened, I placed a tri-pod stand beneath the bellhousing and lowered the transmission jack. Tripod stand rates 2,000 pounds. Each of these tools is able to support far more weight than the transmission and engine.

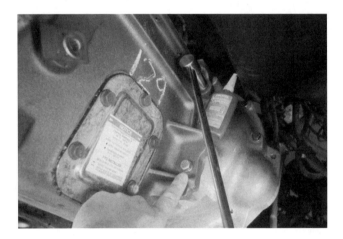

Fig. 3-87

I upgraded the kit's hardware to Grade 8 bolts of proper thread pitch and length. Split ring lockwashers are also Grade 8. Note use of Loctite 242 on threads for added insurance. Four-wheeling torque and vibration require this kind of protection. Torque bolts to specification for the transmission's OEM application.

Fig. 3-88

This adapter is actually the stock Dodge piece, complete with factory seal and output shaft. Advance Adapters makes this swap easy for Dana 300 users. Dana 300 mating face bolts directly to this adapter face! Here, I place a film of '518' sealant on mating surface to keep moisture out of cavity.

◀ **Fig. 3-89**

Note input front bearing retainer on Dana 300 transfer case. This is a custom piece in Advance Adapters' kit. Retainer locates and helps keep transfer case centered. Inner splined hub engages NV4500 output shaft. NV4500 output shaft seal wraps around the splined hub. This is an emulation of the factory sealing method, very reliable and sensible. *(See **Chapter 4** for details on the adapter hub installation.)*

NOTE—

4WD Hardware, Inc., supplied the transfer case shift linkage pieces shown in Fig. 3-89. Lithium grease helps lube shift components without attracting dirt. Renew these parts during transfer case installation.

3

◀ **Fig. 3-90**

Here's that transmission jack again! Tilts enable installation without risk of stressing or binding parts. Protecting seals in this manner prevents nuisance leaks later. Align holes with a bolt or two. Tighten bolts evenly to squarely pull the transfer case to the transmission.

◀ **Fig. 3-91**

Once the transfer case hardware is torqued to specification, I place a tripod stand beneath the thick bellhousing. Bellhousing-to-engine block bolts are Grade 8 and have been torqued to specification during earlier assembly. I use Loctite 242 on all fasteners in addition to the use of factory locking hardware.

 Fig. 3-92

Advance Adapters provided a rear motor mount. I chose to thicken this piece to set the transmission height where desired. This piece is made from a thick-walled, split rectangular steel tube. I added the piece on top to allow the transfer case to sit flatly on the mount without interference. A/A's kit is thorough, however, individual applications vary and often require fabrication work like my mount.

> *CAUTION—*
>
> *Use care when aligning and locating the transmission and transfer case. I used new Mopar front motor mounts to position the engine before centering the transmission/transfer case assembly. Driveshaft angles, body and frame clearance, the engine's fan position, and even the vehicle's center-of-gravity, weight distribution and roll center, will be affected by engine and transmission positioning. The engine's fan angle, the level of the carburetor base or throttle body base, and correct driveshaft angles are each indicators of the powertrain's alignment.*

 Fig. 3-93

Painted and positioned, powertrain components look much like original equipment pieces. Before aligning the crossmember/skid plate, take great care to measure the driveshaft angles, the level of the carburetor or EFI throttle body's mounting surface and the cooling fan's angle. The carburetor or throttle body base should be level.

NOTE—

For lateral alignment, carefully measure and center up the rear driveline between the frame rails. (This works on Spicer 20 and Dana 300 equipped models.) Be aware that some retrofit installations require offsetting the entire powertrain for front driveline clearance. Also note that the '76-'79 Borg-Warner 'Quadra-Trac' transfer case is not a through-drive type. The front and rear driveshafts are offset to the right like the early Jeep's Model 18 side-drive transfer case.

 Fig. 3-94

Advance Adapters rear motor mounts for the NV4500 are effective and stable. A broader foot than the OEM Jeep mount, this design helps prevent torque wind-up. Jeep uses a torque arm. The torque arm is unnecessary with this A/A mount design. Interlocking two-piece motor mount cushions are a proven design.

Fig. 3-95

I modified the skid plate to align the NV4500 rear motor mount, provide clearance for the deep transmission case and maintain the original skid plate alignment. The plate was set in the rearmost of its frame holes, and this section of plate was marked out. I cut out the raised section and fabricated a flat piece of plate to replace the section. Penetrating MIG welds on both sides assure integrity of the modified plate. I then ground plate to restore finish.

Fig. 3-96

In the welding process, careful preparation, stitch tacking at corners and application of correct heat will prevent warpage and distortion. My final passes penetrated from both sides with no risk of occlusions. Finish grinding removes crowns but not the strength or integrity of the metal and welds. This is not a load-bearing section of the plate, and the intent is to reshape and restore only.

> **CAUTION—**
>
> *Were this a load-bearing section, I would leave weld crowns in place. Welds should not be ground down in a stressed or loaded section of metal. Frame and crossmember fabrication is not like sheet metal work where welding and grinding the surface is common.*

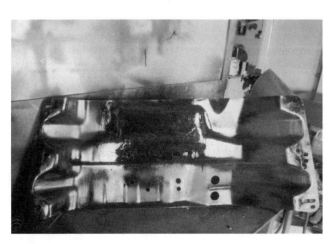

Fig. 3-97

Prepped for paint, a coat of primer sealer fills minor grinding scratches. Several light coats of quality black engine enamel, and the skid plate modification could not be detected. Note that the motor mount holes (larger, wider pair near OEM holes) have been drilled and painted. I enjoy this kind of creative and functional work.

 Fig. 3-98

Bottom side of plate/crossmember reveals newly shaped section. This enables rectangular mount to fit squarely and provides clearance for the deep transmission case. Some builders would consider dropping the skid plate for clearance. I elected to leave the plate in its OEM location (positioned at the rearmost frame and plate holes) for ground clearance and appearance sake.

 Fig. 3-99

Angle view reveals mounting hardware and relationship of interlocking mount cushions. Note that cushions have slight crush when nuts are tightened correctly. Nylock nuts provided by Advance Adapters allow precise adjustment of crush without risk of nuts backing loose. *(Do not over-tighten! Cushions must remain pliant.)* Two upper OEM transmission adapter bolts and split ring lockwashers are Grade 8. Torque to specification, and use Loctite 242 for insurance.

 Fig. 3-100

Final installation in this '86 CJ-7 looks factory! This is a remarkable fit, as the NV4500 is a massive gearbox for such a short wheelbase vehicle. A CJ-5 would not be a candidate, as there would be too little space for a reliable rear driveshaft. Note that I moved the skid plate to rearmost frame attachment points.

Fig. 3-101

I went to Mopar/Jeep for a new speedometer gear. On this vehicle, the change to 4.56 axle gears from 3.54 type necessitated the switch to a gear with more teeth. I did the math and got it right the first time. Tire size remained the same, so the math was not complicated.

Fig. 3-102

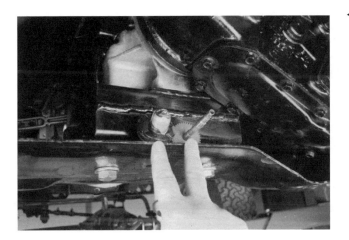

On Dana 300, the OEM sleeve/adapter for the speedometer gear is rotated to different positions for the various tooth counts. Be certain to identify the tooth count and properly index the adapter to assure proper gear tooth mesh.

Fig. 3-103

This '86 had OEM hydraulic clutch linkage. I notched the spacer/shim plate to allow installation of the new Advance Adapters' Girling slave cylinder (similar to OEM). Slave mounts to bellhousing, and A/A provides the release rod and fulcrum end that indexes with the A/A release arm. In this application, I carefully reshaped this CJ's OEM hydraulic hose and pipe to fit.

3

Fig. 3-104

Simple hydraulic clutch linkage is reliable, smooth and ideal for a vehicle that twists and shakes off-pavement! '72-up CJ models with mechanical clutch linkage are prone to problems. Linkage that runs from the frame to bellhousing is subject to twisting and even dislodging. Hydraulic linkage moves with the powertrain and makes the best sense for your Jeep.

NOTE—

This '86 CJ has the hydraulic clutch master cylinder as OEM equipment. If your Jeep does not have hydraulic linkage, there are aftermarket improvements available. See the clutch linkage section in this chapter.

Fig. 3-105

For models where the OEM hydraulic hose is not available, Advance Adapters provides this hose option. OEM hose or aftermarket braided stainless brake-grade hose is required for this installation. Repeated application force at the clutch release arm is similar to hydraulic brake cylinder loads.

Fig. 3-106

For this aftermarket installation, I fabricated an angle bracket for a clutch release arm spring. This is a common universal clutch spring available at any auto supply. Make certain the spring clears the boot and other surfaces over its range of motion. Spring assures complete return of release arm and throwout bearing for proper clearance between the bearing face and clutch fingers. I upgraded the cylinder-to-bellhousing bolts to Grade 8.

> *CAUTION—*
>
> *Full clutch engagement, full release and adequate throwout/release bearing clearance are crucial for performance and long clutch life. See the clutch section of this chapter for details on clutch operation and proper adjustment.*

3

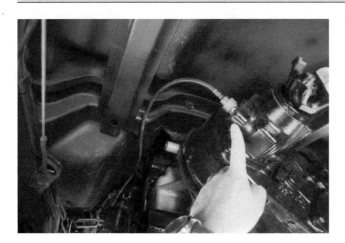

 Fig. 3-107

Installation of speedometer cable into transfer case was relatively simple in this '86 CJ-7 chassis. The OEM cable was long enough for careful rerouting and use. Make sure that cable does not bind or chafe against any surface. Cable needs broad sweeps to prevent binding and premature wear.

Topside Details, Shift Controls and Fabrication Work

Once the powertrain is in place and secured properly, you can complete the shift mechanisms and final sheet metal details. Despite its mass, the NV4500 was not that difficult to address. Jeep's use of a broad transmission cover plate helps here.

The NV4500 and other long transmissions will place the transfer case shifter in a different position. Since some AMC/Jeep transmission applications have rear-positioned shifters (single-rod style), the location of the shifter hole is not the same as truck four-or five-speeds. For these reasons, you can plan on modifying the transmission cover and possibly a section(s) of the floorboard.

Pushing the transfer case rearward also requires a new location for the transfer case shifter. The sheet metal work resembles body shop chores, and some builders may prefer subletting the work at considerable expense. Here I share the sheet metal fabrication involved in the '86 CJ/NV4500 conversion, and you can decide whether to attempt this kind of work.

 Fig. 3-108

Topside view: NV4500, despite its mass, actually fits within the OEM floorpan opening! This is as close as possible. Advance Adapters' rear transmission mount design helps reduce movement, making this a reasonable fit.

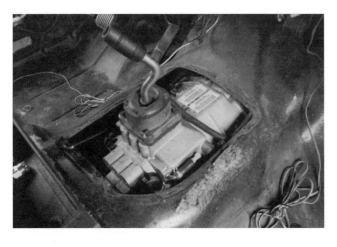

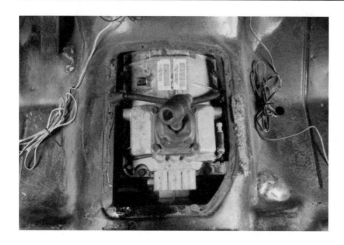

 Fig. 3-109

This works. The NV4500 shifter is well centered but rides high above OEM location. Transmission cover plate will require modification to accept the taller and larger control housing. This is still far easier than modifying a floorboard.

Fig. 3-110

I rough cut the floorpan to adequately clear the shift tower. Here, the shape of the "box" is determined by measuring the rise necessary to clear the tower. Allow plenty of room for movement and boot clearance.

Fig. 3-111

Shaping is easily performed with a "nibbler." This tool is available through body shop tool suppliers and generic tool sources. (Inexpensive offshore tools work fine here if you do not use the nibbler every day.) Accuracy of this air tool enables professional results.

◄ **Fig. 3-112**

Box is coming together here. Basic knowledge of sheet metal forming helps. I use a sheet metal shear to make notches and square cuts in tight spaces.

◄ **Fig. 3-113**

Simple shaping with a body hammer has squared the box. I am not a sheet metal expert, yet the results turned out well. Hammer the metal carefully. This is non-galvanized sheet metal of 22-gauge. Since I have retained the rest of the cover for shape and integrity, the box serves as a stout addition.

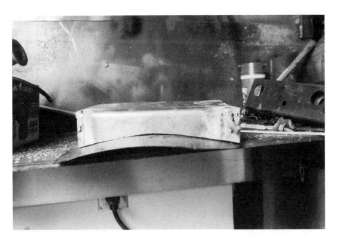

◄ **Fig. 3-114**

I elected to braze the seams of the box. This is a lower heat range and less likely to warp metal. Brass is quite strong and more than adequate for this application. If you can braze, consider this approach.

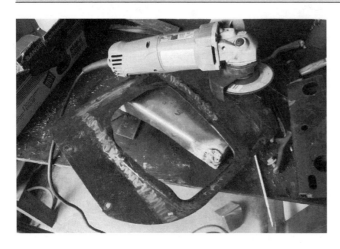

 Fig. 3-115

I removed paint and roughed the OEM cover in areas where I intend to braze. This size grinder is versatile and easy to operate. Use a respirator when brazing or welding around painted surfaces. All burning paint with VOC content is toxic. Old paint can even contain lead.

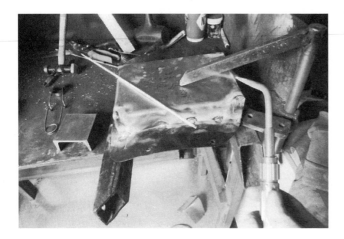

Fig. 3-116

To reduce risk of warpage, I spot braze the box in place. Once tacked thoroughly, brazing should not cause buckling on this gauge metal.

Fig. 3-117

I like brass! The easy filling of gaps and smoother finish require no additional work. Once done, this is a weatherproof, strong bond. Resistant to shear, more ductile than steel, brazing makes a durable alternative to mild steel gas or wire-feed welding on light-gauge metals and small parts repairs. Try it!

3

Fig. 3-118

A coat of primer-sealer and several light coats of black engine enamel produced this result. Make the box large enough to clear the shift tower. Allow for movement! If the boot base is larger than the one I used or has a bigger base, *build a larger box!* You have the entire cover area as a working surface. These were the tools I used.

Fig. 3-119

My hole saw for gauges served well here. I am cutting the hole for the new transfer case shifter location. I began conservatively, with a hole just large enough to fit the shifter through the floorboard.

Fig. 3-120

The OEM shift arm would no longer align properly. Further back and way right, the arm needed bending. I use an oxy-acetylene rosebud tip and apply heat over the bend area. This is an intuitive process; You do not want to burn into or damage the shaft but want the metal to yield as you apply *leather-gloved* hand pressure. Allow metal to cool at room temperature.

> **WARNING—**
>
> *A shift shaft rod requires a good amount of heat to bend. Wear proper eye and hand protection, leather gloves and a welder's jacket if available. Weld and bend in a safe, fireproof area. Wear work boots, not running shoes! Your welding environment must meet OSHA safety standards! Be alert!*

 Fig. 3-121

The nibbler and a rotary grinding bit finish the hole. I made this hole large enough for shifter movement, body shifting and access to the pivot stud on the transfer case. This enables service and removal of the shaft with the transfer case still in the vehicle.

Fig. 3-122

Shifter fits transfer case with stock pieces. The acorn nut must be fastened securely to the pivot pin! Torque this nut tightly and use Loctite to assure that it will not come loose. Lever is shifted fully rearward at this point with adequate clearance to the body.

Fig. 3-123

This primer sealer will help prevent rust on the cut edge and bare sheet metal surface. I always use a quality primer before coating with paint and/or undercoating. Quality black engine enamel on shifter arm is a durable and attractive finish.

 Fig. 3-124

This OEM Jeep shifter boot turned out just right for the new shifter location! Pliant, the boot could be formed to the shape of the floorpan curves. Hefty self-drilling screws now secure the boot. I will spray undercoating/sealant along the edge of this boot to assure a waterproof seal.

 Fig. 3-125

The OEM Jeep backup lamp switch used a different plug type. A weatherproof, two-pronged plug was necessary. I spliced the wires into the OEM circuit, and now the backup lamps will work with the NV4500 transmission.

 Fig. 3-126

I want every wiring circuit to have OEM integrity. Convolution tubing is one way to assure that these harnesses will last the lifespan of the vehicle. Note use of plastic ties and routing of tubing away from sharp edges or any rubbing surfaces. You want your backup lamps to work in the backcountry!

 Fig. 3-127

I route vent hoses high in the body to eliminate any risk of water seepage into the gear cases. Here, I removed the short hose at the transmission and joined the transfer case and transmission vent hoses with a 'T' fitting. I ran the vent hose forward to a valve well up on the firewall.

Fig. 3-128

Transfer case '4WD' wiring, vent hoses and backup lamp wiring are all neatly routed and secure. Protect these wires with a view toward thousands of miles down the road. Will these wires be safe and intact 100,000 miles from now, after years of rough backcountry driving and foul winter weather?

Fig. 3-129

A bead of body caulking restores weather-tight seal between cover and floorboard. Steps like this assure a safe, warm cab. Holes in the floorboard and gaps in the shift cover will defeat your Jeep's heater. If you want fresh air, lower the cloth top or open the vents and windows. Air from beneath the body is road air, complete with toxic tailpipe gases. Seal underside of floor board with rubberized spray undercoating.

3

◀ **Fig. 3-130**

3M Rubberized Body Undercoating provided a durable finish coat on the floorboard and boots. Similar to bed liner coatings and easy to apply at home, undercoating seals and provides a degree of insulation from noise, cold and heat. Simple!

CAUTION—

Use a respirator when spraying undercoat materials.

◀ **Fig. 3-131**

Advance Adapters provides a shift stick, knob and barrel adapter for the NV4500. This is the right length and provides a quality addition to your Jeep!

◀ **Fig. 3-132**

This final location of the shifters is handy. I strived to place both shifters within ready reach, without the need to look down while driving. The passenger has adequate legroom, the levers have good spacing, and the driver can reach either shifter without effort. For the NV4500, this works!

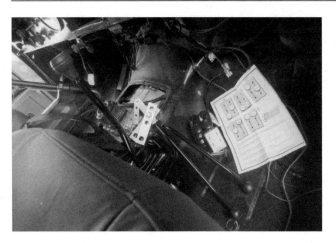

Fig. 3-133
Unfortunately, the Currie 'twin-stick' conversion was not an option for this installation. Currie's kit provides useful options like front wheel drive low-range or low-range rear wheel drive plus the normal shift positions. If you intend to drive in rugged backcountry and have a CJ with the Dana 300 transfer case, consider this versatile accessory sourced from 4WD Hardware, Inc.

Clutch Service and Replacement

The 1972-86 CJs have three-finger and diaphragm type clutches. Conventional, reliable and of popular design, these clutches range from disc diameters of 9.125" (four-cylinder models) to 10.5" and even 11" (sixes and V-8s). While there is nothing extraordinary about these clutches, they do provide the kind of service one would expect from an OEM Jeep clutch. Used properly without excess abuse, the stock CJ clutch holds up well.

For the '86 CJ-7 depicted in this book, I turned to Midway/Centerforce, the popular manufacturer of aftermarket performance clutch assemblies. In each of my vehicle projects since the mid-1980s, I have relied upon Centerforce clutch assemblies for a variety of reasons.

Centerforce's unique centrifugal block weights increase the clamping force as engine rpm increases. The static clamping force of a Centerforce clutch assembly equals or exceeds the performance of a stock Jeep clutch of the same diameter. This means that the Centerforce clutch pedal pressure is similar to the OEM diaphragm clutches, which tend to be a lighter touch than three-finger clutches.

The light touch and ample static clutch pressure provide smooth disengagement-and-engagement. As rpm increases, clamping pressure rises. This delivers substantial resistance to slip under heavy loads. Again, the two benefits of a Centerforce clutch are 1) light pedal pressure and 2) exceptional clamping pressure and resistance to slippage under load.

In my experience, I have never seen a Centerforce clutch fail in service or deliver less than exceptional life. Adjusted properly, which is not a frequent chore for a clutch that simply does not wear much in normal service, the Centerforce clutch could easily last as long as a fresh engine!

Whether you choose a rebuilt or new OEM replacement clutch assembly, or the gains of a custom aftermarket clutch like the Centerforce I or II, the service tips provided here will help assure your Jeep's reliability. There is no service chore more time consuming than the replacement of a Jeep clutch. Selecting the right clutch and properly installing the parts will enhance your Jeep's service life and reliability.

Installation Tips

When you replace your Jeep clutch, make certain that the flywheel face is straight and free of cracks and scoring. Take the flywheel to your local machine shop for inspection and re-surfacing if necessary. If the flywheel is excessively worn or warped, purchase a new flywheel.

Always replace the release bearing and pilot bearing when you change the clutch. These parts are not that expensive, and the labor to replace them later is excessive! It is simply cheap insurance to replace the throwout bearing, pilot bearing, flywheel bolts and clutch cover bolts. Use quality OEM grade pieces, and make certain that all fasteners are properly graded.

Fig. 3-134

OEM Jeep clutches are of diaphragm (left) or three-finger Borg & Beck clutches (right). These two clutches are common to '72-'86 CJs. Readily available as new, rebuilt or heavy-duty aftermarket replacements, the Jeep clutch is popular and similar to other domestic types.

Fig. 3-135

Midway's Centerforce clutch is a modified diaphragm type. Built to exacting standards, with centrifugal weights attached to the fingers, these clutches offer exceptional service life with a light pedal touch.

NOTE—

During disassembly, always relieve torque from the clutch cover by loosening the bolts evenly, a few turns at a time. When installing the clutch disc and cover, use Loctite 242 or equivalent on the bolt threads; install lockwashers as required. Tighten bolts finger tight, then uniformly, a few turns at a time. This will prevent warpage of the clutch cover or distortion of the springs.

Fig. 3-136

This shim (spacer plate) is common to V-8 and six-cylinder AMC engines. The bellhousing pattern is the same for all AMC engines except the four-cylinder 2.5L. This plate must be in place *before* installing the flywheel! There is a hollow dowel on each side of the engine block to index and align the shim. I installed new Mopar dowels on this rebuilt Mopar 4.2L crate engine.

Fig. 3-137

Clean the crankshaft and flywheel flange of any debris. Align the flywheel with the crankshaft flange's threaded holes. I use Loctite Threadlocker on a set of new Mopar flywheel bolts. Start bolts with fingers then tighten evenly until the flywheel is flush against the crankshaft flange. Torque the bolts in cross, uniformly tightening them in stages to full torque. Wait a few minutes, then re-check torque to specification.

Fig. 3-138

These parts assure a long-life clutch installation! A new Jeep/Mopar flywheel, dowels and bolts guarantee safe flywheel operation. The flywheel comes with a new starter ring installed. Centerforce clutch assembly and a new throwout/release bearing complete the package. Always install new OEM or specified clutch cover bolts.

 Fig. 3-139

On this installation, the NV4500 conversion, Advance Adapters provides a bronze pilot bushing. Drive the bushing with an appropriate driver tool. Make certain that a pilot tool or transmission input shaft nose will fit readily into the bushing.

AUTHOR'S TIP!

One time-honored method for removing the old pilot bushing is to pack grease into the crankshaft's pilot cavity. Using the guide tool or a shaft of the same diameter as the pilot bore, drive the tool into the grease. This hydraulic ram effect will force the bearing out of the bore.

CAUTION—

Follow instructions that come with the new pilot bearing or bushing. Some pilot bearings call for a small amount of appropriate grease in the cavity behind the bushing. Other bushings and bearings require no grease. Some Jeep applications use an oil wick in the bore behind the pilot bearing.

 Fig. 3-140

Here, I use the GM input gear for the NV4500 as a guide tool. Place the clutch cover over the disc, and insert the guide tool into the pilot bore. Use Loctite Threadlocker on the bolt threads. Tighten the cover bolts slowly and evenly in cross. Do not hurry this process. By turning bolts a small amount at a time, you will keep the disc on center.

CAUTION—

Make sure that the clutch disc's offset hub faces in the correct direction! The hub flange must not interfere with the pilot bearing or crankshaft flange when the clutch cover fits against the flywheel. Be certain that the guide tool slides freely in and out of the clutch hub splines and the pilot.

 Fig. 3-141

Here is the notch I cut in the shim to allow proper fit-up of the hydraulic clutch slave cylinder. Note hardware grading on the clutch cover bolt. Always use approved high-strength OEM or equivalent fasteners engineered for use on the clutch, flywheel and linkage.

> **WARNING—**
>
> *I am old enough to recall horror stories from the hot rod and Muscle Car eras when clutches and flywheels would disintegrate or come loose, flying through the floorboard with explosive force. Be careful when installing your flywheel and clutch! Use correct fasteners, locking hardware and thread locking liquid as a backup. Torque hardware accurately.*

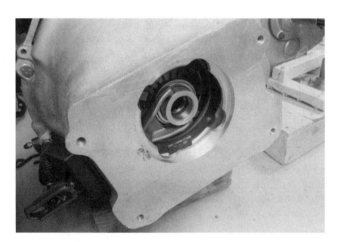

 Fig. 3-142

This is the assembly ready for transmission installation. Make certain that the release arm and release bearing are properly in place. Many Jeep CJ applications use a pivot ball and retainer spring that must be in place before the bellhousing is attached to the engine. Align the release fork/arm and throwout bearing. Check the movement of parts before the bellhousing goes into place.

Ten Tips for a Successful Clutch Installation

Clutch replacement on a 4WD Jeep is a major job. To make certain your clutch works properly and delivers the kind of long service you expect, pay attention to these steps:

1) Always install a new pilot bearing or bushing. Bearing/bushing material must be a correct match for the nose end material of the input shaft. (Follow parts vendor guidelines.) If called for, pack a small amount of high-temp grease in the recess behind the bushing. (*Do not overfill, as this will prevent the shaft from passing through the bushing.*) Wipe away any excess grease.

2) Install a new throwout/release bearing, regardless of how good the old one appears. This, again, is cheap insurance for a bearing that requires hours to access. Check the free movement of the bearing on the transmission's front bearing retainer. If the retainer surface is rough, remove minor galling with emery paper or crocus cloth. If too far worn, replace the bearing retainer.

3) Loosen and tighten the bolts in a cross pattern, a few threads at a time. This will prevent distortion of the cover and springs.

4) When installing the new disc, use a clutch alignment tool. As an alternative to the clutch alignment tool, an old transmission input shaft works nicely.

5) Always center the disc with the pilot bearing, and leave the tool or dummy shaft in place as you tighten the cover bolts. Be certain that the tool or shaft will still slide easily into and out of the disc---and all the way into the pilot bearing.

6) Make certain that the clutch hub faces in the correct direction! Most often, the raised section goes toward the transmission, not toward the flywheel. *Know which way the disc should fit, and do not install the disc backward!*

7) Use new clutch cover bolts of the correct thread pitch, tensile strength (grading), shoulder style and length. Locking hardware should be new and properly graded as well. Use Loctite 242 for added assurance that the properly torqued bolts will stay tight for the life of the clutch.

NOTE—
If anything, consider even higher quality bolts and lock washers designed specifically for clutch installations. Such hardware is generally found at high performance parts outlets and can also be purchased through Mopar Performance sources.

8) Threads should be clean and free of rust or scale. This will assure proper torque settings. Use a torque wrench to ensure uniform torque.

9) Using high-temp grease, lightly coat the release fork pivot and fork contact points. Pack the recessed groove in the collar bore of the throwout bearing. Be careful not to overgrease, as excess grease, oozing from the bearing collar, could damage the clutch disc. Grease helps prevent binding and galling and also helps protect against the water that will inevitably find its way into the bellhousing of a 4WD Jeep.

CAUTION—
Excessive grease could find its way onto clutch friction material and damage the clutch. Grease the throwout bearing's inner groove; place only a light film of grease on the remaining sleeve bore. Wipe grease from ends of the throwout bearing.

10) Make certain that the clutch is aligned for easy insertion of the transmission input shaft. There is nothing more frustrating than trying to align an input shaft with an out-of-center clutch disc---especially with a transfer case hanging from the rear of a hefty transmission!

3

Clutch Linkage and Upgrades

A problem common to the earliest Jeep models is clutch linkage failure. In the Willys/Kaiser era, the use of wear-prone cable linkage, through-the-floor pedals and frail pull rods proved problematic.

At the outset of the AMC-era, some CJs came with housed cable linkage. Others had mechanical linkage. Both designs have been troublesome. Cables, cross-shafts, bellcranks, brackets, bushings and pedal assemblies simply take a beating on Jeep 4x4s.

NOTE—

In the late '80s, I did a photo shoot assignment for OFF-ROAD Magazine. The subject was a radically built Jeep at Phoenix, Arizona. The owner insisted on jumping a ridge with the CJ and having me photograph the leap. When the Jeep landed, I had the photo he wanted. The owner spent the next half hour searching for parts over a 100-foot stretch of ground. Lying beneath the Jeep in the dirt, he attempted to reattach the cross-shaft, bushings and other pieces of the mechanical clutch linkage---only to discover a broken cross-shaft support bracket. Unable to shift the transmission's gears without damaging them, he called for a car-hauling trailer.

The most reliable Jeep linkage to date has been external/hydraulic. On CJs, this starts with a clutch pedal and conventional clutch release arm at the bellhousing. The pedal rod applies the clutch master cylinder piston, sending brake fluid to the slave cylinder mounted at the bellhousing. This allows the engine and transmission assembly to move independently of the body/frame shifting and twisting. No amount of jostling will affect the smooth and predictable clutch operation, as the slave cylinder is firmly affixed to the bellhousing.

 Fig. 3-143

Cross-shaft support bracket (**ARROW**) on this '72 CJ-5 is a heavy-duty replacement item installed by the owner. Linkage from the pedal is hefty enough to survive on the trail.

 Fig. 3-144

Bracket on bellhousing supports the clutch cross shaft. Cross shaft is suspended between the frame and bellhousing. Bellcrank arm pushes the rod against the release arm. Note the adjustment threads on the release arm pushrod. This '72 Jeep CJ does regular duty on the Rubicon Trail. The Jeep's owner claims ongoing success with the beefy, modified mechanical clutch linkage.

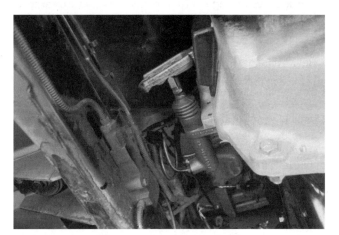

 Fig. 3-145

Hydraulic slave cylinder moves with the bellhousing. The driver steadily presses the clutch pedal, and the reaction at the clutch matches the pedal movement---unlike mechanical linkage that is subject to the movement and twists of the frame and powertrain. A return spring attached to the release arm end will complete this aftermarket installation. (See Fig. 3-106.)

NOTE—

The combined use of Advance Adapters' hydraulic clutch linkage for CJ transmission transplants coupled to a Centerforce clutch creates a remarkably light pedal pressure. You might need time to become accustomed. The engagement and disengagement points are remarkably smooth.

Clutch Adjustment Tips

Proper clutch operation and a long service life depend upon correct clutch adjustment. *Insufficient clearance* between the clutch release (throwout) bearing face and the clutch cover fingers will result in clutch slip and rapid wear of the disc. *Too much clearance* will not allow full clutch release, and this causes gear clash on shifting.

Considering the number of wear points on stock Jeep mechanical clutch linkage, begin by taking all slack out of the linkage with the pedal fully released. (All slack means that the clutch release bearing just rests against the fingers of the clutch without pressing on the fingers.)

At this point, the turns of play on the pushrod adjuster should provide 1" to 1-1/2" pedal free play and, Jeep presumes, the desirable clearance between the release bearing face and clutch release fingers.

On CJs with OEM hydraulic clutch linkage, *there is no adjustment necessary.* The release arm retracts from clutch pressure, and the throwout bearing thrusts back slightly from the clutch cover fingers. There is no provision for adjustment on the stock CJ hydraulic clutch linkage. Jeep does not use a release arm spring with the OEM hydraulic linkage.

NOTE—

On the Advance Adapters hydraulic system, the pushrod is adjusted much like mechanical linkage, and a return spring pulls the release arm back. (See Fig. 3-106.)

Assuming that return springs (if so equipped) are in good condition, enabling the release arm to retract properly, there will be sufficient clearance between the release bearing face and clutch cover fingers. To be certain this crucial clearance exists, I always confirm the actual free-play at the clutch release arm.

Return springs working correctly, check the gap between the release bearing and clutch cover fingers. While looking inside the release lever slot in the bellhousing, move the clutch release lever fore and aft. I look for a minimum clearance of 3/32" between the release fingers and the face of the retracted throwout bearing. *Less than this will result in premature wear of the clutch and throwout bearing. More play than this may not allow enough pedal travel to release the clutch completely.*

NOTE—

The Centerforce clutch uses centrifugal weights for applying additional pressure at higher speeds. Allow slightly more play between the fingers and release bearing face to compensate for the fingers pulling outward (toward the release bearing) at higher speeds.

Make note of how much the release lever end moves when the clutch is adjusted properly. Using this as a reference, you can quickly check the release bearing clearance whenever you service your Jeep---and after any exceptionally strenuous backcountry use of the vehicle. As the clutch disc wears normally, the release bearing-to-finger clearance will decrease. You will note this as less movement at the release lever end. Always keep clutch adjustment in the proper clearance range.

Clutch Data and Torque Settings

Jeep clutch, flywheel, bellhousing and transmission bolt torque settings follow industry recognized torque value limits for graded hardware. At the **Appendix** of this book you will find torque charts with torque limits for U.S. Grade 5 and Grade 8 (plus metric) hardware.

Identify the size of the bolts you are using. If you cannot find a torque setting in the torque specifications chart below, refer to the peak torque settings listed in the **Appendix**. In the case of aftermarket conversion hardware, use good judgment. If the manufacturer provides instructions, follow them. Without recommended torque settings, use the chart at the **Appendix**.

3

CAUTION—

Aluminum metallurgy has evolved, and modern assemblies with threaded aluminum castings can withstand reasonable torque settings. Do not, however, exceed the settings recommended for the aluminum component involved and the grade of fasteners. Use a torque wrench and good sense. Note the torque for the thread pitch and tensile strength/grade bolt involved. Whenever possible, refer to an OEM shop manual or equivalent trade book for proper torque specifications---especially on threaded aluminum castings!

Clutch Repair Data and Torque Specifications for CJ Jeep Models

TORQUE SPECIFICATIONS

Component	Service Set-To Torque	Service Recheck Torque
Clutch Bellcrank Pivot	47 N·m (35 ft-lbs)	41-54 N·m (30-40 ft-lbs)
Clutch Housing-to-Engine Block Bolt (6-Cyl)		
Top	47 N·m (35 ft-lbs)	41-54 N·m (30-40 ft-lbs)
Bottom	61 N·m (45 ft-lbs)	54-68 N·m (40-50 ft-lbs)
Clutch Housing-to-Engine Dowel Bolt Nut (Six-Cylinder)	61 N·m (45 ft-lbs)	54-68 N·m (40-50 ft-lbs)
Clutch Pedal Rebound Bumper, Bolt, Nut, and Lockwasher Assembly-to-Pedal	54 N·m (40 ft-lbs)	47-61 N·m (35-45 ft-lbs)
Clutch Pedal Shaft Locknut	45 N·m (33 ft-lbs)	41-49 N·m (30-36 ft-lbs)
Starter Motor-to-Clutch Housing Bolt (Six-Cylinder)	24 N·m (18 ft-lbs)	16-34 N·m (12-25 ft-lbs)
Transmission Case-to-Clutch Housing Bolt	74 N·m (55 ft-lbs)	68-81 N·m (50-60 ft-lbs)
Clutch Cover Bolts (4-Cyl)	31 N·m (23 ft-lbs)	27-35 N·m (20-26 ft-lbs)
Clutch Master Cylinder-to-Dash (4-Cyl)	26 N·m (19 ft-lbs)	20-31 N·m (15-23 ft-lbs)
Hydraulic Fluid Line Fitting-to-Master Cylinder	15 N·m (11 ft-lbs)	14-16 N·m (10-12 ft-lbs)
Hydraulic Fluid Line Fitting-to-Slave Cylinder	21 N·m (16 ft-lbs)	18-25 N·m (13-18 ft-lbs)

SPECIFICATIONS
Clutch Specifications

Model	Engine (CID)	Clutch Diameter	Release Lever Height (Above Gauge Hub)	Pedal Free Play
CJ-7/ CJ-8	150	2.46 mm (9.687 in)	40.5 to 43.7 mm (1.595 to 1.720)	N/A
	258	26.7 cm (10½ in.)	51.8 to 68.6 mm (2.04 to 2.16)	25.4 to 31.7 mm (1 to 1¼ in.)

Clutch Housing Alignment Specifications

Clutch Housing Bore to Crankshaft
Centerline . . . . 0.25 mm (0.010 max.)
Clutch Housing Transmission Mounting Face
to Crankshaft Centerline . . . . 0.25 mm (0.010 max.)
Clutch Housing to Transmission Adapter
Bore to Crankshaft Centerline . . . . 0.25 mm (0.010 max.)
Clutch Housing to Transmission Adapter
Face to Crankshaft Centerline . . . . 0.25 mm (0.010 max.)
Flywheel Runout at Face . . . . 0.12 mm (0.005 max.)

3

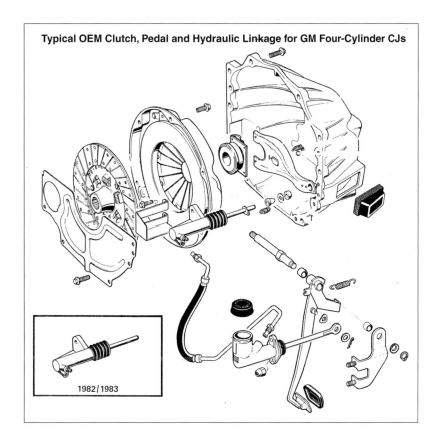

Typical OEM Clutch, Pedal and Hydraulic Linkage for GM Four-Cylinder CJs

1982/1983

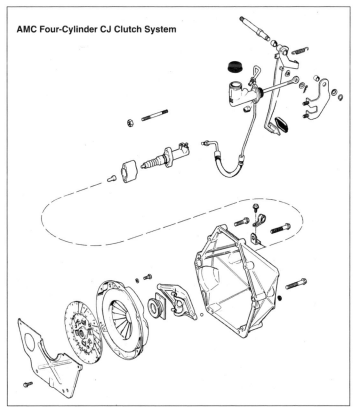

AMC Four-Cylinder CJ Clutch System

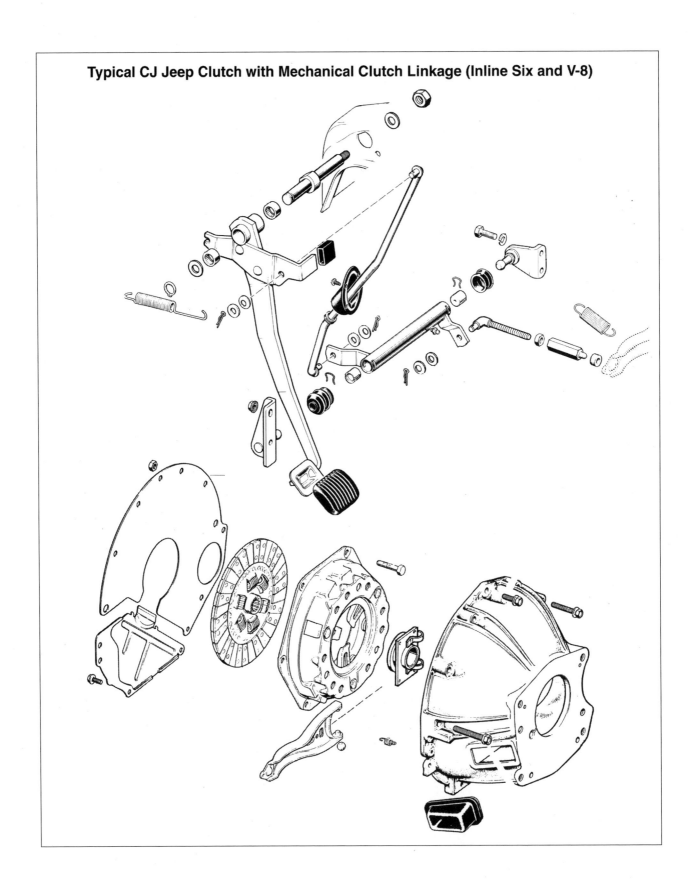

Typical CJ Jeep Clutch with Mechanical Clutch Linkage (Inline Six and V-8)

Chapter 4

Transfer Case

4

General

Three transfer cases served in the 1972-86 AMC-era Jeep CJs: 1) the Spicer 20 ('72-'79 models), 2) Borg-Warner's Quadra-Trac ('76-'79 CJ-7s with THM400 automatic transmission) and 3) the Dana 300 ('80-'86 models). Each is a durable, distinct design.

The Spicer 20 is a through-drive design, as is the Dana 300. The primary design difference between these rugged iron-cased units is the constant mesh, helical gearset in the Dana 300 versus the straight-cut, sliding gear engagement in the Spicer 20. Also, the Dana 300 in stock form boasts a 2.61:1 low range ratio versus the taller and less desirable 2.03:1 ratio in the Spicer 20. Until recently, this has made the Dana 300 the prized unit.

There are now gearset conversions allowing a Spicer 20 changeover to a 3.15:1 low range ratio. (This upgrade is available for earlier Model 18s as well.) The kit is a sensible alternative to the Dana 300 conversion since the Dana 300 and Spicer 20 have different transmission mounting patterns. The conversion from a Spicer 20 to a Dana 300 requires a transmission adapter.

The Borg-Warner Quadra-Trac is a chain-drive unit designed for use with the THM400 GM automatic transmission. This is a *full-time* 4WD system. You will find this transfer case in CJ-7s only, as the shorter CJ-5 wheelbase did not provide enough length for the THM400 transmission and the Quadra-Trac transfer case.

Quadra-Trac is a side-drive design, intended to place the front driveline away from the broad THM400 transmission case. The Quadra-Trac unit requires a differential offset (to the right) on the front and rear axles. By contrast, the through-drive Spicer 20 and Dana 300 models have a centered differential at the rear axle.

The Spicer 20 and Dana 300 units feature part-time 4WD in stock form. Aftermarket part-time 4WD conversion kits are available for the Quadra-Trac. The Mile-Marker version provides a 16% overdrive ratio in high range. Part-time conversions enable use of front locking hubs on Quadra-Trac equipped models. Free-wheeling/locking hubs offer less wear on the front axle parts and a slight improvement in highway fuel economy in 2WD high range.

Origins: The Model 18 Transfer Case

NOTE—
A token number of '72-'73 Jeep CJs have the Spicer Model 18 transfer case. Again, these are carryover models from the Kaiser era and therefore represent Willys/Kaiser technology.

Introduced with the original 1941 Model MB, the Spicer 18 provides a rugged two-speed gearbox. Power flows from the transmission directly to the attached transfer case via a drive gear affixed to the transmission output/mainshaft. (The Spicer 20 also uses an affixed gear.) "High Range" features a 1:1 drive ratio; "Low Range" offers a 2.46:1 reduction ratio.

The Model 18 transfer case is a "side-drive" design. An intermediate gear flows power from the drive (mainshaft) gear to the output shaft and lower gears of the transfer case. This unique design provides for a Power Take-Off (P.T.O.) outlet directly behind the transmission mainshaft.

As an option to this auxiliary P.T.O. power source, the Model 18's P.T.O. port offers a means for installing an aftermarket Warn-designed Saturn overdrive system from Advance Adapters. This is not possible with the Spicer 20 or Dana 300. For details on rebuilding a Model 18 side-drive transfer case, refer to ***Jeep CJ Builder's Manual: 1946 to 1971***.

4

Rebuilding a '72-'86 Jeep transfer case is not a complicated task. Performing endplay checks on bearing clearances will require the use of a dial indicator. Air impact tools are helpful. Larger impact sockets will be necessary, and some specialty or improvised tools will round out your usual assortment of hand tools.

Generally, unless the unit suffered extreme use or has been run without gear lubricant, a set of new bearings, seals, gaskets and snap rings are often the only parts required. The Spicer 20 and Dana 300 seldom suffer gear damage under normal usage. Even the chain drive Quadra-Trac unit usually needs nothing more than bearings, a new chain, thrust washers, gaskets, seals and possibly sprockets.

NOTE—
In this chapter, I illustrate the use of air impact tools and even some home-fabricated specialty tools. For transfer case and axle rebuilding, air tools not only speed the process, they can reduce the need for expensive specialty tools and obsolete fixtures that once accompanied gear assembly work. Simpler, contemporary air service tools serve me and other professional mechanics well. If you do not have access to these tools, you can fall back on basic hand-tool service techniques.

AUTHOR'S TIP!
Store all parts in the order of disassembly. Keep hardware separated, as size and grading vary. Clean parts accordingly, and lay them out in order for easier reassembly.

'Spicer 20' Rebuild Steps

NOTE—

I refer to the '72-'79 Jeep gear-drive transfer case as the 'Spicer 20.' This is technically correct, although Dana and Spicer transfer cases and axles are clearly similar. (Ford popularized the use of the Dana 20 transfer case in '60s 4WD light trucks and the '66-up Broncos.) Years ago, Lloyd Novak politely advised me that the Jeep version of the '20'-type transfer case was clearly a Spicer product, not Dana. For the sake of accuracy and respect for Lloyd's apt observation, I call this unit the Spicer 20. Be aware that many aftermarket parts sources will not draw this distinction, referring to the Spicer 20 as a "Dana 20" unit. Simply put, know your parts when ordering replacement pieces!

Spicer 20 unit used in the Jeep CJs is not difficult to rebuild. At teardown, have suitable means for tagging and segregating parts. If you take time to separate pieces, the unit will be easy to inspect and reassemble. Clean the parts in sequence to avoid mixing the pieces and hardware. Note the grade of hardware, the special length of bolts and studs in various locations, and the bearing sizes. This will help identify parts for replacement and assure a quality assembly job.

The Spicer 20 rebuild sequences shown in this chapter were photographed at Jeff and Karen Sugg's M.I.T. shop, El Cajon, California. If you are not interested in performing your own axle or geartrain work, consider subletting the assemblies work to M.I.T.

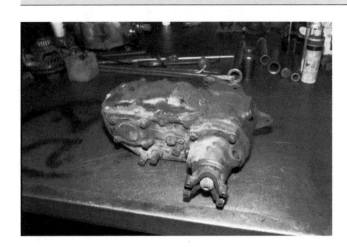

Fig. 4-1.

Gear drive Spicer 20 transfer case has an iron case, much like the earlier Model 18. The most significant difference is the 'through-drive' design that has high range power flowing straight from the transmission mainshaft directly through the transfer case to the rear driveshaft.

Fig. 4-2

First step after draining gear lube from the transfer case is removal of the oil pan, the intermediate shaft lock plate and the rear bearing cap bolts. The output shaft and yoke will come out with the bearing cap and bearing assembly. Pry gently to protect castings.

Fig. 4-3

The bearing retainer, output shaft and yoke come outward as an assembly. This is a serviceable unit. If a mechanical problem like a bad rear bearing and seal were the only defects, the retainer assembly could be serviced without further disassembly of the transfer case.

◁ **Fig. 4-4**

Loosening the companion flange nut is easily done with an air impact gun. Traditional method was to secure the flange with a special, long-armed holding tool. Exerting hefty force with such leverage, these nuts will come loose---or you can make haste of this task with the use of impact tools!

◁ **Fig. 4-5**

Pressing the output shaft from the yoke will separate these parts. You need a hydraulic press for this task. A simple bottle-jack press will work here, as the fit is not exceptionally tight. I use an air hammer as an alternative.

NOTE—

*For understanding the proper use of an air hammer to separate bearings and yokes from the shafts, see the Dana 300 section of this chapter and the axle building details in **Chapter 5**.*

◁ **Fig. 4-6**

These pieces now apart, you can see the relationship of the parts. The self-locking yoke nut is discarded. Always use new seals, gaskets and OEM replacement locknuts during transfer case assembly.

4

 Fig. 4-7

The intermediate shaft lock plate and bolt removed, you can drive the intermediate shaft through the case. The two sets of needle bearings and three spacers will fall out if you do not install a dummy shaft to hold them in place. Since this unit will undergo a complete overhaul, the loose small parts can be accounted for after teardown.

Fig. 4-8

Needle bearings and spacers are loose. Make certain you account for all of them. Needle bearings must be assembled to full counts, and the spacers must be in correct position. Always replace needle bearings and spacers with new parts during assembly. Such parts are contained in the common "small parts kit." At this point, the intermediate gear drops out the bottom of the case.

Fig. 4-9

Shift link is easily removed. Small pivot pins come out after removing the cotter pins. Single lever shift mechanism is simple. This shifter was a major improvement over the earlier Model 18's twin-stick setup.

◄ **Fig. 4-10**

Again, the air gun and impact socket make quick work of the front output yoke nut removal. The washer can also come out at this point. Spicer 20's U-joint "U-bolt" was common with earlier Spicer cross-type joints. This design is strong and often preferred over the later model half-straps with tiny bolts. U-bolts and nuts with lockwashers are a sure means for securing U-joints.

◄ **Fig. 4-11**

Removal of yoke reveals this spacer ring. Yoke may loosen with a few taps using a sand-head plastic hammer. More likely, you will need to use a two-jaw puller or a blunt-end air drive tool, taking care to protect the output shaft and threads. Do not damage the output shaft threads or U-joint saddles!

◄ **Fig. 4-12**

This shift rail guide/seal protector is common to the Spicer 20 and Dana 300 transfer cases. Remove guide to access shift rails.

4

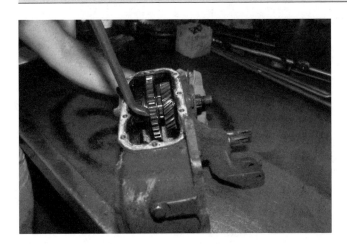

 Fig. 4-13

Pry gears out of the way to access the shift rail setscrew. To remove the shift fork, you will need to first remove the shift rail. This will lead to gear removal. Note that the longer, offset fork and its rail are first to come out.

 Fig. 4-14

Both shift rails in neutral, carefully loosen the long fork's setscrew. Do not damage the setscrew! These would be very difficult screws to access if the heads were damaged. Use the correct tool and carefully remove the setscrew.

Fig. 4-15

Remove the shift rail with a pin punch. Place the pin through the rail's pinhole and rotate the shaft 90-degrees counterclockwise. This will free up the spring-loaded poppet ball from the notch in the shaft and enable removal of the rail. Do not force parts!

◀ **Fig. 4-16**

The poppet ball and spring will come loose as the rail clears the bore. Lift the shift fork and gear from the case. Note the relationship of these parts and the sequence for reassembly. You will inspect the gears and shafts carefully after thorough cleanup.

◀ **Fig. 4-17**

Loosen bolts for the front shift rod housing. Keep track of all hardware, as grading and bolt length dictate the location of these fasteners.

◀ **Fig. 4-18**

Pry the housing loose without binding the shift rail. Use care not to damage castings when you pry. Lift the housing off the shift rail.

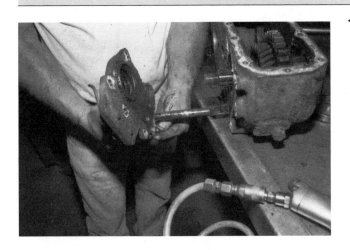

◀ **Fig. 4-19**

Slide the housing carefully off the shift rail. Keep track of poppet ball(s), springs and interlock pieces. Proper shifting depends upon the correct placement of balls and springs.

4

◀ **Fig. 4-20**

Remove the rear plate from the front output shaft. This shaft has shims that are crucial to endplay and the bearing load setting. In the likelihood you will reuse this stack of shims in its original thickness, take care not to damage the edges. I tie shims together with mechanic's wire and mark them for reinstallation.

◀ **Fig. 4-21**

Tap the front output shaft rearward through the back bearing bore. Use a rawhide or sand-head plastic hammer. The bearing cone will come loose as the shaft and bearing push through.

◀ **Fig. 4-22**

Using a brass punch, continue driving the shaft rearward until the shaft is free of the front bearing and gears.

◀ **Fig. 4-23**

Shaft free, the bearing and this spacer are loose. The gearset can be readily lifted from the case at this point.

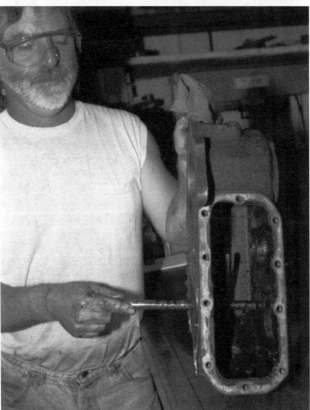

◀ **Fig. 4-24**

The setscrew loose, you can remove the second shift fork and rail. Notice the notches in the rail. These align with the poppet ball and spring sets. Due to the interlock mechanism, you need to rotate and align the rails properly during disassembly and assembly steps.

> **CAUTION—**
>
> *Do not force these shift mechanism parts. Take your time and carefully determine the relationship of these pieces. Improper assembly will prevent normal shifting and could cause severe, damaging gear clash.*

◀ **Fig. 4-25**

Here is the Spicer 20 disassembled, cleaned and laid out in order. The parts washing cabinet makes haste of cleaning chores and scours grime, grease and dirt from the castings, gearsets and even small parts.

4

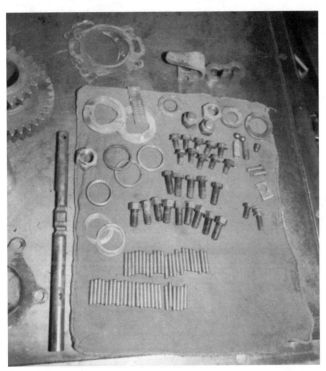

◀ **Fig. 4-26**

Account for these parts. Be certain that the shift mechanism is apart and cleaned thoroughly. On the backcountry trail, fighting the gearshift lever is not safe. These simple springs, balls and the interlock pin must each fit properly and slide freely.

◀ **Fig. 4-27**

Inspect gear teeth and the shift fork's wear points. You need to replace these parts if excess wear is evident. On the Spicer 20, you will usually find negligible wear on the forks and sliding gears' rubbing surfaces. These parts can most often be reused.

◁ **Fig. 4-28**

Use a light grease to hold needle rollers and spacers in place. When the last bearing is in position, the needle/roller assembly will stay put. This is keystone effect, and the bearings should fill the whole circumference of the bore.

◁ **Fig. 4-29**

Here is the bearing set installed properly. Note relationship of spacers: one between the bearing clusters and one at each end of the bearings. You will find that the bearing set endplay is minimal once the bearings and three spacers are installed.

◁ **Fig. 4-30**

You can drive out old bearings with a brass punch. Use safety goggles when tapping against hard bearing steel. Tap at opposite sides of the bearing cup, driving the piece out evenly and straight. Do not cock the cup in its bore, as this could damage the casting.

4

 Fig. 4-31

When holding a part in the vise, do not chew up the flanges. If necessary, use aluminum covers on jaws to protect the piece. Drive cups out carefully with a brass punch. Wear safety goggles.

Fig. 4-32

This is a cup driver for setting the cups into their bores. If you do not have this tool, use a brass drift punch. Drive side-to-side, carefully driving the cup squarely into the bore. Make certain the cup is seated. Avoid leaving brass debris between cup and shoulder. Cup must seat completely to achieve accurate bearing clearance settings.

◀ **Fig. 4-33**

Second cup seats squarely in its bore. For proper endplay measurements, make sure these cups seat fully. Otherwise, the endplay could increase in service as the cups continue to seat. By seating these cups firmly, you will get accurate endplay readings.

◀ **Fig. 4-34**

Shims are selective fit, measured with a micrometer. When assembling the unit, begin with the original shim stack. This is likely the correct fit, as quality new bearings should have the same dimensions as the original bearings.

◀ **Fig. 4-35**

Don't leave the speedometer gear out! This is the assembly sequence of these parts. You can press the bearing onto the shaft with an inexpensive bottle-jack press or even a simple sleeve driver and hammer. You can make a driver sleeve with common black pipe. The inside diameter must fit over the shaft. The outer diameter of the sleeve must fit inboard of the bearing rollers and bearing cage. Do not damage the cage or rollers!

NOTE—

*In **Chapter 5**, I use a variety of inexpensive and handmade tools to build axle assemblies. There you will find my improvised bearing press sleeves and other methods for safely handling bearing and shaft chores without the need for expensive specialty tools.*

◀ **Fig. 4-36**

Outer bearing is a light press fit onto the shaft. The shims between the speedometer gear and outer bearing will set the bearing endplay or clearance. The U-joint yoke holds this bearing securely in place.

4

◀ **Fig. 4-37**

Here, a simple bearing driver is made of a capped sleeve, long enough to clear the end of shaft. Outside diameter of sleeve is inboard of the bearing cage and rollers.

◀ **Fig. 4-38**

The sealing surfaces can wear or become grooved. Use emery paper or crocus cloth to clean up this surface. Make certain the sealing face is smooth and free of burrs or nicks that could damage the new seal's lip. If too worn, replace this flange.

◀ **Fig. 4-39**

Flange held with a large pipe wrench, the old washer and original nut are installed for a trial fit. At this stage, the new seal is not in place.

◀ **Fig. 4-40**

The nut tightly secured, endplay can now be checked with a dial indicator. The shaft will move endwise during this operation. Endplay of 0.001" to 0.003" is correct. If you need to change the clearance, remove the yoke and press the shaft through the outer bearing. Measuring with a micrometer, add or delete shims as necessary to achieve proper clearance.

NOTE—

I lean toward 0.001" endplay on new bearings, as there is always a slight amount of seating and wear-in, each creating slightly more endplay over time. Setting to the closer tolerance will also allow for normal wear over time with less risk of shaft wobble and oil seepage. Be careful not to make endplay too tight, however, or the bearings will run hot and score. Stay with a minimum of 0.001" endplay.

◀ **Fig. 4-41**

You can now remove the nut and yoke. Install a new seal carefully. If the seal does not come with a sealant coating on the outer edge, coat the outer shell with Permatex 'Super 300.' Drive the seal straight and evenly. Seal fits flush with the end of the bearing retainer bore.

 Fig. 4-42

Sealant on splines of yoke and inner mating surface will reduce risk of gear lube wicking. This simple step can prevent a nuisance leak. Some builders replace the felt seal with a new one. Others find that the modern replacement seal is ample enough without the felt seal. Coat the lip of new seal with grease before installing the yoke.

Fig. 4-43

Tapped onto the shaft with a sand-filler plastic hammer, the yoke reveals Super 300 sealant on splines. I lightly coat the washer face that mates with the flange. This should provide a lifetime seal.

Fig. 4-44

A new OE style self-locking nut is installed. As added insurance, apply Loctite 242 or equivalent to threads. Torque the nut to 225-250 lb-ft. Most mechanics know their air gun's torque and tighten the nut accurately with impact force. This eliminates the need to hold the flange while exerting 225-plus lb-ft of torque to the nut with a handheld torque wrench!

NOTE—

See Chapter 5 for details on building a holding tool for U-joint yoke flanges.

◀ Fig. 4-45

Press the front output shaft bearing onto the shaft. Oiling this bearing will provide more accurate assembly measurements.

◀ Fig. 4-46

Brass punch is suitable tool for dislodging bearing cup from case. When using a brass punch, make certain that you remove all flecks of brass that might shed from the tool. Wear goggles. Install the new cup with care, oiling the bore lightly to aid assembly.

◀ Fig. 4-47

Slide the front wheel drive shift rail through the case and shift fork. When installing this setscrew, make certain the screw aligns with the recess in the rail! Use Loctite 242 or equivalent on clean threads. Torque this screw securely to 15 lb-ft. You do not want these setscrews to come loose in service.

NOTE—

If your transfer case uses a square-headed setscrew with mechanic's tie wire, secure the wire carefully and wrap it around the shaft in a manner that will not interfere with any moving parts.

 Fig. 4-48

According to factory and trade service manuals, these seals require special thimble tools for installation on the shafts. Few mechanics have ever seen these tools. With care, you can install these seals and feed the rails through them without damage to the lip seals. Begin with coating the outer shell of the seals with sealant. You can drive the seal with a suitably sized impact socket and softheaded hammer. Seat seals squarely!

Fig. 4-49

Front output bearing retainer seal is easy to install. Coat the outer surface with sealant. Drive the seal evenly and squarely into its bore. A large diameter socket and softheaded hammer will work for this purpose.

Fig. 4-50

This seal will seat in the base of the bore, allowing clearance for the inner shield of the yoke. Original installations use a felt seal and an oil seal gasket in addition to the lip seal. Note fresh grease smeared between sealing lips.

NOTE—

Many builders install a modern lip-type oil seal without using a replacement felt seal or paper gasket. Some builders remain faithful to the OEM felt and paper seals in addition to the lip seal. There are reasonable arguments for either approach.

 Fig. 4-51

Liberally grease the small seal lips. Note the relationship of the shift rails. Recall the need to rotate the rails during installation to press the check balls into their recesses. Grease will reduce risk of seal damage as you install the shafts. Use crocus or a wire wheel to remove any burrs or roughness from the shift rails.

◀ **Fig. 4-52**

Springs must go in correct bores. If these springs show any kind of wear, replace them! They are readily available from vendors like 4WD Hardware, Inc., or Spicer parts sources. Poppet balls and the interlock must be in top condition. Replace any worn parts.

4

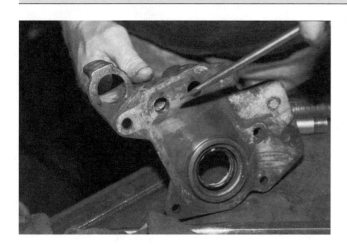

◀ Fig. 4-53

You can press the poppet ball into the spring as you feed the shaft through. The spring goes into the bore, followed by the ball. A ball rides against the rail. Use the flat edge of a screwdriver to depress the ball until the rail passes over the spring and ball.

◀ Fig. 4-54

Rail pushed through the bore, note that the interlock pin is now in place. To provide proper clearance for the second rail, the rail can be rotated. This allows the interlock to seat in the notch, dropping out of the way.

◀ Fig. 4-55

Rail in position and rotated, the interlock is out of the way. Note that the bore is open with no interference from the interlock pin. Do not force any of these parts. Make sure springs and poppet balls stay in place. This handful of small parts will assure safe and accurate shifting.

◀ **Fig. 4-56**

Coat each side of gasket with Super 300 or equivalent sealant. Make sure surfaces are clean and free of nicks or raised scratches. Gasket must seat flatly.

◀ **Fig. 4-57**

Spring goes into place before the retainer slides over rail. Poppet ball will be installed as the retainer drops toward the gasket.

◀ **Fig. 4-58**

Here, screwdriver presses the poppet ball and spring out of the rail's path. Hold the ball down as you move the retainer. The rail will pass the ball and keep it in place. Note the relationship of these parts during this assembly. The two springs, the interlock and the two poppet balls are now in place.

 Fig. 4-59

The front bearing retainer is now located properly, both rails in position. Align the castings with the gasket. If retainer bolts originally had lockwashers, install new lockwashers. Always use Loctite 242 or equivalent on bolt threads. This serves as both a sealant and thread locker. Torque the hardware to specification (32 lb-ft).

4

Fig. 4-60

Remember to rotate the rail to enable the interlock to clear. Do not force these parts. Rotation (typically ¼-turn) will shift the interlock pin into the opposing rail's detent and allow the shaft to pass freely toward the case. Lay the rear wheel drive gear in position. Engage the rear wheel drive shift fork with the gear before you slide the rail into the shift fork. Be certain the gear faces in the correct direction!

Fig. 4-61

The rear wheel drive shift fork and gear should be properly in place as the rail enters the case. (See Fig. 4-63.) You will align the setscrew hole once the rails are both in position. Use Loctite 242 on the setscrew threads. Tighten securely to 15 lb-ft. If required, use fresh wire for ties.

Fig. 4-62

This is a good time to install the front output bearing cup. Whether you use a cup driver or a brass punch, drive the cup evenly and carefully into the bore. Clean any brass debris from the case.

Fig. 4-63

This is the rear wheel drive shift fork and rear drive gear. Make sure these are in place before assembling the balance of the gearsets. The shift fork is now engaged on the rail, and the setscrew has been tightened securely.

Fig. 4-64

This is the front output gear (helically cut teeth) and the front output sliding gear (straight cut teeth). Lightly grease these pieces before installation.

 Fig. 4-65

Front output shaft picks up these gears and the thrust washer as shown here. Make sure the shift fork is engaged with the sliding gear as you move the shaft through these pieces. Use care not to damage the bearings. Oil them to reduce friction during assembly.

4

◀ **Fig. 4-66**

Once all pieces are engaged, and in proper position, you can tap the shaft through the front-facing bearing. Continue tapping until the bearing and its cup have been seated.

◀ **Fig. 4-67**

Do not force any of these pieces. Installing the front U-joint yoke will seat the front bearing cone. Fastening the rear bearing cover will pull that bearing cup into position.

◀ **Fig. 4-68**

This tool (a large socket) will drive the bearing cup into the case. *Avoid contact with the bearing cage!* Protect the bearings during installation. Adjusted properly, these bearing cups and cones will offer long, reliable service.

◀ **Fig. 4-69**

Install this spacer washer! The washer will set the proper depth and clearance for the U-joint yoke and flange. The yoke will compress this washer against the bearing. A thrust/spacer washer seats against the inner end of this bearing to align the front output gear.

◀ **Fig. 4-70**

Once again, the splines get coated with gasket sealant. This is insurance against gear lube seeping from the unit.

◀ **Fig. 4-71**

Using sealant, lightly coat the washer face where it rides against the yoke. Put Loctite 242 or equivalent on the output shaft threads. Use a new self-locking OEM replacement nut.

◀ **Fig. 4-72**

Here, an air impact gun, impact socket and large pipe wrench quickly torque the nut into place. Setting is 225-250 lb-ft. If your gun's torque is predictable and accurate, this is the easiest way to tighten the nut.

◀ **Fig. 4-73**

Front output shaft's rear bearing plate is next. Begin with the original shims, cleaned in isopropyl alcohol to remove old sealant. Trial fitment will require a dial indicator.

 Fig. 4-74

Torque the bolts uniformly to specification (32 lb-ft) to assure accurate endplay reading. The original shims should give a close reading, often being right on specification. Again, 0.001" to 0.003" is specification. I prefer closer to 0.001" than 0.003". Do not eliminate all endplay, as this will cause the bearings to run hot and score.

Fig. 4-75

Once the shims are correct thickness, lightly coat the shims with Super 300 or equivalent sealant. Do not allow sealant to dry before installing shims, as you want the sealant to crush out.

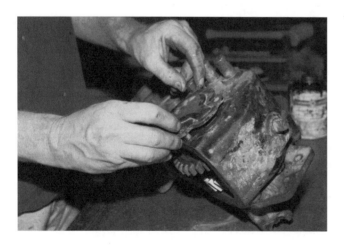

Fig. 4-76

Seal bolt threads with Loctite 242, whether or not lockwashers are utilized. Follow OEM fastener method. If lockwashers were used, replace the lockwashers with same grade new lockwashers.

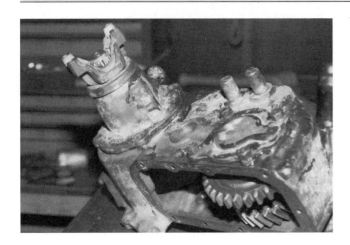

 Fig. 4-77

Using a new gasket coated with Super 300 sealant, install the rear output assembly. This unit was assembled earlier and is ready for installation. You simply need to install correct fasteners and torque in cross, uniformly to specification (32 lb-ft). Seal the bolt threads with Loctite 242. Use new, properly graded lockwashers as required.

4

Fig. 4-78

Lightly grease these thrust washers. Install first one as the shaft just enters the case. Align the shaft's slot for the lock plate, as the shaft will otherwise be difficult to rotate once it has been fitted through the case. Lightly coat the shaft's case bores with sealant.

Fig. 4-79

Needle rollers and spacers should be new and in place with grease. A thrust washer should be at each end of the gear. If all is set, the shaft will slide through the gearset without upsetting the rollers. Alternative insurance is to make a wooden dummy shaft to lead the intermediate shaft through the bore. Carefully push the dummy shaft through with the intermediate shaft. Coat the shaft's case bores with sealant to prevent oil seepage.

◀ **Fig. 4-80**

Align the lock plate and bolt. If so equipped, use a new lock-washer and put Loctite 242 on the bolt threads. Torque the bolt to 15 lb-ft.

◀ **Fig. 4-81**

These units have used a gasket on the oil pan. RTV sealants like Ultra-Black do a fine job of sealing. They actually work better than a gasket in this application if the pan is flat and has no excessive gaps. RTV sealant will swell slightly in the presence of gear lube, and this flexibility is valuable for quality sealing.

◀ **Fig. 4-82**

Here's a completed Jeep/Spicer 20 transfer case. The input drive gear is attached to the transmission output/mainshaft, so this is the assembly, ready to accept the transmission. A coat of shiny engine enamel will showcase your work!

NOTE—

If an OEM gasket was used between the transmission and transfer case, coat a new gasket with a thin coat of RTV sealant on each side. Install the gasket and transmission with new, properly graded lockwashers. Use Loctite 242 for added insurance…Use of a gasket between the transmission and transfer case serves as a seal and also indexes the input gear with relationship to the gears within the transfer case. Do not eliminate an OEM gasket here. To avoid the characteristic tendency for this gasket to break down and seep gear oil, use RTV sealant as a gasket sealer, a light coat on each side of the cut paper gasket. This helps resist gasket failure and provides a better seal.

NOTE—

The nut that holds the transmission drive gear to the output/mainshaft of the transmission is either slotted for a cotter pin or a self-locking type. The castellated nut requires a minimum torque of 80 lb-ft torque and maximum of 300 lb-ft. A self-locking nut requires a 130-170 lb-ft torque setting. I set the castellated nut to a minimum of 150 lb-ft and align the cotter pin hole. If necessary, I will advance the nut to align the holes. (Never back off the nut to align the cotter pin hole. Do not exceed the 300 lb-ft maximum.) For the self-locking nut, I torque to 170 lb-ft plus. In either application, I use Loctite 242 for added insurance.

The Dana 300 Rebuild

Many regard the Dana 300 transfer case as the best unit ever offered in a Jeep CJ or military counterpart model. I would put my vote here, too. This iron-cased unit offers unparalleled stamina, shifts readily and performs better than any other Jeep CJ offering. Added horsepower presents no obstacle. The stock low range ratio of 2.61:1 is respectable. For most owners, the Dana 300 is ideal.

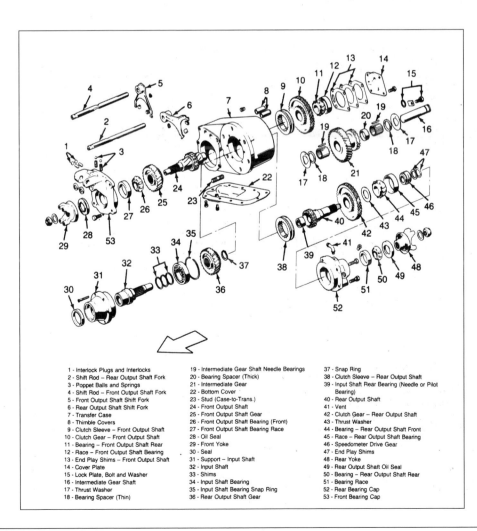

1 - Interlock Plugs and Interlocks	19 - Intermediate Gear Shaft Needle Bearings
2 - Shift Rod – Rear Output Shaft Fork	20 - Bearing Spacer (Thick)
3 - Poppet Balls and Springs	21 - Intermediate Gear
4 - Shift Rod – Front Output Shaft Fork	22 - Bottom Cover
5 - Front Output Shaft Shift Fork	23 - Stud (Case-to-Trans.)
6 - Rear Output Shaft Shift Fork	24 - Front Output Shaft
7 - Transfer Case	25 - Front Output Shaft Gear
8 - Thimble Covers	26 - Front Output Shaft Bearing (Front)
9 - Clutch Sleeve – Front Output Shaft	27 - Front Output Shaft Bearing Race
10 - Clutch Gear – Front Output Shaft	28 - Oil Seal
11 - Bearing – Front Output Shaft Rear	29 - Front Yoke
12 - Race – Front Output Shaft Bearing	30 - Seal
13 - End Play Shims – Front Output Shaft	31 - Support – Input Shaft
14 - Cover Plate	32 - Input Shaft
15 - Lock Plate, Bolt and Washer	33 - Shims
16 - Intermediate Gear Shaft	34 - Input Shaft Bearing
17 - Thrust Washer	35 - Input Shaft Bearing Snap Ring
18 - Bearing Spacer (Thin)	36 - Rear Output Shaft Gear

37 - Snap Ring	
38 - Clutch Sleeve – Rear Output Shaft	
39 - Input Shaft Rear Bearing (Needle or Pilot Bearing)	
40 - Rear Output Shaft	
41 - Vent	
42 - Clutch Gear – Rear Output Shaft	
43 - Thrust Washer	
44 - Bearing – Rear Output Shaft Front	
45 - Race – Rear Output Shaft Bearing	
46 - Speedometer Drive Gear	
47 - End Play Shims	
48 - Rear Yoke	
49 - Rear Output Shaft Oil Seal	
50 - Bearing – Rear Output Shaft Rear	
51 - Bearing Race	
52 - Rear Bearing Cap	
53 - Front Bearing Cap	

 Fig. 4-83

This is the Dana 300 transfer case on my workbench. Most regard the '300' as the best gear-drive transfer case in Jeep CJ history. Iron case and through-drive design, the Dana 300 features rugged, helically cut gear teeth.

There are no straight-cut sliding gears within the Dana 300, and this reduces risk of gear tooth damage on shifting. The through-drive design makes the unit both energy efficient and powertrain friendly. Best yet, this is not a difficult unit to rebuild, and even at higher mileage, most units require nothing more than a thorough cleaning, new bearings and fresh seals.

 Fig. 4-84

Welcome to my shop! Dana 300 perches in Bench Mule device from Mark Williams Enterprises. Fresh out of the parts washing cabinet, the transfer case disassembly begins with removing the bottom cover bolts and cutting the sealant loose with a sharp putty knife.

NOTE—

I equipped my shop with the Bench Mule unit from Mark Williams Enterprises. This is the ideal bench fixture for rebuilding transmissions, axles and transfer cases!

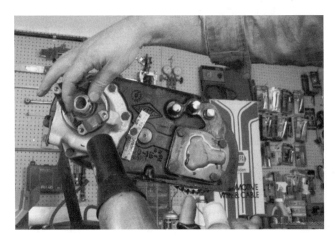

 Fig. 4-85

This '86 CJ-7's transfer case had 109,000 miles on it and still performed flawlessly. This will be a straightforward rebuild that begins with removal of the shift linkage. Here I remove the output shaft yoke nut with an air impact gun and deep-set impact socket.

◁ **Fig. 4-86**

A simple two-jaw puller is sufficient for removing the yoke. In this rebuild, I have purposely used basic tools wherever possible. You will find such work accessible and cost-effective.

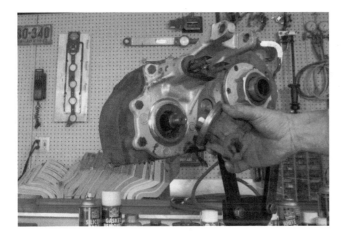

◁ **Fig. 4-87**

Using the air impact gun and two-jaw puller, I remove the front drive companion flange/yoke. The seal is now visible.

◁ **Fig. 4-88**

The input shaft support is readily accessed. Allen-head screws retain the support. Note that Dana 300 has a simpler, splined hub that indexes with the transmission's output shaft. There's no drive gear attached to the transmission output shaft (with a nut) like the earlier Spicer 18 and 20 models!

 Fig. 4-89

Gently pry the support from the case. Use the factory recess as a pry point. Note that modern transfer case does not require paper gaskets. On earlier Jeep transfer cases, trail pounding took its toll on cut paper gaskets, leading to leaks and loose hardware. RTV and anaerobic sealers have eliminated the use of many gaskets.

NOTE—
One of the Allen screw heads broke off during removal. This was easily remedied once the support came loose. Enough thread was accessible to grasp with a Vise Grip.

 Fig. 4-90

On Dana 300, this input assembly is now serviced as a subunit. Note condition of the gears. This transfer case shows minimal wear at 109K miles! Mounting flange pattern is a modern design, readily adapted to transmissions like the NV3550 or NV4500.

 Fig. 4-91

At rear bearing cap, remove the clamp for the speedometer drive gear housing. Note the notches on the top of speedometer housing. The shaft offset can be positioned to fit a variety of driven gear diameters. When adjusting speedometer ratios for oversized tires and axle gearing changes, this housing design is very useful.

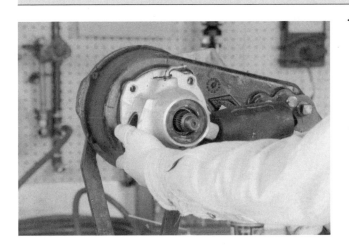

Fig. 4-92

Tail housing is aluminum, and the use of a sand-filled plastic hammer is my tool of choice for tapping on these parts. Although I have loosened the hardware and tapped the housing to unseat it from the iron case, I will leave the bearing cap in place at this stage. I do this to relieve binding and tension on parts. You can leave a few bolts finger tight.

4

Fig. 4-93

I loosen front drive bearing retainer bolts and tap the cap gently. This part will stay in place for a few more steps. For now, you can leave a bolt(s) finger tight at this casting.

Fig. 4-94

Remove the bolt that secures the lock plate at the intermediate shaft. Do not lose the identification tag!

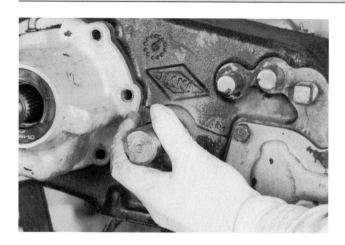

 Fig. 4-95

Drive the intermediate shaft out the rear of the case. To prevent bearings and small parts from dropping, you can make a wooden dummy shaft of the correct diameter and length to follow the intermediate shaft out of the case.

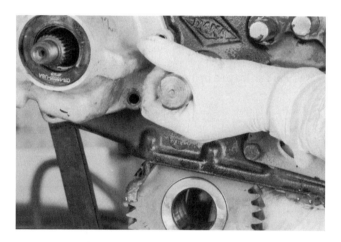

Fig. 4-96

When the intermediate shaft exits the intermediate gear, be prepared to catch the gear. A dummy shaft the width of the gear will keep the rollers and spacers in place. In this instance, I did not use a dummy shaft and allowed parts to drop out. If you do this, account for every piece!

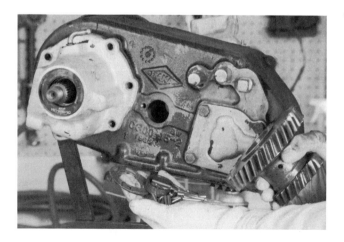

Fig. 4-97

Account for these parts. They can fall from position during disassembly, but make sure these parts are all in place during installation of the intermediate shaft. Upon assembly, use a wooden dummy shaft with the inside diameter of the bearing set and the width of the gear and outer thrust washers.

◄ **Fig. 4-98**

This is a technique I use to save time and reduce risk of stressing parts. An air hammer with a blunted point will quickly drive this shaft through its bearing. Stay in the recess at the shaft end, and protect the threads. (An old shaft nut can be run onto the threads to protect them during this operation.) Impact force will effortlessly loosen and separate this shaft from the outer bearing.

NOTE—

You can use the customary approach, a hydraulic press and fixtures, to remove shafts. A snug bearing will require substantial pressure on a hydraulic press...In some instances, a press is the only safe way to remove a shaft or bearing. On a shaft like the one depicted in Fig. 4-98, however, I prefer my air hammer technique. Impact force minimizes the stress to parts during this operation. Use extreme care not to damage threads and surrounding parts. Do not allow the blunted chisel point to dislodge from the end recess in the shaft. I dull the point with a grinding wheel, leaving the taper in place to keep the point centered. Wear gloves and safety goggles when applying impact force to metal parts!

◄ **Fig. 4-99**

Outer bearing and housing removed, you can see the relationship of the rear output shaft to the splines that receive the rear U-joint yoke. Note that endplay is controlled by shims between the inner face of the outer bearing and the shoulder on the shaft. Spacing of the bearings determines the endplay and bearing clearance.

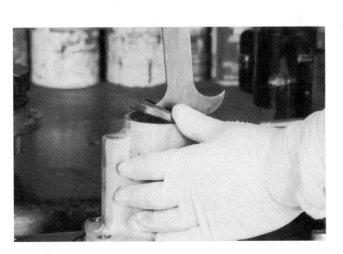

◄ **Fig. 4-100**

Popping out this seal with a seal removal tool will access the loose bearing. Lay parts out in a manner that will help you identify their relationships. Inspect for wear, galling and heat damage or scoring.

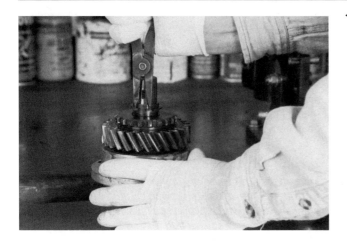

 Fig. 4-101

You can begin disassembling the subassemblies. Input shaft and input shaft gear come apart easily. Loosen snap ring with a snap ring pliers.

Fig. 4-102

Gently pry input shaft gear from the shaft. Do not damage gears, and pry evenly.

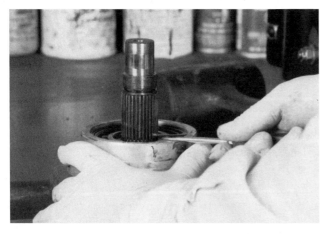

 Fig. 4-103

Remove bearing snap ring. Do not damage or gouge the aluminum housing. The shaft and bearing should slide out of the housing. If tight, tap the input nose on a block of wood. Support the bearing retainer with both hands as you tap the shaft and caged ball bearing from the housing.

4

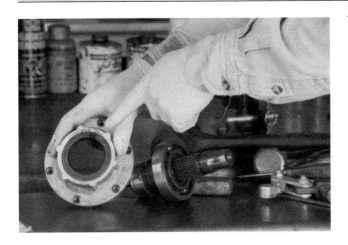

◀ **Fig. 4-104**

Seal is now accessible for removal. A hydraulic press and bearing clamp will remove the caged ball bearing from the input shaft.

◀ **Fig. 4-105**

Loosen the hex-head screw to allow shift rail to slide out of the case. Use extreme care not to strip out the head. This would be a very difficult screw to access with a drill and screw extractor!

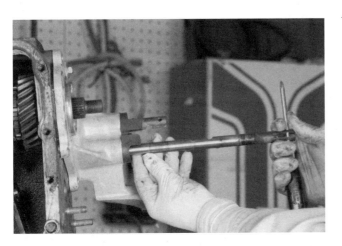

◀ **Fig. 4-106**

Rotate this shaft 90-degrees as you slide it carefully from the case. Note that the bearing retainer is lightly attached with a bolt. This prevents rotation of the retainer while relieving pressure and binding.

◄ **Fig. 4-107**

Now you can carefully remove the bearing retainer. There should be no binding or need to apply force.

◄ **Fig. 4-108**

Remove the cover plate for the rear bearing. Do not damage these shims! Tie them with mechanic's wire for reassembly. The shims set proper endplay of the front output shaft bearings.

◄ **Fig. 4-109**

A hydraulic press is needed for shaft removal. Note the position of the 'V'-plate beneath the shaft. This supports the gears as the shaft presses through. Take your time. This inexpensive bottle-jack press at my shop has a 20-ton capacity!

CAUTION—

Do not force or bind these parts. Protect the threads on the shaft. Place a soft metal plate atop the shaft if necessary. A non-locking nut can be run down flush with the top of these threads for further protection.

4

Fig. 4-110

Parts come apart in sequence. Do not damage gears or bearings during disassembly. You will replace all bearings during a thorough overhaul.

Fig. 4-111

Continue removal of the shaft and remaining gear. Do not drop expensive shaft and gear assemblies.

Fig. 4-112

Now you can disassemble the balance of the shaft. Bearings and gears come apart in this sequence. This hydraulic press works very well. Carrier plates with 'V' and circular cutouts aid in disassembly work. If you do any amount of this work, such a press is cost-effective.

 Fig. 4-113

A seal pry tool makes quick work of seal removal. This is an aluminum casting. Do not use excessive force. Avoid gouging or nicking the retainer! Protect these parts.

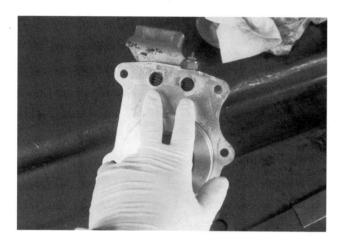

Fig. 4-114

If there is any wear on these springs or other shift mechanism parts, replace them. Keep track of the springs, poppet balls, the interlock pins and the plugs.

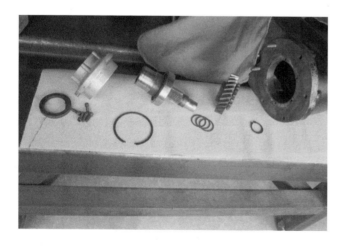

Fig. 4-115

Sub-assembly related parts include the input shaft and bearing retainer.

◁ **Fig. 4-116**

Here are related front output shaft parts. Note the bearing retainer, shaft and adjoining parts.

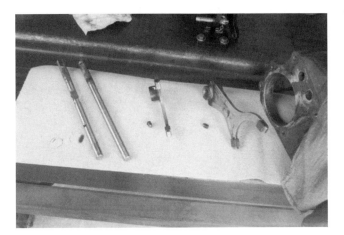

◁ **Fig. 4-117**

Shift rails, forks and setscrews: Make sure these parts are free of burrs and in good condition. Roll the shafts on a flat surface to check for warp. Look closely at the forks. Check them for straightness, wear and signs of fatigue. Most often, these parts are reusable.

◁ **Fig. 4-118**

Rear output shaft and related parts: Inventory these pieces, clean them thoroughly, and inspect for wear and damage.

4

 Fig. 4-119

Intermediate gear and related pieces are shown. (The thicker bearing spacer that fits between the roller sets is not visible here.) You will see these parts in their proper sequence as I assemble the unit.

 Fig. 4-120

Cleaned and inspected, these parts show minimal wear. Bearing cup and cone set will be replaced as a matter of course. Note that I do not remove the shift rail end caps (thimbles) from the case. If they were not seeping gear lube, these caps do not need service.

Assembling the Dana 300

By now, you have thoroughly cleaned and inspected the parts. Your new parts ready, you can begin the assembly process. Bearing replacement is insurance that the Dana 300 will deliver very long and reliable service. Replace all bearings and seals.

CAUTION—

During assembly, use a light chassis grease and/or motor oil to lube rubbing surfaces. This will prevent parts and bearings from scoring during initial startup. Do not use heavier greases that could distort your endplay readings. As a final step, coat gears and shafts with recommended gear lube before attaching the bottom oil pan.

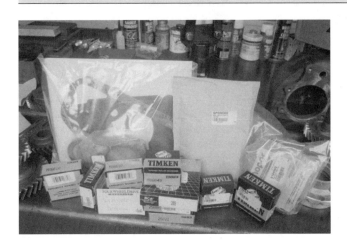

 Fig. 4-121

I relied upon two parts sources for the Dana 300 rebuild job: Genuine Mopar/Jeep parts, available through your Jeep dealer, and 4WD Hardware, Inc. Do not compromise on parts quality.

NOTE—
4WD Hardware offers quality OEM replacement Timken and BCA bearings. Genuine Mopar/Jeep is always your assurance of parts that meet OEM engineering standards and fit.

4

◀ **Fig. 4-122**

Front output shaft and gear fit up now. Make certain these parts move freely. Gear teeth should mesh well and have a healthy sheen.

◀ **Fig. 4-123**

Press the new bearing into position. Pressing sleeve must clear the shaft and press on the inner bearing collar. Make certain the tool clears the bearing cage and rollers! Do not stress or damage the new bearing during installation.

◀ **Fig. 4-124**

Stack the gearset pieces. Carefully feed the gearset assembly through the case.

> **WARNING—**
>
> *A bearing press everts tremendous force. Always line parts up squarely. Watch carefully for any signs of shifting or misalignment. Use extreme caution when applying heavy pressure!*

◀ **Fig. 1-125**

Here, the gearset stack is free standing within the case. You need to press the rear bearing into place. Be certain that all pieces are in place and aligned before you press the new bearing. Note that I protect the case and shaft ends from damage during this operation. Sleeve tool (a deep socket) clears shaft and presses on bearing collar inbound of cage.

◀ **Fig. 1-126**

I use a two-jaw slide hammer puller to remove the caged needle pilot bearing. (See Fig. 1-127 for insight on where to place the puller tangs.) This is the least stressful means for performing this task. Note that I hold the shaft in the vise between two blocks of wood. Protect the shaft and the bearing bore.

4

Fig. 1-127

Bearing removed, the bore is visible. Note the slots where the outward facing jaws of the puller should fit. Always use caution when applying force. Do not damage the flanges in the bore.

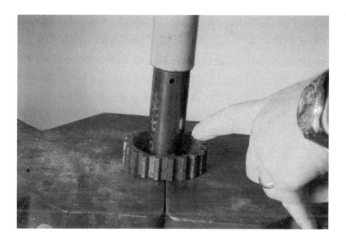

Fig. 1-128

I use a deep-set impact socket to press the new caged roller bearing into its bore. A light film of viscous motor oil on the outside of the cage will reduce risk of binding. Seat the bearing squarely.

Fig. 1-129

Assemble this gearset. Note that shafts and gears are still not supported in the case. Bearing cups will be installed later.

◁ **Fig. 1-130**

Pieces in place, note that I coat the pilot bearing with light chassis grease. This will aid installation and rotation of parts during assembly and assure adequate lubrication during initial startup.

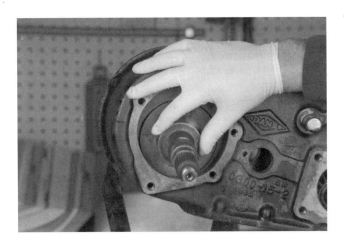

◁ **Fig. 1-131**

Thrust washer goes in place. A light film of grease on each side of thrust washer is appropriate.

◁ **Fig. 1-132**

I made the tool shown here. This sleeve is nothing more than black pipe with the correct inside/outside diameters and a piece of flat plate welded on top. The gearset is still "floating" in the case. Properly support the case while pressing the rear output shaft bearing into position.

 Fig. 1-133

Note that the sleeve's outside diameter is inboard of the bearing cage. Opposite end of shaft is supported (see Fig. 1-134) as you press this bearing into place. Seat bearings carefully and squarely. Make certain all bearings are fully seated to assure proper endplay readings.

4

Fig. 4-134

To support the rear output shaft during installation of the rear bearing, I use this spacer from my hoist. Note that the diameter of this piece fully clears the pilot bearing and bore. Do not damage the pilot caged needle bearing!

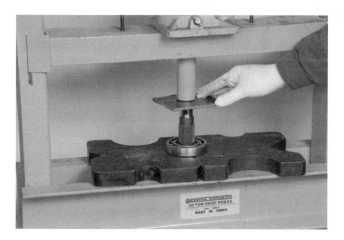

Fig. 4-135

To remove the input shaft bearing, I use support plates against the bearing. A piece of mild steel plate protects the nose end of the shaft. You do not want to damage or distort the nose, as this must fit precisely into the pilot bearing.

> **CAUTION—**
>
> *Pressing against the outer bearing race (as depicted in Fig. 4-135) places stress on the bearing and risks the possibility that a worn bearing will break apart. Be aware that this is a bearing about to be replaced with a new one. Use caution not to overload any bearing, causing it to dangerously fly apart under pressure!*

 Fig. 4-136

On right is the OEM front bearing retainer. Source of new caged ball bearing is 4WD Hardware, Inc. The custom retainer on left is part of Advance Adapters' kit for mating the Dana 300 to an NV4500 transmission. (See **Chapter 3** for further details.) The A/A adapter bearing is a sealed, ball-type bearing.

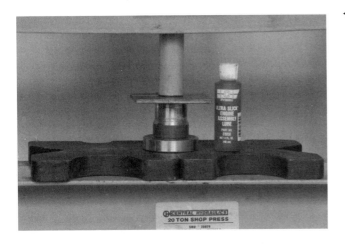

Fig. 4-137

I apply engine assembly lube to the input shaft surface. This aids bearing installation by reducing friction. Note that I very carefully make certain the inner bearing race/collar is fully supported as I press the shaft into the bearing. Supporting only the outer bearing race can damage a new bearing during installation! Gear endplay shims fit between the shaft shoulder and the bearing shoulder.

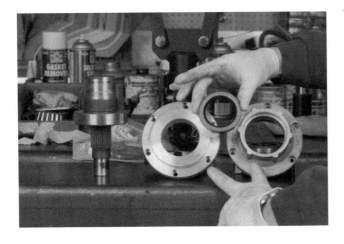

Fig. 4-138

Advance Adapters' retainer does not require a seal. OEM retainer on right requires a new seal. Coat the outer shell of new seal with Super 300 or equivalent.

◁ Fig. 4-139

I coat the A/A retainer bore and outer edge of sealed bearing to prevent seepage of oil past the outer surface of bearing. Permatex Super 300 works well here.

◁ Fig. 4-140

Bearing in the retainer, install the snap ring.

◁ Fig. 4-141

Coating with 'Super 300' and a properly seated snap ring have this input retainer oil-tight. Why the new retainer for NV4500 installations? The flat, machined inner shoulder fits the NV4500's tail housing bore. A/A finds that the permanently sealed bearing works well in this application. This bearing is similar to rugged semi-floating axle shaft bearings---without the load demands placed upon an axle shaft bearing.

4

◀ **Fig. 4-142**

Deep impact socket and sand-head plastic hammer serve as driver tools for rear output shaft gear. Input shaft sets on a block of wood.

◀ **Fig. 4-143**

Install a new snap ring. Use the proper tool for this task, and make sure the snap ring is properly seated.

◀ **Fig. 4-144**

Measure gear clearance between the snap ring and gear. Clearance should not exceed 0.003". If clearance is excessive, you must disassemble the shaft components and install a shim(s) between the bearing and the input shaft shoulder. (See Fig. 4-137.)

◀ Fig. 4-145

This is a place for anaerobic sealant. Permatex 518 Sealant is my choice here. A uniform film will match the OEM approach. There is no gasket, this is it!

4

◀ Fig. 4-146

Loctite 242 (medium strength) is a suitable safeguard for the Allen head retainer screws. '242' will serve as a thread locker and sealant. '518' sealant offers additional adhesion in the area of these new OEM replacement screws.

◀ Fig. 4-147

I thread several screws into the case to keep retainer aligned properly as I tap it into place. Use of a plastic sand-filler hammer is ideal for this task. Plastic does not damage aluminum. Tap retainer evenly and squarely into the iron case.

Use of the Stock Input Bearing and Retainer

If your rebuild does not involve the use of a custom retainer for a transmission swap, here are the steps for installing the stock input bearing retainer:

Fig. 4-148 Here is a stock bearing retainer installation. Open caged ball bearing receives oil from within the transfer case. In this application, the retainer seal keeps gear lube from leaking at the front of the case.

Fig. 4-149 Coat outer shell of seal with sealant and drive it into the retainer. The seal should be flush with the end of the housing bore. Coat the seal lip with grease before installing the shaft.

Fig. 4-150 Bearing fits into the retainer bore. A light tap around the outer edge of the bearing with a plastic hammer will help seat the bearing. Tap evenly and seat bearing squarely.

Fig. 4-151 Install the snap ring to secure bearing. Make certain bearing and snap ring seat; the snap ring should fit fully in its groove around the full circumference of the retainer bore.

Use of the Stock Input Bearing and Retainer (continued)

Fig. 4-152 Rear output shaft gear now fits onto shaft. A light amount of oil will aid installation. (See Fig. 4-142.)

Fig. 4-153 Install a new snap ring. Check clearance between the snap ring and gear. (See Figs. 4-143 and 4-144 for details.)

4

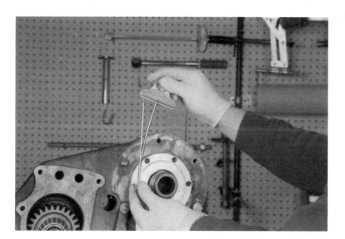

◄ **Fig. 4-154**

You could easily "snug" these Allen head screws, however, there is a torque specification, and I use it. 10 lb-ft is correct, and my ¼-inch drive torque wrench does this as 120 lb-in. Remember to use Loctite 242 on the screw threads!

◄ **Fig. 4-155**

Two means for removing the rear bearing cap cups: 1) the common brass punch and hammer method, and 2) the two- or three-jaw slide hammer. I prefer the slide hammer, which pulls uniformly. In either case, wear safety goggles.

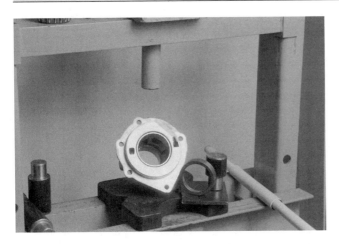

◄ **Fig. 4-156**

The original bearing cup can serve as a driver for pressing the new cup into place. Tap new cup gently with plastic hammer to square it in the bore. I place the old bearing cup atop the new bearing cup (thin edge to thin edge). Place the mild steel plate above the old bearing cup. With all parts square and aligned, gently apply pressure from the hydraulic press. Seat the new cup squarely against the stop flange in the bore. Wear safety goggles when operating a hydraulic press.

◄ **Fig. 4-157**

Lightly oil and start the new outer bearing cup into the bore. With cup aimed squarely, I set old cup atop the new cup, thin edge to thin edge. Wear safety goggles. Apply pressure against the old cup with a suitable adapter, driving the new cup squarely into the bore. Seat the cup squarely.

◄ **Fig. 4-158**

Make certain cup is clean, and install the new bearing cone. Now you can coat outer edge of seal with Super 300 and drive it into the bore. Large socket and a sand-head plastic hammer seat the seal. This seal does not fit flush with the end of the housing. Drive it squarely to the bottom of the bore.

Fig. 4-159

I coat the outer face of the seal and sealing junction with Super 300 for added insurance. This helps form an additional weather, water and debris barrier. (Earlier transfer case designs used an outer felt seal as a barrier.) Keep sealant away from seal lip. Grease the lip to reduce friction.

4

Fig. 4-160

Blocks of wood and the old bearing cup serve as installation tools. Press the new cup into the front bearing cap/retainer.

Fig. 4-161

Front bearing cap seal fits into recess of bore. Coat the outer shell with sealant. Square up and gently bottom the seal (like the rear bearing cap seal). The outer gap is correct. As an added precaution and barrier, I seal the outer gap of the bore and seal face with Super 300 sealant. Keep sealant away from the seal's lip.

Fig. 4-162

Coat the sealing lip and bearing cups with light chassis grease. This will protect these parts during initial operation of the unit.

Fig. 4-163

These shims set endplay of input/rear output shaft. For proper bearing clearance, you must set this endplay accurately. Use the original shim stack for initial setup. This will often be precisely right for the new bearings. We shall see…

Fig. 4-164

518 Gasket Sealer is anaerobic sealant, the kind required for the rear bearing cap-to-case surface. '518' seals these surfaces without a gasket. Tolerances are properly maintained and parts fit flush. This system is far better than earlier transfer cases with cut paper gaskets!

◀ Fig. 4-165

Here, I use Super 300 sealant on splines and the inner end of the yoke. This sealant will prevent gear lube from seeping out the splines.

4

◀ Fig. 4-166

The extra minutes spent on sealing the yokes will pay dividends in a leak-free transfer case assembly. High lubricity, modern gear lubes, especially synthetic types, will otherwise find their way out of the case.

◀ Fig. 4-167

Coat bolt threads with Loctite 242. A thread locker and sealant, '518' will add further sealing effect. Torque these bolts to specification, in cross and steps. Final torque is 35 lb-ft. I recheck this torque after letting parts set for several minutes.

 Fig. 4-168

Use the original shaft/yoke nut to set the yoke in place. At this stage, you're making a trial fit to see if shaft endplay is correct. Set nut to approximately 120 lb-ft torque.

 Fig. 4-169

Here, I check endplay. My approach is a magnetic stand stuck to the iron case. Bring the dial indicator squarely to the output shaft end. Push the shaft all the way forward, and zero the dial indicator. Carefully pull the yoke outward with firm pressure. Note the thousandths of an inch play. Correct play is 0.001" to 0.005".

NOTE—

I prefer a setting of 0.001"-0.002" with new bearings to allow for normal parts settling and wear during service life. Too much play will allow the bearings and shafts to run out, causing seal leaks and noise. Too little play will cause bearing heat-up, scoring and premature failure. I often run 100% synthetic oils. These lubricants are highly viscous and cooler running. Closer tolerances are wise if you plan to run synthetic gear lube.

 Fig. 4-170

Endplay on specification, you can install the new self-locking yoke nut. Put Super 300 on threads and the yoke washer faces. Torque nut to 120 lb-ft of torque minimum. Re-check the torque after parts settle for several minutes.

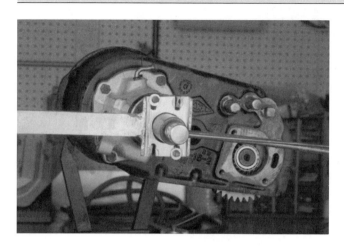

 Fig. 4-171

This is a tool I made in 1969 to restore my 1950 CJ-3A! (I was only one year older than the Jeep at that time.) The yoke holding device, a facsimile of an expensive, factory-recommended tool, enables torquing the shaft nut to specification.

NOTE—

Professionals turn to air tools and a sense for torque settings on their favorite air impact gun. I will attest that this can be reasonably accurate, as working daily with air tools provides this insight. However, it makes good sense to confirm torque settings with a torque wrench.

4

Fig. 4-172

Nut will now seal well. Use of Loctite Threadlocker 242 on the nut offers sealing quality plus additional insurance against loosening. This new self-locking nut is from 4WD Hardware, Inc., a prime source for Dana 300 and other Jeep parts.

Fig. 4-173

All bearings came from 4WD Hardware, Inc. Here, I tap the bearing cup into the rear bearing's bore. Note use of engine assembly lube to enable easier installation of these parts. A few drops spread over the bore of the case will do the trick.

◄ **Fig. 4-174**

Clean original shims with isopropyl alcohol and coat very lightly with Super 300. Do not allow sealant to set up. You will want to squeeze any excess from the shims when you torque the bolts to specification.

◄ **Fig. 4-175**

Use Loctite 242 on bolt threads, and torque bolts in cross and steps to a specification of 35 lb-ft. Re-check torque after parts settle for several minutes.

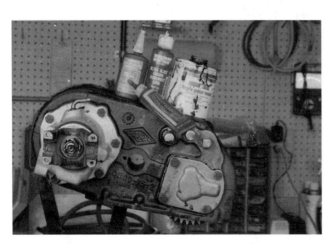

◄ **Fig. 4-176**

These "soft tools" assure a quality rebuild. Invest in quality soft tools before assembling your Dana 300. Note my repeated use of these four products. Keep them handy.

◀ **Fig. 4-177**

Coat of Super 300 on face of shift rail seals is insurance. I coat the outside edge of the seals on installation.

4

◀ **Fig. 4-178**

'518' sealant is appropriate for bearing retainer. Here I strive to leave an even, thorough coating. Excess is not necessary, as this sealant against flat surfaces works exceedingly well. It's also very expensive, and waste is costly.

◀ **Fig. 4-179**

Loctite 242 time! Coat bolt threads for sealing and thread locking. Tighten in cross and steps, reaching a setting of 35 lb-ft. Re-check torque after parts settle for several minutes.

◄ **Fig. 4-180**

Magnetic stand on iron case, dial indicator reads endplay of front output shaft. Dial indicator stem pointed straight toward shaft, endplay should fall between 0.001" and 0.005". Again, I strive for 0.001"-0.002" for proper running clearance and long service life. Endplay adjustment is at rear cover plate, determined by adding or removing shim thickness.

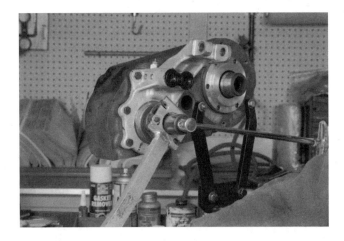

◄ **Fig. 4-181**

Now you can install yoke. Coat splines, washer faces and yoke threads with Super 300. Install a new self-locking nut and torque to 120 lb-ft minimum.

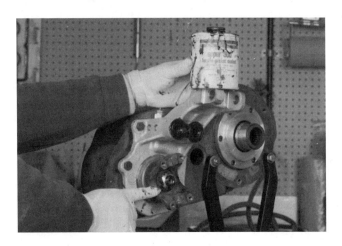

◄ **Fig. 4-182**

New nut and proper sealing assure success. Re-check torque and check the endplay once more to confirm results.

Fig. 4-183

Small parts from 4WD Hardware, Inc., include the shift fork slippers. These nylon parts wear and cause sloppy shifting and grating of metal-to-metal. Replace them if wear is present or nylon appears brittle. Using snap-ring pliers carefully spread the slipper.

4

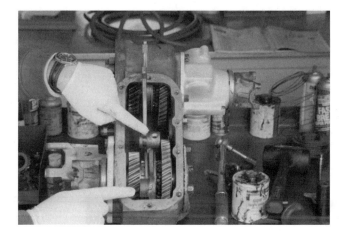

Fig. 4-184

Note the direction forks face. Setscrews must be accessible, and forks must fit properly into the clutch sleeves. Make certain the nylon shift slippers fit correctly.

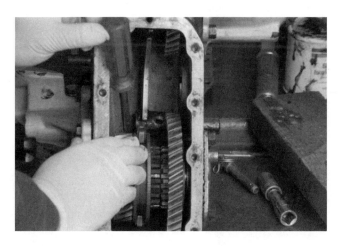

Fig. 4-185

Check alignment of each fork. Make sure the shift rail will fit through the fork and that the setscrews are accessible.

 Fig. 4-186

Replace worn parts with quality new pieces. Note the setscrew hole offsets. Compare with the location of the shift forks and setscrews. Be certain you are placing each rod in the correct bore.

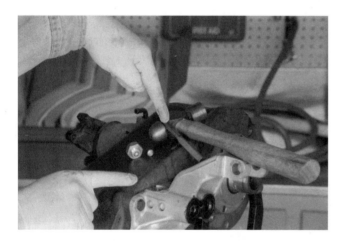

◀ **Fig. 4-187**

Remove the 4WD switch and drive out the adjacent soft plug to access poppet balls and springs. Make certain you have new parts before driving out old plug. This plug must seal well. If you need to replace the interlock pins, remove the pair of soft plugs at the side of bearing retainer (**ARROW**).

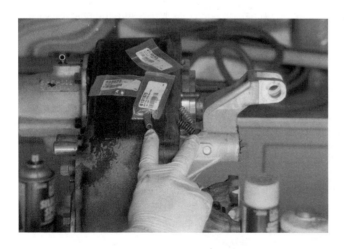

◀ **Fig. 4-188**

Install new springs and poppets to assure that rails will stay in each gear position. This arrangement dates to the earliest Jeep transfer cases. You will appreciate the crisp shifts and renewed detents.

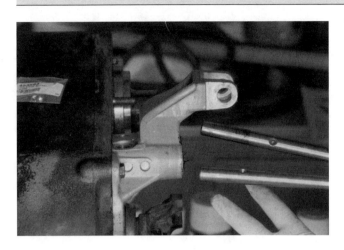

 Fig. 4-189

Note the offsets of these setscrew holes. Be sure rod's notches face the poppets properly. Compare the alignment and length of each rod. These pieces must fit the correct bore and shift fork. Grease the rod seals liberally.

◀ **Fig. 4-190**

This is the relationship of the shift rods. Place the clutch sleeves in neutral while you determine which rod/rail fits each bore.

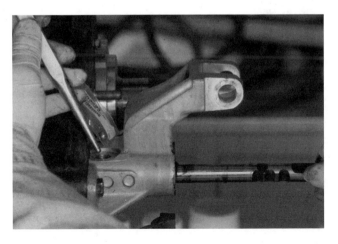

◀ **Fig. 4-191**

Install a spring and poppet in its bore. Push the ball down with a tapered punch to a point just below the rod bore. Slide the shift rod over the ball. This will hold the spring and ball down.

 Fig. 4-192

As you insert rails, know that they must be set in a position that will allow the interlocks to fall out of the way. If it takes much effort to push a rail, rotate the opposite rod to allow the interlock pin to slide out of the way. Look closely at the relationship between the rails and the two interlock pins. In service, these important pins prevent the clashing of gears.

Fig. 4-193

Use Loctite 242 on setscrews. Make sure threads are free of burrs. Align setscrew recess in rod with setscrew. Torque the setscrew to 15 lb-ft. Shift the rail several times then re-check the torque.

NOTE—

You can move each rail by inserting a screwdriver or pin punch through the hole at the rod end. Push and pull each rod straight inward and outward while watching the clutch hub movement. Note that the interlock pins will not allow simultaneous movement of the rails.

Fig. 4-194

Align setscrew recess in rod with setscrew, and tighten the second setscrew. Use Loctite 242 on threads. Torque setscrew to 15 lb-ft. Shift the rail several times then re-check torque.

 Fig. 4-195

We're close! Note shift rail and fork positions. Each clutch hub is in its intermediate mode. Shift rods extend equal lengths from the front bearing retainer bores.

4

◀ **Fig. 4-196**

Care taken to assure sealing, the rail seals are in place, centered and intact. The shift link guide will add further support, keeping these seals secure.

◀ **Fig. 4-197**

You can install a new spring/poppet soft plug, coating the plug's edges with Super 300 sealant. This round shaft and hammer work well for installing the soft plug.

 Fig. 4-198

Coat threads on the "4WD" switch with Super 300. Secure the switch snugly in the bearing retainer/cap.

 Fig. 4-199

Again, 4WD Hardware, Inc., offers all of the new pieces shown. Install new thrust washers, needle/roller bearings and spacers. Use genuine Mopar/Jeep or quality aftermarket parts like these. Do not compromise.

NOTE—

Built properly and run on quality gear lubricant, a Dana 300 transfer case should be good for at least 150,000 miles of trouble-free driving! The '86 unit did not require any hard gear parts at 109,000 miles. Without anything more than oil changes, this transfer case could have gone many more miles behind its original four-cylinder engine. I chose to freshen up the unit for the sake of this book and the 160-plus horsepower of Mopar's 4.2L remanufactured engine with the Mopar Performance MPI conversion.

 Fig. 4-200

With thrust washers in place, measure the end-to-end width between the outer edges of the thrust washers. This measurement will enable construction of a wooden installation tool.

◀ **Fig. 4-201**

Here's the objective: Find a 1-1/8" diameter piece of dowel/round stock. Cut a 3-1/8" length, square on ends. This is your dummy shaft for easily installing the intermediate gear and its bearings.

4

◀ **Fig. 4-202**

Begin by stacking a row of new needle rollers in the intermediate gear bore. Light grease or petroleum jelly will keep these rollers in place during assembly.

◀ **Fig. 4-203**

Drop the dowel into the bore. This and keystone effect hold the rollers from dropping out of position. Wide spacer sleeve (**ARROW**) fits between the two sets of roller needles.

 Fig. 4-204

With first row of needle rollers and middle spacer in place, you can begin building the second set of rollers. When all rollers are in place, they will stay intact by keystone effect. The only way to collapse the bearing set would be sliding a roller out endwise.

NOTE—

If a full-count set of new rollers will not stay in place due to too much clearance between rollers, the gear's bore is over-sized from wear. The proper count of bearings should stay intact when the last roller goes into position. Use grease to keep rollers in the bore until the last roller fits.

Fig. 4-205

Dummy tool is long enough to extend through the two outer spacers and the two thrust washers. Here, the outer spacers bring the stacked bearing width to the edges of the gear.

Fig. 4-206

Petroleum jelly will hold the thrust washers against the case sides. Be sure to index the thrust washer locating tabs with the notches in the case.

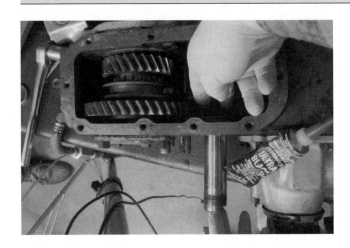

◀ **Fig. 4-207**

Align the intermediate shaft lock plate notch and carefully push the shaft through the back bore of case. Note that I put Ultra-Black RTV sealant around the intermediate shaft where the new O-ring seats in its groove. This will help protect the O-ring, enable easier movement of the shaft, and improve sealing. Stop as the shaft just catches the first thrust washer.

4

◀ **Fig. 4-208**

Now I carefully place the intermediate gear assembly in to the case. Align the gear, and insert the dummy shaft. Slowly tap the shaft with a plastic hammer while holding the dummy shaft flush against the steel intermediate shaft. The intermediate shaft slides through the thrust washers, bearings and spacer washers.

◀ **Fig. 4-209**

Put a small swab of Loctite 242 in the bore of the case. By now, the shaft is fully supporting the gear and bearings. All parts are in place. Make sure the lock plate notch aligns properly, and continue driving the shaft into the case. Seat the shaft and align it for lock plate installation.

◀ **Fig. 4-210**

A dab of Super 300 at the outer edge of shaft provides additional protection. This shaft fits snugly in both bores. RTV, Super 300 and Loctite 242 satisfy sealing needs for this shaft!

◀ **Fig. 4-211**

Put Loctite 242 on threads of lock plate bolt. Place the plate in position and install the bolt. Torque the bolt to 25 lb-ft.

◀ **Fig. 4-212**

Slowly pour a pint of gear lube over the gearsets while rotating all shafts and yokes. Make a final inspection of the rolling mechanisms. The capacity of the Dana 300 is two quarts (four pints). You can perform the balance of the fill-up with the transfer case in the vehicle and level.

Fig. 4-213

If you use a bottom gasket, coat each side of a new gasket with Super 300 sealant. Some prefer the use of RTV sealant in place of a gasket. If so, place a uniform 1/8-inch high bead of RTV sealant around the mating surface. Visualize how the sealant will compress and fill. It must cover the mating surface of the pan and case without gaps.

> **CAUTION—**
>
> *If you plan to eliminate the bottom gasket, make sure there is adequate clearance between the oil pan and moving parts!*

4

Fig. 4-214

If you do not use a gasket, put Loctite 242 on the bolt threads, and lightly thread the bolts up---just loosely finger tight. Let RTV sealant set up for awhile before securing the bolts with a torque wrench. If using a gasket and Super 300 sealant, you can tighten bolts immediately and securely, torquing in cross sequence to 15 lb-ft.

NOTE—

Read the instructions for RTV sealant to determine when you can torque bolts to specification. An alternative to RTV sealant is '518' anaerobic sealer. This enables immediate torquing to 15 lb-ft, as anaerobic sealant will cure in the absence of air. RTV, by contrast, requires some amount of air-cure before you fully tighten the bolts.

Fig. 4-215

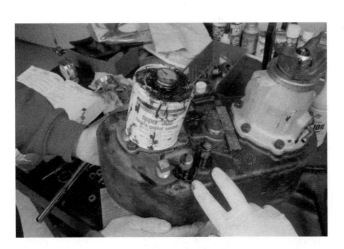

Swab a bit of Super 300 at the base of each shift rod thimble cap. If these were not disturbed and sealed well before you disassembled the transfer case, they should seal fine.

 Fig. 4-216

Install the speedometer driven gear assembly. Make sure you index the support housing to match the driven gear's tooth count. The housing offsets to accommodate several driven gears. Replace the sleeve/housing outer O-ring and the shaft seal if needed. Use Loctite 242 on the clamp bolt. Torque to 15 lb-ft.

 Fig. 4-217

Install the shift link guide. Put Loctite 242 on bolt threads, and secure bolt to 15 lb-ft. The balance of linkage is very simple. Replace the cotter pins and worn nylon bushings on the shift linkage.

This completes the Dana 300 transfer case rebuild. In **Chapter 3**, you can see this unit painted in gloss black engine enamel, installed and looking better than new! For details on the shift linkage, review the illustrations in **Chapter 3**. If your CJ can benefit from the Currie 'Twin-Stick' shifter conversion, consider that option for the Dana 300 transfer case.

Borg-Warner's Jeep 'Quadra-Trac'

NOTE—
*A relatively small number of Quadra-Trac units were produced for CJ-7 use. For that reason, step-by-step overhaul coverage is not warranted within this book. I have limited the scope of coverage to an overview and my impressions of the Quadra-Trac's design. For the rebuilder intent on overhauling a Quadra-Trac unit, I encourage access to a **Mitchell**, **Motors** or **Chilton** professional-level manual or, preferably, a Jeep factory workshop manual from the '76-'79 era. Rebuilding a Quadra-Trac unit is not a difficult procedure.*

4

For the 1976 CJ models, AMC/Jeep made bold advances. A new, fully boxed-rail frame was evident. While the wheelbase for the CJ-5 remained at 84-inches, the CJ-6 of 104-inch wheelbase was no longer available, and an all-new model CJ-7 of 94-inch wheelbase came on line.

This new CJ-7 wheelbase afforded the use of an automatic transmission option, a first for the CJ models. The transmission of choice, a GM THM400 had served in the Jeepster/Commando, J-trucks and Wagoneers. Notably, the three-speed THM400 was the most rugged GM transmission available for automobile and light truck use.

The aluminum Quadra-Trac transfer case is a chain-drive type. Long before the New Process chain-drive units became standard fare for later model Jeep vehicles, the Quadra-Trac advanced the use of a heavy-duty chain for delivering power to both the front and rear driveshafts. This "side-drive" design harkens back to the Spicer Model 18 gear-drive transfer cases.

Models with the Quadra-Trac unit are easy to spot, as the rear differential is offset to the right side. This alignment matches the front axle offset, much like the '46-'71 CJ models and the WWII MB. While other '76-'79 CJ models benefit from the through-drive Spicer 20 transfer case with a centered rear axle differential, the CJ-7 equipped with Quadra-Trac has a unique version of the Model 20 AMC rear axle.

Additionally, Quadra-Trac is a full-time 4WD system. The shifting options include a high and low range, full-time 4x4 plus 4x4 "lock" mode. These features involve a vacuum shift mechanism for 4WD lock. Minor troubles with the Quadra-Trac include faulty vacuum controls or loose vacuum hoses. Before condemning the unit for failure to shift properly, trace the vacuum hoses and devices. Make certain routings are correct and that the devices hold vacuum.

An option to the vacuum controls is an aftermarket conversion to part-time 4x4. The Quadra-Trac lends itself to a manual shifting conversion that will enable use of a bona fide 2WD mode. A kit is currently offered by Mile-Marker and sold through aftermarket suppliers. Converting to part-time 4x4 permits the use of front wheel locking hubs like those available for the Spicer and Dana part-time 4x4 systems. This saves wear-and-tear and slightly improves gas mileage.

A bonus is the optional kit available to build 16% overdrive into the part-time conversion. This is optimal for highway driving, especially when a builder retrofits a very low axle ratio for off-pavement benefit. If you plan to keep the Quadra-Trac system, the part-time conversion can be a part of your transfer case overhaul.

Is the 'Quadra-Trac' Worth Rebuilding?

If your '76-'79 CJ has a worn Quadra-Trac unit, should you rebuild it? This is a time-honored question. Let's take a look at the merits and liabilities of the Quadra-Trac options.

 Fig. 4-218

This is the Warner Quadra-Trac unit. Used in '76-'79 CJs equipped with the THM400 automatic transmission, the chain-drive transfer case has vacuum and mechanical shift linkage components. Note the offset drive for both the front and rear axles.

There are currently replacement parts available and even the option of a part-time conversion. The unit is fundamentally strong and offers good service. More importantly, your switch to another transfer case design would involve additional expense and work.

A prime consideration is that the Quadra-Trac CJ's rear axle differential is offset to the right. The only gear drive transfer case of similar design is the Model 18 Spicer unit. A conversion to that transfer case would be retrograde. Many builders of early Jeep vehicles shy away from the Model 18's side-drive design, often abandoning this unit in favor of a Dana 300 or Spicer 20 transfer case. In these swaps, the rear axle must be replaced with a later rear axle featuring a centered differential.

 Fig. 4-219

This is the '76 rear axle for a Quadra-Trac model. That model year, all CJs shifted to the AMC Model 20 axle assembly. Unique to Quadra-Trac/THM400 models is the rear differential offset to the right side of the vehicle.

Abandoning the Quadra-Trac in favor of a Spicer 20, Dana 300 or an Advance Adapters' Atlas (aftermarket) transfer case requires changing the rear axle. You need an axle with a centered differential, and a Jeep's Dana and AMC axle with a centered differential is not difficult to find.

NOTE—

Keeping the Quadra-Trac solely because of the rear axle offset is not sensible. It is easier and cost-effective to change out the rear axle. If you keep the Turbo 400 transmission, however, you would be wiser to stay with the Quadra-Trac and the offset differential rear axle.

4

◀ **Fig. 4-220**

The THM400 is a very desirable automatic transmission. If you keep your AMC engine, the original THM400 case is a rare find. It matches the round AMC bellhousing/converter pattern. If you use this transmission with other transfer case types, you may need an expensive adapter kit to mate the transmission and transfer case.

NOTE—

If you intend to change the transmission type for any reason, the swap to another transfer case and a center-differential rear axle would be a likely change as well. The Quadra-Trac had limited applications and was primarily used with the THM400 automatic.

So, should you swap transfer cases? Add this up: the cost of another transfer case, adapters and another rear axle. There is also the possibility that the chosen transfer case will not provide enough clearance for the THM400 or the front driveshaft routing.

The switch to a through-drive transfer case will also increase the rear driveshaft angle considerably. This may not be desirable, especially on vehicles with suspension lift kits, as a radical driveshaft slope stresses the driveline and other components. Such a problem requires additional modifications and expense to rectify.

If your CJ's rear axle is in good condition, you may decide the cost-effective route is to rebuild the Quadra-Trac unit. At the same time, you could upgrade with the overdrive/part-time conversion kit. As long as such parts are available, these options exist.

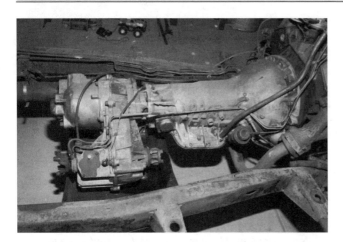

◀ **Fig. 4-221**

Note the location of the driveshaft yokes. Side-drive design places driveshafts in line with each other. The length, wide case and oil pan of the massive THM400 presents clearance issues. If you swap transfer cases, make certain you have adequate clearance for the front driveshaft. Consider the incredible length of this transmission and transfer case combination!

NOTE—

The Quadra-Trac's origins were earlier '70s J-truck/Wagoneers with longer wheelbases and a heavy chassis. The CJ-7 use of this setup is quite amazing, as no effort was spared to build a system that would have tremendous stamina in such a lightweight vehicle. The THM400 is 'Class A' motorhome material!

Consider, too, that THM400 units were available for popular GM V-8 engines. For builders intending a GM engine conversion using the THM400 as well, you can find a GM version of the THM400 case and use the output shaft and tail section components from the '76-'79 CJ-7's original THM400 unit as an adapter. In such a swap, you would likely want to keep the Quadra-Trac transfer case.

Testing for Wear

One version of the Quadra-Trac system has a two-speed reduction unit. This planetary gear mechanism provides the Low Range ratio for severe pulling and 4x4 crawling ability. There is also a single-speed unit used on some applications.

Barring grating noises and clear indications that your transfer case is defective, you can determine relative wear without tearing the unit down. The Quadra-Trac has the equivalent of a limited slip differential that transfers torque between the axles as traction demands.

You can test the operation of this differential by running a "torque bias" check:

1) Place the transmission in "Park" mode. Make sure the shifter is in 4-High and not in "Lock" mode. Lift your Jeep off the ground. (If you do not have a hoist, jack the front end up and place a pair of properly rated safety jack stands beneath the front axle.) Remove the rear driveshaft.

2) Rotate the rear yoke nut with a 0-250 lb-ft torque wrench. Note the torque reading when the cone clutches start to slip. Ideally, this should occur between 110 and 270 lb-ft.

3) If no slippage occurs at 270 lb-ft, the clutches are sticking. This could be nothing more than the wrong lubricant in the transfer unit. Slippage below 110 lb-ft means time to rebuild the transfer case's differential!

You can test for chain wear:

1) Remove the drain plug and allow lubricant to drain out.

2) There is a transfer case chain inspection plug mid-way between sprockets on the bottom side of the case. Remove the plug and insert a depth gauge or narrow ruler.

3) Reference the chain's wear from the normal depth for a new chain: 1.575" from the outside edge of the case to the chain surface while pushing against the chain. Wear in the ½-inch to 3/4-inch range is considered excessive and means that the chain needs replacement.

4) After checking chain wear and tightening the inspection and drain plugs, refill the transfer case with Jeep/Quadra-Trac lubricant or an equivalent, recommended product.

The Quadra-Trac is much like later model transfer case designs from New Process and Borg-Warner. The parts breakaway diagram helps identify components for purchasing service parts. Despite its numerous parts, the Quadra-Trac is not difficult to rebuild.

If you have tested your Quadra-Trac unit and determined the need to rebuild it, a professional-level truck service manual or Jeep factory workshop manual will provide the steps necessary.

NOTE—

If you cannot obtain a Jeep factory workshop manual, I find that the **Motors**, **Mitchell** *and* **Chilton** *professional-level truck service manuals covering the '76-'79 era provide detailed coverage of the 'Quadra-Trac' unit overhaul. These books are readily available from used book sources, as contemporary reprint books and at public libraries.*

4

Borg-Warner 'Quadra-Trac' Transfer Case
Found in 1976-79 CJ-7 Models
Equipped with THM400 Automatic Transmission

Sealing Ring

Snap Ring

Drive Hub

Power Take-Off Cover

Drive Chain

Drive Sprocket Front Needle Bearing

Oil Seals

Drive Sprocket

Thrust Washer

Drive Sprocket Rear Needle Bearing

Transfer Case

Case Front End Cap

Small Spring Thrust Washer

Large Spring Thrust Washer

Pinion Mate Gears

Preload Springs

Brake Cone

Transfer Case Cover

Front Case Gasket

Shifting Shoe

Shift Fork

Pinion Mate Shaft

Pinion Shaft Lock Pin

Side Gear

Preload Spring

Side Gear

Pinion Mate Thrust Washers

Differential Front Needle Bearing

Output Shaft Oil Seal

Brake Cone

Case Sprocket

Bearing Snap Ring

Yoke

Felt

Case Rear End Cap

Large Spring Thrust Washer

Small Spring Thrust Washer

Annular Bearing

Lock-Out Indicator Switch

Thrust Washer

Poppet Spring And Ball

Front Output Shaft

"O" Ring

Bearing Snap Ring

Lock-Up Hub

Retaining Ring

Diaphragm Control

Yoke

Rear Output Shaft

Annular Bearing

Output Shaft Oil Seal

Felt

Expansion Plug

Cable Clamp

Cable Clamp Bracket

Reduction Collar Plate Hub

Ring Gear

Snap Ring

Needle Bearing

Sun Gear

Snap Ring

Spring Pin

Reduction Holding Plate

Snap Ring

Reduction Shift Fork

Taper Plug

Spring Pin

Poppet Ball And Spring

Pinion Cage

Taper Plug

Baffle And Tube Assembly

Pinion Cage Lock Plate

Reduction Collar Plate

Shift Rail

Spring Pin

Reduction Shift Collar

Shift Collar Hub

Reduction Main Shaft

Snap Ring

Direct Drive Sleeve

Reduction Collar Hub

Spacer

Reduction Housing

Shift Lever Assembly

Snap Ring

Spacer

Needle Bearing

Control Lever

Snap Ring

Annular Bearing

Power Take-Off Cover

Power Take-Off Cover Gasket

Chapter 5

Axle Rebuilding and Upgrades

General

The front axles of 1972-86 CJs are rugged Dana 30 units. Incorporating a live, hypoid axle system with open steering knuckle joints, "solid axles" have proven exceptionally versatile and durable. Both drum type (1972 to early '77) and disc (late 1977 to '86) brakes have been used with the Dana 30 front axle.

A hypoid (solid) rear axle is common to all CJs. The '72-'75 models and some 1986 models feature a rugged Dana 44 rear axle. AMC's own Model 20 axles, used in 1976-86 models, have proven very reliable as well. The Dana 44 has an 8.75" ring gear diameter, and the Model 20 ring gear is slightly larger at 8.875".

NOTE—
The AMC Model 20 axle has received criticism from some owners. This, however, has more to do with the axle shaft/wheel hub design than any issue with the axle's differential or housing stamina. In the AMC Model 20 section, I address the axle shaft/hub issue.

Axle service is a challenging task, most likely a job for subletting to a qualified shop. For this reason, I have devoted this in-depth chapter to procedures that will enable *any* Jeep CJ builder to service or completely rebuild a Spicer/Dana integral-type axle or the Model 20 AMC axle assembly.

I have constructed this chapter to serve as a useful guide for builders of the Model 20 AMC rear axle or any Spicer-Dana open-knuckle front or hypoid rear axle. Once you master the basic assembly and set-up principles for these integral type axles, you will be able to confidently set up any Jeep axle.

NOTE—
Precise service specifications for Dana-Spicer axles not covered here can be found in trade service guidebooks and OEM shop manuals. The full-floating Warn aftermarket rear axle conversion described in this chapter offers insight into Spicer's own use of full-floating axles on MBs, the earliest CJ-2As and heavy-duty truck applications.

Within the service sections of this chapter, you will find detailed data for the Dana 30, Spicer/Dana 44 and AMC Model 20 axles. At the end of the chapter, the pinion height shim chart, tooth contact pattern illustrations and quick-reference data for Dana/Spicer axles will enhance your work.

Subletting Your Axle Work

Axle setup is not for everyone! You may not have the tools or patience for this process, and that's okay. I would, however, encourage every builder and serious backcountry traveler to read this chapter thoroughly.

Some Jeep builders will determine that axle rebuilding is a worthwhile and interesting effort. Others may decide such detailed and precise work is best left to a professional who specializes in the art of axle setup. \

My personal work history includes years as a journey level light- and medium-duty truck mechanic. This involved truck fleet service plus work as a truck dealership line mechanic with a front end/axle and manual/automatic transmission specialization. I have, for this reason, always performed my own axle and powertrain/geartrain work.

If, after reading this chapter, you find this work too challenging or time consuming, see my sublet shop recommendations in the **Appendix**. Shops like Jeff and Karen Sugg's M.I.T. can handle any gear-related task or sublet work, and M.I.T. will readily ship by freight.

NOTE—
Jeff Sugg and I go back to my early writing days with **OFF-ROAD** *Magazine in the mid-1980s. We share an appreciation for quality workmanship and have similar work habits. I have worked alongside Jeff on projects, and he is, in my opinion, among the very best 4WD transmission, transfer case, and axle builders in the United States. If I were to sublet axle or geartrain work to anyone, Jeff Sugg would be my choice.*

Overview; Ring-and-Pinion Gear Work Made Easier

Whether you're upgrading with a locking differential, changing axle ratios or simply renewing the axle bearings and seals, the outcome of ring-and-pinion gearset work will determine the reliability of your CJ Jeep. This work involves the use of specialty tools, precise measurements and an awareness of axle building objectives.

Uncertain of the outcome, many mechanics refuse to rebuild a differential. My professional experience has taught that the outcome is fully predictable---*if you know the fundamentals and goals of ring-and-pinion gear fit-up!*

General Concepts:

1)There are four elements to setting up a ring-and-pinion gearset: 1) pinion gear depth in the case, 2) pinion gear bearing pre-load, 3) pre-load on the differential carrier bearings* and 4) ring gear tooth mesh/backlash with the pinion.

*The differential carrier supports the ring gear.

2) All adjustments reference from the pinion gear's depth in the case. If the axle is original and has never been worked on before, the shims for pinion depth must be carefully measured. If you change the pinion gear but have the original shims, you can use the pinion chart *(at rear of this chapter)* to set up the new pinion gear's height/depth in the case. This measurement is crucial. If you have lost the shims that determine the shim stack thickness, you will need a special fixture to calculate the proper pinion gear depth in the axle case. The only other alternative is to rely strictly on a tooth contact pattern for gauging the proper pinion gear/shaft position.

NOTE—
The cost of securing a pinion depth gauge fixture is so great that most one-time axle builders will abandon the project at this point and sublet the task to a 4WD specialty shop like Jeff and Karen Sugg's M.I.T. You can, however, use the tooth contact pattern as a guide. This takes a bit more effort but can be done without the aid of a pinion depth gauge fixture. (See tooth contact pattern illustrations at rear of chapter.)

3) Once the pinion gear depth is set properly, you can set the pinion bearing preload. (See illustrated steps within this chapter.) This task will assure proper gear/shaft alignment and the lifespan of the pinion bearings. Done properly, setting pinion bearing pre-load will keep your Jeep axles working for many seasons!

4) Now you have a properly positioned pinion shaft. The next steps involve the differential carrier: carrier bearing pre-load, ring-and-pinion gearset backlash, and run-out of the ring gear. As described in the service steps, a simple bearing renewal (reusing the carrier and original ring gear) should involve nothing more than installing the original left and right side shim stacks in their respective positions.

NOTE—
If shims were damaged during disassembly, take an accurate measurement of their thickness, and install new shims that will make up the original stack thickness.

5

Overview; Ring-and-Pinion Gear Work Made Easier (continued)

5) Install the carrier by tilting the new bearing cups and tapping (not beating!) cups evenly, side to side, using a plastic sand-head hammer. Oil the cups to reduce friction. The axle housing will spread as the carrier moves into place. This is the preload on the carrier bearings, which determines both the trueness of the rotating ring gear and the lifespan of these highly stressed bearings. (See service steps in this chapter for details.)

NOTE—

In nearly all instances, you can carefully tap the oiled bearing cups into place. Service books, however, often call for use of a housing spreader tool when either the carrier fit is too snug or the bearings can become damaged due to excessive hammer force. Should you encounter such rare difficulty, you're faced with buying the tool, fabricating a similar tool, or subletting this procedure to a shop.

6) If you must spread the axle case for carrier bearing installation, the axle housing has two holes cast just outboard of the inspection cover opening. The spreader tool's pins fit these holes. Professional tools made for this task have an adjustable threaded sleeve. During this operation, a dial indicator is used to measure the maximum side-to-side stretching of the axle housing/case. 0.015"-0.020" is plenty, anything more than this will distort the case or worse!

7) Unlike pinion depth, you can set up carrier bearing preload without a special gauge. With no shims installed, drop the carrier and bearing cups into the axle housing. Pry the differential/ring gear assembly toward the pinion gear. Wedge feeler gauges between each bearing cup and the housing until only 0.001"-0.002" backlash exists at the ring gear. Note the feeler gauge thickness at each side…

8) Now, for the bearing away from the ring gear teeth, build a shim stack the thickness of the bearing cup-to-axle housing gap. For the tooth side bearing on Dana/Spicer axles, build your stack to the thickness of the measured gap, and then add 0.015" additional shim thickness. This should establish the proper preload (0.015") plus set the desired ring gear backlash---between 0.005" and 0.010". (I like a 0.006"-0.007" reading with new bearings, backed up by a correct tooth contact pattern.) You may need to move shims from one side of the carrier to the other in order to achieve desired backlash.

See sections of this chapter for the tooth contact pattern test. This carrier bearing preload and ring gear backlash formula applies to the variety of Spicer/Dana axles found in 1941-86 Jeep 4WD vehicles. These range from the Spicer 23-2 full-floating rear axle found in the MB and earliest CJ-2A (prior to serial number 13453), the common Spicer '41-2' and '44' (Spicer and Dana) rear axles, the Spicer 25, 27 and 30 (Dana) full-floating front axles.

9) Once the backlash and preloads have been set, recheck the ring gear bolt torque (before Loctite 271 has cured on the bolt threads). Then check runout of the ring gear for warpage of the gear or carrier. 0.006" is maximum runout allowable for Dana/Spicer axles, although I find this amount excessive. A few thousandths would be the sensible limit. Measure runout with the dial indicator's roller tip running on the flatly machined face of the ring gear (outboard of the carrier flange). If you discover an excessive amount of runout, remove the ring gear and check the carrier flange for runout. Determine the cause, and repair the problem accordingly!

NOTE—

Even a minute amount of debris or encrusted oil, trapped between the ring gear and carrier flange, will cause excessive run-out. Keep these parts thoroughly clean during assembly!

10) Run a tooth contact pattern to confirm your work. The tooth contact pattern is always a good follow-up to the setup process. (See later section of this chapter for details on running a tooth contact pattern check.)

Front Axle Disassembly

Front axle teardown is similar for all '72-up AMC/Jeep CJs. Proper teardown of the Dana 30 front axle is an important element of rebuilding.

 Fig. 5-1

If your CJ has disc brakes, loosen the calipers from their brackets and carefully slide the calipers free of the rotors. (See **Chapters 1** and **7** for more details.) If your locking hubs have tabs, begin by loosening the lock tabs on the locking hub bolts.

AUTHOR'S TIP!

On disc brake models, the calipers can be slid from the rotors and tied out of the way with mechanic's wire. This leaves the caliper and hose sealed and intact while freeing the rotor and hub for removal. Do not put stress on the brake hoses!

5

 **Fig. 5-2**

Remove bolts that hold locking hub to wheel hub flange. This older aftermarket hub application features a six-bolt design, much preferred over 5-bolt hubs beginning with 1981 models and continuing through 1986. (See later reference to hub changes.)

NOTE—

Models without aftermarket locking hubs have a drive plate in this position. On such models, carefully remove the hub cap. This will expose the axle shaft end and retaining snap ring. Remove the snap ring, then the drive flange bolts. Use an appropriate puller or cautious method of persuasion to remove the OEM drive flange plate from the axle shaft.

 **Fig. 5-3**

This is the '81-up 5-bolt hub. OEM bolts use liquid thread locker on this '86 application. Removal of snap ring will enable access to inner hub components.

 Fig. 5-4

The snap ring removed, slide the inner hub pieces out. Clean the hub area and identify the outer wheel bearing jam nut and thin steel lockwasher/plate.

Fig. 5-5

Bend the tab to free up the lock nut. Use a tapered chisel point and avoid damaging the nut or lockwasher/plate.

Fig. 5-6

The spindle wrench will fit the nut when the tab is flat and out of the way.

 Fig. 5-7

Using a spindle nut wrench, loosen the outer hex nut. Remove the nut.

◀ **Fig. 5-8**

If the lockwasher/plate is difficult to grip, use a mechanic's magnet to remove it. Loosen the wheel bearing adjuster/inner nut. You will find an inner thrust washer just outboard of the outer wheel bearing. Rock the wheel hub gently to dislodge the thrust washer and outer wheel bearing. Remove the bearing cone.

5

◀ **Fig. 5-9**

Grip the brake drum or rotor, attached to the wheel hub, and gently pull the assembly from the spindle. Now you have access to the spindle.

 Fig. 5-10

On drum brake models, the wheel brake assembly is now exposed. The drum can also be removed before hub removal, as routine brake work is often performed with the hub and wheel bearings still in place. Some mechanics prefer removal of the hub and drum as an assembly.

NOTE—

On drum brake models, you will need to loosen the brake hose from the chassis pipe. This will allow removal of the brake backing plate from the steering knuckle. Always cap off the hoses and pipes to prevent any contaminants from entering the hydraulic system during service.

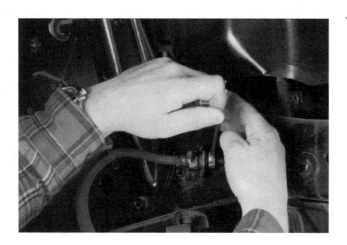

Fig. 5-11

Loosen each brake pipe flare nut from its wheel cylinder brake hose. (Note my use of flare nut wrenches on pipe nut and hose.) Pull the clip loose that holds the brake hose to the support bracket. Slide the hose loose from the bracket. After pipe is detached, tape off or cap the hose and pipe ends to prevent debris from entering the hydraulic brake system.

Fig. 5-12

You can now remove the rotor dust shield or the drum brake backing plate from the spindle/steering knuckle. Loosen the self-locking nuts. You should replace these nuts with new OEM replacement nuts on reassembly. The drum brake backing plate assembly will come loose in similar fashion.

5

◁ **Fig. 5-13**

The spindle tends to bind in the knuckle. With all nuts removed, lightly tap on the shank with a plastic, sand-filled hammer. This will dislodge the spindle. (Avoid striking threaded section.) Once dislodged, the spindle will slide free of the axle shaft.

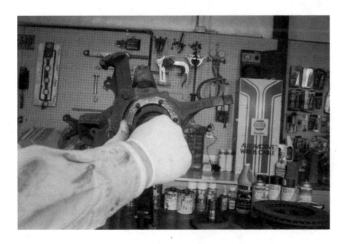

◁ **Fig. 5-14**

Spindle removed, you can slide the axle shaft from its bore. Support the axle joint, and keep the shaft as level as possible to prevent stress to inner axle shaft seal and guide edges. Pull straight out.

Fig. 5-15

Loosen the lower ball-joint/stud nut with a box-ended wrench. This is a self-locking nut and should be replaced with an OEM replacement type nut during assembly. Leave the nut loose on the threads.

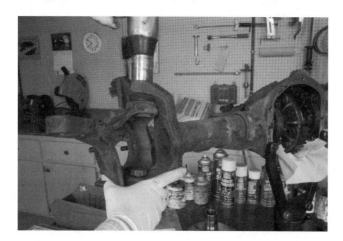

Fig. 5-16

Remove the cotter pin and loosen the upper ball-stud nut. This nut is accessible, and an air gun and impact socket will work here.

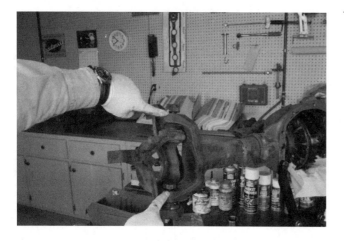

Fig. 5-17

Note that I leave the two nuts loose enough to allow the knuckle to drop away from the taper of the studs without falling to the bench or floor.

◀ **Fig. 5-18**

The plastic, sand-filler hammer once again comes in handy. Set the castellated top of the nut flush with the top of the ball stud. This helps protect the ball stud threads from damage. A solid couple of whacks should drop the knuckle.

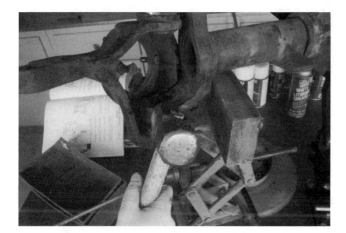

◀ **Fig. 5-19**

If the lower knuckle fails to loosen, here is a proven method for dislodging the ball stud from the taper in the knuckle casting. A solid whack on the side of the flange will "squeeze" the stud loose. Sometimes, a backup hammer on the backside of the flange will help. *Avoid hitting the stud or damaging the expensive axle flange! Use a sharp, jarring force.*

◀ **Fig. 5-20**

Once the knuckle drops, you can loosen the nuts and re-move the knuckle. The axle housing is now freed of the knuckle and axle shaft. Repeat these steps on the opposite end of the axle, removing that knuckle in the same manner. Mark parts for correct reassembly.

5

Fig. 5-21

It is possible to rebuild the axle assembly in the chassis. This is common under warranty or during installation of an after-market traction differential. Here, I perform the task on the Bench Mule, beginning by scribing the housing and bearing caps. *Caps must fit in original location and direction on reassembly!*

Fig. 5-22

Loosen four bolts, and remove both bearing caps. Although most manuals talk about a case spreader to relieve this case preload, I have good success with two long pry bars. Apply pressure evenly at ring gear bolt heads.

> **CAUTION—**
>
> *Be prepared to catch the differential case/ring gear assembly as it comes out. Do not allow these parts to become damaged. Protect the bearings.*

Fig. 5-23

Success! The differential case/carrier came out without fuss. I caught these parts as they came free of the axle housing. Note that the bearing cups slide out with the carrier case.

◀ **Fig. 5-24**

The pinion shaft can be removed at this point. (The pinion shaft can also be removed with the axle in the chassis. For the sake of thoroughness, proper cleanup and professional results, I perform this task on the workbench.) Begin with removal of the pinion nut. I use an air gun. My faithful, home-made flange tool helps hold the yoke flange steady while loosening or tightening the flange nut.

NOTE—

New vehicle warranty axle work, which I performed as a professional truck mechanic, most often takes place in the chassis. Higher mileage axles, however, are grimy and often contaminated with metallic residue. For this reason, I shift this job to the workbench. Spring U-bolts loosened, springs detached, the axle's first stop was the parts washing cabinet! A clean axle assembly is far more inviting.

◀ **Fig. 5-25**

Two-jaw puller makes quick work of the pinion flange removal. I use a long pry bar to keep the flange from rotating. Note that I pry beneath the flange on a surface that will not distort the U-joint saddles.

5

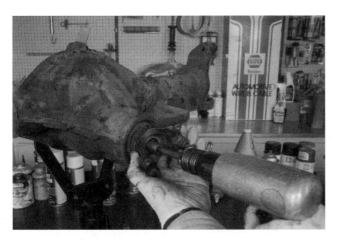

◀ **Fig. 5-26**

If you have an air hammer, you might find this approach handy. I blunted the end of a chisel point. Hammering carefully at the recess of the pinion shaft, I "dance" the shaft right through the outer pinion bearing. I find this method least stressful to all parts involved. Use care not to slip out of the recess. Protect the pinion shaft threads!

Axle Rebuilding and Upgrades

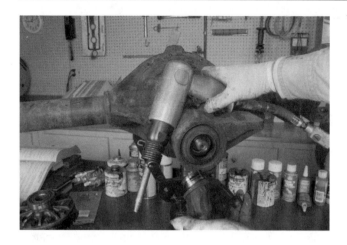

 Fig. 5-27

Here it is! The flange loose, the shaft free of the outer pinion bearing, these parts come apart readily. Note the blunted end of the air hammer chisel. This approach does not damage the shaft and quickly disassembles parts.

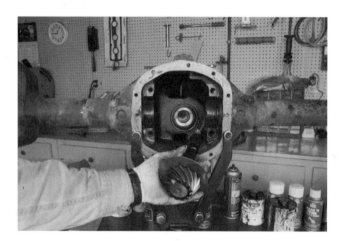

Fig. 5-28

Pinion shaft slides easily from inside the axle case. You now have the ring and pinion assembly removed from the axle housing. All that remains is the pinion seal removal and capturing the outer bearing and shim stack.

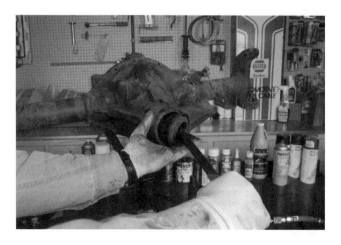

Fig. 5-29

You can remove the oil seal with a seal pry tool. Such tools are readily available at your local auto supply. Use caution not to damage the loose oil slinger. Keep clear track of the order in which the parts come out. Lay out parts in order, and tag them for reassembly work.

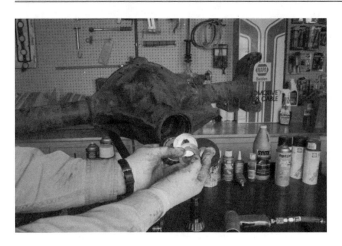

Fig. 5-30

Slinger fits between bearing cone and pinion flange. Shims fit inboard of the bearing cone between the cone and pinion shaft shoulder. These shims set the pinion bearing preload, crucial for proper axle function and long bearing life. Tag and wire-tie these shims together for reassembly work.

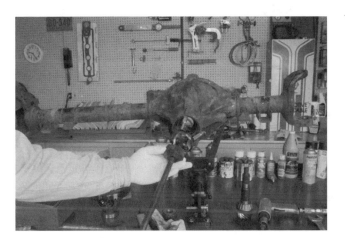

Fig. 5-31

I pull the outer bearing race/cup with a three-jaw slide hammer puller. Always protect the axle housing. Carefully place the jaws to avoid damaging the housing in any way.

Fig. 5-32

Drive the inner cup out with a brass punch. Do not damage the axle housing, and try to protect this oil baffle (**ARROW**). Take care to keep the shims intact and together. These shims are critical! They determine the pinion depth in the axle housing. All other setup steps originate and reference from the proper pinion depth!

NOTE—

The pinion depth shims indicate the pinion location for the ring-and-pinion setup. I view the pinion depth as the most important setup measurement in any axle buildup. Keep these shims and the oil baffle together. They will either reset your current pinion gear properly or serve as the baseline for installing a new and properly marked pinion shaft. See later sections in this chapter for configuring the use of the original shims with a new pinion shaft.

◀ **Fig. 5-33**

Axle shaft seals for the Dana 30 front axle are at the inboard end of the axle shaft, just outboard of the differential case in the axle housing. There is a seal on each side that I pry out with the seal removal tool.

> *CAUTION—*
>
> *Do not confuse the oil seals with the axle shaft guide sleeves. The guide sleeves keep the axle shaft centered during installation to prevent damage to the axle seal.*

◀ **Fig. 5-34**

Axle housing is now stripped of parts. (I left the driver's side axle knuckle in place, as the ball-joints met OEM specifications and were not in need of replacement.) Note the simplicity of handling this axle assembly with Mark Williams Enterprises' "Bench Mule" holding fixture.

NOTE—

Designed for the Ford 9-inch center section, the Bench Mule will support a CJ Jeep's Dana or AMC axle. I use caution with the loaded assembly, as weight far exceeds that of a drop-in 9-inch center section! The device is ideal for transmissions, transfer cases, center sections and lighter full axle assemblies.

◀ **Fig. 5-35**

A bearing collar will be needed for pinion inner bearing removal. Secure the tool evenly and in a manner that will not damage the oil slinger. Keep the collar tight during bearing removal. If necessary, release pressure, check the clamp nuts, then resume use of the press. My inexpensive bottle-jack (20-ton capacity) does fine for this work.

◀ **Fig. 5-36**

Bearing off, note that the bearing and oil slinger are intact and undamaged. Reasonably, you will replace all bearing sets, however, the oil slinger is a reusable part. Make sure it remains so!

◀ **Fig. 5-37**

Carrier bearing removal benefits from the collar tool and a press. (A professional puller set also has the fixtures for performing this bearing removal. The press, however, is much faster.) Note that the collar rests on plates that clear the carrier and ring gear assembly. Keep these parts from falling when the bearing comes loose!

◀ **Fig. 5-38**

Note that I have separated the bearings and tagged the shims. These shims determine the ring and pinion backlash and the carrier bearing preload. Clean the shims with alcohol or in a parts washer to assure accurate measurements.

NOTE—

You will discover that quality replacement bearings meet exacting standards and fit-up. Assuming that the axle had correct factory settings, a simple overhaul (new bearings, seals and reuse of the original ring-and-pinion gearset with the original differential carrier) most often requires nothing more than the original shim stacks in their original locations.

Rebuilding the Front Axle Assembly

The most challenging aspects of axle work are the bearing preload settings and adjusting the ring-and-pinion backlash. In this chapter, I address the Dana 30, Dana/Spicer 44 and AMC Model 20 axles. Among these rebuilds, I have included the popular use of aftermarket Truetrac and ARB Air Locker differentials plus a switch from tall 3.54:1 gearsets to lower geared 4.56:1 ring-and-pinion sets.

Most Jeep CJ axle rebuilds involve some kind of aftermarket traction upgrade. The two aftermarket differentials described in this chapter have seen wide use in the backcountry, and for that reason, it is sensible to include these upgrades within the axle buildups. Your Jeep requirements, however, may require nothing more than an OEM "blueprint" overhaul. The steps described will be nearly identical whether you use a stock differential assembly or one of these aftermarket traction devices.

NOTE—

For those rebuilding a stock, non-limited slip differential, the wear points are the side gears and pinions ("spiders"), the thrust washers and the pinion shaft. In inspecting the differential, you will check for play between the side and pinion gears. I cover this procedure later in the chapter for the benefit of OEM "open differential" rebuilders.

Rebuilding an open-knuckle Dana 30 front axle consists of two phases: the center section/differential overhaul and the outer steering knuckle/axle shaft work. We'll begin with the center section work, which is similar to Dana/Spicer rear differential and carrier work. *(See the Spicer/Dana 44 rear axle rebuild later in this chapter.)*

Accuracy of Shims and Bearing Tolerances

If a shim has become damaged beyond use, measure its thickness in an undamaged area. Replace damaged shims with new shims of the same thickness.

Bearing standards and tolerances are so close that simply changing bearings should, in most instances, have negligible impact on the preload or backlash settings. *If the axle was running true before*, and you simply change the bearings while reusing the exact shim stack thicknesses at each adjustment point, the result will most likely be an axle set to original factory specifications! Clean the shims thoroughly to achieve accurate settings. Seat bearings squarely and flush.

Verify each setting:

1) With only the pinion gear installed, perform a pinion bearing preload rotational torque check as described.

2) Confirm the carrier bearing preload/spread as you assemble the carrier and bearings.

3) Measure the ring-and-pinion backlash with a dial indicator.

4) Always perform a final ring-and-pinion gearset tooth contact pattern test.

On Spicer/Dana axles, you will install shim stacks behind carrier bearings. Here, I improvise a suitable bearing installation tool using an old bearing piece. This prevents damage to the new bearing and also allows the bearing to seat fully, as the flange of the carrier protrudes slightly beyond the installed bearing.

5

The Most Important Step: Setting Up the Pinion Shaft

NOTE—

In the front axle rebuild section, I describe an ARB Air Locker installation into a Dana 30 front axle. Whether you upgrade your front axle or rebuild a completely stock unit, all axle work begins with the setup of the pinion shaft. Each of the precise axle/differential adjustments depends upon proper pinion height and bearing preload settings. Here, I share the key elements of how to properly set up the Dana-Spicer axle's pinion shaft.

The tools for setting up the pinion shaft and other axle components can be very expensive. In this chapter, I demonstrate inexpensive alternative tools for setting up an axle. If you have avoided axle work because of the complex and costly tools involved, perhaps these suggestions and detailed 'how-to' steps will make axle work accessible.

All differential work relies upon a properly installed pinion shaft. Once you have set up the pinion shaft, the balance of the work will fall neatly into place. Pinion shaft installation consists of two concerns: 1) pinion height or the gearhead location in the case and 2) pinion bearing preload. These adjustments involve choosing the right shim stack thicknesses and locating the shims in the proper places.

The illustrations depict a change from the OEM 3.54:1 ring-and-pinion sets to 4.56:1 gearsets, supplied by 4WD Hardware, Inc.

A change from 3.54:1 to 4.56:1 gearsets requires a new shim stack height. The new pinion is at left. Note "+6" on that gearhead and "+2" on the OEM 3.54:1 pinion. This requires a change in shim stack height of 0.004", the difference between these two markings expressed in thousandths of an inch. For these two pinion shafts, I remove 0.004" of shim stack thickness from the original stack that fits behind the inner bearing cup. (See chart and further details at the end of this chapter.)

NOTE—

Adding or subtracting shims from behind the inner bearing cup can have an effect on pinion bearing preload. Make sure that you do not over-tighten and damage the bearings when you run the old yoke flange nut into position during trial fit-up of the pinion bearing preload. If you add shims behind the inner bearing cup, you may need to add shims at the outer bearing. If you subtract shims behind the inner bearing cup, you may need to subtract shims at the outer bearing. Tighten yoke flange nut slowly and cautiously during preload tests.

All original shims, the oil baffle and the oil slinger have been tied with mechanics wire and identified for their locations. Here, you see the pinion shaft shims, oil baffle and outer slinger in my left hand, the carrier bearing shims resting at the left and right sides of the case.

For inner pinion bearing, you must install this slinger before pressing the new bearing onto the shaft. Slingers and shims make up the stack heights and must therefore be replaced in their original locations. Otherwise, stack heights and position of various parts will be wrong.

The Most Important Step: Setting Up the Pinion Shaft (continued)

This oil baffle is very important, making up a portion of the shim stack behind the inner pinion-bearing cup. Oil baffle and shims determine the crucial pinion gearhead height. This oil baffle must go back in place with the shim set and face in the correct direction.

NOTE—

If damaged beyond repair, the oil baffle must be replaced. Compare the new baffle's thickness, and relate to the oil baffle as one of the shims in the stack. Adjust shim set thickness accordingly. Similarly, the inner oil slinger (between the gearhead and bearing) also plays an important role in the stack height of the pinion gear.

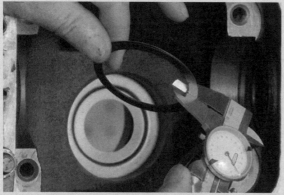

Here, I quickly measure this pair of shims with a dial caliper. You can use an accurate caliper or a micrometer for this task. If shims are worn or damaged, replace them with new matching thickness shims available in shim sets. Note the oil baffle positioned in the bearing cup bore.

This is my solution to special cup drivers and fussing: a hefty, ¾-inch diameter length of Grade 5 rod-stock, a bunch of Grade 8 flat washers and some Grade 5 nuts. Add to that a ½-inch thick plate with a hole drilled in the center.

Oil baffle and shims in place, you can install the bearing cup. My rod-stock tool and a clean old pinion bearing cone in adequate shape will serve well here. Coat the new bearing cup face and outer edge with light grease or gear lube to prevent friction or galling as the used bearing pulls the cup into place. Swab clean grease over bearing rollers. Oil the housing bore lightly.

WARNING—

Lubricate the new cup properly! Failure to lubricate the bearing surfaces---or use of excessive pulling force--- can mar or score the new bearing cup! Make certain the bearing cup is square with the bore. If necessary, stop intermittently and rotate the bearing cone to re-spread grease or gear oil. Prevent metal-to-metal friction as you pull the cup into place. If this procedure is not working easily, consider alternative installation methods such as specialty cup drivers.

The Most Important Step: Setting Up the Pinion Shaft (continued)

Here is opposite end of rod stock and other puller pieces. If inner cup is straight with bore, the pull correct, and components are properly lubricated, the new cup should pull into place without excessive force. If effort required is excessive, *stop and find the reason*. Make sure the oil baffle and shims are in place as the cup seats.

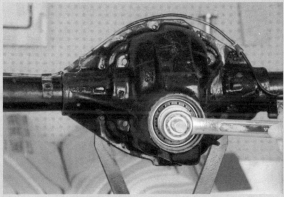

Repeat this approach with the outer bearing cup. Grease the surfaces of new bearing cup and clean the old bearing thoroughly to prevent damage to new cup. Swab clean grease on bearing rollers. Oil the housing bore lightly.

Steel plate is at inner side of housing, straddling the pinion bore. Start the cup squarely and evenly. Install the outer bearing cup carefully. *Do not use excessive force.*

New cups seated squarely, pinion shaft with oil slinger and inner bearing now fits into housing. Now, pinion pre-load shims can be placed on the shaft. A critical measurement, these shims set the distance between pinion bearings to achieve the right pre-load for proper shaft alignment, gear mesh and long bearing life. This fitment will be trial-and-error, as the new shaft required a shim change for correct pinion height.

5

The Most Important Step: Setting Up the Pinion Shaft (continued)

Install shims then lightly oil a modified dummy bearing. *(See Fig. 5-40 for details on dummy bearing set.)* Slide the dummy/trial fit bearing onto the shaft, followed by the outer oil slinger. When you install and tighten the companion/yoke flange with the old nut, the bearing will seat against the preload shims.

NOTE—

When purely guessing preload shim thickness, trial start with a thicker stack to prevent bearing damage. Leave out the oil seal for now, as you will check preload without the seal in place. Pull up the old nut slowly, checking the whole time for any binding of the bearings. To prevent costly damage, do not over-tighten the bearings!

When the trial shim stack is reasonably close, install the yoke with the old pinion nut and washer. Torque to 220 lb-ft minimum with an air gun and impact socket. You will check pre-load by rotating the pinion shaft with an inch-pound torque wrench. Start shaft rotating, then read the scale as you keep the shaft in motion.

Measure the torque needed to keep the pinion shaft rotating. Jeep recommends that you disregard the startup torque reading, which is typically higher and not consistent with the rotational torque effort. Adjust shim stack thickness until a 20 lb-in rotational preload is achieved with the used, trial-fit bearing. (The Dana 30 setting should read 20-40 lb-in with new bearings or 10-20 lb-in with original bearings.) Install the new bearing and test preload once more. Strive for a 20-40 lb-in setting. I prefer 30-40 lb-in with new bearings.

Fitting Bearings and Shafts the Easy Way!

Jeep Dana/Spicer and AMC axle assemblies use shims for setting bearing preloads, pinion depth, gear tooth mesh and axle shaft endplay. Shims placed behind bearing cones or cups require the use of pullers or a hydraulic press to trial fit the bearings. This time-consuming, often frustrating approach has caused many mechanics to lose patience and not perform this kind of work.

Professional and home mechanics alike can simplify these trial fit-ups. In the service field, there are tools available for quick setup and trial fitting of pinion shaft bearings and carrier bearings. They enable trial fit-up in an effort to more easily achieve correct preloads and gear tooth contact patterns. These mockup tools duplicate the shape of a bearing, but they install on the shafts or the carrier flanges with a light fit. Imagine not having to use a puller or press to remove bearings each time you need to make a shim correction!

In the interest of those who cannot afford such specialty tools, I have an alternative that works very effectively. Begin by rounding up a set of used OEM bearing cones and cups that show no appreciable wear---perhaps the ones you just removed.

Wearing safety goggles and holding the bearing cone securely in a bench vise, grind the inside (mounting) surface with an inexpensive, drill-mounted 1" diameter grinding stone. The stones I use for this task are flat-sided and at least as deep as the bearing.

This is very hard steel, but if you continually circle the interior surface, using the flat edge of the stone and uniform pressure, the diameter will gradually increase. Periodically clean the bearing, and check its fit on the shaft or carrier flange. Only a slight increase in diameter is necessary to achieve the desired result: the ability to install and remove the bearing with just light pressure from your fingers!

At this stage, you can easily remove and install the trial fit bearing(s) and shims any number of times---without the use of a puller or press and no risk of damaging the shims! Once you have achieved optimal measurements, clean all parts thoroughly and install the new bearing cone(s) in place of your dummy set.

AUTHOR'S TIP!
When you set up your final shim stacks, allow for the very slight fit-up difference between new and old bearings.

You can even use this approach for setting the pinion gear position or height on the Dana/Spicer axles. This should only be necessary if the original shims and pinion gearhead marks do not provide a proper reference, *and* you do not have the special gauge for setting pinion gear position.

Assuming that a tooth contact pattern test has revealed a misalignment of the pinion shaft, you can proceed by making a trial fit inner bearing cup. Dana-Spicer pinion gearhead location/height is controlled by the thickness of the oil baffle and shims behind the inner pinion-bearing cup.

Leave the large diameter oil slinger and new inner pinion bearing on the pinion shaft. Make a trial-fit bearing cup from a used cup in good condition. Grind the cup lightly on its *outer* edge to provide a finger-press fit into the bearing bore of the housing. *Keep the cup clean and free of metal debris to prevent contamination of the new pinion bearing!*

Use trial shimming to achieve the proper pinion gear position. Set the bearing preloads and ring-and-pinion backlash. Confirm pinion depth and tooth mesh with a tooth contact pattern test. Once preloads and tooth patterns are correct, you can remove the pinion shaft. Install the new bearing cup with the oil baffle and proper shim stack in place.

5

 Fig. 5-39

Housing cleaned and the outside painted, this rebuild includes an ARB Air Locker. I carefully follow ARB directions, drilling and tapping the case for the locker air line. This step is strictly for ARB and similar locker installations. Trial fit the ARB differential in the case to determine a safe, out-of-the-way location for this fitting. The air line and bulkhead fittings must not interfere with moving parts.

Fig. 5-40

This is my dummy bearing set. I grind the inner race of the bearing evenly, very carefully removing a uniform amount of material to keep the bore concentric. The outer edge of bearing cup can be sized on a grinding wheel. *This is very hard bearing steel. Use caution and always wear goggles when grinding this material!*

Fig. 5-41

Trial fit of bearing onto differential flange will determine whether you have removed enough material. Continually clean the bearing of all debris and strive for a light press fit, a finger pressure fitment. The bearing should slide on and off the flange yet fit without perceptible play. Old bearings, in good shape, work very well for this task.

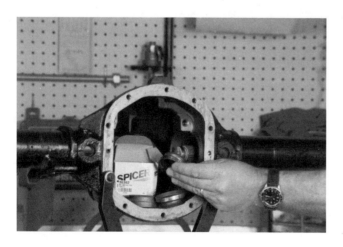

Fig. 5-42

OEM/Spicer quality inner axle seals were sourced from 4WD Hardware, Inc., also my source for the 4.56:1 ratio ring-and-pinion retrofit gearsets for the Dana 30 front and Model 20 AMC rear axles. Timken bearing sets, seals, new yoke flange nuts, shims, washers and all other axle buildup hardware also came from 4WD Hardware, Inc. Parts quality readily meets OEM standards.

5

◀ Fig. 5-43

Put sealant on outer edge of the seal. I use traditional Form-a-Gasket, the Super 300 type. These are seals that you definitely do not want to leak! Replacement requires removal of the differential carrier assembly!

◀ Fig. 5-44

This is my improvised driver. I select a socket that will fit the steel shoulder just inboard of the seal's outer shell. Make certain the socket clears the outer shell and the lip section of the seal! Use a very long extension(s) to tap seal into bore from the open tube at knuckle end. A plastic, sand-filled hammer will serve well here.

◀ Fig. 5-45

This is the correct socket fit. Seal fits to proper location in the bore. Note the sealant thoroughly coating the bore and seal's outer edge. I don't want a leak here, and you don't, either! Note that seal lip must face inward to contain gear oil in the differential.

 Fig. 5-46

Here, the trial bearing fits the carrier's bearing flange. First, place the original shims between the bearing cone and carrier shoulder. When installing an ARB differential with the shim set outboard of the "seal housing" piece, you can install the new bearing now. New bearing on this side of the ARB Air Locker carrier does not require shims between the cone and shoulder during installation.

> **CAUTION—**
> *The ARB-supplied bearing cup is of different size than the OEM type. This bearing fits on the air supply side of carrier, not the "crown" (ring gear bolt) side of the carrier.*

> **NOTE—**
> *The 'Truetrac' aftermarket rear differential's installation, shown later in this chapter, requires shims between each carrier bearing and the differential case---just like the OEM Spicer/Dana method. The ARB installation is unique, as the seal housing piece enables use of shims outboard of both the bearing and seal housing. Too bad Spicer/Dana did not do this! As you will also see, AMC's Model 20 axle is easier to service due to its outboard location of carrier shims.*

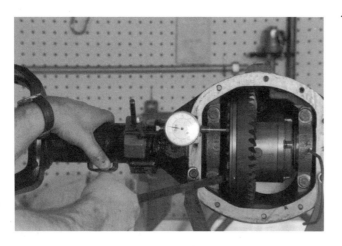

Fig. 5-47

The new ring gear is carefully mounted on the differential case. *(See 'Ring Gear Installation Tips.')* Here, I am checking the ring gear runout and endplay of the carrier. Before checking ring gear backlash, adjust carrier shims to create zero endplay. Note the air line notch/hole in the right side bearing cap. *Make certain that you have centered the ring gear/carrier with the pinion gear before marking, drilling or notching the bearing cap!*

> **WARNING—**
> *The air tube must fit freely without interfering with the bearing cap! ARB recommends a preliminary ring-and-pinion backlash setting to within +/- 0.010" of final set before you mark the cap and drill or notch the ¼-inch diameter air tube hole!*

Ring Gear Installation Tips

Before installation, make sure you heat the ring gear. (I use my parts washing cabinet, which will heat dense metal to 180° F. 180-212 ° F is recommended.) Center the gear then tap it into place with a plastic sand-filled hammer, evenly and carefully.

When several threads can be safely utilized, you can install the old bolts and pull the gear into place by tightening bolts a few turns at a time in cross. Remove old bolts and install the new ring gear bolts with 'High Strength' Loctite 271 on their threads. Torque bolts in steps/cross to full torque. Let bolts and parts set for several minutes then recheck torque.

5

◁ **Fig. 5-48**

With carrier endplay at zero, you can do a preliminary check of the ring gear backlash. Backlash on the Dana 30 front axle calls for 0.005"-0.009". Trial set the carrier at zero sideplay with zero gear tooth backlash. According to factory recommendations, you can then preload the tooth side of the carrier with 0.015" of extra shim to preload the bearings and set the backlash.

NOTE—

With new bearings, I strive for a final backlash setting of 0.006"-0.007" before reading the tooth contact pattern carefully. Preloading the tooth side 0.015" will push the ring gear away from the pinion and supposedly create the correct backlash. This seldom happens. While 0.015" preload on the carrier bearings is correct, you will likely need to adjust shims from one side of the carrier to the other when striving for the right backlash setting. Trial-fit carrier bearings will ease this phase of ring gear backlash adjustment.

◁ **Fig. 5-49**

Place a light grease or petroleum jelly on the O-rings to protect them during installation. On ARB Air Lockers, these O-rings are crucial to sealing. Use extreme caution when installing the seal housing. You don't want a leak here! In some ARB installations, I have taken the time to polish the O-ring grooves and the seal housing's O-ring mating surface. Using crocus cloth, the result was a non-abrasive, smooth O-ring seal. My installations have not leaked over very long service lives!

NOTE—

Just outboard of the bearing cup, the seal housing acts as a spacer at the right side of the carrier. ARB's shims fit into the recess at the outer face of the seal housing. The thick shim goes to the outside, sandwiching the thinner shims against the seal housing.

 Fig. 5-50

On ARB and OEM rebuilds, this bearing requires shimming to center the carrier and contribute to bearing preloads. If you use a trial/dummy bearing set, you can set preload and ring-and-pinion backlash to precision then remove the dummy/trial bearings and install the new bearings with the correct shim pack. If you do not use trial bearings, a two-jaw puller will be needed to remove the bearings.

> **CAUTION—**
>
> *Removing and reinstalling a new bearing runs the risk of damaging the bearing. Trial/dummy bearings eliminate this problem. You only need to install the new bearings once---after you have trial fitted the ring-and-pinion and selected the right shims to achieve correct preloads and backlash!*

Fig. 5-51

If you set the carrier to zero endplay (sideplay) with zero backlash, you can now add 0.015" shim to the tooth side of the carrier. (This is the seal housing side on an ARB installation.) While this is the correct bearing preload and a place to start, you may need to adjust shims side-to-side in an effort to achieve 0.005"-0.009" ring gear backlash.

NOTE—

Since the 0.015" preload is a fixed amount of shims, setting backlash is simply a matter of moving shims from one carrier-bearing flange to the opposite carrier-bearing flange. Use trial-fit bearings for this adjustment. This will preserve the new bearings and prevent damage to the shims…If you need to change backlash, a 0.005" shim moved from one side to the other will change backlash approximately 0.003". This step is usually trial and error and benefits from the use of the dummy bearings. Dummy/trial fit bearings can be quickly removed from the carrier flanges during the trial tests. I strive for 0.006"-0.007" backlash with new bearings.

Fig. 5-52

Once all settings have been confirmed, you can install the new bearings and fit the bearing caps for the last time. Put Loctite 242 on the thoroughly clean (wire brushed) threads of the bearing cap bolts. Make sure the cap-to-housing mating surfaces are clear of any debris. Install the caps, and tighten the bolts in cross.

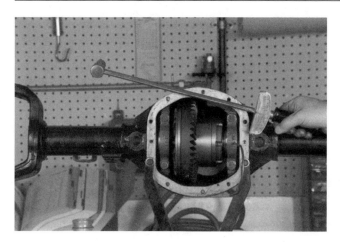

 Fig. 5-53

Torque in three steps to specification. Wait a few minutes, and recheck torque (55 lb-ft) after parts settle. You will find that a re-torque will often pull up at least one bolt.

5

◀ **Fig. 5-54**

Using an old toothbrush, I coat the ring gear teeth with yellow titanium dioxide. Wrap a shop rag around the pinion flange to form a tourniquet. Establish tension as you rotate the ring gear with a box wrench on the ring gear bolts. First turn the gear in the direction of forward rotation (drive pattern) then rotate in the opposite direction (deceleration/coast). Apply some resistance in each direction to get a clear imprint on the teeth. Compare pattern with the backlash reading.

◀ **Fig. 5-55**

I like a 0.006"-0.007" range of backlash with new bearings and a new ring-and-pinion gearset. My goal targets where this setup will be 80,000 miles from now. This kind of back-lash, with a normal tooth contact pattern and proper preload-ing of new bearings, will assure longevity.

 Fig. 5-56

Zero the dial indicator in one direction with all play out of the gearset. Gently rock the ring gear to the point that the backside of the teeth contacts the pinion teeth. It is often wise to check backlash at either two (180°) or four (90°) positions of the ring gear. Any variance is ring gear runout.

NOTE—

According to Spicer/Dana, ring gear runout must not exceed 0.006", measured at outer edge of ring gear from the crown side of the carrier. As a rule, I prefer a maximum runout in the range of 0.002". (See Fig. 5-47. Dial indicator will mount in this manner with stem and roller contacting the backside, flat outer face of the ring gear.)

Fig. 5-57

Note how tooth contact is well centered in both the "heel to toe" and "working depth." This, in conjunction with proper backlash, will provide long and noise-free service. (At the chapter's end, you will find the chart for proper gear tooth contact patterns and causes for incorrect contact patterns.)

Fig. 5-58

Check tooth contact in both directions. This is a wholesome looking pattern, confirmed by backlash reading. If runout and bearing preloads are within specification, the axle is ready to go!

NOTE—

In my experience, ring gear runout of 0.000"-0.001" is ideal, 0.001"-0.002" is still quite good. 0.006" runout, allegedly within specification for Dana axles, appears extreme to me. I would be looking for a new ring gear (sold as a ring-and-pinion matched gearset) or another differential carrier. Confirm whether the carrier flange or ring gear is at fault. Remove the ring gear and check the runout on the ring gear side of the carrier's flange. Also, be aware that even a burr on the mating surface between the ring gear and carrier flange can cause substantial runout.

5

 Fig. 5-59

I had installed the pinion gear and shaft, the bearings, shims, oil baffle, the oil slingers, the flange yoke and old yoke nut with washer, setting the bearing preload to specification without the oil seal in place. (This allows a more accurate bearing preload check and easier access for changing the pinion depth if needed.) Now I can remove the yoke and carefully install the seal. Place sealant on outer edge of seal, yoke flange end, yoke splines and washer faces.

NOTE—

An OEM oil baffle and inner oil slinger are part of the pinion height measurement and factored with the shim stack thickness. Always begin by installing the slinger with shims of the original thickness. When changing pinion shafts, add or subtract shim material as indicated by pinion gearhead markings. (See sections on pinion height and bearing preload adjustments to determine how much shim thickness to add or subtract.)

Fig. 5-60

Loctite 242 is added insurance. Install a new OEM replacement nut.

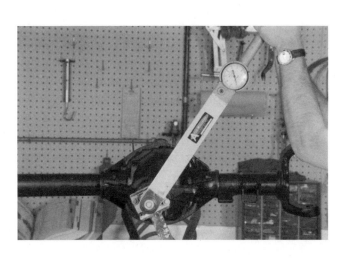

Fig. 5-61

Torque the nut to 200-220 lb-ft. Allow the nut to set for a few minutes and recheck torque. Some use an air gun for this operation. Here, I confirm torque with a 0-250 lb-ft torque wrench and my holding fixture's handle wedged against bench top. Axle setup is now complete.

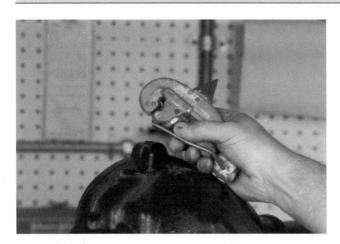

 Fig. 5-62

The ARB Air Locker line runs through the drilled and pipe-tapped hole. I cut off excess, allowing for proper shaping when the tube retracts into position. De-burr copper from the cut end. Use a shop vacuum to extract any copper debris from the tube or axle housing.

 Fig. 5-63

I shape copper tube to avoid moving parts. Envision effect of vibration over time. Route the tube away from abrasive edges of the case and the bearing cap. The tube fits into the brass bulkhead fitting with a 3/16" ferrule. Install the cover with Ultra-Black RTV, using Loctite '242' Threadlocker on bolt threads. Drive axle center section is now complete.

For details on installing the ARB air compressor, wiring, switches and the chassis air lines, see **Chapter 10**. For a reliable ARB Air Locker system, route the lines properly. Safely install the compressor and electrical wiring.

Steering Knuckle Service

The open-knuckle steering system is not complicated. Servicing and replacing the ball-joints, however, does require some special tools. For builders who do not care to invest in expensive commercial level front-end specialty tools, I offer some simpler alternatives.

Use Highest Quality Steering Parts

When selecting ball-joints and other safety hardware, I seek OEM quality components. For steering linkage and knuckle service, the best components available are genuine Jeep/Mopar pieces. See your Jeep dealer or suppliers who carry OEM quality replacement parts.

Mopar provides these kits for ball-joint replacement. Replace the ball-joints and boots, preload adjustment sleeves, cotter pins, grease fittings and nuts. New lower nut is self-locking type. Upper OEM nut is castellated for use with a cotter pin. Mopar is my first choice for steering, brake and other safety-related components.

NOTE—

Some installations use a snap-ring at the base of the lower ball-joint flange. On many CJs with the Dana 30 axle, the snap-ring is not required, and there is no provision for installing it. Know whether your Jeep uses the snap-ring at the lower ball-joint. Replacement ball-joint kits will often contain a ball-joint with the snap-ring groove and a new snap-ring. On some CJ applications, the snap-ring is not needed.

5

◁ **Fig. 5-64**

To replace a worn ball-joint, I use my air hammer and blunt chisel point to drive the ball-joint from the knuckle. You can use a hydraulic press for this chore as well. Take care not to damage the knuckle in any way. Wear safety goggles when operating air tools or a press.

 Fig. 5-65

Here, my ¾" Grade 5 rod stock and nuts with Grade 8 flat washers perform as a suitable spreader tool. I place an impact socket on the upper ball-joint base and tighten nuts in a manner that lengthens the rod. Pushing against the lower ball-joint flange, the spreader loosens the upper ball-joint. This can be done in a press if you prefer.

Fig. 5-66

This hardware is off-the-shelf steel electrical tubing from the local hardware store. I sought a piece with the correct inside and outside diameter to fit the ball-joint without interfering with its boot. Cut the tubing squarely. Round off or wire brush the edges to prevent chafing of the boots.

Fig. 5-67

Here's the "spreader" again. Note that sleeve clears the ball-joint boot and safely rides on steel shoulder of joint. I have $15 tied up in all of the tool hardware shown. This simple set-up is highly versatile.

> **CAUTION—**
> *Start and press the ball-joint straight! Prevent binding. Protect the knuckle's bore to achieve a secure ball-joint fit.*

 Fig. 5-68

Joint is safely installed without stress or damage to boot! These tools did the job. As an alternative, you could use a hydraulic press if available.

5

◁ **Fig. 5-69**

Here I use the cut off piece of electrical tubing to support the base of knuckle. This piece clears the protruding ball-joint and rests squarely on the knuckle casting. Upper tool is a sleeve deep enough for the steel plate to clear the ball stud. A hefty sledgehammer will readily drive the joint into place. Drive the joint squarely to prevent binding.

 Fig. 5-70

Drive ball-joint until the joint seats squarely in the knuckle. It is very important that joints seat completely. Make sure ball-joint's shoulder seats flush with the knuckle surface!

> **CAUTION—**
>
> *Some parts illustrations show the use of a snap-ring near the base of the lower ball-joint. The thick-style knuckle flanges do not provide space for this snap-ring. Know which knuckle flange type and ball-joints your Jeep requires. Determine whether a snap-ring is required for your installation. The replacement ball-joint likely has a snap-ring groove, which may or may not be needed.*

> **WARNING—**
>
> *The ball-joint preload setting would be ineffective if either the upper or lower ball-joint does not set flush in its seat during assembly. If not fully seated, the ball-joint(s) could settle further in service, which would change the crucial preload settings!*

 Fig. 5-71

Make certain that the axle housing's tapered seats are free of debris and any burrs. You want the ball studs to seat fully and securely! Catch the first few threads of the lower ball-joint to hold the knuckle in place. Note that this '86 CJ's knuckle does not require the use of a snap-ring below the lower flange. The new ball-joint kits included a snap-ring, which was not needed in this application.

 Fig. 5-72

New ball-joint preload sleeve gets a light coating of Anti-Seize on the threads. This will ease adjustment and also assure easier removal or adjustment of this sleeve many years from now. *Do not get anti-seize on the inside, tapered seat of the sleeve.* Sleeve/preload adjustment is in lb-ft of torque, so easy movement of the sleeve is important.

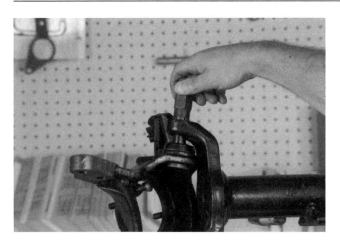

 Fig. 5-73

Sleeve installation tool is available at the local auto supply. K-D, OTC and Snap-On each make this tool, the K-D variety working just fine at less cost. (I've had this tool for over twenty years.) Thread the sleeve into a clean set of knuckle threads. Leave the sleeve extra loose for now.

◄ **Fig. 5-74**

Loctite on new nut's threads is good insurance. Nut is self-locking type. I still use Loctite Threadlocker on these nuts.

5

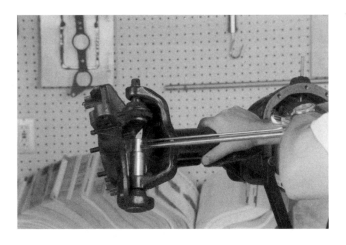

◄ **Fig. 5-75**

Some installers place a large two-jaw puller atop the knuckle and pull the knuckle assembly upward to seat the lower ball stud. Here, I am able to pull the knuckle upward by hand and seat the ball stud using a few light taps on the lower knuckle casting with my sand-filled plastic hammer. Once the stud is seated, you can torque the lower nut to specification (85 lb-ft). Recheck torque before Threadlocker sets up.

AUTHOR'S TIP!
If tapping the knuckle base does not seat the lower ball-stud securely, there is a simple technique that often works. With the split-ring adjuster sleeve removed, tighten the upper ball-stud nut to approximately 20 lb-ft. This will pull up the knuckle and hold the lower ball stud in its seat. See if this allows tightening of the lower ball-stud nut. Once the lower nut is tightened to 85 lb-ft with the ball stud secure, you can install and torque the upper split-ring sleeve to 50 lb-ft.

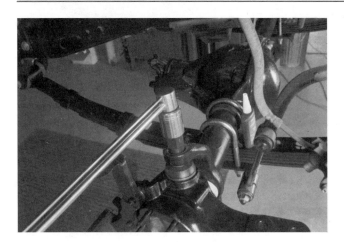

 Fig. 5-76

Carefully torque the preload sleeve adjuster to 50 lb-ft. Keep the tool's four tangs squarely within the split-ring's slots as you tighten the adjuster.

 Fig. 5-77

Despite the use of a cotter pin, I apply Loctite Threadlocker to the threads. Coat the first few threads before installing the castellated nut.

 Fig. 5-78

Torque this nut carefully to 100 lb-ft. Align castellated nut's slots with the cotter pin hole in the ball stud. If slots and hole do not align, tighten the nut just enough to align the slots. Re-check torque after the parts set for several minutes.

> **CAUTION—**
> *If the slots do not align with the cotter pin hole, do not attempt to align the cotter pin hole by loosening the nut! Torque the nut to 100 lb-ft and continue tightening until the slots and cotter pin hole align.*

 Fig. 5-79

Install a new cotter pin. Pin should be of same diameter as hole. Pull cotter pin firmly into position as you bend the upper portion of pin over the top of the ball stud. This is how I install a ball-stud cotter pin: no ends stick out, and the pin sets snugly in position.

 Fig. 5-80

This is the finished installation of the ball-joints and knuckle. Note that on this '86 CJ, there is no snap-ring near the base of the ball-joints. These high-quality Mopar ball-joints have snap ring grooves but do not use snap rings in this '86 CJ application.

NOTE—

Always rotate the steering knuckle through its full range of steering movement to be certain that the new ball-joints do not bind. There should be uniform resistance, as properly adjusted ball-joints are preloaded. If you suspect too much resistance, consult a Jeep workshop manual for your year CJ. Follow factory guidelines for measuring ball-stud pre-load and making corrections. If you have followed the assembly procedure in sequence and adjusted the split-ring sleeve properly, there should be no binding and no indication of looseness in the knuckle joints. Any play or binding indicates bent, misaligned or improperly installed parts. This could include a damaged steering knuckle or axle flange---or it could be as simple as a misadjusted split-ring sleeve.

5

Using a Hydraulic Press to Install Ball-Joints

If a hydraulic press is available for ball-joint installation, you may prefer the press to using a spreader tool or hand drivers. There are some techniques that can assure safer, quicker installation with a press.

◄ **Fig. 5-81**

This is a quick method for ball-joint removal. At M.I.T. in El Cajon, California, a weighted hammer serves as a driver. Do not damage the knuckle flange or ball-joint bore if you use this method! Wear safety goggles.

◄ **Fig. 5-82**

This method will work, although accuracy with a hammer and punch is critical. Always wear safety goggles when hammering hard metals.

◄ **Fig. 5-83**

This is a simple enough method for installing the lower ball-joint with a quality hydraulic press. Socket is deep enough to clear the ball stud. Make sure the socket safely clears the boot and rides securely on the joint's flange.

 Fig. 5-84

Bar presses against the socket and ball-joint. Power press makes quick work of the installation. Make sure parts align correctly and will not fly out of position under pressure! Force here could cause severe injury.

5

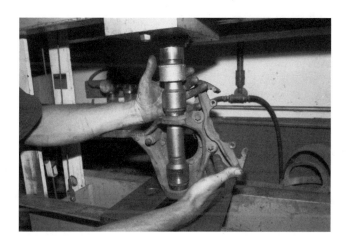

◄ **Fig. 5-85**

Now this is different! For quick production work, this method installs both joints at the same time! Again, be very careful not to misalign parts. Avoid any risk of this stack flying out of position under load. If you're not familiar with the use of a hydraulic press, do not try creative methods like this double joint installation!

◄ **Fig. 5-86**

M.I.T. technicians use this very accurate stack of tools. They can get both joints to seat completely at the same time. It is crucial that the lower joint seat completely in this approach, as you would have very difficult access to the joint if it did not.

Axle Shaft U-Joints and Shaft Installation

Axle shaft service is a part of front axle rebuilding. The axle shaft joints on the Dana 30 are common Spicer cross-type or cross journal and bearing cap joints. They are non-service design, without any grease fitting, permanently sealed by grease seals. Despite their exposure to the elements, these open knuckle axle shaft joints have been designed for very long service lives under normal operating conditions.

You will discover that these OEM Spicer joints offer exceptional service. When replacing them, I always return to Spicer-built joints. Under no circumstances should you use any other joint than a permanently sealed, solid-cross type. Do not use joints with a grease fitting, as the drilled cross is weaker than a solid-cross, permanently sealed joint. If you want long, OEM service life, use OEM-quality parts!

 Fig. 5-87

There are several means for disassembling a U-joint. All start with the removal of the C-clips (circlips).

 Fig. 5-88

The fastest method for joint disassembly is shown here at M.I.T. Using an anvil and a weighted hammer, the first bearing cap removal is the result of a few solid whacks in this manner. Remove this bearing cap.

> **WARNING—**
> *When using this method, protect the axle shaft pieces and the bearing cap flanges of the shafts! Do not strike the hammer near the bearing bores of these axle flanges. Do not distort the flanges!*

Fig. 5-89

First cap removed, rotate the shaft 180°. Tap in this manner to loosen the second cap. Tap until the inner edge of this cap is just flush with the flange. Do not remove the cap yet.

5

Fig. 5-90

Cap at bottom was loosened in same manner as the first bearing cap. (Second cap now faces outward.) Note that the short outer shaft is supported by hand as the hammer drives the longer shaft downward. This will loosen the topmost cap.

Fig. 5-91

Top cap is now driven loose. Remove this cap, and the cross should come out. Remove the remaining two bearing caps, twisting them outward with pliers if necessary. That's it!

Fig. 5-92

This is the new U-joint. Sealed with special grease, this joint should not be washed in solvent or wiped off. Keep these parts away from contaminants and dirt during assembly.

Fig. 5-93

Joint is placed in the flanges. Held in this position, the first cap can be installed carefully.

Fig. 5-94

Start the opposite bearing cap. Center the cross-shafts carefully to prevent the rollers from dislodging. This is a crucial part of U-joint assembly. Tap gently while keeping the cross-shafts within both bearing caps.

 Fig. 5-95

Keep the joint's shaft in the bearing cap to prevent the rollers from coming loose. Carefully tap the bearing cap inward while holding the cross journal in the cap. Tap until the C-clip groove just clears the inside of the flange.

5

◄ **Fig. 5-96**

Install the first C-clip. Make certain these clips seat firmly and fully in their grooves. Check carefully over full surface of the clip.

◄ **Fig. 5-97**

Center the second bearing cap. Note that an old inner bearing race serves as a tool for supporting the opposite flange. (This tool's inner space clears the first bearing cap, allowing the second cap to move downward into the flange.) Drive the second bearing cap until the C-clip groove is accessible. Install the C-clip.

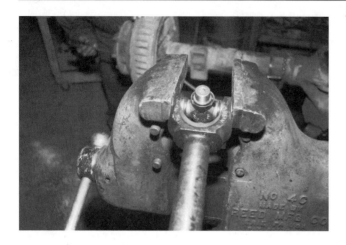

 Fig. 5-98

A bench vise will also serve as a press for installing the bearing caps. I have found that sockets of various sizes can serve as sleeves and pressing tools.

CAUTION—

When working on driveshaft joints using external snap rings, be aware that snap-ring grooves are fragile and cannot withstand a stray hammer blow! I use a vise/press approach when working on Jeep driveshafts. A vise also works well with axle shaft joint installation, providing a safe means of control over the movement of parts.

 Fig. 5-99

Third cap goes in place much like the first one. Make certain bearing rollers stay in place during assembly. Keep bearing shaft engaged in the bearing cap while tapping the cap into place.

 Fig. 5-100

Fourth cap goes into place like second bearing cap. Again, make certain the bearing shafts stay centered between the bearing caps to keep the rollers from coming loose. This is critical. Loose rollers will become broken and prevent the caps from seating. Rollers are only available with a new U-joint, a costly loss.

Fig. 5-101

Rotate the shafts to be certain movement is free. If you find any binding at all, tap on the U-yoke (**ARROW**) of the axle shafts. Stay clear of the bearing cap flanges. A sharp rap will restore the original shape of the yoke, freeing up the bearing caps at the same time.

Fig. 5-102

Be certain this end of the axle shaft is free of burrs and clean. Note the area where the inner axle seal lip rides. Polish this with crocus if there is any sign of roughness. If the groove is excessive, there is a high likelihood that the new seal will leak.

Fig. 5-103

Thoroughly clean and dry the spindle before repacking with fresh grease. Double-lipped seal (middle) installs with thicker lip toward the U-joint flange (**ARROW**). Thrust washer (left) fits against U-joint flange, inboard of the double-lip seal, with chamfered edge toward the U-joint. Ring seal (right) fits into bore of spindle as shown.

NOTE—

I thoroughly pack the thrust washer, spindle bearings and spindle with Starplex 2 grease, the same lubricant as my wheel bearing pack. Grease protects bearings and helps prevent moisture damage to these parts over long service life. The spindle's needle bearing may need replacement. If so, you can protective-wrap the spindle surface with duct tape and hold it in a vise. Use a slide-hammer puller with jaws facing outward to pull the bearing. Drive a new bearing into the bore with a suitable driver or an impact socket of the correct diameter, using a sand-filled plastic hammer.

Axle Rebuilding and Upgrades

◄ Fig. 5-104

Reference points: This is the direction that the chamfer on the thrust washer faces. Note that thin lip of axle shaft seal faces toward the spindle. On earlier Dana 30s, the thrust washer is bronze. Later model CJs use nylon/plastic. Either holds up well. Replace washer if wear exists.

◄ Fig. 5-105

Grease inner splines and slide the axle shaft carefully into the axle tube. Use caution to prevent damaging inner axle seal. Keep the shaft centered. When shaft splines engage the side gear, push the shaft inward. Place the spindle over the axle shaft end, making sure seals, thrust washer and bearing fit properly. Install the spindle gently onto the studs, protecting the threads. Seat the spindle in the knuckle bore.

◄ Fig. 5-106

I use Loctite Threadlocker as added insurance when installing new spindle nuts. Always install new, properly graded (OEM replacement) self-locking spindle nuts. Here you see a disc brake dust shield installed. If this were a drum brake model, you would install the drum brake backing plate with renewed OEM locking fasteners.

NOTE—

I torque the Grade 8 spindle nuts to 40 lb-ft, first in cross then rechecked after they set for a few minutes. Studs and nuts prove an excellent design, far superior to the bolts used on earlier Jeep closed-knuckle axles. Overall, the open-knuckle Dana 30 is a reliable, reasonably strong unit. These axles hold up very well under normal use and have survived serious abuse in many applications. If you intend to install an engine beyond the 225 horsepower mark, however, I suggest conversion to a custom Dana 44 axle assembly.

Dana 44 Front Axle Swap

The Dana 30 is suitable for most usage, including the installation of an EFI 4.2L six (160 horsepower range). When bigger horsepower or large tires are in the plan, you should consider installing a custom Dana 44 front axle. As no CJ has come stock with such an assembly, you will either buy the unit from a reputable aftermarket source or consider another, perhaps innovative approach.

Fig. 5-107 This is a highly effective alternative: Jeep J-truck/full-size Wagoneer Dana 44 front axle assembly in a '72 CJ-5! The driver's side axle tube has been narrowed, a shorter axle shaft custom cut for this application. Large, factory disc brakes came with the package, all stock components, including the massive J-truck steering linkage upgrade.

NOTE—

This '72 CJ sees regular service on the Rubicon Trail and other rock piles. Owner wanted a beefy front axle for large front tires and a wider wheel track, a muscular V-8 engine and a substantial suspension lift! (The wider track width helps offset the lift's negative effect on center-of-gravity.) This swap, including the axle shaft machine work and tube welding, was far less expensive than a custom aftermarket Dana 44 axle package.

Fig. 5-108 Left/driver side axle tube has been cut, its end (knuckle support) re-welded onto the tube. This requires precise measurement for caster angle and SAI. Spring perches must be fitted to CJ spring locations, meeting correct caster requirements. Brake hoses and other hookups require attention, too. Steering linkage from J-truck/Wagoneer chassis is substantially beefier. This CJ has power-assisted steering and a steering gearbox brace.

5

Rear Axle Service and Upgrades

Service steps described for the front axle's differential overhaul, including the ring-and-pinion gearset fit-up, are much the same for the Spicer-Dana type rear axles. The two axle types used in '72-'86 CJs are the Spicer-Dana '44' ('72-'75 and some '86 models), and AMC's Model 20 axle (1976-86 models). All Spicer-Dana axle models have one-piece flanged axle shafts. AMC axle models use tapered axle shafts with detachable wheel hubs ("two-piece" axle shafts).

All '72-up CJ rear axles are of semi-floating design. Each axle shaft receives support from one large bearing at its outer end. The inner end of the axle shaft receives support from the splined side gear of the differential.

By contrast, the Dana 30 front axles are full-floater type. Front wheel hubs have an inner and outer bearing that rides on the hollow spindle. The axle shaft fully "floats" between the differential side gear and the outer drive plate hub or locking hub.

In this section, you will find the distinctions between front and rear Spicer/Dana axles plus service details not covered under the front axle section. You will also follow the step-by-step installation of an aftermarket "automatic" locking differential, the Truetrac, and a full-floating aftermarket Warn axle shaft upgrade as well!

Both the Spicer-Dana 44 and AMC Model 20 axles have excellent stamina when used in a CJ Jeep. The '44' tradition began with the postwar CJ applications, first as the similar '41-2' in the CJ-2A, which then became the '44' in CJ-3As. 44s have been popular in ½- and even some ¾-ton capacity domestic trucks. The AMC Model 20 saw service in J-10 and even some 20-series Jeep trucks.

Your CJ has a rear axle designed for use in trucks weighing thousands of pounds more in both curb weight and gross vehicle weight rating (GVWR)! For this reason, as long as the rear axle has received proper maintenance and is not making ring-and-pinion gear noise, your Jeep's rear axle may need nothing more than a bearing and seal renewal to restore first-rate performance.

Many CJ builders seek a ring-and-pinion ratio change or plan to install a locking differential. This is the opportunity to renew bearings and seals as well. Within this section, rear axle modifications unfold alongside the routine overhaul of the Spicer/Dana '44' and AMC Model 20 axles.

 Fig. 5-109.

Models with this hubcap and the castellated nut have a two-piece axle shaft. This is common to the Model 20 AMC axles. Dana-Spicer 44 units used from '72-'75 and in some 1986 models have a one-piece flanged axle, a quick identification feature.

5

◀ **Fig. 5-110.**

On models that use brake drum retainer screws, an impact tool (motorcycle variety) makes easy work of loosening stubborn brake drum screws. This application is a 1986 CJ with a Model 20 AMC axle.

◀ **Fig. 5-111.**

Solid whack at reinforced, beveled edge of drum helps dislodge the drum. Strike drum at a 45-degree angle then tap as shown here. Drum will come loose.

> **WARNING—**
> *Beware of asbestos hazard from brake dust. Use an appropriate respirator and brake parts washing method. All '72-'86 CJs have asbestos content brake lining. You can find a contemporary non-asbestos replacement lining to reduce exposure to this hazard.*

Quick Steps for Removing Flanged Axle Shafts

The '72-'75 and 1986 Dana 44 axles use flanged, one-piece axle shafts. To perform axle center section work, you must first remove the axle shafts. These steps will quickly remove both axle shafts:

1) Remove the brake drums.

2) There is a hole in the axle shaft flange that enables access to the nuts that hold the axle shaft's bearing retainer. Remove the nuts. (Some models have a plug in the flange hole that must be removed before nuts are accessible.)

3) Retainer and brake backing plate should now be loose. Once you remove the axle shaft, the backing plate can be removed.

NOTE—
Remember to detach the brake pipes before removing the backing plates!

4) The axle shaft is ready for removal. You will need a hefty slide-hammer puller, attached to the wheel studs with a plate, to pull the axle shaft loose. Secure the puller flange to the wheel studs, and slam the hammer outward. The axle shaft and bearing will come loose from the axle's tube end.

Here is a technique for pulling the axle shaft. Pictured is an early Jeep axle with two-piece tapered axles. My son, Jacob, easily pulls the shaft with a three-jaw puller. A similar approach will work with flanged, one-piece axle shafts.

5) Unless you have a press and bearing collars, you must sublet the axle shafts to an automotive machine shop for bearing replacement. Generally, this is not an expensive labor procedure.

6) Replace the seal in the axle's housing bore. Use caution to place the seal in the proper location, sealing lip facing inward toward the differential, the outer metal shell coated with Super 300 or equivalent sealant.

NOTE—
This seal helps prevent axle shaft bearing failure and brake lining damage caused by gear lubricant contamination.

Reversing the jaws of the slide hammer puller enables removal of the axle housing tube seal. Replace this seal to prevent axle lube from entering the axle bearing and brake lining areas. Seal lip faces inward toward the differential, keeping gear lube in the housing.

7) If your bearing is a tapered roller type with cup and cone, you must pack the bearing and its adjacent space with appropriate grease. I use Texaco's Starplex 2 bearing grease, which offers excellent service life and reasonable resistance to moisture. Use suitable sealant on the retainer and bore mating surface of the seal. Create safe barriers to moisture! Coat the sealing lip with grease.

NOTE—
AMC Model 20 axles use a special silicone paste/sealant on the retainer plate. Use the recommended sealant! See the AMC rear axle section for details.

8) With new seal installed, the bearing, retainer and axle-shaft assembly can be tapped into the bore with a sand-filled plastic hammer. Be certain to install the brake backing plate before installing the axle shaft assembly!

In the section covering Model 20 AMC axle rebuilding, I detail the assembly of axle bearings, seals and the retainer. Refer to that section for further details.

Disassembling the Spicer/Dana 44 Axle

Teardown of the Spicer and Dana 44 axle units is similar to the Dana 30. For clarity, this section details the Jeep CJ's Spicer/Dana '44' rear axle disassembly procedure. (An earlier CJ assembly is depicted.)

 Fig. 5-112

Mark the bearing caps for direction and location. (Each must be installed in its exact, original position.) Pressure applied evenly at opposing pry bars, my son Jacob pries differential carrier and ring gear out of the housing. Keep bearing cups even as you pry.

Fig. 5-113

Jacob smiles as he lifts the carrier assembly free. He's smiling because I said this CJ frame-off rebuild project would take only three months to complete. Jacob was a high school sophomore when the project began and a senior when I finished all of the mechanical work!

NOTE—
As this book enters the market, Jacob will graduate college with a Civil/Structural Engineering degree (B.S.C.E.). Enjoy the read!

Fig. 5-114

Here, impact air gun quickly removes the pinion shaft flange nut. Minimal pressure on homemade holding fixture prevents pinion shaft from spinning. Note that Jacob wears eye protection.

Axle Rebuilding and Upgrades

 Fig. 5-115

Simple two-jaw puller extracts yoke flange from pinion shaft. Jaws seat safely beneath U-joint flanges.

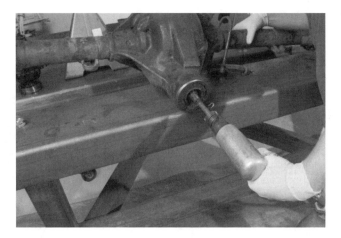

◄ **Fig. 5-116**

Pressing a blunted point against the pinion shaft's recessed end, Jacob uses an air impact hammer to quickly "walk" the pinion shaft from its outer bearing. Use of impact force, applied carefully to keep the tool centered, is far less stressful to bearings than swinging a wieldy mechanic's hammer.

> **CAUTION—**
>
> *Wear safety goggles when using impact tools. Protect threads and castings when using an air impact hammer. Become familiar with the tool's behavior before performing these procedures. Air hammers can be difficult to master. A tip: Hold the blunted chisel point solidly against the object. This will reduce the chisel's tendency to dance around.*

◄ **Fig. 5-117**

Here's the pinion shaft! Bigger than '25' or '30' version, '44' still uses pinion bearing preload shims. Two appear here. As a precaution, look for other shims stuck to the back of the bearing or in the axle cavity. You need a full shim stack for reassembly and fit-up. Tag and store the shim packs.

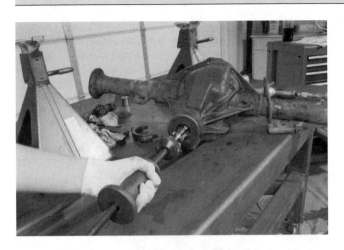

 Fig. 5-118
Pinion shaft removed, three-jaw slide hammer puller makes simple task of pinion seal removal.

Fig. 5-119
Pinion seal out, the original paper gasket (if used), steel oil slinger and bearing can be lifted free from the housing bore. Make careful note of the parts sequencing and layout. You can now proceed with the differential rebuild.

NOTE—
Refer to the Dana 30 front axle section for details on pinion shaft fit up and installation procedures.

5

Installing an Aftermarket Locker

NOTE—
If you simply want to restore or rebuild your stock Spicer rear axle's differential and ring-and-pinion gearset, you can still follow these steps. (For further details, I address the disassembly and assembly of a stock Jeep "open" differential later in this chapter.) This section focuses on the installation of a locker unit and preparation for the installation of a Warn aftermarket full-floating axle shaft conversion. Review of this section will enhance your overall knowledge of axle rebuilding and aftermarket upgrades.

A common upgrade for trail-use Jeep 4x4s is the locking differential. There are a variety of locking differential types, which I describe in detail within the ***Jeep Owner's Bible***. For this section, I have elected to install an "automatic" locker, the "Truetrac" model built by Tractech, Inc.

The Truetrac version of choice fits the Spicer/Dana 44 axles with ratios of 3.92 and lower (numerically higher). The axle involved here will use 5.38:1 gearsets for an exceptional off-pavement crawl ratio.

In the interest of upgrading the overall axle stamina, I added a Warn Industries' full-floating rear axle conversion kit. Custom Warn axle shafts feature the stronger 30-spline design. This Truetrac unit, therefore, is for a 30-spline application and will not work with lesser-spline OEM axle shafts. (For details, see section on full-floating axle conversion. Due to the popularity of 30-spline upgrades, the Truetrac is only available for 30-spline axle shafts as of this printing.)

The 'Truetrac' Locker

The Truetrac locker unit provides substantially greater traction for backcountry trail use. Since assembling this CJ Jeep, I have tested the Truetrac and found it capable of meeting every advertising claim. Sure and rugged, the unit is highly effective. For my use on this vehicle, the Truetrac unit, installed at the rear axle with an "open" (non-locking) axle up front, was a wise choice.

On the snail-paced, Rubicon type trail, where a wheel might hang well off the ground, a light touch of the brake pedal (or first clicks of the parking brake lever) will encourage torque flow to the wheel with traction. Under all other conditions, the transfer of torque is automatic, sure and effortless.

When wheelspin begins, the Truetrac delivers equal torque to both rear wheels. In the rough backcountry, the vehicle will gain sure footing in rock shale, mud and even moderately deep snow.

I caution, however, that any locker (including factory limited-slip types) can also contribute to vehicle handling quirks, either on- or off-highway. Both wheels spinning on an icy, off-camber road or trail can cause the vehicle to spin out or drop to the low side of the road. With any locker or axle traction device, use extreme caution and light throttle application when driving on icy or otherwise slick surfaces! (See the *Jeep Owner's Bible* for details on how a locker operates.)

 Fig. 5-120

Truetrac unit comes ready to install. This 30-spline application replaces the "open" conventional differential (right). Again, shims are used for setting ring-and-pinion gear backlash and carrier bearing preload. Use of trial fit bearings will speed the process.

NOTE—

At the sidebar "Fitting Bearings and Shafts the Easy Way!" in the 'Front Axle' section of this chapter, you will find details on making dummy bearings. Use these easy-to-make tools for trial check of the pinion shaft preload and the crucial differential carrier/ring gear fit (which combines gear backlash and carrier bearing preload).

 Fig. 5-121

Common Spicer/Dana shims, victims of a two-jawed bearing puller, need replacement. Using a micrometer, read thickness at undamaged sections of shim. Trial-fit dummy bearings will save time.

Review: Carrier Bearing Preload and Gear Tooth Contact

Ring gear installed, you can start fit-up by mounting trial bearing cones and cups on the differential carrier---without shims. Pry the carrier assembly and ring gear toward the pinion teeth, closing gear backlash to 0.001"-0.002". Take play out of bearing cups, and measure (with feeler gauges) between each carrier bearing's cup and the axle housing's cup seats.

Build shim stacks equal to the feeler gauge measurements for each side. On the side facing the ring gear teeth, add 0.015" of shims. When you assemble the shims and bearings, this should provide the 0.005"-0.010" gear backlash while properly preloading the carrier bearings.

Install the carrier assembly. Check ring gear backlash with a dial indicator. (0.006"-0.007" will provide a good range for the new bearings.) If backlash is off, remove carrier and shift the shim thickness from one side to the other, without changing the total thickness of shims. (Example: If you add five thousandths to one side, subtract five thousandths from the other.)

When backlash is correct, check the tooth contact pattern. If that pattern is correct, on both coast/deceleration and acceleration sides of the teeth, then replace trial fit bearings with new bearings. Install the carrier and make a final check of ring gear backlash and the tooth contact pattern.

Fig. 5-122

I heated the ring gear in my parts washing cabinet, which at 160°F+ drives heat into the metal. While still retaining heat, the gear tapped into place with a plastic sand-head hammer. Two old ring gear bolts pull gear up even and squarely, a few threads at a time.

5

Fig. 5-123

Always use new ring gear bolts. Old bolts stretch and fatigue. (High tensile strength makes such hardware vulnerable to shearing.) For insurance, I use Loctite 271 on clean threads of new replacement bolts. Tighten in cross and steps, several times around. Before Loctite cures, recheck the torque.

NOTE—

You will find torque figures at the end of this chapter.

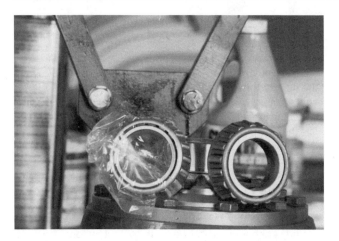

◄ **Fig. 5-124**

Here is a trick. To install a 30-spline axle shaft's carrier requires a unique bearing. Bearing on right is OEM for original Jeep 10-spline carrier. Note that bearing on left will work with OEM type cup yet this bearing has a larger inside diameter to fit the Truetrac's larger (30-spline) diameter flanges.

◄ **Fig. 5-125**

Past the trial testing and fit-up, new bearings now go on the carrier flanges of Truetrac unit.

◄ **Fig. 5-126**

Original bearing caps, clean and marked for proper position, work fine with Truetrac unit. New bearing cups fit original saddles. This is an aftermarket locker that installs without fuss, identical to an OEM differential installation. Use Loctite 242 on bearing cap bolts, Loctite 271 on ring gear bolts.

 Fig. 5-127

While feeler gauge readings were between the outer edge of bearing cups and the axle housing (with no shims in place), shims install inboard of bearings. Shims provide the correct bearing preloads and gear backlash. Oil bearing cups, and tilt the cups slightly to start installation of the carrier. Tap evenly.

5

Fig. 5-128

Just as with OEM differentials and the carriers, dial indicator measures ring gear backlash.

Fig. 5-129

Final, important step is the tooth contact pattern test. Here, I apply yellow titanium dioxide paint to teeth. Old toothbrush is good tool for this task.

◄ Fig. 5-130

"Drive" and "coast" patterns are crucial. For an accurate tooth impression, I learned a trick from friend and axle specialist Jeff Sugg: Create some resistance at the pinion shaft by holding the yoke flange with a shop rag in tourniquet fashion. Rotate carrier slowly with a box wrench applied to ring gear bolts.

◄ Fig. 5-131

Continuing to apply resistance at the pinion yoke, rotate the ring gear in the opposite direction. Force applied with box wrench should be just enough to make quality tooth impressions but nowhere near enough to loosen torqued bolts!

◄ Fig. 5-132

An aftermarket locker installation, by itself, does not require removal of the pinion shaft. To replace the pinion seal, remove old flange nut and washer, then the U-joint yoke.

NOTE—

This axle job was a complete rebuild. The pinion seal was left out to facilitate testing the pinion bearing preload.

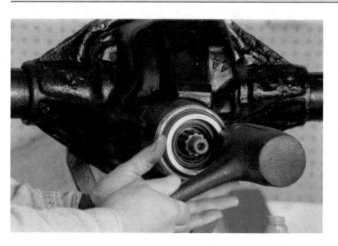

 Fig. 5-133

Some replacement seals, like this one, have sealant coating around perimeter and require no sealant. Apply chassis lube to the seal lip recess. Seal drivers work, though I prefer a hands-on approach with a sand-head plastic hammer. Keep seal straight during installation. Tap gently around the perimeter of the seal face.

NOTE—

Modern replacement seals often make no provision for the OEM paper gasket that Spicer fit between the seal shell and base of the seal bore in the housing. Here, I coat the bore area with a film of Super 300 sealant.

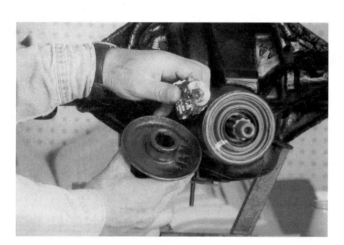

Fig. 5-134

Again, I apply Ultra-Black to base of yoke and onto splines. This insures against gear lube seepage. A new yoke washer and self-locking nut will also fit now. I apply Loctite 242 to the nut then torque to specification. (See torque charts at end of chapter.)

5

Fig. 5-135

One modification that I find sensible for older Jeep axles is proper ventilation of the axle housing. At one time, OEM venting was satisfied by the tiny bleed holes at the outer ends of the axle housing. Later Jeep vehicles feature vents high up in the chassis or body. For a vintage axle, I copy that approach.

◄ **Fig. 5-136**

Female thread air coupler fitting, its chuck end cut off to 1/8" length, fits hole I drilled in axle cover. Fitting mounts above oil fill level, away from any moving parts. A few minutes with my brazing torch, and here's the place for a vent hose fitting to attach! Once repainted, cover looks "factory."

NOTE—

The front axle also sports a custom vent hose running well up into the body. Attaching a hose fitting in place of the early Jeep's front cover vent, I run the front hose high in the body and alongside the radiator, placing a late Jeep CJ one-way check valve in the upper hose end. (Route front and rear axle vent hoses out of harm's way, and use metal clamps to secure hose.) This provides the vital protection needed for water crossings and deeper fording---protection that early Jeep engineering neglected.

◄ **Fig. 5-137**

Since this vintage ('55) Jeep CJ housing is being converted to a full-floater with Warn's kit, I also brazed the tiny vent/re-lief holes atop the axle housing. My intent is to seal the entire axle from contaminants and axle-deep water. The new oil re-sistant hose and one-way check valve provide ample vent-ing at the differential cover.

NOTE—

None of the modifications depicted in Figs. 5-135 and 5-136 should be necessary on later Spicer/Dana 44 axles that pro-vide for a vent hose fitting on the axle tube. On later models, you simply mount the check valve high up in the chassis and increase the hose's length.

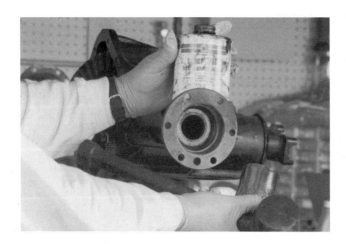

◄ **Fig. 5-138**

Install the axle seal, using Super 300 sealant on the outer jacket of the seal. These seals are crucial, keeping gear lube within the differential and axle tubes. Install seals with care to prevent seepage of gear lube into the axle shaft bearings or the brake parts.

NOTE—

In the next section of this chapter, this Spicer/Dana 44 rear axle receives a Warn full-floating axle conversion kit. For that conversion, some installers eliminate the outer axle shaft seal depicted in Fig. 5-138. The wheel bearings then receive axle lube. My axle still seals gear lubricant in the OEM manner, with the rear wheel hub bearings periodically packed with wheel bearing grease just like front (full-float-ing) Jeep wheel hubs. My reasoning for this approach: Gear lube running all the way to the hub end could cause oil star-vation at the differential and pinion shaft if the vehicle were to negotiate a tilted trail for too long!

271

 Fig. 5-139

Although I brazed the vent holes atop the housing, you can still see the OEM grease fitting in place. With the full-floating axle conversion, the fitting will be ornamental. (No harm done to leave it in place, or I could install a plug here.) Vintage Jeep tapered axle shaft models need these fittings for periodic greasing of the axle shaft bearings. These needs do not apply to '72-up Jeep CJ axles.

Full-Floating Rear Axle Shaft Conversion

Several motives prompt users to convert the rear axle to a full-floater. Warn Industries makes exceptionally high quality conversion kits, including some of the best axle shafts and custom hub assemblies in the industry.

 Fig. 5-140

Rebuilt Spicer/Dana 44 rear axle with 30-spline Truetrac locker installed makes an impressive package. Torque now available to a bound up wheel can place maximum load on the axle shafts. The strongest axle shafts available are seen here as part of Warn Industries' full-floater conversion kit.

30-spline shafts found in later high performance Dana/Spicer axles have superior strength. The addition of a modern, high-torque locking differential requires this kind of stamina.

Some builders also want to upgrade the braking system. While the use of 11"x2" drum brakes and backing plates was a major improvement in the '72-'77 CJs, drum brakes at all four wheels are now obsolete in Jeep 4WD vehicles. Builders should be aware of the disc brake options available.

Warn's full-floater conversion kits are only part of that company's offerings. Along with the full-floater is the availability of disc brake caliper mounting brackets that enable Jeep and other 4WD owners to convert their rear brakes to disc type. (Most vehicles intended for these kits already have disc front brakes.) These kits will also fit the front axles of Jeep CJs equipped with OEM drum front brakes.

Considering the tremendous improvement in both axle stamina and braking options, the Warn full-floating rear axle conversion kit provides a number of durability and safety improvements.

NOTE—

*In **Chapter 7**, you will also find Warn's front wheel hub upgrade to internal-spline hubs. Four-wheel disc brake conversions are available for all '72-'86 CJ models.*

Internal spline wheel hubs, used on full-size trucks including the (Grand) Wagoneer/J-truck, have substantially more stamina than the CJ's OEM five-bolt and even the six-bolt drive flange or locking hub setup. Much to Warn's credit, the conversion wheel hub design allows the option of using either disc or drum brakes.

Warn engineers patterned the wheel hub and bearing spacing to provide for use of 11" OEM drum brakes and backing plates, the OEM disc brakes or the Warn disc caliper/conversion mount. (Consult Warn literature and tech information for appropriate matching of parts.) The custom Warn disc mounting plate accepts a common GM caliper that works with late CJ OEM rotors. When using these rotors, long-shoulder wheel bolts must be installed with the Warn internal spline wheel hubs.

NOTE—

*The Spicer/Dana rear axle housing outer flange bolt pattern is also the flange pattern for the live front axles! As a result, I was able to create the first known use of disc brakes mounted to a Spicer 25-type closed-knuckle front axle. (This conversion fit my otherwise stock '55 CJ-5 front axle. See **Chapter 7** for details.) Warn's caliper mounting plate will fit front or rear axles on '41-'45 MBs, M38s, M38A1s and all years of CJs. You can also use the Warn internal spline locking wheel hub conversion kits with later OEM Jeep CJ disc brake knuckles and rotors. (See later sections of the book for details on the '86 CJ's conversion to Warn's internal spline front wheel hubs. OEM brakes work with that conversion.)*

Providing that you use the correct size wheel bearing cups and cones, any CJ front spindle will work with the Warn internal spline wheel hubs. (Read Warn's technical notes to determine which bearings to use.) When setting up the front wheel bearing adjustment, you can even maintain the double hex nuts and OEM lockwasher plate for a "factory" wheel bearing adjustment method.

NOTE—

*See **Chapter 7** for details on wheel hub, wheel bearing and brake parts fit-up. In that chapter, I outline the upgrading of Jeep braking systems to bring a CJ's brake performance/safety into the modern era.*

 Fig. 5-141

Warn provides a precisely machined spindle that mates to the OEM axle housing outer flange. I elected to install an OEM axle seal and intend to periodically pack wheel bearings with grease. I apply an even film of Ultra-Black RTV sealant to the spindle mating face and install the parts before sealant cures.

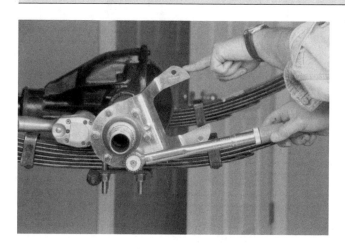

◁ Fig. 5-142

Matching the front disc caliper conversion bracket, I clocked the caliper location one flange bolt rearward. This provides reasonable protection from trail debris plus adequate chassis clearance. The caliper readily clears the wheel rim. (See **Chapter 7** for details on the complete disc brake conversion.)

NOTE—

High strength T-head bolts, provided with Warn kit, replace OEM rear backing plate bolts. Grade 8 top-lock (self-locking) all-steel nuts, with Loctite 242 Threadlocker on threads, will take care of mounting fasteners. I tighten nuts in cross and steps to a final torque of 40 lb-ft.

5

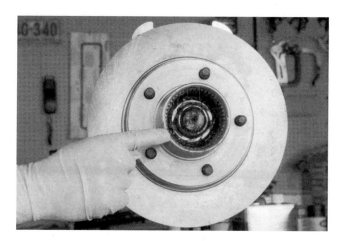

◁ Fig. 5-143

Grease axle shaft splines to protect seals as you slide the shaft into the housing. Keep axle shaft centered; engage splines with side gears in the differential. Thorough instructions provided in the kit, Warn's internal spline freewheel/locking hubs serve like modern, more rugged Jeep (full-size) Wagoneer and J-truck assemblies.

◁ Fig. 5-144

Installation looks similar to front wheel disc brakes on a later model J-truck or full-size Grand Wagoneer! Caliper is GM/S-truck type; rotor is late CJ OEM disc brake type. Warn supplies spindles, all bearings, axle shafts, seals, caliper brackets and mounting hardware. This is my '55 CJ-5's Spicer 44 rear axle with disc brakes. A '72-up CJ's Jeep Spicer/Dana 44 axle converted to disck brakes will look just like this! Locking hubs are Warn's internal spline, full-size truck type,

AMC Model 20 Axle Rebuild

1976-86 era CJs have AMC's Model 20 rear axle. (The only exceptions are those '86 CJs equipped with the Dana 44 rear axle.) Jeep/AMC axles may have narrow or wide-track housings; they may have a centered or an offset (Quadra-Trac model) differential. Regardless of axle tube configuration, the rebuild steps remain the same.

By design, the AMC Model 20 is easier to rebuild and set up than the Spicer/Dana axles. The location of shims is far more convenient, and setting up backlash or bearing pre-load is much easier with the AMC Model 20. I enjoy working on these axles. They present far less challenge to rebuild than other integral axle types.

◀ **Fig. 5-145**

Removing drum exposes wheel flange and brake parts for service. (See **Chapter 7** for brake work details.)

◀ **Fig. 5-146**

Remove cotter pin from the axle shaft nut. Air gun makes quick work of removing nut. Model 20's axle shaft nut may take a stout gun and impact socket for removal. Mark the hub and axle shaft to assure reassembly as a matched set. Do not mix parts.

◀ **Fig. 5-147**

Tapered axle and hub means the need for a special puller. If you do not own one, consider renting one. This can be an expensive tool.

Fig. 5-148

Once hub pops loose, removal is easy. Note that there is a small woodruff key in the shaft. This key keeps hub in position during installation. Do not lose the key...Brakes and seals are now visible.

On Model 20 AMC axle, rear brake work does not require hub removal. The hub should be left in place to prevent disturbing the axle shaft/hub fit-up.

> **WARNING—**
>
> *For work around brakes, it is now believed that a brake parts washer, using an aqueous solution, is better than any kind of vacuuming method. A washer not only cleans brake parts but also holds hazardous dust in liquid suspension. Never vacuum brake dust with your shop vacuum! Asbestos will find its way through the vacuum's filter and into your shop air.*

Fig. 5-149

Loosen brake pipe. Keep contaminants out of the wheel cylinder. Seal pipe end and cylinder with a plastic or rubber sealing cap, or tape off the openings with duct tape. Note use of a flarenut wrench to protect the flare nut from rounded corners.

Fig. 5-150

To perform routine brake work, there is no need to remove backing plate or wheel hub. For axle bearing or axle shaft access, you do need to remove the backing plate. Remove the flange nuts and gently pry out the dust guard. Beware of brake dust hazard. Wear an asbestos- rated respirator.

NOTE—

Wetting the brake area with an aqueous cleaning solution dramatically reduces the risk of dust exposure. Modern brake parts washers use a water-based cleaning agent that does not harm rubber parts and helps hold brake dust in suspension while service is underway.

 Fig. 5-151

You now have access to the outer axle seal. Pry this seal out gently. You will want to replace this seal on reassembly, using special sealant between the plates. Again, beware of brake dust hazard. Consider washing all of these parts down before performing shaft and seal work.

Fig. 5-152

These shims are critical to axle endplay setting. Keep track of the shims, and mark them for placement in their original positions. When you reassemble the axle, if the settings were correct to begin with, you will likely find these shim stacks remain the same. This is the left side of the axle.

NOTE—

Replacement bearings should match the tolerances of the original bearings. There is an international standard for bearing sizes. If shims remain where the factory put them, and if the axle housing and shafts have no damage, new bearings should require the same shim stacks as the original bearings. Verify shaft endplay with a dial indicator when assembling the axle shafts. (See Fig. 5-237.)

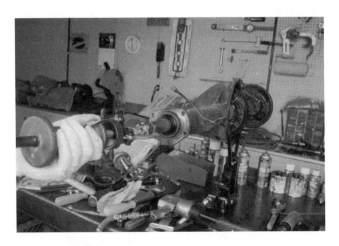

Fig. 5-153

This is my recommendation for pulling the axle shafts. The multipurpose three-jaw puller grabs the washer and axle nut. Keep jaws tight against washer. A few solid whacks will pull the bearing cup loose with the shaft and bearing cone.

 Fig. 5-154

When cup clears the housing, be prepared to catch the shaft and guide it straight out of the axle. Avoid dragging the axle shaft against the inner seal.

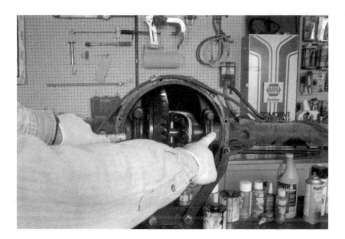

Fig. 5-155

Loosen the bearing cap bolts. At this point, I leave the bolts in place with several threads. This will prevent the differential from falling out of the housing and getting damaged.

Fig. 5-156

Use two hefty pry bars to lift the differential carrier. Pry evenly, and do not allow parts to cock or bind.

 Fig. 5-157

The differential carrier and ring gear are now out. Note that bearing cups set inboard of the adjusting shims. AMC was practical with this setup! Adjusting the ring gear backlash and carrier bearing preload is easy with this design. New bearing cones will press directly against carrier flange and only need to be installed once---no need for dummy trial-fit bearings!

Fig. 5-158

For bearing removal, this two-jaw puller works fine. (You can also use a hydraulic press with a bearing collar to perform this task.) Note the use of heavy washers to ride against the carrier hub. Washers fit inboard of the bearing, allowing the bearing to move past the washers. This may take two people: one to hold the case, the other to turn the puller's stem.

Fig. 5-159

If needed, my flange holding tool will keep U-joint yoke from turning while you remove the pinion shaft nut. I use an impact gun and impact socket to quickly and effortlessly remove the nut. You will replace the nut with a new OEM self-locking type.

Fig. 5-160

Seal prying tool makes quick work of seal removal.

Fig. 5-161

Again, my air impact hammer with blunted point works well as a pinion removal tool. I drive the shaft through the bearing. Keep the point centered in the pinion shaft end. If necessary, run an old nut flush with the end of the threads to protect the shaft.

Fig. 5-162

Place a block of wood under the carrier flange. A heavy brass drift punch will drive the ring gear from the carrier. Tap at opposite sides of the ring gear, and keep the gear even.

Differential Side Gear and Pinions Rebuild

The conventional differential is easy to rebuild. If the differential case is not excessively worn, you can restore performance with new pinion thrust washers and side gear shimming.

 Fig. 5-163

Begin the differential disassembly with the pinion shaft roll pin removal. Leave the shaft in place at this stage. You need to measure the side gear-to-case play.

 Fig. 5-164

This is the method for checking side gear-to-case play. Use matching feeler gauges at each side. Increase feeler width equally until all play is removed. Keep maximum play to less than 0.007". More than this will create axle clunk on gear engagement. Inspect gears for wear and scoring. Make sure the shaft is not worn. Replace the pinion thrust washers, and shim gears to specification. I strive for 0.002"-0.003" play.

 Fig. 5-165

These parts make up the differential. Inspect gear teeth and wear surfaces carefully. Shaft requires a tight fit into the differential case. Examine the shaft and the axle shaft thrust block carefully.

Keep in mind that all of the engine and gear reduction torque transfers through the differential parts. These pieces are subjected to extreme loads. Make certain differential pieces are in good condition or replace them. Check the differential case carefully for scoring, wear and pitting. Assemble parts carefully.

5

 Fig. 5-166

Bearing cup removal is done readily with the slide hammer puller. Make sure the jaws catch the cup fully. Take care not to damage the housing.

◣ **Fig. 5-167**

Pinion shaft inner bearing has a shim/spacer behind the cup. This shim sets the critical pinion gearhead depth/height within the case. If you plan to reinstall the same ring-and-pinion, the same shims would be placed back in this position. Keep track of the shims!

◣ **Fig. 5-168**

These new parts, all secured from 4WD Hardware, Inc., make up a complete overhaul. Included is the change from the OEM 3.54:1 to 4.56:1 gearsets. This '86 CJ-7 went from a T-4 non-overdrive 4-speed transmission to a transplant NV4500 with 27% overdrive. With this degree of overdrive, the 4.56:1 gearing is not extreme.

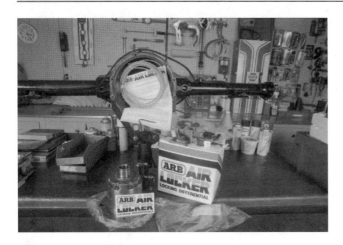

Fig. 5-169

For this Model 20 axle, the upgrades include an ARB Air Locker. The CJ-7 went from open differentials front and rear to ARB Air Lockers. (See **Chapter 10** for details on installing the ARB air lines, electrical wiring and air compressor system.)

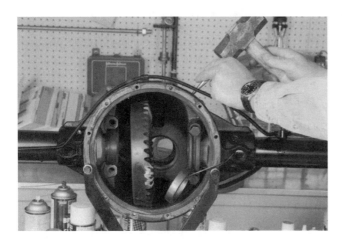

Fig. 5-170

Here, I set ring gear in its approximate location. My intent is to find a place in the axle housing for the ARB air fittings. You want this air coupling to be accessible to the air tube without interfering with moving parts.

Fig. 5-171

I drill the hole for the bulkhead fittings, following the ARB instructions. All of these drill filings must be vacuumed carefully from the housing!

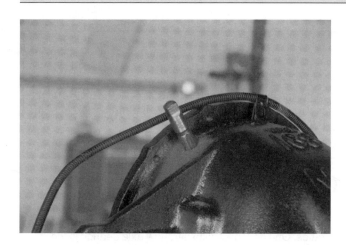

 Fig. 5-172

This is a ¼-18 NPT tap, the size recommended by ARB. Iron case does not present a problem when cutting threads. Be careful: This is your axle housing! Clean up all metal debris throroughly.

5

Fig. 5-173

You can heat up the ring gear in water before installing it. I place the gear in my parts washing cabinet at 160-180 degrees F. Use old ring gear bolts to pull up the gear gradually and evenly. Remove the bolts and replace them with new ring gear bolts.

Fig. 5-174

This is the recommended Threadlocker for the ARB Air Locker carrier/ring gear installation. I installed new ring gear bolts, part of the rebuild package from 4WD Hardware, Inc. Torque the bolts evenly, in cross. In three steps, bring torque to 105 lb-ft, the Jeep/AMC factory specification. Re-check torque before Threadlocker cures.

Bearing Cap Footnote

Make certain bearing caps fit in correct location and direction. These pieces are machined to match case saddles and must be installed in their original positions. Always clean the case and base of cap thoroughly to assure a proper mate-up of these parts.

Use Loctite Threadlocker on bearing cap bolts. Tighten the bolts in cross and to specification. Take up slack uniformly and in cross. This assures proper seating of the bearing cups and the safe spread of the case. Let the bolts set for a few minutes after reaching final torque setting. Recheck the bolt torque.

◀ **Fig. 5-175**

The dramatic difference in these two gear heads is simply the result of changing from OEM 3.54:1 (right) to 4.56:1 (left) ratios. One drawback with ultra-low axle gearing is the reduction in pinion gear head stamina. The reduction ratio offsets this, however, as it is far less effort for the vehicle to get rolling, pull a trailer or sustain speed.

◀ **Fig. 5-176**

My bottle-jack press and homemade sleeve pressing tube make quick work of installing the inner pinion bearing. Recall, the pinion depth for the AMC Model 20 axle is controlled by a shim(s) between the inner bearing cup and the axle case---much simpler than Dana/Spicer arrangement. I use engine assembly lube to reduce friction as I press the bearing onto the shaft.

◀ **Fig. 5-177**

Protect the lower bearing as you install the upper one. Do not damage the lower bearing cage or rollers! If necessary, use an old inner bearing race as a spacer. I use assembly lube to prevent binding and friction. Press makes quick work of bearing installation.

◀ **Fig. 5-178**

Considering the delicate flange at this end of the ARB carrier, you must be very cautious when pressing bearings into place. Make certain that the flange and grooves are intact with no rough edges. Key to long O-ring life is a polished set of grooves in the carrier flange.

◀ **Fig. 5-179**

Compare the two pinion gear head marks. You will use the OEM shim stack thickness as a baseline, adding or subtracting thousandths of an inch in shim material. The amount added or subtracted is determined by the difference in the gear head numbers.

NOTE—

If your original gearset ran properly, you can set a very accurate pinion depth simply by following the guidelines for adding or subtracting shim material. Carefully study and follow the pinion depth chart and instructions, found within this chapter.

◀ **Fig. 5-180**

If necessary, use a magnifier to confirm the plus-or-minus and the number. The number represents thousandths of an inch. The plus or minus indicates the amount of shim that was added or subtracted to match this pinion's depth with the "0" factory baseline.

NOTE—

*"+5" means a pinion that stood 0.005" higher in the case than the standard baseline position. The factory, therefore, would remove 0.005" of shim stack height to place this pinion head at the desired location, moving the pinion away from the axle centerline...A "-5" means a pinion that was 0.005" too low in the case. The factory added 0.005" of shim material to achieve the standard pinion head height, moving the pinion **away from** the axle centerline.*

 Fig. 5-181

Once the proper shim stack height has been determined, you can place the shim(s) in the case. Shims fit between the bearing cup and the axle housing's bearing flange. Once you seat the cup completely with the proper shim stack in place, you have the primary measurement done. Once the pinion depth/height in the case is correct, all other adjustments will follow readily.

 Fig. 5-182

Here, you can see through the bore to the inner pinion bearing's shim stack and installed bearing cup. The outer cup now fits into the case as shown in the foreground. To install bearing cups, you can use a press, cup drivers or my rod stock-and-nuts puller tool. (Look earlier in this chapter for details.) If you use a brass punch, use care to clean all debris from the case.

 Fig. 5-183

Seat the bearing cups completely. They must fit squarely into a clean bore and drive up flush with the flange. This will assure accurate pinion depth and bearing preload readings. Unseated cups are dangerous: They can move in service and alter the bearing adjustments.

 Fig. 5-184

Oil the bearing and install the pinion in the case. If you did your math correctly for the pinion depth/height shimming, you are very close to having the pinion shaft installed. All other adjustments will reference from the pinion depth and the correct preload on the pinion bearings.

5

Fig. 5-185

AMC uses a crush spacer (sleeve) for the pinion bearing preload adjustment. For initial setup of the ring-and-pinion gears, I leave the spacer sleeve out.

> **WARNING—**
>
> *If you crush the new spacer/sleeve too much (resulting in too much pinion bearing preload), you cannot simply loosen the nut to reduce preload. You will need to replace the spacer/sleeve with another new one! This is the reason I perform the initial ring-and-pinion set-up without the crush spacer/sleeve in place.*

Fig. 5-186

To drive the outer bearing cone onto the shaft, I place the 4"-square block of wood on the head of the pinion and tap the bearing onto the shaft. I will pull the bearing to position with the yoke and nut.

Fig. 5-187

For the initial fit-up, I install the yoke, old washer and nut. Note that the seal is not in place at this time. This is a trial fitment without the crush sleeve in position.

Fig. 5-188

I use my holding tool to support the yoke and use the air gun to very gently bring the nut up. Do not over-tighten the nut, as this could damage the bearings! The aim is to just take the endplay out of the pinion shaft. You merely want an accurate location of the pinion for setting up the ring-and-pinion backlash and verifying the tooth contact pattern if necessary.

Fig. 5-189

Were this a simple restorative rebuild, using the same ring-and-pinion gear and OEM differential case, you would be using the OEM carrier shims in their original locations. This is still a place to start, even with the ARB Air Locker.

◄ Fig. 5-190

Again, this is a great design! The carrier bearing preload and ring gear backlash are controlled by shims outboard of the bearing cups. For fit-up, the carrier bearings, in this design, can be the new ones. You will not need to remove bearings to make adjustments.

◄ Fig. 5-191

The recommended hole (1/4" diameter) should not be drilled until you have removed all sideplay in the carrier and established a rough backlash setting. You do not want to drill this hole in the wrong place! This is a factory machined bearing cap that cannot be replaced in any simple manner.

◄ Fig. 5-192

You can check for zero sideplay with a dial indicator in this location. Note that I'm prying the carrier away from the dial indicator. After eliminating end/side play, you can attach a wheel to the dial stem and check for ring gear runout. For checking runout, move dial indicator stem outboard to the flat surface at the back face of the ring gear. (See Fig. 5-213.)

5

 Fig. 5-193

On ARB Air Locker installations, the O-rings require special consideration. The O-rings are made of a durable material designed for holding air during clutch actuation. These rings must hold pressure in order to prevent air leaks, minimize wear on the air compressor and avoid wasted time in tearing the axle apart to stop a leak!

 Fig. 5-194

Handle O-rings with care. Grease these sealing rings, the inner seal housing and the surface around the grooves. Bearing cone, supplied by ARB, is specially sized to fit seal housing side of carrier.

 Fig. 5-195

Carefully slide the seal housing over the O-rings. Be certain these O-rings are in good shape when you assemble the system. You have a major problem if these O-rings begin leaking. ARB supplies the correct bearing set for the seal housing side of the carrier. Model 20 OEM bearing cup (held outboard of seal housing) is wider than ARB bearing.

NOTE—

My ARB Air Locker installations have been leak-free and provided long, trouble-free service. I take care to polish out any roughness in the grooves or inner seal-housing surface. You may wish to leave the O-rings out when trial fitting the carrier for bearing preload and ring-and-pinion backlash.

◀ **Fig. 5-196**

Fitting just outboard of the bearing cup, the seal housing acts as a spacer at the right side of the carrier. ARB's shims fit into the recess at the outer face of the seal housing. The thick shim goes to the outside, sandwiching the thinner shims against the seal housing.

◀ **Fig. 5-197**

Once you have confirmed settings, you can remove the carrier with ring gear. Remove the yoke, and drive the pinion shaft through its outer pinion bearing. Install the new crush spacer/sleeve, and lightly oil the new bearing. Support the pinion head, and drive the new bearing into place as illustrated earlier. Grease the seal lip.

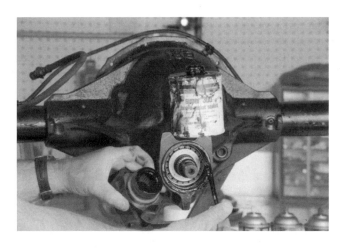

◀ **Fig. 5-198**

Coat the seal bore, yoke splines and yoke inner end. Install the new oil seal. Tap seal until its face is flush with the end of the housing bore. Grease the seal lip. Place the yoke on the pinion shaft. Bracing the pinion head, drive the yoke onto the shaft.

 Fig. 5-199

Install a new yoke washer. Apply Loctite 242 to threads of a new self-locking yoke nut. Carefully pull up the new nut as illustrated earlier, using extreme care not to over-tighten the nut. Continually check pinion bearing preload, and tighten the nut slowly.

 Fig. 5-200

Continue checking preload as you crush the spacer/sleeve. Go very slowly here, as the finish torque is only 15-25 lb-in. This is rotational force. As soon as you sense any resistance, stop and check the preload torque carefully. I like a setting of 25 lb-in with new bearings, read while rotating the shaft with the seal in place.

 Fig. 5-201

You'll want to start preloading the bearings with the aim of achieving proper tooth backlash at the same time. Confirm ring-and-pinion backlash. With shims adjusted to achieve no carrier sideplay (measured with the dial indicator), adjust ring gear backlash. Shift shims side-to-side until backlash reads correctly.

 Fig. 5-202

Here, shim goes to left side of carrier to close up backlash. AMC calls for 0.005"-0.009", 0.008" preferred. I strive for 0.006"-0.007" with new bearings and use of synthetic gear lubricant. At this stage, the aim is still correct backlash and zero sideplay. Continue to confirm zero end/side play by prying the carrier side-to-side with a pry bar.

5

Fig. 5-203

Without preload, removing the carrier is not difficult. A light prying and lifting brings the carrier out for shim changes. You can readily shift shims side-to-side with this design. Once backlash is correct with zero sideplay, you will preload each carrier bearing with 0.004" of shim material (total carrier preload of 0.008").

Fig. 5-204

Backlash correct with zero sideplay, 0.004" shim material is added to each side of the carrier. This is the preload (0.008" total) for carrier bearings. Place the appropriate shims in each bearing cup bore then tilt each bearing cup slightly on its cone. Guide the carrier into the case, straight and carefully.

Fig. 5-205

Using the plastic sand-head hammer, I tap the tilted cups into their saddles. Take care not to damage the bearings or shims. Keep the cups even as you tap side to side. Make sure the cups center over the bearing cone rollers as the cups drop into place.

Fig. 5-206

Tighten the bearing caps into place once more. Measure backlash of ring gear. Make any final adjustments needed. Hold preload at 0.008" (overall) with correct ring-and-pinion backlash.

Fig. 5-207.

I like to run a final rotational torque check. This takes both the pinion shaft bearings and carrier bearings into account. There is no particular setting to strive for. I am simply making sure that the overall torque exceeds the rotational torque of the pinion shaft alone. This indicates that the carrier bearings have preload.

 Fig. 5-208
Once the preload and backlash are correct, you can remove cap bolts and put Loctite Threadlocker on their threads. The caps in correct placement, tighten the bolts in cross and sequence.

5

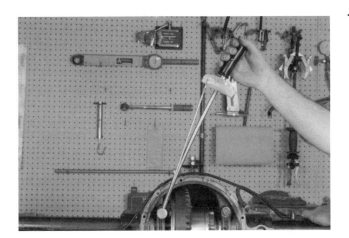

◀ **Fig. 5-209**
Torque called for is 87 lb-ft. Tighten the bolts in steps to full torque. Allow hardware to set for several minutes then confirm the torque. I set torque to 90 lb-ft on the recheck. Note that all of this work has been performed in the Bench Mule fixture (available through Mark Williams Enterprises). The versatility of this fixture makes axle work far easier.

◀ **Fig. 5-210**
I paint the gear teeth with titanium dioxide (yellow). Coat the drive and coast sides. Use the rag tourniquet on the yoke to create resistance. Rotate the ring gear with resistance on the yoke. This will make a tooth pattern impression. Rotate in both directions.

Fig. 5-211

This is the pattern you want. Centering heel-to-toe and proper depth assure room for run-in of parts. Pattern shown will run quietly and offer exceptional service over a very long service life.

Fig. 5-212

Check tooth pattern in opposite direction. Coast and drive patterns are both critical. Again, this is a pattern you want to see. Axle will run quietly and precisely. An axle set up properly will offer a very long and trouble-free service life. Use correct, high quality lubricant to insure against any kind of premature parts damage. Cost effective in the long run, Texaco synthetic gear lubricant, designed for over-the-road trucks, is my choice.

Fig. 5-213

A final check of ring gear runout with a dial indicator is the last step. Note the roller end on the dial stem. A dial indicator, magnetic stand and inch-pound torque wrench are must tools for precise axle measurements. Tooth contact pattern and dial indicator confirm that runout of ring gear is negligible and well within specification.

5

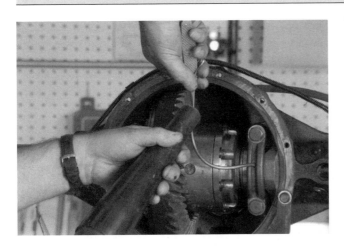

 Fig. 5-214

Finishing up the ARB Air Locker work, I cut bundy tubing with a tubing cutter. When trimming the cut end, I hold the vacuum on the tubing to prevent contamination of the air system and axle.

◄ **Fig. 5-215**

Careful routing of the tubing reaches to the bulkhead fittings. Use ARB-recommended sealant on the bulkhead fittings. Be cautious about keeping the tubing away from moving parts and surfaces that could chafe the tubing. When assembling these parts, envision where they will be 100,000 miles from now---or when jarring along a rock pile like the Rubicon Trail.

◄ **Fig. 5-216**

This is the finished axle assembly: new bearings, seals, small parts, an ARB Air Locker and new ring-and-pinion gears make this a better-than-new setup. With ring-and-pinion gear backlash and bearing preloads set properly, this axle should easily serve for 150-200,000 trouble-free miles if oil is changed on schedule. Synthetic lubricant could extend that lifespan further.

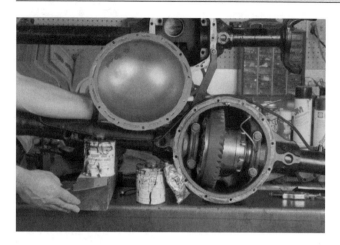

 Fig. 5-217

I use Permatex's Super 300 or High-Tack to hold cork gasket in place. Added use of RTV sealant, spread evenly on the differential cover, assures a leak-free axle. Loctite 242 on threads of cover screws is added safeguard. Build this axle to last ---as it will.

AMC Model 20 Axle Shaft Installation

The AMC Model 20 axle shafts have tapered ends and separate wheel hubs/flanges. The axle shafts have serrations that cut into the tapered bore of the wheel hub. When properly tightened, the axle shaft and hub act as a tight unit. The small woodruff key on the axle shaft is simply a means for keeping the hub and shaft aligned during assembly.

Whenever possible you should not remove the hub from the axle shaft. Some AMC service literature encouraged replacement of the hub any time a hub was detached from the axle shaft. I will reuse a shaft and hub only if the original hub can be placed on the original axle shaft in the precise original location. The other factor is torquing the nut properly, which I discuss in this section.

If you need to replace a hub or axle shaft, consider the aftermarket axle shafts available. Moser and others produce one-piece flanged axle shafts. Flanged, one-piece axle shafts serve builders who run large tires and/or locking differentials. Considering the cost and waning availability of new OEM axle shafts and hubs, quality aftermarket flanged axles make sense.

Aftermarket One-Piece Axle Shafts for the Model 20

Oversized tires, high horsepower engines and locking axles place a heavy demand on axle shafts. An axle equipped with a locker will bind on hard surface turns---not only on asphalt but slick rock or granite as well.

On a corner, the outer wheel needs to rotate faster than the inner wheel. This is not possible with a locked differential, and something has to give. The "give" could be the stock hub spinning on the axle shaft!

If you have concerns about the use of a two-piece axle shaft arrangement, consider a pair of aftermarket-sourced flanged axles. These one-piece axles resemble factory applications like the flanged, one-piece Dana 44 axle shafts used at the end of the Kaiser/Jeep era.

Moser Engineering (product seen here) builds a flanged axle kit that has wide popularity. Available for standard and wide-track Model 20 AMC rear axles, the kit installs readily and features high quality axle shaft materials. Axle bearing endplay adjustment is simplified.

NOTE—

*Another option is the Warn full-floating axle shaft conversion for various Jeep and Dana axle applications. (See **Chapter 7** for details on Warn's full-floater rear axle conversion with optional disc brakes.) A full-floater uses a spindle to support the wheel hub. The wheel hub rides on inner and outer wheel bearings. This arrangement is similar to the OEM full-floating wheel hub setup found on the front ends of 1941-86 Jeep 4WD light utility trucks (military models and all CJs).*

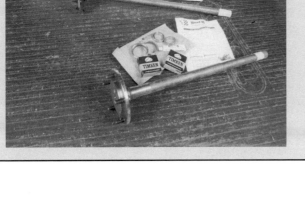

5

When you reuse the OEM axles, you will need to pay close attention to the fit-up of the axle assemblies and proper tightening of the castellated nut. In this section, you will discover just what it takes to tighten the nut properly and securely! Begin installation with the right (passenger) side axle shaft.

 Fig. 5-218

These are the two axle shaft seals. The outer seal is a seal/plate design. These axle shaft seals will last a very long time if installed properly. At 109,000 miles, the '86 CJ's seals were still functioning. These OEM replacement seals are available from Mopar and aftermarket suppliers like 4WD Hardware, Inc.

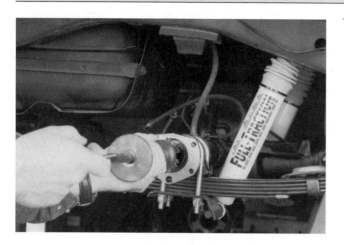

 Fig. 5-219

Beginning with the right side axle shaft installation, I use my three-jaw slide hammer puller to remove the inner seal. Jaws face outward, grabbing the seal without chafing the axle housing.

NOTE—

Shims to adjust axle shaft endplay are used only at the left side axle shaft. Do not split the shim stack between left and right sides! Since the right side axle shaft has no shims, install the right shaft first.

 Fig. 5-220

I coat the outer edge of the new seal with Super 300 sealant. A handy driver for this seal is the Jeep front spindle nut wrench or a large diameter socket. The sand-head hammer and socket can drive the seal squarely and snugly into position.

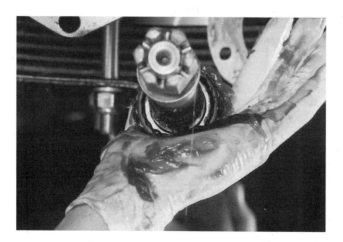

 Fig. 5-221

The OEM and some aftermarket axle bearings are tapered roller design. Bearings must be packed with a quality wheel bearing grease. Make certain the grease presses through each of the rollers, much like hand packing a front wheel bearing.

NOTE—

*See **Chapter 7** for details on proper bearing packing methods. Grease must fill the gaps between the rollers.*

5

◀ Fig. 5-222

Grease the lip seal with wheel bearing grease. I use Texaco's Starplex 2 for this application, swabbing a large amount of extra grease around the packed bearing. Lightly fill the housing cavity with grease, too, but do not overfill. This bearing pack can last for 100,000 miles or more with the right grease and proper packing method.

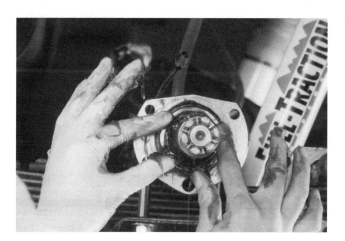

◀ Fig. 5-223

Place the bearing cup over the tapered roller bearing. Grease the inner axle shaft splines lightly. Use care to center and slide the axle shaft through the inner seal without damaging the sealing lip. Proper sealing is essential. Visualize fording streams with your Jeep. This is your barrier to moisture damage.

◀ Fig. 5-224

Seat the right side axle shaft and bearing cup. Tapered surface of cup faces the bearing cone. Note that I run the castellated nut flush with the end of the axle shaft. This and a plastic sand-filled hammer prevent damage to threads. You can tap the bearing cup flush with the edge of the housing.

> **CAUTION—**
> *Make certain axle shaft inner splines align with the side gear splines before tapping the shaft into place! Do not force parts.*

◄ **Fig. 5-225**

Moser, a manufacturer of quality one-piece flanged axle shafts, provides this special sealant. This silicone-based product will prevent moisture from seeping into the bearing. Lightly coat surface of axle flange, shims, backing plate, and inner face of the outer seal plate. Think in terms of keeping moisture and contaminants out of your bearings.

◄ **Fig. 5-226**

Outer sealing plate matches the axle flange shape. This plate fits outboard of the brake backing plate. The retainer plate seal sandwiches the backing plate to the axle flange. Dust shield fits outboard of the seal plate. Moser's one-piece axle shaft conversion kits still rely upon the OEM inner seal and outer sealing plate.

◄ **Fig. 5-227**

Shims (at left axle flange only) are *behind* the backing plate. Make certain these pieces are clean of debris. Silicone sealant or Moser's sealing paste serves as the moisture barrier behind the backing plate.

◀ **Fig. 5-228**

Back face of retainer plate seal now coated with sealant or paste, you can install the retainer/seal and dust shield outboard of the backing plate. Bolts should come through from inside the axle flange. Here, I am merely aligning the parts. I will remove bolts one at a time and insert each bolt from the rear. Nuts will tighten against the retainer and dust shield.

◀ **Fig. 5-229**

OEM bolts are Grade 8 tensile strength. If you need to replace any of these bolts, use exactly the same type, thread and length. Thread pitch and shoulder type must be the same. Seek this hardware from Mopar if possible. The matching nuts are Grade 8 top-lock (all-steel) variety. Bolts should fit through from the inner side of the axle housing's flange.

NOTE—

I am using the bolts backwards in this illustration, simply to hold pieces in place.

◀ **Fig. 5-230**

Coat a set of new OEM type self-locking nuts with Loctite 242. Loctite serves as added insurance. Bolts must be removed, one at a time, and installed from the backside axle flange.

5

◁ **Fig. 5-231**

Bolts now face properly with heads at the inner side of the axle housing's flange. Tighten the nuts in cross and evenly, reaching a torque of 35-40 lb-ft. Allow hardware to set a few minutes then recheck the torque. Set these bolts and nuts securely and uniformly. Right side axle shaft installation is now complete.

◁ **Fig. 5-232**

Now I move to the left axle shaft. The inner seal installation is the same as at right side.

◁ **Fig. 5-233**

Starplex 2 grease has exceptional viscosity and resistance to heat and pounding. I hand pack the bearing, pressing grease through each of the rollers. Swab a thick coating of grease around the outside of the bearing. Note that I also place grease in the bore, outboard of the inner axle seal. I want this cavity to provide a safe backup of grease.

NOTE—

*See **Chapter 7** for details on proper bearing packing methods. Grease must fill the gaps between the rollers.*

5

 Fig. 5-234

Bearing cup seated, the flange receives a coating of sealant paste. Use Mopar's recommended grease or a product like Moser Engineering offers. Shim(s) receive a light, even coating of sealant. This seals against the backing plate.

◀ **Fig. 5-235**

Sealant paste on backside of retainer plate will seal the outer face of the brake backing plate. Note that bolt studs face outward to receive nuts. This is correct orientation.

◀ **Fig. 5-236**

I reinstalled the original shimming in its left side axle flange location. Since the differential thrust is new (ARB Air Locker), and the only change here was the installation of new OEM replacement bearings and cups, I am reasonably certain that the endplay will be correct. I apply Loctite to threads and torque up nuts to specification.

 Fig. 5-237

To confirm axle shaft endplay, use a magnetic stand and dial indicator. This left axle shaft, pushed fully in and out, measures 0.0045" movement. 0.004"-0.008" is acceptable, 0.006" preferred by AMC/Jeep. I am very comfortable with this endplay measurement, which allows for slight wear-in of the new differential thrust to achieve the ideal.

 Fig. 5-238

Once the axle shaft endplay is correct, you can install the wheel hub. Remember, you must install the original hub in precisely the original position. Be sure the woodruff key is in place. Install the washer and castellated nut. Now the challenge begins: You must tighten the nut to a minimum of 250 lb-ft with 1-5/16" of shaft extending beyond the outer end of the hub flange.

NOTE—

If cotter pin hole does do not align, do not back off the nut! Continue tightening the nut to the next alignment slot. Install a cotter pin that is the same diameter as the hole. Make certain the cotter pin fits securely, and spread the pin ends properly.

Tightening the OEM Axle Shaft Nut on Model 20 AMC Axles

The axle shaft nuts on the AMC Model 20 axle are not easy to tighten! Torque minimum is 250 lb-ft, which can be established with an air gun or larger torque wrench. The trick, however, is to achieve the required 1-5/16" measurement between the hub flange end and the end of the axle shaft. (See Fig. 5-238 for illustration of how to measure between the flange and shaft end.)

On the '86 CJ-7, one axle shaft came somewhat easily into specification with the use of a 450 lb-ft rated air gun. The goal is to reach, not exceed, the 1-5/16" measurement. Stop tightening as soon as the nut exceeds 250 lb-ft and reaches the 1-5/16" shaft extension measurement.

The second axle shaft was not as easy. After breaking a socket extension with a ½" breaker bar, I stepped up to a ¾" drive breaker bar and impact socket. Still short of the 1-5/16" measurement, I could not move the nut with this ¾" breaker bar! The next step was the use of the handle from my floor jack.

I slipped the handle over the ¾" drive breaker bar. Using extreme care and a tugging action, I gradually moved the nut to achieve the necessary 1-5/16" measurement. I did not damage the hub or shaft in any way, and this was the necessary force to cut the shaft's serrations properly into the wheel hub's tapered flange.

Experiences like this one offer insight. The common complaint with the AMC/Jeep two-piece axle shaft is that the wheel hub might spin on the shaft. If there is looseness or improper pressure in the fit-up, the hub surely could spin. (The small woodruff key is of no help here.) Oversized tires and a locking differential increase the risk of the wheel hub spinning on the axle shaft.

The only sure way to secure the AMC wheel hubs is to tighten them properly. My guess is that many installers have simply not tightened the nut enough! Or the nuts required a retorque during their service life, and nobody bothered to check the fit-up. Follow the 1-5/16" formula, and your two-piece axle shafts just might work!

Fig. 5-239 If you think that an air gun is enough to tighten the castellated axle shaft nut, think again! After stepping from a ½" breaker bar to a ¾" and, finally, to a floor jack handle for leverage on the ¾" breaker bar, I finally got it. The other shaft nut tightened more readily with an industrial strength ½-inch air gun (rated 450 maximum lb-ft).

I recommend a periodic check of the axle shaft nuts, especially if the axle has a locker unit or large tires. The minimum setting is 250 lb-ft, followed by confirmation of the 1-5/16" measurement between the hub flange end and the end of the axle shaft. This effort could assure that your OEM wheel hubs will not spin on the axle shafts.

NOTE—

Using a locking differential on a hard road or rock surface places tremendous loads on the wheel hub and shaft. If you do not use the locker properly, the hub could loosen. Builders planning severe duty use of lockers, a high output V-8 engine swap and/or exceptionally large tires should consider axle shafts like the Moser one-piece flanged type.

5

 Fig. 5-240

I use new Mopar/Jeep brake drums to assure quality. This brake drum design uses spring washer retainers to hold the drum in place. If your application uses spring retainers instead of screws, make certain the spring retainers do not keep the wheel rim from fitting flush against the drum.

> *CAUTION—*
>
> *Some aftermarket wheels do not have recesses cut to clear these retainer washers. In such cases, do not install the spring retainers. These retainers are available from your Jeep dealer or at local auto supply houses under a Dorman part number.*

 Fig. 5-241

New cotter pin should be same diameter as the hole in the axle shaft. Bend the pin as illustrated here. If your brake drums have hold-down screws, reinstall them with a hand impact driver.

 Fig. 5-242

Last steps are plastic hubcap installation and connection of brake pipes with a flare nut wrench. Keep brake fittings, pipes and wheel cylinders free of any debris when installing the pipes. Bleed the brakes. (See **Chapter 7** for details on hydraulic brake pipes and other brake system details.) Tap the hubcap into place with a plastic hammer.

Driveline Service and Upgrades

Whether you are restoring your Jeep or modifying the powertrain, driveshaft service is a vital part of the process. Generally, driveline service consists of routine lubrication and U-joint replacement. For the stock driveline with splined couplers in good condition, restoration is nothing more than periodic U-joint replacement.

When modifying your Jeep with a suspension lift, high horsepower engine, oversized tires or a transmission swap, driveshafts will need modification and, likely, upgrading. (In my ***Jeep Owner's Bible***, I discuss driveshaft design and performance needs.)

Be aware that a change in torque loads or a steeper driveshaft angle places more load on the driveshaft tube and joints. For excessive angles, there are modified approaches like a double-Cardan joint at the transfer case end and a rotation of the rear axle housing to bring the rear cross-joint to approximately 2° angle at static chassis height.

5

Measuring Driveshaft Length and U-Joint Angles

Under load and in the backcountry, your CJ depends upon reliable driveline performance. Popular modifications like suspension lifts, axle assembly swaps and engine/transmission conversions have a large impact on driveline performance. Most of these changes will require new driveshafts. (See driveline building and upgrade details in other sections of this chapter.)

When ordering new drivelines, you need to accurately measure the required lengths. The driveline shop must know your reference points for these measurements. Here are some tips for determining driveshaft lengths and quick-checking the U-joint/flange angles:

The NV4500 transmission swap put the transfer case rearward in the '86 CJ-7 chassis. This demands a shorter rear and longer front driveline. Here, I carefully line up the U-joint yokes on a horizontal centerline and tape the saddles as a reference point. The axle is at "curb" height, with body weight bearing on the springs. My measurement is between the midpoints of the U-joint bearing caps.

NOTE—
I have the CJ on my hoist with tri-pod stands beneath the axle housings. The vehicle weight is on the tri-pod stands, compressing the springs and establishing a true curb weight. You can do the same with four quality jack stands or even with the vehicle parked on level ground. The idea is that the axle/chassis is at its curbside ride height. Shops will use this reference to determine the slip collar midpoints.

Measuring Driveshaft Length and U-Joint Angles (continued)

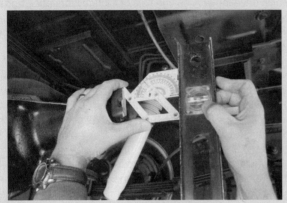

To check or establish proper U-joint angles, this inexpensive protractor/angle gauge from Sears will work. Notice how the bubble level determines the vertical line. Although not as accurate as a commercial U-joint angle gauge, this method gets results. Again, the axle is at weighted, curb height for this measurement. Measure the output flange at the transfer case. Compare these angles, and determine whether the axle and pinion shaft need rotating.

NOTE—

It is possible to shim the rear axle-to-springs, much like the caster change shimming at the front axle. Wedge-shaped alignment shims are available for moderate degrees of change. (I prefer hard steel rather than aluminum shims for this task.) If a radical rotation is needed, the spring perches must be repositioned. Bring the U-joint flanges into proper angularity before measuring the driveline length requirements.

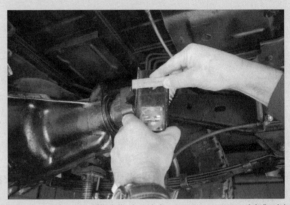

Here is the fastest (field) check I can muster: a spirit/bubble level and a quality 1/64" increment ruler. Although not as precise as more expensive means, this will put flange angles into rough alignment. For a preliminary measurement, this method works.

Installing U-Joints

At regular service intervals, you should check driveshafts for excessive play. Play at U-joints is easy to remedy, and quality new joints are not expensive. A worn spline coupler or bent/sprung driveshaft tube requires more steps and extra cost to remedy.

The most basic driveline service is the replacement of U-joints. This can take place at routine service time or even alongside a trail. Many of us have been on 4x4 backcountry outings and witnessed someone snapping a universal joint. Fortunately, the common Spicer cross joint used in CJ Jeep models is not difficult to change.

NOTE—

On two-piece, splined coupler driveshafts, proper phasing of the U-joints is important. You must mark the driveshaft before separating the two parts of the driveline to reestablish phase and shaft balance upon reassembly. You must always assemble the driveshaft "in-phase," which means that the U-joints align precisely with each other.

 Fig. 5-243

A simple method for changing a U-joint is to use a bench vise as a press. The only tools needed are the vise and an assortment of sockets. For the purpose of illustration, I am using a Spicer/Dana front axle shaft joint. I begin with removal of the lower bearing snap ring. I place a large socket over the cap and drive the joint down.

Fig. 5-244

Snap ring removed, the large socket on left is the receiver. Smaller socket fits inside right bearing cap. Vise serves as the press. Simple.

5

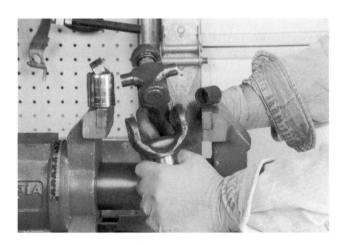

Fig. 5-245

Two bearing caps are now out of the way. On U-joints using external snap rings, like the driveshafts, use a similar approach.

◀ Fig. 5-246

Repeat the process with the other two bearing caps. Even an old nut can serve as a spacer for this operation. Use care to protect and not stress the U-joint yoke and flanges of the driveshaft.

◀ Fig. 5-247

With the new bearing cross in place, start the first bearing cap squarely. Do not apply pressure unless you are certain the caps are going in straight. Once the cap is flush with the flange, you can use a socket to press the cap far enough into the bore to insert the snap ring. Make sure each snap ring seats thoroughly around its groove.

◀ Fig. 5-248

Whether you have seated the first cap or not, center up the cross-journal and carefully start the opposite bearing cap. Keep caps straight, and make certain that the cross remains inside the bearing rollers. Do not dislodge the rollers. Rollers must remain in place during bearing cap installation.

 Fig. 5-249

On axle shaft joints, you can tap the snap ring into place now. On a driveshaft joint, you need to seat the caps past the external snap ring grooves to install the snap rings. Always make sure the rings seat completely in their grooves.

◀ **Fig. 5-250**

Repeat the bearing cap installation on the other two caps. The vise can press the first two caps into place readily. Keep cross-journal aligned to prevent dislodging the rollers. If you cannot seat a pair of opposite caps, suspect that a roller has fallen out of place. Disassemble the joint. Never use excessive force.

5

◀ **Fig. 5-251**

On an axle shaft joint with internal snap rings, you may need to seat one cap further to install the opposite snap ring. Again, the receiver socket works well here. The old nut or a socket pushes on the opposite cap.

NOTE—

I purposely illustrate how simple tools and common hardware will do the job. You may have even less to work with in the outback!

 Fig. 5-252.

Once the snap rings are in place, you can move the joint to be certain there is no binding. Joint should move freely in all directions.

NOTE—

If you feel binding in a newly installed U-joint, tap on the shaft's yoke saddles. (Avoid hitting the U-joint or the flange's snap ring grooves!) This jarring will spring the yoke saddle to its original shape and free the joint binding. If binding persists, and all bearing caps are seated against their snap rings, a roller may have dislodged.

Custom Driveshaft Upgrades

For the '86 CJ-7 depicted in this book, I installed an NV4500 transmission and a Mopar rebuilt 4.2L inline six with Mopar Performance EFI/MPI conversion (good for 160+ horsepower). I also added a very mild one-inch over stock height suspension lift.

The rear driveshaft angle increased, and the shaft shortened. (In the new powertrain layout, the front driveline needed to be lengthened.) These kinds of changes place far more stress on the driveshaft. I turned to Drive Line Service of San Diego, California, for a pair of driveshafts that would meet these demands.

 Fig. 5-253

Steeper angles, shorter length or an increase in horsepower---each demands a stronger driveline. Drive Line Service of San Diego specializes in OEM replacement and custom driveshafts. They ship anywhere U.P.S. goes. The original '86 CJ shafts had 109,000 miles on them and were under-capacity. New custom shafts and Spicer support hardware were all sourced from Drive Line Service of San Diego.

NOTE—

The arrows indicate the proper phasing of the U-joints and balancing position. Drive Line Service balances the driveshafts in this position. You must always assemble the driveshaft "in-phase," which means that the U-joints align precisely with each other.

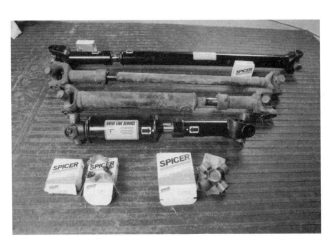

5

◀ **Fig. 5-254**

The joints are stronger Spicer "solid-cross" type, permanently sealed with grease. These are now recommended as superior to any cross-drilled joint with a grease fitting. Solid-cross joints are common for axle shaft use and should always be replaced with a similar solid-cross joint. Drive Line Service also recommends new Spicer straps and bolts with each installation.

◀ **Fig. 5-255**

Make sure the U-joints seat in their saddles squarely. Small 12-point heads on new strap bolts require care in tightening. New Spicer bolts come with thread-locking agent on the threads. Straps and bolts new, I torque these uniformly and in cross to 18 lb-ft.

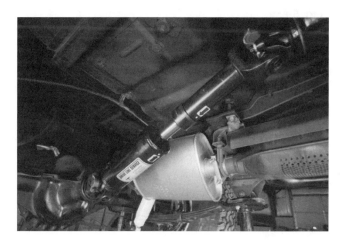

◀ **Fig. 5-256**

This driveshaft features heavier tubes, a stronger splined coupler assembly, and precision balancing. A Drive Line Service/San Diego hallmark, high performance driveshafts are your backcountry assurance of safety and reliability.

 Fig. 5-257

Front driveshafts are longer and not as subject to angle issues. U-joint angles must still conform to factory specifications, and front-end caster angle is also important. Drive Line Service increased the tube size and coupler strength, followed by installation of solid-cross joints. This is a high-performance front driveshaft. Permanently sealed Spicer U-joints require no service over exceptional lengths of time.

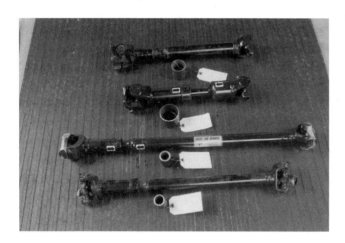

◄ **Fig. 5-258**

This earlier Jeep application also benefits from Drive Line Service of San Diego workmanship. I have assembled samples of the OEM tubes and compare them with the upgrade tubing. The quality of these upgraded drivelines means many more years of reliable service.

NOTE—

The arrows indicate the proper phasing of the U-joints and balancing position. Drive Line Service balances the driveshafts in this position. You must always assemble the driveshaft "in-phase," which means that the U-joints align precisely with each other.

◄ **Fig. 5-259.**

New Spicer U-bolts, nuts and lockwashers were available for this package from Drive Line Service, San Diego. If high horsepower, severe duty use is your plan, new hardware is advisable. This is not as critical with U-bolts as with the lighter strap-and-bolts approach.

NOTE—

Many regard U-bolts as a superior design. 18 lb-ft is appropriate torque for Jeep CJ/Spicer U-bolt nuts. Nuts should be tightened evenly with equal thread showing at each U-bolt end when done.

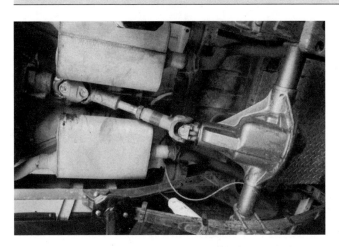

◄ **Fig. 5-260**

This is a contemporary fix for steep U-joint angles due to chassis/suspension lifts. A stock design driveshaft would have the U-joints on radical angles. Use of a double-Cardan joint at the transfer case with a conventional joint at the rear works well. Rear axle housing and pinion shaft have been rotated to establish a U-joint angle of approximately 2-degrees at static (curb) chassis height.

NOTE—

The front double-joints (double-Cardan) on this driveshaft cancel each other's angularity. The shaft in Fig. 5-260 *has worked very well with the suspension lift and high torque demands of this short wheelbase, V-8 powered CJ-5.*

◄ **Fig. 5-261**

Spring perches were relocated to rotate the axle pinion shaft upward. This novel use of an Isuzu Rodeo version of the Dana 44 axle required spring perch work for installation on the '72 CJ's springs. Note unique "factory" Isuzu disc brakes. Pinion shaft now angles toward the driveshaft tube with the U-joint tilt measuring a mere 2° at static chassis height.

NOTE—

Double-Cardan joints have been popular on full-size 4WD trucks and SUVs for many years. Commonly used to help cancel out vibration, they work well to offset the traditional driveline problems encountered with shorter wheelbase CJ Jeep models. In situations where angles are awkward, double-Cardan joints can often solve problems. The rear (single) joint needs a very slight angle of approximately 2-degrees to provide normal service and proper lubrication of the U-joint's bearings. For driveline details, consult with specialists like Drive Line Service of San Diego. (See **Appendix**.)

Axle Data and Specifications Section

Setting Pinion Gear Position

Pinion gearhead location is crucial to the ring-and-pinion tooth contact. To understand the charts, presume you have an original pinion gearhead mark of "0" as the base reference. If your new gear has a "+2" mark, the gearhead would be 0.002" too high with the original shims. To put this gear in position, remove 0.002" of shim from the stack (the inner pinion bearing shims that fit between the bearing cup and axle case).

If, instead, the new gearhead scribed mark reads "-2", you would need to raise the gearhead by inserting an extra 0.002" of shim in the original stack.

NOTE—

The pinion gear's height shims fit between the inner pinion bearing cup and the axle housing's bearing cup bore.

Another example: Changing from a "-2" original pinion gear to a "+2" new pinion would call for subtracting 0.004" shim thickness from the original stack (chart reads "-0.004"). Read the original and new pinion head marks, then consult the chart to find how much shim material to either add or subtract from the original shim stack.

NOTE—

If you kept the original stack of shims together, you can position the pinion gear without difficulty. After setting the pinion bearing preload and carrier bearing preload with proper ring gear backlash, always confirm results with a test of the tooth contact pattern.

 Differential Shim Pack Locations (Dana/Spicer axles)

If you remove shim(s) from gearhead (locating) end of pinion, shim(s) of equal thickness must be placed at the companion flange end to restore pre-load (as indicated in illustration). The addition of a shim(s) at the gearhead end will require removal of equal shimming at the companion flange end.

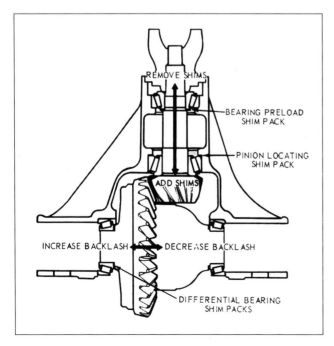

Pinion Gear Marking Chart

Old Pinion Marking	New Pinion Marking								
	-4	-3	-2	-1	0	+1	+2	+3	+4
+4	+0.008	+0.007	+0.006	+0.005	+0.004	+0.003	+0.002	+0.001	0
+3	+0.007	+0.006	+0.005	+0.004	+0.003	+0.002	+0.001	0	-0.001
+2	+0.006	+0.005	+0.004	+0.003	+0.002	+0.001	0	-0.001	-0.002
+1	+0.005	+0.004	+0.003	+0.002	+0.001	0	-0.001	-0.002	-0.003
0	+0.004	+0.003	+0.002	+0.001	0	-0.001	-0.002	-0.003	-0.004
-1	+0.003	+0.002	+0.001	0	-0.001	-0.002	-0.003	-0.004	-0.005
-2	+0.002	+0.001	0	-0.001	-0.002	-0.003	-0.004	-0.005	-0.006
-3	+0.001	0	-0.001	-0.002	-0.003	-0.004	-0.005	-0.006	-0.007
-4	0	-0.001	-0.002	-0.003	-0.004	-0.005	-0.006	-0.007	-0.008

5

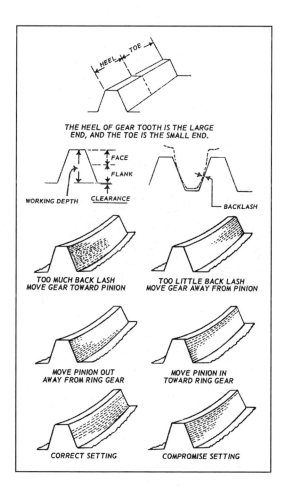

◄ Ring-and-Pinion Gearset Tooth Contact

A tooth contact pattern serves as the final test for proper gear tooth mesh. For long service and a quiet axle, make certain your ring-and-pinion sets produce the correct pattern! (See Fig. 5-129 to Fig. 5-131.)

Spicer/Dana Axle Data and Tightening Chart

The data supplied here applies to the Dana 30 and 44 (Spicer and Dana) axle assemblies. Refer to other sections of this chapter for additional specifications and service details. You will find torque settings and service data for AMC/Jeep's Model 20 rear axle within the "AMC Model 20" service section of this chapter.

Torque Settings for Dana 30 Front Axle

Housing cover bolts	25 lb-ft
Steering tie-rod end nuts:	45 lb-ft minimum (if cotter pin hole does not align at 45 lb-ft, tighten to nearest cotter pin alignment)
Spring to axle U-bolts: ½"-20 thread 9/16"-18	65 lb-ft 105 lb-ft Note: Aftermarket U-bolt specs may vary; consult manufacturer's instructions!
U-joint strap bolts/nuts	20 lb-ft maximum
OEM wheel nuts	minimum of 90 lb-ft for original wheels (For aftermarket wheels, see manufacturer's recommendation.)
Pinion shaft bearing preload (torque to keep shaft rotating; no seal in place)	15-20 in/lb with original bearings 20-40 in/lb with new bearings
Differential bearing cap bolts	55 lb-ft with Loctite 242 on threads
Ring gear-to-carrier bolts (use new bolts only)	55 lb-ft with Loctite 271 on threads
Differential side gear clearance	0.006" maximum (measured with two feeler gauges of same thickness at opposite side thrust washers)
Maximum spread of housing to install carrier assembly	0.020"
Added shims for preload of carrier bearings	0.015"
Maximum ring gear runout	0.006"* *Maximum runout of 0.002"-0.003" preferred.
Ring gear backlash	0.005"-0.010" (optimal 0.006"-0.007" for new gears and bearings)
Pinion shaft nut	200-220 lb-ft (210 lb-ft preferred)
Brake backing plate/spindle to knuckle	OEM bolt-type 40 lb-ft
Free-wheeling hub or drive plate bolts	35 lb-ft

NOTE—

When torquing axle, differential and wheel hardware, I always torque in cross pattern and tighten in several incremental steps. (Do not pull to maximum torque in one step.) After reaching torque setting, allow hardware to settle for a few minutes, then recheck torque to specification.

5

Torque Settings for Spicer/Dana 44 Rear Axle

Brake backing plate-to-axle housing flange fasteners:	40 lb-ft using new OEM self-locking hardware and Loctite 242 on threads
Inspection cover bolts: 3/8" stud size 5/16" stud size	 25 lb-ft 20 lb-ft
Differential bearing cap bolts:	70-90 lb-ft (preferred uniform 80-plus lb-ft) with Loctite 242 on clean threads
U-joint flange yoke nuts:	200-220 lb-ft (210 lb-ft optimal)
Ring gear-to-carrier bolts (new):	55-65 lb-ft 60+ lb-ft preferred (A uniform torque setting is important, using Loctite 271 on threads.)
"Open" differential side gear-to-case clearance:	0.000"-0.006" (maximum) measured with two feeler gauges of same thickness at opposite side thrust washers (I prefer 0.000"-0.003" clearance.)
Pinion shaft bearing preload (torque to keep shaft rotating with no seal in place):	15-20 lb-in with original bearings and 20-40 lb-in with new bearings (I strive for minimum of 30 lb-in with new bearings.)
Maximum spread of housing to install carrier assembly:	0.020"
Added shims for preload of carrier bearings:	0.015"
Maximum (factory recommended) ring gear runout:	0.006"* *My preferred maximum runout is in the 0.002"-0.003" range.
Ring gear backlash:	0.005"-0.010" (My optimal setting is 0.006"-0.007" for new gears and bearings.)
Pinion shaft nut:	200-220 lb-ft (210 lb-ft preferred).
Spring to axle U-bolt nuts: ½"-20 thread 9/16"-18	 65 lb-ft 105 lb-ft (For aftermarket U-bolts, see manufacturer's specifications.)
U-joint attachment hardware:	20 lb-ft maximum for U-bolts with lockwashers and hex nuts; 18 lb-ft maximum for straps with bolts (Loctite 242 or equivalent on threads)
OEM wheel nuts:	minimum of 90 lb-ft for original steel wheels (For aftermarket wheels, see manufacturer's recommendation.)

NOTE—

On models with straps and bolts, driveshaft shops recommend new straps and bolts with each replacement of the U-joints. Spicer-made bolts come with thread locker on bolt threads. If your Jeep has a higher horsepower engine or will see severe duty usage, new Spicer-made straps and bolts are a must. On models with U-bolts, make certain you tighten nuts uniformly, leaving an equal amount of thread showing at each bolt end. Install new, properly graded lockwashers with the U-bolts.

Chapter 6

Frame, Suspension, and Body Repair

6

General

Among the many components that fatigue over time, the Jeep frame, springs and body are also subject to wear-and-tear. Extreme rust may render the frame and body beyond repair. In such cases, the best approach is to salvage the powertrain and axle components, and then find a better frame/body to restore.

The best Jeep for restoration has no frame rust or body perforation rust. Under severe use, the AMC/Jeep CJ frame can distort or otherwise lose its shape. Exposed to salted winter roads or corrosive chemicals and atmosphere, the Jeep frame and body can rust through.

Your Jeep's frame/body provides the platform for a safe, reliable vehicle. This chapter addresses the inspection, proper repair and mechanical restoration of the Jeep's frame, body structure and suspension system.

NOTE—

This chapter is not intended to teach body-and-paint technique. There are many useful books written to that subject. In this chapter, you will find details on how to repair the frame, perform basic repairs on the body tub and other sheet metal, and upgrade the suspension system in ways that can best serve your Jeep's backcountry and multi-purpose uses.

◁ Fig. 6-1

In the Far West, we seldom see a Jeep with serious rust problems. Even my four-decade-old '55 CJ-5 had only minor surface rust on exposed sheet metal and no frame or spring rust whatsoever. Without the risk of rust exfoliation, inspection of the frame and body becomes easy.

◁ Fig. 6-2

The condition of the tub was unclear until I scraped out the old carpet, tossed out the broken down retrofit seats, and dumped a pile of trash stored in the bed! Now, the body metal, fuel tank and floor pan are ready for inspection. This vehicle had minimal wear for its age.

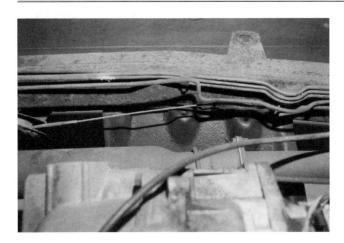

 Fig. 6-3

Body removed from this '76 CJ-7, the frame and suspension system are exposed for close inspection. If an area looks suspect, thorough cleaning and de-scaling will reveal trouble spots. Here, the frame rail below the E-brake cable shows rust perforation. Yes, a CJ frame can rust through!

◁ **Fig. 6-4**

This same frame has a crack in the rail (**ARROW**) near the junction of the steering gear and front crossmember. This can be repaired but indicates a severely stressed frame. The power steering attachment points and brackets are a common fatigue point on AMC-era CJs.

6

◁ **Fig. 6-5**

Somewhere in this Jeep's history, a steel rod was welded to the frame. The rod braced the fender and helped support weight of a spare tire carrier and an add-on rear rack. Aftermarket accessories often lead to frame modifications, an area of concern.

 Fig. 6-6

This CJ-7 tub has serious rust trouble. The primary rust is in the pan. Restoration of this tub will require considerable labor. At current labor costs for sublet work, I would look for another tub unless you can do this work yourself.

Fig. 6-7

Severe body rust is very difficult to address. I look for this kind of damage beneath carpets and floor matting. Moisture accumulates and forms rust like this over time. When looking for a CJ or estimating its value, this is a tub to avoid. If you want this kind of vehicle, expect to replace the tub with a complete fiberglass or steel body.

Fig. 6-8

A floorpan replacement is possible. The top tub section was salvageable, and in this case, the floorpan had rust perforation. Separating the upper tub from the floorpan is possible with the CJ-7. Aftermarket body parts like the pan are available for restoration.

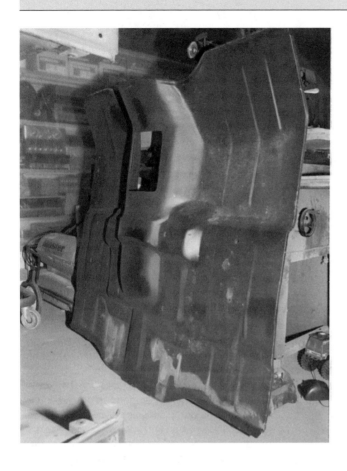

◀ **Fig. 6-9**

This is an aftermarket replacement floorpan. The pan can be spot-welded, wire-welded or even oxy-acetylene welded with mild steel rod. Holes for plug welds can be drilled at each original spot-weld location. The most critical step in such a repair is caulking.

NOTE—

The tub (upper section and floorpan) must be a sealed unit when completed. There are bonders available to serve as both a seal and metal-to-metal adhesive agent. A concern is warpage when welding the tub and pan. If you undertake this welding, isolate heat to the spot holes (plug welds) to reduce risk of warpage. Caulking and primer/sealer must prevent moisture from seeping into seams.

6

◀ **Fig. 6-10**

This tub is worth saving. The builder found a reasonably priced new floorpan through an online source. You need to weigh all of these costs before considering the work. In some cases, installing a new tub (steel or fiberglass) would make better sense.

 Fig. 6-11

Another rust spot on AMC-era CJs is the taillight area. Any attachment point for accessories or lighting is a possible rust location. Surprisingly, this vehicle was not from the Midwest. It was a vehicle used in a farm/ranching environment out West, exposed to corrosive chemicals and irrigation.

Frame Repairs

Restorers and backcountry trail runners can benefit from knowing how to perform minor frame repairs. Obviously, there are limits. If the frame is either too rusted or twisted in such a way that repairs are impractical, you must look for another frame.

A reputable frame and axle shop can perform precise measurements and even straighten a mildly out-of-shape frame. I recommend such shops when you suspect damage or distortion of the frame. For the straight and serviceable frame, basic cosmetic and minor structural repairs are possible---if you can weld properly.

 Fig. 6-12

This rod welded to frame is an eyesore. Preparing for such repairs, I remove all electrical wires and any brake or fuel pipes in the area.

Checking the Frame for Square

Perch the frame unit on level stands above a flat floor. Testing for square and twist, you will take diagonal frame rail measurements and plumb bob the frame at opposing line intersects.

At the end of this chapter, I offer an example of a Jeep OEM frame measurement diagram. If your rough measurements turn up trouble, take the bare frame to a shop for precise light or laser beam measurements and straightening if needed.

Any frame bending should be done *cold*, not with heat, to prevent frame fatigue! Heating a frame to excess can cause

metallurgical damage. In minor repairs, I allow heated areas to air-cool gradually, without quenching. This minimizes risk of "crystallizing" (embrittling) the heated area of metal.

CAUTION—

Any effort to straighten a frame section should be done cold. Typically, a bent frame goes to the frame shop. Shops use floor anchors, hefty chains and hydraulic jacks at high tonnage ratings to properly straighten a twisted frame.

 Fig. 6-13

First frame restoration task is removal of the front bumper. Tow bar plates, welded to the bumper's face, ruined the OEM bumper. I begin by heating rivet head. When metal is ready to puddle, gently blow the rivet head away. Do not aim torch downward, or damage to the frame could occur.

NOTE—

In each of the welding and cutting procedures shown here, I allow the metal to cool on its own. I do not apply wet rags, water from a garden hose or any other means for "quenching" the heated metal. I want the metal to cool evenly, in a slow, steady manner.

Fig. 6-14

Rivet head severed, you can punch drive the remaining section through the frame holes.

6

Fig. 6-15

Repeat by heating the other rivet's head until liquid, and then gently blow material away. Again, avoid blowing through the bumper material and into the frame.

 Fig. 6-16
If you proceed with caution and drive rivets out straight, the frame holes remain round and like new! Replacement bumper installs with bolts and nuts.

 Fig. 6-17
Early CJ-5 battery box has suffered the fate of vibration and trail twisting. (Civilian bracket was an afterthought. Batteries were mounted in the cowl on the prototype M38A1 military body.) Bracket needs re-weld to the frame. As evident, it should not be difficult to meet or exceed the quality and appearance of the OEM welds!

 Fig. 6-18
Wire-feed MIG would work here, however, I do not want to concentrate heat. Excessive heat can damage frame metal. My choice for this repair is an oxy-acetylene weld. Clean thoroughly before welding.

 Fig. 6-19

Use of gas welding and filler rod allows for reinforcement and restoration of the original metal. Mild steel rod works fine for this repair.

◁ **Fig. 6-20**

Factory arc weld at lower edge is very coarse. It could be speculated that the intense heat applied could have weakened the battery bracket. I believe the gas welding technique provides the best means for minor reconditioning and restoration of this metal. Here's the finished product.

6

 Fig. 6-21

Here goes the steel rod! Rod was welded in place with (stick) arc welding method. This weld is shoddy and unsightly. Now is the time for restoration.

 Fig. 6-22

Note angle of cutting torch: upward slightly. *I do not want to remove any frame material*, even if I must leave a slight portion of the weld. Fortunately, the stick weld had penetrated properly, and the actual weld material can stay in place.

 Fig. 6-23

I scarf the surface as clean as possible, without digging into the frame rail material! You may not be confident about using a torch this close to the frame. An alternative would be to cut the metal further outboard, then surface grind to the frame with a disc grinder.

 Fig. 6-24

Rod and weld material have formed a puddle and separated from frame rail metal.

◀ **Fig. 6-25**

Now, a chip hammer lifts the separated metal.

◀ **Fig. 6-26**

Small remnants of weld material remain. A cut-off wheel is my next tool of choice.

6

◀ **Fig. 6-27**

Wearing face and eye protection, I carefully remove remaining high points with the cut-off wheel.

Fig. 6-28

Take your time here. A gentle touch will leave this near paint-ready surface with no signs of undercutting into the frame rail.

Fig. 6-29

A small notch remained where the rod detached. I took this a step further, repairing the metal.

Fig. 6-30

Again, gas (oxy-acetylene) welding produces the kind of result I want. Mild steel filler rod builds up in successive passes.

Fig. 6-31

I like it! This is the weld material that will fully fill the notch. I let the welded metal air cool, evenly and slowly.

Fig. 6-32

Here's the cut-off wheel again. Careful, easy passes remove just enough metal so that the surface is flat. You can also use a surface grinder to accomplish this. Use care and wear safety goggles.

6

Fig. 6-33

Square up the inner frame edge.

 Fig. 6-34

Well, how's that! Looks just like the factory metal. This kind of restorative welding, whether gas, wire or electric arc, is both rewarding and creative. I had no desire to leave this cosmetic scar on a visible section of the frame.

 Fig. 6-35

A coat of black frame or engine enamel, and you can't tell this section from any other area of the frame.

Building a Transmission/Frame Crossmember

NOTE—

*In **Chapter 3**, I cover the AMC/Jeep crossmember and modifications. For fabricating a crossmember using the OEM plate on '72-'86 CJs, review Figs. 3-92 to 3-100 in **Chapter 3**. Here, I share how to fabricate a crossmember for an early CJ. This task serves as a prototype for custom building any crossmember from scratch. Builders who intend hybrid V-8 engine and transmission swaps will benefit from reviewing this section.*

Transmission and engine swaps, even the installation of a factory-type 4-speed transmission like the T-18, may require modifications to the transmission crossmember. As a factory four-speed (T98A/T-18 type) crossmember was not available for my '55 CJ-5, I took precise measurements of driveshaft angularity and fit-up. The original crossmember placed the transmission/transfer case too high in the chassis, so I modified the crossmember to establish the correct powertrain alignment and driveshaft angles.

Fig. 6-36

First step was to align the crossmember in the original location. Using stout steel pieces, I fabricated a transmission pedestal mount (**ARROW**) that fits between the transmission and an OEM-type transmission mount. At this stage, I removed and modified the crossmember.

Fig. 6-37

After precisely measuring the placement of hardware, I built a "dropped" crossmember. The design allowed original equipment attachments to fit appropriately, and the final driveshaft angles remained stock.

6

Fig. 6-38

My crossmember has stout side mounting plates and rectangular spacer blocks to fit against the lower edge of frame rails. Holes at the top of the spacer block bolt to the lower frame rail. Diagonally positioned holes will be drilled through the vertical side plates and the frame rails.

 Fig. 6-39
Holes at top of spacer block bolt to lower frame rail (OEM method). I attach the crossmember with Grade 8 hardware. This is the rear support for the engine, transmission and transfer case. Note use of OEM torque support mount (**AR-ROW**) for transfer case. Crossmember attachments are in OEM position.

Repairing or Replacing Damaged Frame Nuts

One engineering feature of AMC/Jeep vehicles that has frustrated builders and repair technicians is the frame nut. Used at locations along the frame rail, these special nuts are generally used with OEM thread-seeking bolts. They make rapid factory assembly of the bump stops, transmission crossmember and shackle frame brackets possible.

Unfortunately, these nuts can seize to the bolts and break loose at the frame attachment points. Sometimes, simply loosening the bolt may break the frame nut's tack welds from the inner side of the frame rail. Knowing how to properly repair these nuts can save a good deal of aggravation and expense.

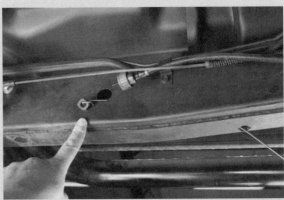

Fig. 6-41 Conveniently, I was able to run a mild steel filler rod from the nut hole to a hole in the side of the frame rail. I bent the rod end to snag the nut. Carefully, I fed the nut to its original location.

Fig. 6-40 This actually happened! In simply loosening the crossmember bolt on the '86 CJ-7, this frame nut broke loose from its weak tack welds on the inner side of the frame. I managed to get the bolt loose and fished the nut out of the frame with a magnet, using a nearby frame hole for access. Here, I have notched the edges of the frame hole with a round file.

Fig. 6-42 Anti-spatter coating a bolt's threads, I very carefully thread the bolt into the nut. The bolt provides a means for holding the nut securely in place during the welding operation. This anti-spatter will prevent the bolt from sticking to the nut when I weld. I used my MIG wire-feed for this operation, welding the nut to the two notches filed at the edge of the hole. I fill the notches and avoid striking the bolt. When done, the bolt will thread readily out of the secure nut.

Repairing or Replacing Damaged Frame Nuts (continued)

Fig. 6-43 Finished with simple surface grinding, the nut weld is a permanent fix. I applied some black paint, and this looked like a reinforced factory installation. You can readily torque the crossmember bolt into the repaired nut. If a frame nut loosens and you have a welder, this is the permanent fix. I made this repair in half an hour!

Reinforcing the '72-'75 Frame

A common fatigue point on '72-'75 CJ frames is just behind the anchor end of the front spring. The anchor at the rear of the spring receives the thrust of the front axle. Especially in rough backcountry rock scaling, the driving force of the springs and axle assembly stresses the frame. It is not uncommon for the frame to crack or break at the point just rearward of the boxed rail section.

For decades, owners have repaired this frame section in a variety of ways. The method shown here has withstood the Rubicon Trail and other severe backcountry trials. Additionally, the spring anchor brackets on these models deserve attention.

Again, stitch welds would reduce concentration of shock force along these lines. I would stitch-weld both the angle inserts and the anchor reinforcements on the frame rail. Stitch welds are common on automotive frames and other stressed members

This is a very sensible repair: shaped metal follows factory angle. This avoids the squared-end approach that would otherwise place a heavier load on one vertical point in the frame. Diagonal cut and welds make this a safer, more functional repair. One additional consideration would be the "stitch weld" technique (a stretch of weld followed by an open section) like those shown in the forward OEM box section.

Another weak point is the spring anchor-to-frame attachments. Here, the owner reinforced the frame section with angle inserts. He also welded the anchor at the frame.

These stitch welds between the frame rail and spring anchor will work nicely. Builders often reinforce the factory attachments at these points. If OEM welds look weak or fatigued, a wire-feed or stick weld pass can remedy the problem. Do not concentrate heat over long sections of the frame. To maintain tensile strength, allow metal to air cool gradually---do not quench with water!

Springs, Shackles and Bushings

The springs on a Jeep 4x4 are perishable. Whether you prefer an OEM-type set of springs or an aftermarket suspension system, the springs, at some point, will need attention. Fatigue is just as likely to occur as damage. Periodically inspect your springs. Broken spring leafs are not uncommon.

Spring leaf design affects the ride quality and the amount of axle/wheel travel. The early CJs with military-type leaf stacks have a stiff, harsh ride with relatively good load carrying capacity. AMC/Jeep CJs were far more adapted to highway and moderate trail usage, using compliant, more versatile spring (load) rates.

You may have good reason for keeping the original springs. If they need repair, there are shops that can build OEM replacement springs and leafs. Often, a spring shop can rebuild your original springs.

If your vehicle is headed for use on the highway and backcountry trails, you may prefer upgrading the springs and shock absorbers. Fortunately, due to the popularity of Jeep 4WD vehicles, there are a variety of suspension kits available in the aftermarket. For my purposes, unless I plan to build a museum piece or parade vehicle, aftermarket suspension makes the best sense.

My picks for aftermarket suspension lean toward longer travel, "soft ride" springs. Oversized tires often dictate the need for a "lift kit" approach. You can combine these needs with most aftermarket suspension kits.

For the '86 CJ-7, there was no need for a radical lift. The tire size of choice would be 31"x10.50"x15 on eight-inch rims. This required nothing more than a stock-to-one inch lift. I went with a custom one-inch lift suspension package from Full-Traction Suspension intended to accommodate these trail use tires.

When raising the vehicle with a chassis/suspension lift, you must be conscious of the impact on center-of-gravity. Safety needs should take precedence over all other considerations.

NOTE—

*I substantially explain suspension upgrades in the **Jeep Owner's Bible**. If you have curiosity about the broad range of concerns that accompany suspension changes and related topics, including the use of oversized wheels/tires, my comments and recommendations are found in that book.*

Massachusetts Has the Formula for Safe Suspension Modifications

Here's an example of one lift law that applies to sensibly modifying Jeep vehicles. Massachusetts has devised a formula for allowable mechanical (body and suspension) lift that accounts for both vehicle stability and safe handling: Wheelbase multiplied by Wheel Track (tire tread center to center measurement at the wider axle) divided by a factor of 2200. The wheel track width may be increased up to four inches by way of rim offset only, no wheel spacers allowed.

The formula is relatively easy. Suppose your Jeep has a 94" wheelbase and wide rims that provide a 62" tread width. 94" x 62" = 5828, divided by 2200 = 2.65" of lift.

Under Massachusetts' section 6.04 and 6.05, tire diameter (based upon largest size available as an OEM option) may also be increased the same amount as the mechanical lift.

Simply put, the Jeep could have tires up to 2.65" larger in diameter than stock, plus a 2.65" mechanical lift by way of chassis and/or a body lift kit. (Accordingly, the body/door height could set a total of 3.975" over stock.)

All parts must be equal to or better than OEM standards, and the vehicle safety cannot be compromised. Here, Massachusetts has addressed OEM vehicle design, roll center, center of gravity, and all other handling concerns with this statute. Other equipment on the truck must comply with general safety standards.

This is a sound approach, allowing reasonable lift for both off-pavement and highway usage. I am very pleased that Massachusetts took the iniative to advance such a formula. The guideline serves those who earnestly want a safer, versatile 4x4 truck.

Suspension Lifts and Driveshaft Upgrades

A suspension lift alters the driveshaft angles. When a driveshaft operates on a steeper angle, the stress loads on the shafts and U-joints increase. Typically, longer driveshafts are needed to compensate for the increase in distance from the transfer case to each axle's pinion flange. Driveline Service of San Diego, California, built custom driveshafts for my '55 CJ-5 featured in *Jeep CJ Rebuilder's Manual: 1946-1971* and the CJ-7 shown in this book. *(See Chapter 5 for details on the CJ-7's driveshafts. Driveline Service can ship driveline products throughout the United States. See Appendix.)*

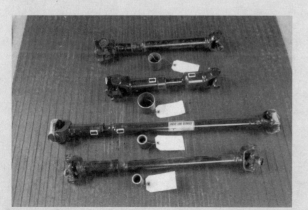

Driveline Service of San Diego built these two custom driveshafts with heavier wall tubing and improved spline cou-

plers. Steeper driveline angles required heftier components. Note the difference between OEM and new shafts.

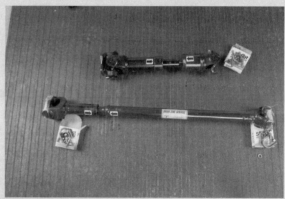

Rugged shafts are engineered and balanced for long service life. Due to the length of a 4-speed transmission installation, the rear shaft is now shorter than OEM. The front driveshaft is longer than stock. Arrows index shafts for proper "phasing" and balance.

NOTE—
*Driveshaft phase is critical. Splines must align so that front and rear U-joint positions match. For readers interested in driveshaft concerns, I cover driveshaft issues in depth within the **Jeep Owner's Bible**.*

6

Frame, Suspension, and Body Repairs

Suspension Lifts and Driveshaft Upgrades (continued)

Steeper driveline angles and short driveshafts (like 81-inch wheelbase '55 CJ's rear shaft with a T-18 conversion!) require a different transfer case U-joint flange. Spicer offers the flange at left, which has a shallower flange plate and taller bearing cup stands for the U-joint. This flange, available from Spicer suppliers like Driveline Service of San Diego, allows steeper operating angles than the OEM flange at right. I use new Spicer U-bolts as well.

Shorter rear driveshaft, with suspension fully dropped, shows steep angle of shaft. Without the use of the special Spicer flange at the transfer case, U-joint or shaft damage would occur.

CAUTION—

This is as far as any driveshaft angle should drop! A combination of driveshaft challenges: 1) an early Willys/Kaiser CJ-5's short, 81-inch wheelbase (i.e., shorter driveshafts overall), 2) the 3-inch (suspension) lift kit and 3) a longer transmission. Suspension lifts are easier to deal with on the 101-inch wheelbase vintage CJ-6s or later model CJs like the 94-inch wheelbase CJ-7 or 104-inch wheelbase CJ-8/Scrambler. The '72-up CJ-5 has only an 84-inch wheelbase length.

By contrast, the relatively long front driveshaft, with its milder slope and moderate drop distance, seldom presents problems. As with the rear driveshaft, the concern here is U-joint angles, which should closely match at each U-joint flange. Another consideration is proper front axle caster angle for correct steering geometry.

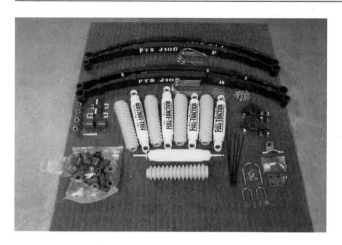

 Fig. 6-44

This custom suspension package from Full-Traction Suspension *(see Appendix)* features a mild 1-inch lift. This is essentially a spring system designed for use with 31"x10.50"x15" tires on 8-inch width rims. Tuning includes well-matched shock absorbers, a full set of urethane replacement bushings, U-bolts and hardware, a steering stabilizer shock assembly and a pair of Full-Traction's heavy-duty front shackle frame brackets. New bushings include the stabilizer bar and all spring mount points.

Fig. 6-45

Bolts removed from the front shackle's frame bracket, I pry enough to slide out the frame bracket. These brackets are a weak link on '76-'86 CJs. Inspect the bracket in the area of the punched hole that surrounds the frame rivet. Over time, many of these brackets have fatigued and cracked in this area.

6

Fig. 6-46

This quality Full-Traction Suspension aftermarket bracket reaches forward to the bumper's bolt hole. The bracket receives support in front of the shackle, where the factory bracket does not. Consider this upgrade. *(See Appendix for address of Full-Traction Suspension.)* Here, I use Loctite Threadlocker on the steering gear support bracket bolts.

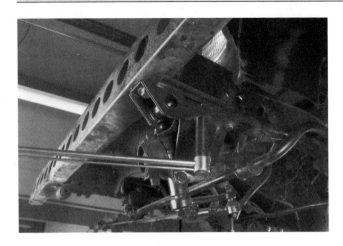

◄ **Fig. 6-47**

Torque these bolts to specification (70 lb-ft maximum with clean threads and Threadlocker). Pull up evenly and do not tax the frame nuts. These frame nuts are vulnerable to seizure and breaking loose within the frame rail. Bolts and washers are Grade 8.

NOTE—

If necessary, gently clean and chase the frame nut threads with a tap before installing these new bolts. Lube the tap to minimize risk of removing material. The goal is simply to "shape" the threads and not to cut new ones.

◄ **Fig. 6-48**

Torque these bolts to 70 lb-ft. The steering gear support brackets are vulnerable to cracking and breaking on '72-'86 CJs. Aftermarket trusses are available to brace the gear to the opposite frame rail. Especially on power steering models, inspect these brackets regularly. If this bracket breaks in the remote outback, you have a real problem! Use Threadlocker on the bolt threads.

◄ **Fig. 6-49**

This is the right side bracket. Note the difference between OEM bracket and aftermarket Full-Traction suspension design. Picking up support at the front bumper's bolt hole provides the stamina needed.

Springs, Shackles and Bushings

◄ **Fig. 6-50**

Installing urethane aftermarket bushings begins with greasing the bushings and frame sockets. Spring bushing kits should indicate what kind of grease to use. Full-Traction's kit comes with special silicone lubricant.

◄ **Fig. 6-51**

Aftermarket urethane anchor-end bushings use a steel sleeve spacer. (OEM spring bushings have a built-in sleeve.) This controls the tension applied to bushing shoulders. These sleeves will work with the OEM frame brackets. The shackle end *(at right)* uses the OEM shouldered shackle pins instead of a spacer sleeve.

6

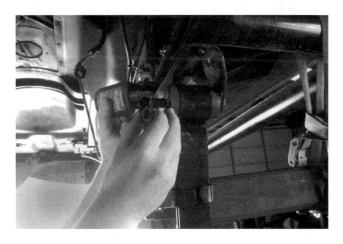

◄ **Fig. 6-52**

Steel sleeve in place with the greased bushings, the OEM bolt and an OEM self-locking nut go into the anchor end of the spring. This is rear end of front spring, similar to the front end of the rear spring. Use Threadlocker as insurance.

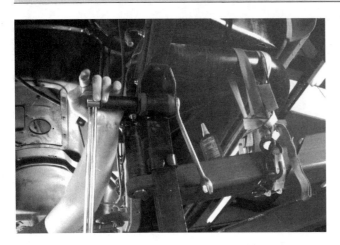

◀ Fig. 6-53

Torque these bolts and nuts to 100 lb-ft. Tighten nuts to specification, and recheck torque after parts settle.

◀ Fig. 6-54

These OEM shackles have shouldered pins that serve as spacers for the side plates. This assures proper preload/tension at sides of OEM or aftermarket bushings *(shown)*. I torque these self-locking nuts to 30-35 lb-ft and use Threadlocker as insurance. Recheck torque after parts settle.

> **CAUTION—**
>
> *Be cautious with aftermarket shackles that do not provide spacers or shouldered bolts! Typically, these shackles use self-locking nuts. Do not tighten nuts to the point of seizing the bushings! Eliminate clearance/sideplay, but do not prevent the bushings from flexing.*

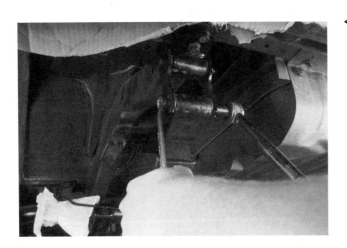

◀ Fig. 6-55

Tighten the front shackle nuts to specification: 30 lb-ft. Apply Threadlocker as insurance. These shackles have spacer pins to preset the tension on the bushing shoulders. This is a factory setting. Urethane replacement bushings must have the proper shoulder thickness to achieve this setting. Grease bushings, including shackle faces.

 Fig. 6-56

Hefty U-bolts come with the Full-Traction Suspension package. OEM 9/16" U-bolt nuts typically torque to a *maximum* of 105 lb-ft. OEM ½" U-bolt nuts torque to a *maximum* of 65 lb-ft. Always follow aftermarket kit instructions for recommended torque settings. Re-torque these bolts after driving the vehicle. Recheck periodically.

 Fig. 6-57

Wearing safety goggles, I use a cut-off wheel to quickly remove excess bolt length. Do not overheat the bolts. To assure that U-bolts are evenly tensioned and centered, make sure exposed threads are even in length before cutting off the excess.

6

Fig. 6-58

Repeat the process for installing rear springs. Anchors are at the front end of these springs, bolt/nut torqued to 100 lb-ft. Note that I have the axle assembly perched above the springs on my ½-ton capacity transmission jack. With springs now secured in place, axle drops into position and U-bolts can be easily installed. This jack serves a variety of uses.

Aftermarket Suspension Footnotes

There are a variety of suspension products that CJ builders find useful. Often, a better or stronger part is available, or a particular modification is desirable for off-pavement use. Here are some common aftermarket items.

Aftermarket "H" shackles are the best design. Steel sleeves through bushings maintain spread of the shackle. At the shackle mid-point, a steel crossbar or spacer helps stabilize the shackle. This is far stronger than OEM shackle plates. Torque the supplied hardware to manufacturer's specifications.

New aftermarket springs, with U-bolts installed, show extra arch and improvements. This is a 3-inch (over stock chassis height) lift spring set. Aftermarket spring set offers: 1) longer travel for off-pavement axle articulation, 2) a softer highway ride, and 3) the lift needed for taller tires.

Rear suspension of my '55 CJ is now ready for shock absorbers. Quality aftermarket springs feature nylon slippers between each leaf. This reduces friction, aids movement and extends spring life. Suspension package shown offers excellent backcountry wheel travel.

Lowering the bump stops will prevent hyperextension of long travel springs and also prevents tires from rubbing the body tub when axles twist to extremes. Aftermarket drops like these are available, or you can make stops to suit your chassis needs.

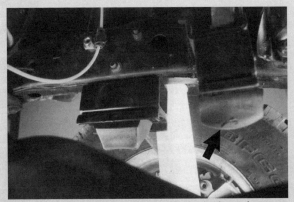

I try to match the drop distance with the inches of suspension lift. Here, the front bump stop drops on the '86 CJ have their match in a dropped snubber for the axle housing (**ARROW**). The axle snubber prevents the housing from winding up or rising high enough for the front driveshaft to hit the clutch/bellhousing.

Body Modifications and Metal Parts Restoration Tips

While auto body and paint masters have produced great guidebooks on their subject, the focus of this section is to illustrate how a Jeep mechanic can perform utilitarian, restorative metal work and fabrication. You will discover, too, that the difficult to find metal items can sometimes be salvaged and restored.

NOTE—

*In **Chapter 3**, I describe the modification of a CJ floor pan. This procedure addresses the common changes surrounding transmission swaps and modifying linkages. Refer to that section of this book for details on floorpan modifications.*

◄ **Fig. 6-59**

Rocker sill protector is custom built and a serious means for preserving this '72 CJ. Body lift kit spacers provide additional clearance for oversized tires. Note the tub bottom reinforced with channel rail, welded to the base of the tub. This helps overcome tub flexing on '72-'75 CJs.

6

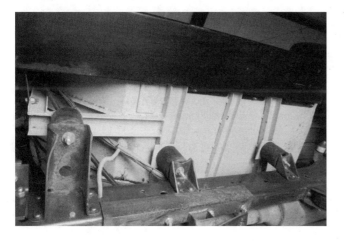

◄ **Fig. 6-60**

Tub reinforcement channels double as mounting points for frame-to-body cushions. This '72 CJ-5 sees severe duty use on the Rubicon Trail and other rock piles. Here, body stress and twisting run to the extreme. Floorpan reinforcement and barrel cushions keep the body tub sheet metal from fracturing.

CAUTION—

Urethane body mounts have several advantages. However, changing from OEM body cushions to body lift urethane cushions creates the need for several adjustments! These can include radiator or fan relocation, steering column alignment issues, fuel and brake line repositioning, and more. Unless you plan to follow through with these modifications, do not install thicker body mounts or a body lift kit! When you do not want to alter the OEM body/frame relationship, replace body mount bushings with OEM-thickness cushions (rubber or urethane type).

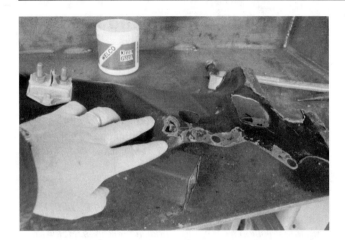

 Fig. 6-61

Even a Nevada vehicle can have sheet metal perforation, though in this case the damage is from wear, then minor rust.

 Fig. 6-62

Torch removes loose, thin metal, taking material back to stable sheet metal.

 Fig. 6-63

Using oxy-acetylene welding technique, I carefully ran successive beads of filler rod until the hole was completely filled with quality, mild steel weld.

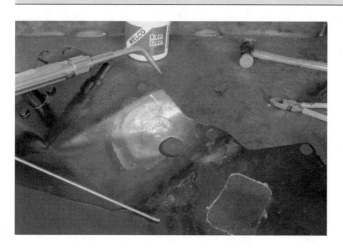

◀ **Fig. 6-64**

Finished weld forms a strong, permanent repair. For the visible portion of the floor pan, light grinding with carbide bit and drill motor will restore the surface. Use a quality primer/sealer to protect against rusting. Apply final paint coat over the primer/sealer.

◀ **Fig. 6-65**

For better seal and weatherproofing, use body caulking when fitting up panels.

6

◀ **Fig. 6-66**

When modifying a floorpan, I prefer working with the original pan. This provides a template for the shape, but more importantly, minimizes the modifications to a pristine body tub.

352

Frame, Suspension, and Body Repairs

 Fig. 6-67

I built this custom panel of stout sheet steel. This panel wraps around the relocated and modified levers, including the Warn overdrive stick on my vintage CJ. Contours of the body and the tall 4-speed control housing were addressed. This is a very strong, bolt-in piece that enhances floorboard integrity.

 Fig. 6-68

Finish details include use of an OEM transmission boot. Other levers require custom boots and innovation. Overall, the look is "original," and this is one strong place for resting a passenger's foot!

Repairing Worn and Hard-to-Find Parts

Jeep CJs have many links and levers. Vintage Willys and Kaiser Jeep vehicles are notorious for high-friction joints and pivots. (Fortunately, the AMC/Jeep CJs use modern, lower friction joints.) When vintage parts wear out, and they surely will, owners can spend a good deal of time finding serviceable used or NOS pieces. I find that many of the worn original parts are restorable.

Using oxy-acetylene welding technique, I build up the worn area with mild steel filler rod, carefully avoiding the drilled cotter pin hole. Then I file and reshape the stud.

This vintage CJ throttle link has worn over time, a common development. The part is not easy to find, and a used piece would likely be no better than this one. This is a repairable part.

Repairing Worn and Hard-to-Find Parts (continued)

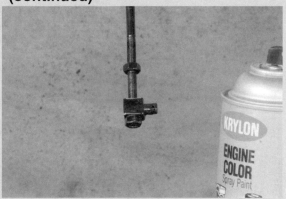

Carefully file the stud to original shape, then coat with a quality engine enamel. This part will once again deliver the service intended.

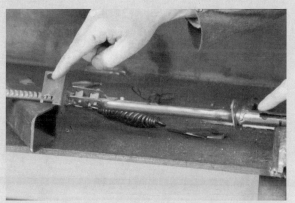

Emergency/parking brake mounting bracket broke loose over time. This is a difficult-to-find piece and can be repaired. Once cleaned thoroughly, the tube-to-firewall bracket separation *(at right)* is an easy wire-feed or oxy-acetylene welding fix. Dashboard lever mount *(left)* needed closer attention.

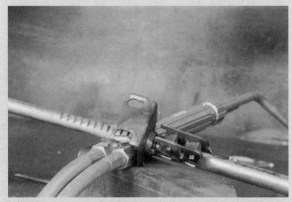

Again, the oxy-acetylene technique works well here. Carefully build material to rough shape of original form.

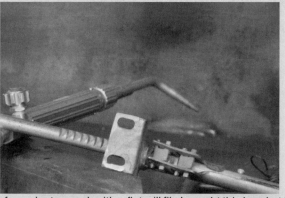

A few minutes work with a flat mill file brought this bracket to shape. I use a round or chainsaw (tooth sharpening) file to shape the slots.

A coat of primer and engine enamel bring this piece to like-new appearance. For my '55 CJ-5, restoration is much cheaper and far less time consuming than chasing down a rare, nearly half-century old part! Thoroughly cleaned and lubed, the assembly will now work as designed.

This vintage oil bath air filter came from the Midwest. Outer shell looked grimy but otherwise intact.

6

Repairing Worn and Hard-to-Find Parts (continued)

Internal pieces were okay. Oil had protected metals from corrosion.

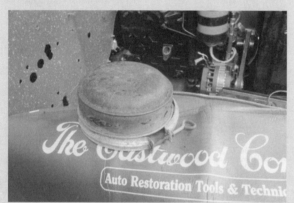

Bottom of oil cup was severely rust damaged. Corrosion ate this section to paper-thin stage! Upon cleaning the metal, daylight could be seen at several points.

I carefully cut away the bottom from the rest of the oil cup as-sembly. Yes, a quality vacuum-tight coffee can offers enough structural integrity to serve as a "deep sump" oil cup bottom! Here, after carefully wire brushing the can section, I brazed the section to the remaining solid portion of the oil cup, flowing brass smoothly to provide a leak-proof seal.

Removed cup base reveals degree of rust damage. Oil would have poured through this metal like a sieve.

Finished piece with coat of engine enamel (exterior only) looks like a custom part. Oil cup now holds more oil and functions exactly like the original. Though I would have been content with an intact original cup, this extra capacity sump works for me---and saved searching for an OEM/NOS replacement part to fit a 1955 CJ-5 Jeep!

Sheet Metal Restoration Basics

CJ Jeep bodies, thanks to their spartan military roots, have simple panels and curves. There are a variety of tasks that you can perform without professional-level metal finishing and painting skills. Though I'm not a body-and-paint specialist, I once restored a CJ-3A body to completion, including a quality paint finish. The result was very satisfying.

> **WARNING—**
>
> *In the late 1960s, when I painted the '3A,' automotive paint chemistry was far less toxic than modern paint systems. I avoided the use of catalyst hardeners, which at the time were the most toxic agents. I wore a respirator. Today, you need a fresh-air supply system/respirator to be safe with the VOCs in sealer/primers, paints and reducers. Most owners sublet painting to professionals who have the right safety equipment.*

Perhaps you feel competent, although most builders choose to do minor prep work, then have a professional shop paint the vehicle. These days, I leave this kind of work to professionals, like my pal since high school days, Brent Howerton!

6

Brent and I determined that the smartest approach to restoring and painting the CJ-5 was off the frame. You will likely find this method works best. For sealing and priming, assuring full attention to preventing future rust and deterioration, working "frame-off" makes sense! Panels separated, you can prime/seal and paint every crevice of your Jeep!

◁ **Fig. 6-69**

Often, an older Jeep will have aftermarket or add-on accessories that require body modifications. The '55 CJ-5 had support tubes for a canvas top that no longer were useful and created a body eyesore. Here, Brent removed these pieces with a cut-off tool.

◁ **Fig. 6-70**

Brent demonstrates minor straightening technique with a simple dolly and hammer. Thick metal gauge and simple contours make the CJ an easy vehicle for honing your minor bodywork skills. Tools shown are inexpensive.

 Fig. 6-71

Brent repairs a crack in the sheet metal with an oxy-acety-lene torch. This is much like the work I performed on the links, levers, frame and floorpan construction, however, sheet metal requires minimizing heat exposure. Note smaller tip used for this process.

 Fig. 6-72

Brent isolates heat to weld area, getting torch away as quickly as possible. On sheet metal, allow metal to cool slightly as you weld. 1/16" mild steel filler rod works well here. A smaller tip, light quenching with a wet rag, and vintage Jeep's hefty gauge sheet metal help prevent buckling problems.

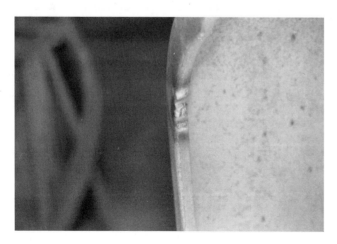

 Fig. 6-73

This is sufficient weld for strength and filling. Brent will grind the surface with a disc grinder to bring the shape back. Light use of plastic body filler, and the area will then be ready for priming, sanding and painting.

◀ **Fig. 6-74**

This outer sheet metal wrap was separating from the fender stampings. Brent prepares for spot welding.

◀ **Fig. 6-75**

Spot welding speeds the process of attaching loose panel. Heat concentration and the binding force help minimize buckling or warpage. This is a common way to pin sheet metal panels together.

6

◀ **Fig. 6-76**

Spot welds in place, Brent gas welds a hard-to-reach area. Again, heat is held to minimum. Stamped sections and over-lapping sheet metal areas are less likely to warp or buckle.

 Fig. 6-77

Disc sander takes metal and spot-welds to a flat surface. Light use of plastic body filler will take care of the slightly low spots. This is one step closer to priming and painting.

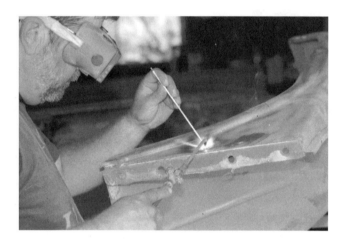

 Fig. 6-78

Brazing offers lower heat and a durable filler material for filling unwanted screw holes. A gritty disc will cut through brass quickly. Bonding of primer/sealer is an issue with brass. Tap the brazed area inward, just slightly, and fill with plastic body filler to assure proper primer adhesion.

 Fig. 6-79

Brent continues to fill extra holes from add-ons. These three spots are hard to reach with a grinder. Often, this kind of repair, if done without a great deal of weld bulge, can simply be sprayed and covered with primer/sealer and a stiff coating of quality undercoating.

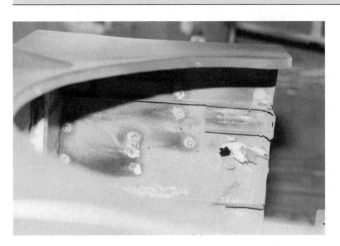

 Fig. 6-80

Brent uses a sheet metal backup when MIG or wire-feed welding these holes. Backer prevents wire from jumping through hole or puddling on the other side. Tack weld the patch, then "plug" or "button" (circular welding motion) fill the hole. When done, the patch will either fall off or break loose with light encouragement from a sharp chisel point.

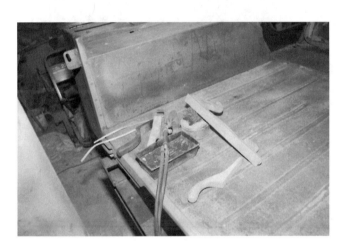

 Fig. 6-81

Here, Brent has demonstrated modern methods for working sheet metal. He thought it fun to bring out his father's lead working tools, items that were much a part of the body business when the '55 CJ was new! Modern methods and plastic body filler are much easier processes.

6

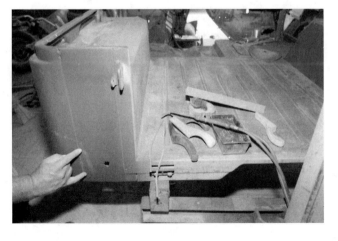

 Fig. 6-82

After filling holes and restoring the sheet metal, light filling with plastic and priming with a quality primer-sealer, the body tub nears pre-painting stage. Careful sanding and re-priming complete the prep work. Red '55 CJ on the back cover of *Jeep CJ Rebuilder's Manual: 1946-1971* represents the finished paint job. Nice work, Brent!

AMC-Era CJ Rust Repair

Builders who have a copy of my *Jeep Owner's Bible* will recall the *Chapter 14* section covering Louie Russo's rust repairs on the '81 CJ-5's body. This vehicle was a project for *OFF-ROAD* magazine, and the bodywork met magazine color photo standards! Here, again, is insight from Louie's quality repairs of very common AMC-era CJ rust issues.

When carpet rolls back, so does metal! The small bulge at outer body surface never suggested this severe rust. Aftermarket roll bar extensions mount to front floor of CJ models. Unless you seal properly around drilled metal, carpets may hide an area where water can accumulate. Here, menacing rust will form. Always take rust bubbles ("exfoliation") seriously.

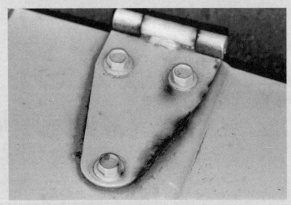

Hinge joint shows surface rust. A professional body worker sees this as salvageable. Separate the hinge from the hood and sand blast all surfaces to restore metal.

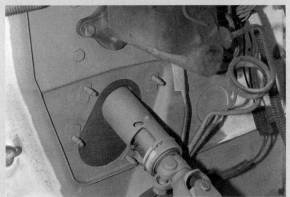

Surface rust on firewall, although unsightly, does not reduce the integrity of base sheet metal. Sandblasting reveals that underlying metal is strong and serviceable.

This is insidious rust. Hidden behind an aftermarket trim panel on the CJ-5, rust now presses through sheet metal. Watch for high spots like this, especially when considering a used Jeep buy.

AMC-Era CJ Rust Repair (continued)

Sandblasting at this metal bulge reveals a broader problem. Hidden between an aftermarket trim panel and interior carpet, severe rust damage resulted from inadequate metal priming/sealing job when owner drilled holes through sheet metal to install an aftermarket roll bar.

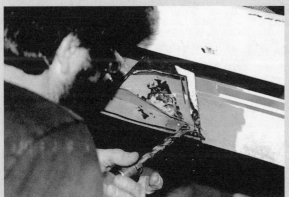

Factory rivets drilled, Louie Russo separates floorpan from interior body brace. Extent of rust is still illusive, even at this point.

Louie carefully removes rotted metal. Here, a carbide disc cuts quickly through the sheet metal brace. Structural integrity of the body tub is a consideration with this repair. Wear a particle mask and safety goggles when grinding with carbide discs!

Remove or treat all rust-effected metal. At this point, wire brushing and sandblasting will determine strength of metal and uncover any pinholes to fill.

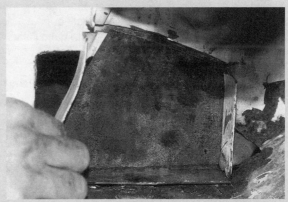

Heavy-gauge flat metal section from a hefty 1930s car fender has become a replacement piece for the original tub brace. Louie welds the handformed repair section into place. Note use of salvageable segments of the original brace. This small portion of metal helps maintain alignment and contours.

6

Frame, Suspension, and Body Repairs

AMC-Era CJ Rust Repair (continued)

MIG welded into place, section now fits against the cleaned floorpan. Heat applied to lower bracket flange allows shaping with a body hammer until new brace matches OE fit perfectly. Louie also welded pinholes in floorpan. Surface grinding of welds will restore original appearance.

Surface grinding reveals Louie's careful handling of metal. Masterful heat isolation, shrink/stretch control and correct heat diffusion results in near perfect surface straightness.

Louie cuts and forms flat piece of sheet metal to fit cutout. He purposely keeps the original lower roll of body lip to avoid re-shaping edge. Drilling and spot-welding outer panel to inner brace duplicates OE engineering. MIG confines heat. Louie strategically lays down welds while carefully quenching hot sheet metal to maintain shape.

Louie applies a light coat of plastic body filler to sanding scratches and very light depressions. Once shaped and sanded, only a tiny amount of plastic will remain. Louie Russo prefers the challenge of metal working to the simpler, plastic fill approach. His work shows "good -as-new" quality.

Frame Measurement Methods

Always check the frame for square and plumb height. These original factory service illustrations provide a guideline for measuring points. The goal is to assure that "diamond" measurements conform to original standards. To perform these measurements, take diagonal (side-to-side) measurements from one frame rail to the opposite rail. Use the factory reference points when measuring point-to-point.

For determining whether the frame is twisted (not shifted diagonally), set the frame on stands. Make certain that the frame reads level *and that the floor is level.* Pick matching frame points and features on opposite sides of the frame. Hang a plumb bob from these points, and measure accurately from the floor to the frame points.

NOTE—

*As a Jeep factory guideline, stated in the **1972 AMC/Jeep Technical Service Manual**, "If the diagonals in each pair are within 1/8", that part of the frame included between points of measurement may be considered as satisfactorily aligned. These diagonals should also intersect at the center line."*

6

If you cannot determine the side- and plane-view integrity of the frame, take the assembly to a frame and axle shop that has specialty equipment for performing accurate measurements of an isolated frame unit. Modern measuring techniques include point-to-point light beam and laser checks--- far more precise than Jeep ever intended!

1972 CJ-5 and CJ-6 Frame Dimensions and Measuring Points

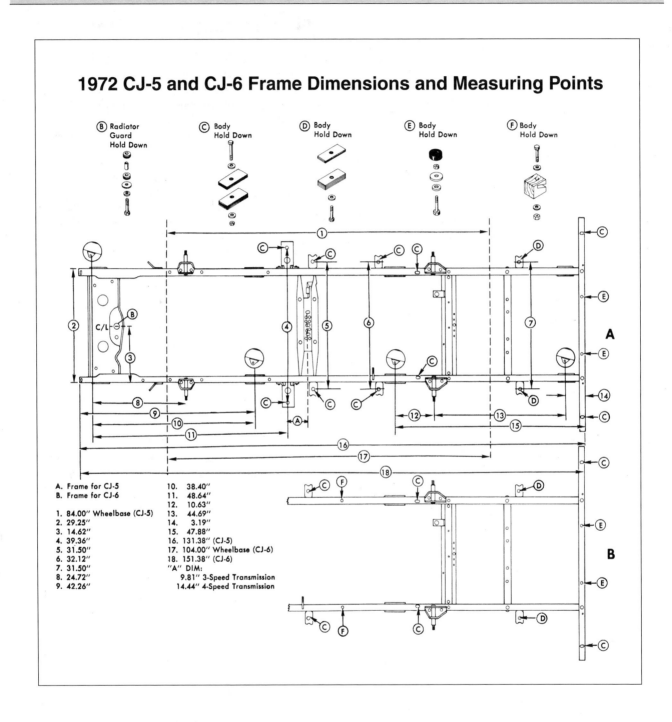

A. Frame for CJ-5
B. Frame for CJ-6

1. 84.00" Wheelbase (CJ-5)
2. 29.25"
3. 14.62"
4. 39.36"
5. 31.50"
6. 32.12"
7. 31.50"
8. 24.72"
9. 42.26"
10. 38.40"
11. 48.64"
12. 10.63"
13. 44.69"
14. 3.19"
15. 47.88"
16. 131.38" (CJ-5)
17. 104.00" Wheelbase (CJ-6)
18. 151.38" (CJ-6)
"A" DIM:
   9.81" 3-Speed Transmission
   14.44" 4-Speed Transmission

Chapter 7

Steering and Brake Service

7

General

The steering and brake systems on '72-'86 Jeep CJs are superior to earlier CJ models. Of all pre-AMC/Jeep CJs, only the later V-6 models had adequate brake sizing and reasonably responsive steering. Anyone disputing whether or not '72-up brakes work better need only drive a stock Willys or Kaiser era four-cylinder model with 9-inch drum brakes!

True to my aims for this book, this chapter addresses the original brake and steering system needs. More importantly, in my view, this chapter also details the sensible safety upgrades that can improve the steering and brake systems of '72-'86 Jeep CJ models.

The AMC/Jeep Steering Systems

When the model MB went to war, steering gear technology was primitive. General Motors had just developed the low-friction, more rugged ball-and-nut (re-circulating) manual steering gear, however, Willys and Ford had no access to this advanced design. Instead, Willys settled for the simple Ross cam-and-lever gear, among the most wear-prone, high friction designs of the era. This gear survives nearly all the way through the Willys/Kaiser era.

Various Ross steering gears remained in the Jeep truck inventory until the AMC era. (Due to carryover models and parts inventories, small numbers of Kaiser-type vehicles were still manufactured as late as 1973.) Although the Jeepster and J-trucks/Wagoneer benefited from Saginaw steering gears during the last years of the Kaiser era, the universal use of Saginaw gears in CJ models did not occur until the introduction of AMC/Jeep-designed CJs in 1972.

 Fig. 7-1

My vintage '55 CJ-5 sported its original steering system. Steep rake of steering column is an early Jeep trademark. Ross cam-and-lever gear bolts to the frame, just below and forward of the cowl. Pitman arm, drag link, bellcrank and two tie-rods make up the steering linkage. Note large steering wheel.

Fig. 7-2

Here's the Ross gear assembly removed from my vintage Jeep. The fore-and-aft movement of the pitman arm is part of the busy steering linkage. AMC terminated this approach with the '72 CJs.

Fig. 7-3

Steering bellcrank is common to per-AMC era CJs. Steering gear's pitman arm moves fore-and-aft, draglink attaches to one arm of bellcrank. The bellcrank's other arm moves both tie-rods, which in turn move the two steering arms. On pre-AMC/Jeep CJs, wear here can cause loose, erratic steering and wander.

> **CAUTION—**
>
> *Always mark the steering wheel and shaft relationship before disassembly. Assemble the wheel in the same position unless you suspect that the wheel is not indexed with the center (high) point of the gear. With the draglink disconnected at the pitman arm, the gear's center point is ½ the turns from the lock-to-lock position. When turning lock-to-lock, do not jam the gear against its extremes! Turn slowly as you approach each end of the gear's range of motion. This will prevent damage to the steering gear components.*

Use of Saginaw manual and power assisted steering was a milestone for the CJ models. Additionally, the steering linkage underwent a major improvement just prior to the AMC-built models.

Your '72-'86 CJ benefits from the very best manual or power steering systems in the light truck industry. Gone is the draglink-to-bellcrank linkage with archaic two tie-rod steering linkage. A single piece tie-rod connects the two steering arms. The "short tie-rod" or draglink is a single rod running from the steering pitman arm to the right side steering arm location.

For the ***Jeep CJ Rebuilder's Manual: 1946-1971***, I show the step-by-step rebuild of a Ross cam-and-lever steering gear. Evaluating whether to include 'step-by-step' coverage for rebuilding the '72-'86 Saginaw manual or power steering gear assemblies, I concluded that such information is not practical.

7

Common Jeep CJ Saginaw gear assemblies are available in new, rebuilt and improved or upgraded aftermarket versions. Suppliers like 4WD Hardware, Inc., and others market these popular gear units, hoses and pump assemblies.

By contrast, individual Saginaw replacement parts can be difficult to source and expensive. Adjustments and service methods are precise, and power gears require special care with their seal installations and clearances. Servicing a power steering gear is much like the detailed work involved with an automatic transmission's valve-body work. Cleanliness is critical.

When working with a GMC truck agency as a line mechanic in the early '80s, I rebuilt Saginaw gears under warranty (a rare occasion for the virtually bulletproof Saginaw power gear!). This included bearings, the power rack, spool valve assembly, the worm shaft and all seals. At current retail parts and labor costs, such a rebuild job would equal or exceed that of a rebuilt unit. For this reason, and due to the ready availability of bolt-on replacement steering gears, I have omitted the rebuilding and adjustment steps for these Saginaw gears.

NOTE—

In my experience with Saginaw steering repairs, which dates back to the late 1960s, a loose gear is always a sign of trouble. Excessive play or backlash typically indicates a worn out ball-and-nut or rack piston assembly, which means an additional need for shafts, bearings and seals.

There is a quick check for wear in a Saginaw steering gear. If the worm shaft/stub shaft pulls up and down in the steering gear housing, with looseness and no perceptible preload on these worm shaft bearings, this clearly indicates wear. If the amount of rotational movement (turning degrees) at the steering stub or wormshaft feels excessive before the pitman/cross shaft moves, this is an obvious sign of wear.

You can easily check for this wear. Place your hand on the worm/stub shaft and attempt to move the shaft up and down. If no play is evident, jack up the front end and turn the steering to precisely the straight-ahead position. Grip the pitman arm in one hand and carefully rotate the stub shaft back-and-forth to the point that you feel the pitman shaft/arm move ever so slightly. This stub/worm movement should be minimal, feeling like nothing is loose.

NOTE—

On power steering models, you will need to have the engine running to perform this simple backlash test. Otherwise, normal torsion bar and spool valve movement might be suspected as "play." Stay well away from the engine's fan! Make sure that steering is in the straight-ahead (gear on center) position. Rotate the stub shaft with great care. Sense the exact moment when the pitman shaft/arm begins to move, and note the amount of movement involved. If necessary, compare this to a newer vehicle's gear.

CAUTION—

There are precise torque measurements for the worm bearing's preload and the sector teeth-to-ball nut or rack piston's over-center resistance (mesh). The tests described here are simply to determine the extent of wear. These tests do not serve as the adjustment procedures for Saginaw manual and power-assisted steering gears.

If play is so slight that you have confidence the gear's friction parts are not worn, you can consider adjusting the gear. I caution any builder about this procedure, however. *Do not attempt to compensate for obvious wear by adjusting the wormshaft endplay or the lash/mesh between the ball nut or rack piston and the pitman cross-shaft/sector teeth!*

Whenever wear is obvious enough to show up under these simple tests, consider replacing the gear assembly. For those builders confident that their steering gear can still be adjusted to specification, see a factory Jeep workshop manual or a readily available *professional-level* service manual covering these Saginaw steering gears.

NOTE—

*My home/work library includes Jeep factory workshop manuals plus model-specific **Mitchell**, **Motors** and **Chilton** professional-level (trade) service books. The Saginaw manual and power gears are widely used in the automotive industry. (Every popular domestic light truck manufacturer has used these units.) For detailed adjustment procedures and vital specifications, seek such a manual in new or used form, or check the reference section at your local public library.*

 Fig. 7-4

On earlier Jeep models with no threaded puller holes in the steering wheel, I use this method for removing the wheel: Wedge a lower grade (more malleable) flat washer on the pointed end of the air chisel bit. Insert bit into the hollow steering tube, making sure the bit does not touch the tube. I pull upward on the steering wheel while applying the air hammer. The washer drives against the top of the hollow tube. The steering wheel should pop loose immediately.

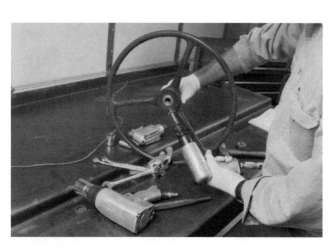

7

◀ **Fig. 7-5**

Regardless of steering gear type, the method of loosening the pitman arm is similar. Remove the nut and lock washer.

◀ **Fig. 7-6**

With a pitman arm puller or two-jaw puller, remove the arm. When changing the steering gear, you will remove and install the pitman arm. Torque on the later Saginaw manual or power gear pitman arm nut is 210 lb-ft *maximum* (185 lb-ft recommended). Renew the OEM lockwasher and nut if any wear or fatigue is evident. Use only OEM replacement parts.

NOTE—

On power-assisted gear systems, Jeep recommends staking the nut to the pitman shaft at one point. When installing a pitman arm on a Saginaw manual or power steering gear, use the OEM lockwasher supplied plus Loctite 242. Tighten the nut to a minimum 185 lb-ft of torque. 200-210 lb-ft of torque is not too much. This is a safety item! To prevent damage to the gear, make sure the steering is in the center position while tightening the nut. Hold the pitman arm steady (preferably in a stable, soft-jawed vise if the gear is off the frame) while tightening the nut.

Pitman Arm Installation Checklist

For safety sake, use care when installing the pitman arm. Follow these safety guidelines:

1) Make sure that the pitman shaft and arm splines are clean.

2) Index the arm to the correct splines.

3) Do not tighten the nut with steering turned to left or right extremes. Support the pitman arm securely in the gear's center position. (Hold the arm in a vise or by similar means.)

4) Tighten the nut securely. If performing torque set in the vehicle, steering linkage should be attached with front wheels pointed in a straight-ahead position to center the pitman arm. This will prevent stressing the gear's ball races and ball-nut.

NOTE—

The modern tightening alternative, of course, is to center the gear, support the pitman arm, and use an air gun, one capable of accurately setting torque within the 185-210 lb-ft range. Once installed in the Jeep, the gear can be centered to re-check the pitman shaft nut. Use a torque wrench.

AUTHOR'S TIP!

When aligning the steering wheel, make certain the steering gear's pitman arm is on dead center (precisely midway between left and right turn extremes). Keeping the gear on dead center, align the steering wheel spokes in the straight-ahead position. This should correspond to any factory indexing marks and assure an accurate reference for the straight-ahead driving and wheel alignment mode. Note that the gear has a high point on center, designed to provide the least amount of play when driving straight down the road.

◀ **Fig. 7-7**

Common Saginaw manual steering gear is popular and found on '72-'86 CJ models. This gear has exceptional stamina and unparalleled ease of operation. Smooth, ball-and-nut concept revolutionized steering gear design.

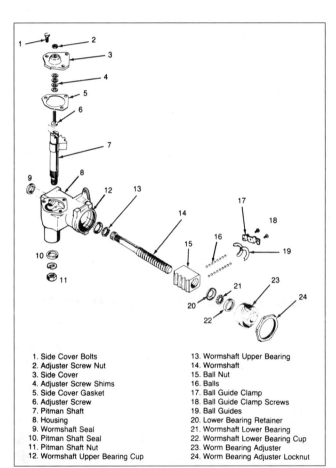

1. Side Cover Bolts
2. Adjuster Screw Nut
3. Side Cover
4. Adjuster Screw Shims
5. Side Cover Gasket
6. Adjuster Screw
7. Pitman Shaft
8. Housing
9. Wormshaft Seal
10. Pitman Shaft Seal
11. Pitman Shaft Nut
12. Wormshaft Upper Bearing Cup
13. Wormshaft Upper Bearing
14. Wormshaft
15. Ball Nut
16. Balls
17. Ball Guide Clamp
18. Ball Guide Clamp Screws
19. Ball Guides
20. Lower Bearing Retainer
21. Wormshaft Lower Bearing
22. Wormshaft Lower Bearing Cup
23. Worm Bearing Adjuster
24. Worm Bearing Adjuster Locknut

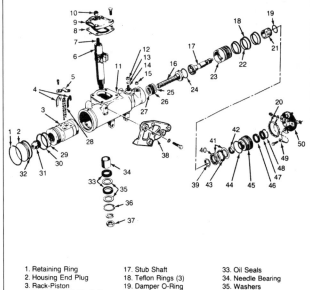

Fig. 7-8

Saginaw power rack piston-and-wormshaft steering gear is the most rugged unit ever used in U.S.-built light trucks and automobiles. In a CJ Jeep, this gear is powerful enough to pull the mounting brackets loose from the frame while freeing an oversized wheel and tire from a rocky trap. Adjust your driving technique accordingly!

> **CAUTION—**
>
> *If you have a Saginaw power steering system, use extreme care to preserve the frame and steering components. I equate this unit to a very powerful source of hydraulic force and energy. When this force is applied to excess, something will give!*

1. Retaining Ring	17. Stub Shaft	33. Oil Seals
2. Housing End Plug	18. Teflon Rings (3)	34. Needle Bearing
3. Rack-Piston	19. Damper O-Ring	35. Washers
4. Ball Return Guide Halves	20. Adjuster Plug Lock Nut	36. Retaining Ring
5. Clamp	21. Valve Spool	37. Pitman Arm Nut
6. Pitman Shaft	22. Backup O-Rings (3)	38. Spacer
7. Adjusting Screw	23. Valve Body	39. Bearing Retainer
8. Gasket	24. O-Ring	40. Spacer
9. Side Cover	25. Race	41. Races
10. Lock Nut	26. Thrust Bearing	42. Bearing
11. Housing	27. Race	43. Thrust Bearing
12. Pressure Port Seat	28. Ball Bearings (24)	44. O-Ring
13. Poppet Valve	29. Backup O-Ring	45. Adjuster Plug
14. Spring	30. Piston Ring	46. Oil Seal
15. Return Port Seat	31. Rack-Piston End Plug	47. Washer and Dust Seal
16. Worm	32. O-Ring	48. Retaining Ring
		49. Ground Wire
		50. Flexible Coupling

Steering Linkage and Columns

When servicing the steering system, steering linkage requires attention. The linkage consists of a draglink ("short tie-rod"), a long tie-rod between steering arms, and the attaching tie-rod joint ends. Wear occurs at any of the pivotal points and joints.

Fig. 7-9

'72-'86 CJ steering linkage is simple and functional. The solid axle lends itself to a one-piece tie-rod. This is a positive arrangement. If the draglink ("short tie-rod") remains reasonably close to the horizontal plane of the long tie-rod, the bump steer is minimal. '86 CJ-7 (shown) features an OEM anti-sway bar and steering stabilizer/shock absorber.

 Fig. 7-10

When installing tie-rod ends, match the thread penetration at each end of the tie-rod sleeve. This way, the adjuster sleeve will always expose the same number of threads at each end. Before tightening sleeve clamps, make sure each tie-rod's ball-stud is in its centered position. This will prevent binding and allow a full range of motion when the linkage travels.

> *CAUTION—*
>
> *Threads must penetrate the tie-rod sleeve ends enough to assure safe attachment! This will be the case if the front-end alignment is within range and you have threaded the tie-rods equally into the sleeve. Secure tie-rod sleeve clamps safely, and make sure the clamps and hardware will not interfere with any parts over the full range of suspension and steering travel.*

Fig. 7-11

Make certain tapered ball stud seats and studs are clean, free of burrs. Stud should seat snugly and not rotate as you tighten the castellated nut. Torque tie-rod stud nuts to 45 lb-ft, and install the cotter pin. If slots in nut do not align with the cotter pin hole, tighten just enough to align the first available slot, and install the cotter pin. Torque the 5/16" (thread size) sleeve clamp nuts to 20 lb-ft.

7

Fig. 7-12

Make certain that the tie-rod ball studs align with each other. When checking alignment, set a stud in its centered position. The stud at the opposite end of the rod should also be on center. If ball studs match at each end of the tie-rod, maximum range of motion is possible. Note my method for bending and shaping cotter pins.

Draglink Slope and Bump Steer

With vehicle on ground, fully weighted, the draglink/short tie-rod should be close to level with the long tie-rod. (A slight downward slope from the pitman arm to long tie-rod is common and acceptable.) Excessive draglink slope can create "bump steer" effect as suspension moves up and down.

On a vehicle with a solid front axle and leaf springs, determine draglink slope with the vehicle at normal curb weight and height. Keep the draglink/short tie-rod slope to a minimum at this ride height. This way, as the suspension and axle move, the draglink will stay within an acceptable arc, as near parallel to the long tie-rod as possible.

Steering linkage requires proper engineering. Always make certain that links move freely and do not bind or interfere with one another. If in doubt about the layout or design of your CJ's steering linkage system, refer to OEM engineering found on other Jeep vehicles.

Always follow lift kit instructions, especially kits that contain a dropped pitman arm. Swing the steering fully in each direction. Envision the position of linkage as the chassis rises and sets to its full travel. Visualize the linkage in all positions at extremes of movement. *Make absolutely certain that parts do not interfere with each other!*

◄ **Fig. 7-13**
When building a steering linkage system, refer to OEM layouts. Mimic practical, proven designs. This '72 CJ boasts a narrowed, disc brake Dana 44 front axle with the J-truck/Wagoneer's factory steering linkage. Steering joints and tube sleeves are very stout. Note use of a brace from the power steering gear to right frame rail.

NOTE—

The '72 CJ is shown with front axle hanging at full drop. The slope on the draglink/short tie-rod is minimal. (Slope is even less with vehicle at static floor height, well within specifications for any stock Jeep system.) This is a well thought out conversion of the '44' axle and steering linkage. When setting up a steering gear and linkage, the gear must be on exact center with front wheels/tires pointed straight ahead. Use extreme care to build a safe, proven steering system! Mimic OEM engineering.

Rough Steering Adjustments

While wheel alignment is best left to a shop with four-wheel alignment equipment, there are rough settings that you can set for at least driving the vehicle. Caster will need to be set at an alignment shop. Camber should always be within specification unless the axle housing is bent. Toe-in, however, is something you can set yourself, at least close enough to drive safely home from a remote trail or to an alignment shop.

To adjust front wheel alignment, raise the front tires off the ground and set the steering straight ahead. Make sure the steering gear and steering wheel are on exact center. Loosen the bracket for the steering damper shock. This is a Full-Traction Suspension damper, part of the suspension kit. Like the shock absorbers, the damper fits in exact place of the OEM damper.

Pick an easy to identify tread pattern on each front tire. With a tape, measure the distance between these patterns at the front of the tires, as close to mid-line between the bottom and the top of the tires. Keep tape level. Pick identical marks at the rear of the tires, and measure as close to the mid-line there as possible.

Loosen both tie-rod ends at these clamps. Rotate the long tie-rod sleeve to change the toe-set. Keep measuring between the front and rear marks, near the mid-line of the tires. When the toe-in (toe'd inward at the front) is 1/16"-1/8", you have a workable setting.

Make sure ball sockets align at each end of the long tie-rod. Torque the clamp hardware to 20 lb-ft. Now center and tighten the damper bracket (**ARROW**). Tighten the damper shock bracket with the shock setting level, making certain the bracket clears the axle's center section and differential cover on full right turns.

NOTE—

Drive the vehicle and note the position of the steering wheel when driving straight ahead. Park the vehicle with the steering wheel in the offset position. Adjust the draglink (short tie-rod) sleeve until the steering wheel sets straight. Make sure the ball-studs/joints are straight at each end of the draglink, and tighten clamps to 20 lb-ft. Confirm the steering wheel alignment.

AUTHOR'S TIP!

Make certain that the damper shock is level. Be sure the clamp bracket clears the axle's center section on extreme right turns. Check all linkage for free movement, no parts interference and no binding. If the steering wheel spokes align properly with the steering gear's center point, never reposition the steering wheel to align it! Center the steering wheel with the draglink sleeve adjuster. (As shown in photo above).

7

 Fig. 7-14

For building custom steering columns, Advance Adapters and Flaming River have teamed up. Here, aircraft quality slip joint/U-joint is enshrouded within a rubber seal. When fitting the shaft into my '55 CJ-5, I centered the slip joint to allow both up and down movement as the chassis and body flex. A rigid joint/shaft arrangement would not be able to change length. Shaft is "double-D" design.

NOTE—

Use of the slip joint style U-joint and boot required enlarging the notch in the '55 frame. For '72-'86 CJs, Flaming River offers simpler, bolt-in heavy duty replacement steering shafts that use these high performance joints. Steering gear depicted in Fig. 7-14 is a new replacement unit for '72-'76 CJs. Mount is Advanced Adapters kit for Saginaw steering retrofit to early Jeep chassis.

 Fig. 7-15

For my '55 CJ-5, the upper steering shaft has a CNC machined-billet (aircraft steel) Flaming River joint, splined to match a standard GM-style steering column/shaft. Using a sized hole-saw and arbor, I carefully cut firewall and dash holes for the column tube. A rubber grommet seals the firewall. Steering column is '70-circa GM truck design. Column is very similar to those used in AMC-era CJs, so this setup serves as a prototype.

NOTE—

Needle bearing Flaming River joints rate 670 lb-ft torque capacity! This is optimal for use with manual or power steering applications in '72-'86 CJs.

 Fig. 7-16

For the vintage CJ-5, an AMC/Jeep-type Saginaw gear conversion, Flaming River shaft and joints, and stock GM truck upper column fit neatly alongside F-head engine. Upper column is a complete, non-tilt type unit from a recycling yard. Appearance and function mimic OEM Jeep engineering for '72-up CJs.

CAUTION—

If you use a double-D steel shaft, cut the stock to proper length with a power hacksaw or other cold method. Drill a slight indexing dimple where U-joint setscrew secures the shaft. Use Loctite 242 on the setscrew and jam nut threads. Tighten screw securely, then tighten jam nut.

7

Fig. 7-17

Determining the fixed column angle and correct steering wheel location took considerable time. I shaped and fitted a flat plate to the GM steering column tube, welding the plate to the thin column material using gas method. (Finished weld looks much like TIG!) New custom mounting plate distributes load to the reinforced section of the instrument panel.

NOTE—

For many AMC-era CJ models, rebuilt OEM steering columns are currently available in the aftermarket. These tilt or non-tilt columns will satisfy most builders' needs. I built the steering column for my '55 CJ-5 around a '70-circa GM truck column, but this is not necessary for those AMC/Jeep CJs that use a similar OEM column. I also converted the '55 to Saginaw-type manual steering, using Advance Adapters' brackets and steering linkage pieces, Flaming River steering shaft components, and a new re-circulating ball-and-nut steering gear with dropped pitman arm, The gear and pitman arm supplied through 4WD Hardware, Inc.

Steering Column Cautions and Footnotes

Make certain the instrument panel will support the load! Manual steering requires far more effort than power assisted steering. If necessary, add reinforcement bracing to assure adequate strength.

The firewall end of my CJ-5's column now features a sealing grommet and the new column's OEM mounting plate/clamp. I made flat reinforcement plates to back up the column's firewall and dashboard mounts. The mounting bolts secure these plates, which distribute the column load over a wider area of body sheet metal. This clamping effect helps prevent the load from concentrating at the mounting holes drilled through the sheet metal. Use of large diameter fender-type flat washers help here, too.

Fig. 7-19 Primed area on dash is space allocated for new steering column's mounting plate. I cut the oblong hole in the dash with a hole-saw, trimming the sides with a die grinder and flat file. Primer protects bare metal and holes from rust.

Mounting hardware, including flat washers, lockwashers and nuts, is Grade 8. Former radio cutout in dash will receive a diamond plate patch. (See **Chapters 9** and **10** for gauge installation.)

Fig. 7-18 All column hardware was purchased from a recycling yard. I disassembled the unit and sandblasted the tube. After gas welding the plate in place, using mild steel filler rod, I cleaned, primed and painted the column, refurbished the turn signal mechanism, and greased the column bearings.

 Fig. 7-20

Steering wheel for builders wanting the flat, vintage look is a large marine application available from Grant. Diameter is within ¼-inch of OEM size for '55 CJ. I prefer a large steering wheel for any short-wheelbase Jeep with manual steering. Grant provides horn adapter kits, in this case patterned for the donor GM truck column and turn signal switch.

NOTE—

My approach for any short wheelbase Jeep is to stay with a larger-diameter steering wheel, the goal being better road feel and safer steering response. System works smoothly, wheel has the right "feel," and a modern, self-canceling turn signal switch, with four-way hazard lamp feature, is certainly a nice touch!

 Fig. 7-21

Small reshaping job at radiator side support was the last modification needed on '55 CJ-5. Steering column has a "stock look," with Flaming River components able to meet severe duty use. An OEM slip shaft is an option. Use a slip shaft of the correct length, measured with the sliding section centered.

NOTE—

The minor body lift created through the use of urethane body tub mounts allowed slightly more grille clearance for the new steering shaft on the '55 CJ-5. None of this is an issue for '72-up CJs designed for Saginaw steering. The '72-up frame was engineered for the forward-mounted steering gearbox plus a longer steering shaft and V-8 engine.

Brake System Service and Upgrades

7

CJ models covered within this book have either four-wheel drum brakes (1972-77) or drum rear/disc front brakes (1977-86). The 11"x2" four-wheel drum brakes serve reasonably well when dry, poorly when wet or overheated. Disc front brakes resist fade and provide better recovery after stream crossings.

AMC/Jeep Corporation brought the CJ's brakes to a reasonable standard. Any of the '72-'86 models have adequate stopping power under most driving conditions and provide ample braking for a full cargo load or pulling a small trailer.

Disc brakes are notably more efficient than drum brakes. In this section, you will find coverage of both systems. I also address the upgrading of CJ brakes, including two- and four-wheel disc brake conversions, improved hydraulic systems, and quality restorative brake work. Included is the installation of aftermarket stainless braided brake hoses and long-life, armor guard stainless steel brake tubing.

AUTHOR'S TIP!

AMC/Jeep's '72-'77 four-wheel drum brake CJs use substantial 11-inch diameter brakes. The only downside remains the wet brake issue inherent to any size drum brakes. Be cautious when crossing streams. Until the brake shoes dry, you may not have effective braking! To dry brakes faster, apply the brake pedal lightly while driving down a stretch of secluded, level trail. The heat/friction generated will help dry the lining. Don't trust the brakes until they dry out!

OEM Drum Brake Service

Anyone who has performed a brake job on domestic drum brake cars or trucks will recognize the '72-up CJ's two-piston wheel cylinders and modern self-energizing brake design. The self-adjuster mechanisms, a wheel cylinder mounted at the upper backing plate, and a self-energizing (duo-servo) layout provide a common, easy-to-service system.

AMC/Jeep CJs use duo-servo drum brakes. In this design, the single anchor pin is above the two-piston wheel cylinder. An adjuster link connects the lower ends of the two shoes. On the duo-servo system, the brake drum's rotational force and the shoe anchor pin create a "self-energizing" effect. For this reason, on duo-servo brakes, the longer lining goes toward the rear of the vehicle; the shorter lining mounts toward the front of the vehicle.

Brake Service Checklist

If you have read my **Jeep Owner's Bible**, you have a good understanding of brake system needs. For the '72-'86 Jeep vehicles, here are some general service tips:

1) Maximum oversize is noted on the drum, typically 0.060". If a drum is excessively distorted or requires more machining than 0.060" over stock diameter (0.030" on radius), replace the drum with a new one.

2) Hydraulic cylinders could be more than three decades old! Replace the hydraulic cylinders if any signs of corrosion, rust, pitting, scratches or deep scoring exist. Unless the cylinders have been replaced, plan on installing new wheel cylinders and a new master cylinder.

3) Replace worn brake hardware (springs, pins and retainers) as needed. Before installing new wheel cylinders, flush the brake lines with denatured alcohol or an ample amount of fresh brake fluid. Blow out the lines with clean (filtered) compressed air to remove all fluid or alcohol, any contaminants and moisture. Do not leave lines open to atmosphere, or moisture will begin to accumulate.

WARNING—

Brake fluid and denatured alcohol are extremely poisonous! Do not get in mouth, nicks, cuts or eyes!

4) Inspect hoses and lines for any signs of fatigue or corrosion. Replace pieces as needed, meeting OEM requirements. Buy D.O.T.-approved (double flared ends) brake tubing with flare nuts already installed. Such tubing is available at auto parts stores in a variety of straight lengths. Bend lines with a tubing bender. (See details later in this chapter.)

5) Always use D.O.T. approved brake hoses, T-fittings and brake hardware. Never substitute generic grade fittings in place of brake hardware! See your parts specialist or Jeep dealership for catalogs of genuine brake-grade hardware and fittings. Use OEM-equivalent replacement brake hoses when restoring or upgrading the brake system.

6) Use only denatured alcohol for cleaning brake cylinder parts. Wear chemical-proof mechanics gloves to prevent exposure to alcohol or brake fluid.

7) When handling parts, make certain your hands/gloves are clean and free of any petroleum solvents, "distillates" or mineral base products.

WARNING—

When cleaning or assembling brake rubber parts, never use petroleum or mineral-base oils or solvents. (When working around rubber parts, do not use brake parts cleaners that contain petroleum distillates!) Contaminated rubber parts can swell or rot, causing failure of the brake system!

8) Never mix silicone brake fluid with conventional D.O.T. 3 or D.O.T. 4 fluid. If the system is completely purged of all conventional fluid, you can convert to silicone brake fluid if you so desire. This is more expensive but provides better resistance to moisture contamination. *Do not add conventional brake fluid to silicone fluid or vice-versa!*

NOTE—

The Jeep 4WD vehicle used for fording streams is at higher risk for water contamination in the braking system. In addition to corrosion problems, diluted brake fluid has a lower boiling point that contributes to "fade." Changing brake fluid regularly can help maintain brake performance and protect hydraulic cylinders from corrosive moisture damage.

Brake Service Checklist (continued)

WARNING—

All OEM brake lining from the AMC/Jeep CJ era has asbestos content. Wear the proper protective mask, rated for filtering out asbestos particles, to prevent inhaling brake dust. Be certain to clean up any brake dust---the acceptable practice is an aqueous solution method. Do not use a conventional shop vacuum cleaner, as particles will pass through the filter and contaminate the air! Commercial brake and clutch shops now use aqueous solution brake parts washers that hold dust and debris in liquid suspension.

9) If the master cylinder or wheel cylinders show any signs of pitting, scoring, scratches or rust, replace them with new cylinders.

10) Hoses, tubing and brake hardware should be closely inspected for fatigue or signs of corrosion. Replace parts as needed, using correct, OEM-quality replacement parts.

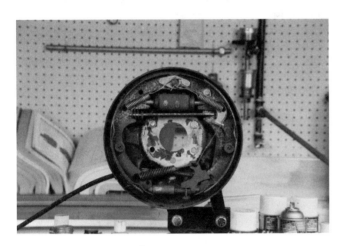

 Fig. 7-22

This is the typical brake layout for the left side of vehicle. Note that long length of very worn lining faces to rear of vehicle, while short lining faces forward. (This is common for duo-servo brake types.) Self-adjuster mechanism is visible. This is a simple, duo-servo/self-energizing brake design. (See brake service section later in this chapter for brake layout on left and right sides of vehicle.)

NOTE—

You can service the brakes with the drum removed and the backing plate assembly still attached to the rear axle flange or front steering knuckle! I have placed the backing plate and brake assembly in the Bench Mule fixture to ease illustration.

7

 Fig. 7-23

Front brake drum can be removed from hub by tapping hammer against the nubs at outer edge of drum. Remove any drum-to-hub retaining screws. If drum is stubborn, consider leaving the drum attached to the hub. Remove the locking hub then the hub/drum as an assembly.

Fig. 7-24

For access to the rear brake assembly, remove any drum-to-hub retaining screws, or spring washers, then the drum. Drum removal is similar to front brake setup. This right rear brake assembly on Model 20 axle shows signs of an axle seal leak that has damaged the brake lining. Although brakes could be serviced at this point, the hub and axle shaft require removal to address the seal leak.

Fig. 7-25

Master cylinder is mounted against firewall just forward of pedal mechanism and the vacuum booster (if so equipped). When loosening pipes, use a flarenut wrench on tubing nuts. Take care not to damage nut or tubing. Master cylinder is held in place with two bolts.

Pedal and Brake Adjustment Tips

The brake pedal-to-master cylinder pushrod is non-adjustable. Clearance is pre-set, and you should verify that there is a slight amount of play between the pushrod and master cylinder piston. The pedal, in its fully retracted position, should provide for clearance here. When you perform brake work, follow these adjustment checks:

1) Brake pedal concerns---When the brake pedal is fully retracted, there should be slight play before the pushrod moves the master cylinder piston. Too much clearance would limit the brake piston movement; too little clearance can keep fluid from returning to the reservoir through the compensating port(s). Fluid remaining trapped in the cylinder bore and brake lines can expand from heat and cause hazardous brake drag.

2) Pedal play check with manual brakes---Make sure pedal retracts to normal height, under proper spring tension, then grip the brake pedal. Play should translate as slight clearance felt between the rod end and piston as you gently move the pedal downward. The piston should retract completely to its snap-ring seat with the pedal released. Adjust pedal return height, if necessary, to assure slight rod-to-piston clearance.

3) Models with power booster---On models equipped with a power booster, there should be slight pedal-to-booster play. There should also be slight clearance between the booster pushrod and the master cylinder piston. This booster rod-to-master cylinder piston clearance is usually measured with a bridge gauge. You can simulate this gauge with a depth gauge/caliper. The goal is to assure that there is slight clearance to allow the master cylinder piston to retract completely when the pedal releases.

4) Drum-to-lining adjustment---On '72-'86 CJs, the brake adjustment should only be necessary during brake service. Adjust the brakes by pushing the self-adjuster lever away from the adjuster star wheel. When adjusted properly, without any sign of drag, you can allow the self-adjuster mechanism to complete the adjustment. Drive the vehicle backward, apply the brake pedal firmly then release the brake pedal fully. Continue backing the Jeep up then again apply the brake pedal firmly. Go forward and apply the brakes, then back up and apply the brakes again. Repeat this pattern a half-dozen times, and all drum brakes should be adjusted properly!

NOTE---

You can rely upon the self-adjusters to keep the drum brakes adjusted properly. To assure proper function of the self-adjuster system, follow steps in the service section of this chapter. If self-adjusters are frozen or do not work properly, the described "drum-to-lining adjustment" procedure will not work effectively.

7

5) Always check the brake fluid level after adjusting the brakes. With brakes adjusted properly, apply the pedal a few times to center lining and to position the brake pistons in the wheel cylinders. Make certain that the area around the master cylinder cap is clean. With clean hands or mechanic's gloves, remove the cap or cover. Top off fluid, and replace the cap or cover.

NOTE---

With brakes seated and bled, I fill the dual master cylinder reservoirs to within ¼-inch of reservoir rims. Make certain the cap seats fully, and place the retainer clip into place securely. Pump the brake pedal, and look carefully for any signs of seepage around the master cylinder cap seal.

6) Test-drive the vehicle to assure that brakes work properly with no pull or grab. If pull is present, make certain that the self-adjusters work properly. Back up the vehicle and drive it forward several times, applying the brakes firmly in each direction. This will set the adjusters and seat the lining.

NOTE—
When servicing brakes with self-adjusters, make certain the adjusters work freely and properly. Clean the adjuster, and apply brake grease or 'Anti-Seize' to the threads. Wipe off all excess grease to avoid risk of sloughing off and contaminating the brake lining.

Parking Brake Adjustment

The rear wheel parking brakes require an adjustment at the E-brake cable. When renewing the brake shoes, the cable will need adjustment.

Parking brake adjustment---With the E-brake lever released fully and slack in the E-brake cable, make sure the cable and equalizer are in good shape and moving freely.

Free up any rough or binding parts. With brake drums completely cool, adjust the cable to provide a slight drag at each rear wheel. Back off the adjuster nut until the drag is just gone. Tighten the lock nut (if used) on the cable adjuster.

Disc Brake Conversions

Most owners will find the '72-up OEM brake system adequate. If the drum or disc brakes are in good condition (good lining, no glazing or warpage, hydraulic system in good condition), the brakes should work well. The AMC/Jeep CJ's OEM steering and brakes work fine for the kind of trail and on-highway use that most owners intend.

Your Jeep needs may, however, require additional brake capacity, perhaps due to the use of substantially oversized tires. Warn Industries and others offer retrofit disc brake caliper mounting kits, heavy-duty wheel hub upgrade kits, and even extreme duty, full-floating rear axle shaft conversion kits.

While retrofitting disc brakes might seem involved, Warn's approach relies upon the commonality of Spicer/Dana axle flange patterns. Warn's well-conceived front and rear disc brake conversion kits for AMC-era CJs and other Spicer/Dana axles provide a straightforward installation.

The Warn heavy-duty internal spline wheel hubs will work with all Jeep CJ front spindles. This provides a platform for use of the OEM 11-inch front drum brakes, the OEM disc front brakes, or a Warn disc brake conversion.

As for semi-floating rear axle flange patterns, Spicer 41-2 rear axles were introduced with CJ-2A models. The '44' rear axle remains popular from CJ-3As into the AMC/Jeep era. (Dana 44s are similar.) This rear axle flange bolt circle pattern is the same diameter as the Jeep CJ's front steering knuckle/spindle flange pattern.

NOTE—

All of these Spicer-Dana axles, including the Spicer 25 and 27 closed-knuckle front axles and Dana 30 open-knuckle front axle, share a common flange circle pattern! You will see how this plays out in four-wheel disc brake conversions.

NOTE—

At the time of this printing, Warn Industries is capable of cutting axle shafts and splines for most popular Spicer/Dana light truck or Jeep axles, including centered and offset differentials. Recall from the axle chapter that I upgraded the Spicer 44's rear differential spline count to the stronger 30-spline type for use of the Truetrac locking differential.

Do you need all of this? Well, that depends upon your use of the Jeep. For safe highway use and light hauling, for flat towing the vehicle, certainly for a larger powerplant and modern accessories, these changes often make sense.

 Fig. 7-26

Warn Industries provides a disc-caliper mounting bracket that bolts in place of the OEM brake backing plate. The plate "clocks" one bolt hole rearward to clear the steering knuckle bearing cap on the earlier Jeep's closed-knuckle front end.

NOTE—

Figure 7-26 depicts my '55 CJ's closed-knuckle front axle with button-head spindle mounting studs installed. This conversion is similar to the open-knuckle retrofit for later Dana 30 or 44 axles, which already use studs and do not require a button-head stud conversion. The Warn caliper mounts will fit the front or rear axles, replacing the drum brake backing plates.

7

Fig. 7-27

Loctite adds insurance with Grade 8 top-lock (all steel, self-locking type) nuts.

 Fig. 7-28

Loctite 242 on nut threads, I torque nuts in stages to a minimum of 480 lb-in (40 lb-ft), first in cross, then re-checked after parts settle.

◀ **Fig. 7-29**

Warn's kit consists of all bearings, seals and hardware needed to install the Warn wheel hubs. These hubs accept 11-inch OEM drums or later CJ Jeep rotors (not supplied in kit). For use with rotors, longer shoulder bolts press through the rotor and hub flange, securing the rotor to the hub. Use a press for this chore. Note the inexpensive bearing packer for inserting fresh grease.

CAUTION—

Use care when installing bearing cups. I carefully install cups with either my hydraulic press or with a hefty brass punch and hammer. The cup must enter the hub bore perfectly straight. Cups must seat completely. When using the press, I take an old bearing cup and place its thin edge against the new cup. Applying even pressure against the old cup, I carefully press the new cup into the wheel hub bore. If you use a brass punch, follow by removing any debris. Do not scratch or damage the bearing cup! Wear safety eye protection when using the press or a punch and hammer!

◀ **Fig. 7-30**

Seals work with OEM earlier Jeep spindle. Pack inner wheel bearings with fresh grease. Swab a liberal amount of grease into the housing recess and space between the bearings. Install inner bearing and grease seal.

NOTE—

Warn will detail which bearings and seals to use in your application. I used the '55 CJ-5's original spindle with this hub, fitting appropriately sized bearings and seals. Warn wheel hub offers internal splines for the free-wheeling/locking hub mount. This is the strongest design available, common to later J-trucks/Wagoneers and many full-size domestic 4WD trucks.

Fig. 7-31

Rather than use the Warn wheel bearing nuts, I opted for the OEM hex nuts common to CJs. This arrangement works fine with the OEM spindle and Warn's wheel hub. Advantage is a common, easy-to-identify wheel bearing adjustment method. New double nuts and lock plate kits come from 4WD Hardware, Inc.

Fig. 7-32

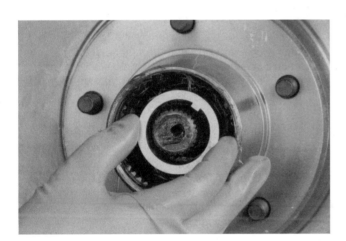

Freshly packed bearings and wheel hub cavity make this hub ready for outer bearing installation. Bearing in place, the thrust washer aligns with the spindle's groove and fits against the bearing.

7

Fig. 7-33

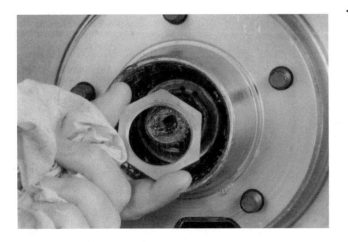

New OEM replacement hex nut fits against thrust washer.

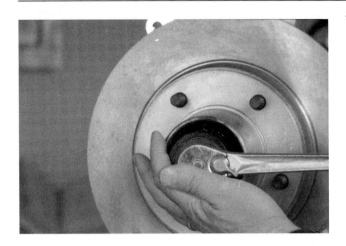

◀ Fig. 7-34

Tighten inner bearing to OEM specifications while rotating the wheel hub assembly. OEM setting is to tighten inner nut until wheel binds (50 lb-ft maximum), then back off approximately one hex flat of the nut. Desired result is no side-play.

◀ Fig. 7-35

Confirming endplay with a dial indicator (after outer locknut has been tightened to 50 lb-ft) is far more precise than "no sideplay." Find endplay by gripping rotor at 3 and 9 o'clock, then pushing straight in and pulling straight out. The measured lateral/axial movement is endplay.

NOTE—

Do not make the bearings too tight! Zero endplay is not bearing preload. If in doubt, loosen slightly, and try again. Once you have slight endplay with the outer nut secured, readjust nuts to just remove axial movement with the locknut secured to 50 lb-ft of torque.

◀ Fig. 7-36

Inner nut adjusted properly, install the lockwasher plate. Install outer locking hex nut. Torque lock nut to minimum 50 lb-ft of torque.

 Fig. 7-37

Outer lock nut tight, I confirm endplay with a dial indicator. Factory wheel hub/bearing adjustment calls for no binding and "no sideplay." Respecting these specifications, I strive for a dial indicator reading of 0.001" endplay movement for this kind of full-size truck wheel hub intended to run with disc brakes.

NOTE—

If you use the original wheel hub and drum arrangement, simply follow the OEM "no sideplay" adjustment procedure: 1) tighten inner nut to 50 lb-ft, then loosen one hex flat (1/6-turn), 2) install lock plate and outer nut---torqued to 50 lb-ft, and 3) check for no binding and no sideplay. This worked for forty years of CJs!

Fig. 7-38

If sideplay or endplay checks correct (with locknut secured to proper torque), the lock plate is ready for tab bending.

7

Fig. 7-39

Carefully bend a tab inward. Do not press against the bearing cage! Bend tab snugly against a hex flat of the inner nut.

 Fig. 7-40

I build a dam of grease outboard of the inner and outer wheel bearings. Grease shown here is packed against the bearing and fills the space around the nuts. I use Texaco Starplex 2 for the bearings and dam. Dam is added grease protection and helps seal against contamination or moisture.

◄ **Fig. 7-41**

Close-up view shows lock tab bent securely against inner hex nut. Combination of two nuts jammed tightly together (sandwiching lock plate) plus bent lock plate offers protection against nuts loosening. This is a safety measure and must be done properly.

 ◄ **Fig. 7-42**

Following instructions furnished with the free-wheel/locking hubs, the splined mechanism fits over the lightly greased axle shaft splines and into the greased splines of the wheel hub. Outer snap ring locks hub mechanism into the housing. Make certain this ring seats properly.

NOTE—

In this vintage CJ application, the earlier closed-knuckle Jeep Wagoneer (27-spline) outer axle shaft's end has a snap ring groove. This snap ring controls shaft end float. Secure snap ring in place. For my '55 CJ's Spicer 25 front axle, I adapted early Wagoneer (closed-knuckle) outer axle shafts. These axle shafts have become rare, and were there enough demand for vintage closed-knuckle conversions, Warn might consider duplicating this shaft in a 4340 steel alloy. When fitting Warn's internal spline wheel hubs to the popular AMC-era CJs, you will not encounter any axle shaft challenges. There will be no need for modifications.

 Fig. 7-43

Here is the closed-knuckle Spicer 25 front axle with its disc brake upgrade! Warn engineers made this possible by patterning the disc brake bracket to the standard Spicer/Dana six-stud spindle and axle flange dimensions. Bracket for the caliper takes the place of OEM brake backing plate. The open-knuckle Dana 30 conversion looks similar.

 Fig. 7-44

Rear view shows clocking of caliper bracket away from steering knuckle bearing caps. Position works well and does not impact performance. Calipers lie out of harm's way for trail use of the vehicle. For Dana 30 installations, follow Warn's instructions for bracket positioning.

7

 Fig. 7-45

Rear/front rotors and hubs are identical. Warn's spindle for rear full-floater patterns off a common (later Jeep) bearing arrangement. Rebuilt 'Sure Stop' calipers from All Drum and Rotor Warehouse (see **Appendix**) came fitted with pads. This is a common GM S-truck/Blazer caliper and mounting pin arrangement that Warn engineered into the conversion.

NOTE—

Warn instructions indicate which components fit and match properly. When securing parts for the disc brake conversion, consult Warn's catalog and technical information to be sure of a safe and correct fit-up!

Necessary Master Cylinder Modification for Disc Brake Conversions

When converting from drum to disc brakes, you must remove the check valves from behind the OE master cylinder's tube seats (the seats where the pipes and flare nuts fit into the cylinder). These check valves, designed to hold enough residual pressure in the hydraulic system to keep wheel cylinder cups from collapsing, will cause brake drag on disc brake calipers.

Disc brake calipers do not require residual pressure. The caliper piston's seal will hold without pressure applied. In fact, residual pressure will only cause the pads to drag against the rotor face. Normally, the disc pads retract only to the edge of the rotor, unlike drum brake shoes, which will retract to allow actual clearance between the shoe lining and brake drum.

On drum brake systems that have check valves at the master cylinder's tube seats, residual pressure is typically 8-12 (maximum) PSI. Residual pressure will only have an impact within the wheel cylinders. This pressure is not enough force to move the pistons and brake shoes. The brake shoe retraction springs produce more pressure than the residual pressure. These retraction springs overcome the residual pressure's lighter force against the wheel cylinder pistons and cups. Pistons stay in the retracted position. Rubber cup lips remain expanded, preventing fluid leaks and keeping air from entering the system.

Where residual pressure is desirable for drum brakes, it is a hazard on a disc brake system. Disc brake pads dragging on a rotor will warp the rotor, glaze the pads and cause brake fluid fade. Disc brake master cylinders do not use check valves on the line(s) feeding the disc brakes.

A combined drum rear/disc front brake system sometimes uses a check valve on the drum brake line. No check valve will be found on the disc brake line.

Some drum rear/disc front brake Jeep master cylinders do not use a check valve at either master cylinder tube seat.

CAUTION—

If you convert from drum to disc brakes, be aware of any check valves, anywhere within the hydraulic brake system. Eliminate residual pressure on hydraulic lines feeding the disc brake calipers.

If you convert to disc brakes, front or rear, note whether the master cylinder has check valves and springs behind the tube seats. Remove the master cylinder's tube seat(s) on the line or lines feeding the disc brakes. Eliminate the check valve(s) and spring(s). Install either the original tube seats or, preferably, new tube seats.

Before you reuse a tube seat, make certain that no burrs are present and the seat is free of debris. Be certain that the tube seats do not leak! New tube seats are available in master cylinder rebuild kits or from your Jeep dealer. The tapered brass seats press into the housing. Use a clean spare flare nut to seat the tube seats (torque to approximately15 lb-ft). Tube seats can be removed by threading a sheet metal screw into the passageway then prying beneath the screw's head with two opposed screwdrivers.

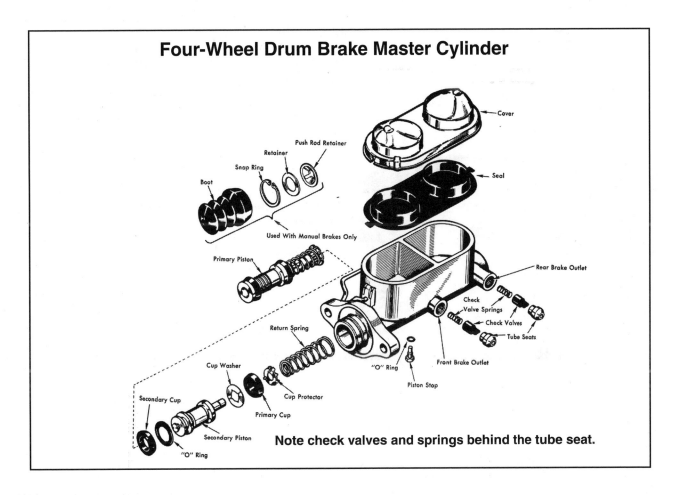

Four-Wheel Drum Brake Master Cylinder

Note check valves and springs behind the tube seat.

7

Warn's Wheel Hub Bearing Adjustment Method

Warn's bearing adjusters appear similar to full-size domestic truck designs. These illustrations provide a look at the alternative methods of securing and adjusting the wheel bearings. The Warn kit includes these adjuster nuts and hardware.

NOTE—

I have provided two methods for adjusting the wheel bearings: 1) the OEM hex nuts with thrust washer and lock plate and 2) the Warn inner and outer four-lug nuts with thrust washer and pin-type lock plate. If you prefer the use of OEM parts, which lend themselves to readily recognizable service procedures in the field, the OEM option works well.

 Fig. 7-46

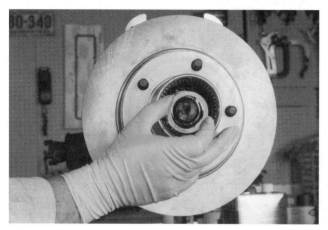

Bearings and hub cavity have been packed with Starplex 2 grease. Here, I have already installed the dust "V-seal" on the Warn spindle. The inner bearing is in place with a grease dam swabbed outside the bearing. Inner seal installed, the hub is on the spindle. The greased outer bearing fitted into place, the thrust washer (shown) now goes outboard of the bearing.

 Fig. 7-47

Warn inner adjuster nut has a locating pin that faces outward. After adjusting the inner nut, this pin will index with holes in the interlock washer/plate. Make certain that the pin faces outward!

 Fig. 7-48

The adjuster and lock nut resemble full-size truck OEM types. These Warn nuts use a common Dana/Spicer four-lug socket.

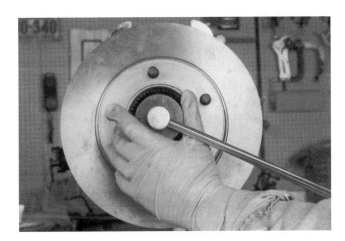

◀ **Fig. 7-49**

Torque the adjuster nut to specification (50 ft-lb) while rotating the wheel hub. Since this is the rear axle, I went with the "no sideplay" approach and backed the adjuster off 1/6 turn (55-65-degrees). Goal here is no bind with zero endplay. I intend to confirm with a dial indicator.

NOTE—

Warn says to tighten at 50 lb-ft, then back off one-half turn and re-torque to 3-5 lb-ft (36-60 lb-in). Carefully install interlock washer/plate before setting outer nut at 30 lb-ft (Warn's recommendation) of torque. I like a tighter outer nut setting than this, which will require checking endplay with a dial indicator. My outer nut setting is at 50 lb-ft.

7

◀ **Fig. 7-50**

Carefully align the lockwasher, indexing a hole with the pin. If necessary, you can flip the washer over to line up a different hole.

 Fig. 7-51

Note that pin seats in notch. Make certain the lockwasher remains flat against the nut, with the pin engaged, as you carefully install the outer lock nut.

Fig. 7-52

Warn's outer nut uses setscrews. Make certain setscrews face outward.

Fig. 7-53

I torque outer nut to a minimum 50 lb-ft. This nut seats the interlock plate/washer and locks down the inner nut.

 Fig. 7-54

Warn has designed the setscrews to pick up at least one notch. Tighten the setscrews securely. Here I use an Allen wrench and adjustable pliers to snug up the setscrews. Make sure that at least one screw seats through an indexing slot.

Fig. 7-55

Using a dial indicator, check endplay of wheel hub. At rear of vehicle, I strive for zero (0.000") endplay without any sign of binding. With torque driving through Warn's straight rear axle shafts, I opted for zero clearance rather than the slightest endplay. This will keep the axle shaft on center.

NOTE—

When adjusting wheel bearings, with caliper off or pads retracted, make sure the wheel hub turns without resistance.

7

Fig. 7-56

Rear axle shaft snap ring fits groove at end of Warn's axle shaft. Build a grease dam outside the outer wheel bearing, and lightly grease all splines. Install the free-wheel hub ("hub-lock") internal mechanism. Install the snap ring at the axle shaft end.

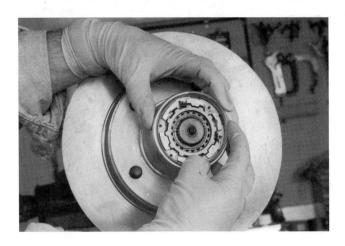

 Fig. 7-57

Seat outer (large diameter) lock ring in the wheel hub groove. This holds the hub mechanism in place.

 Fig. 7-58

The rest of the hub pieces go into place, including this spacer tube used with the rear axle (full-floater conversion) hub-lock installation. Hub-lock cover has a rubber O-ring seal. Grease this seal to reduce risk of damage to the O-ring during installation.

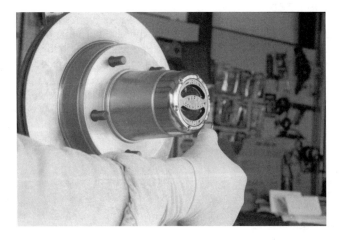

 Fig. 7-59

Final step is hub cover installation. Make certain tiny O-rings seat at heads of long Allen screws. I put Loctite 242 on threads of cover screws. Torque to specification provided by Warn. Do not over-tighten, or damage to the O-rings will occur. Check rotation of wheel hub on "Free" and "Lock" modes to assure safe operation.

OEM Wheel Bearing Service and Adjustment

Jeep wheel bearings have been serviced in the most primitive outdoor settings. The long backcountry trip involving stream and water hole crossings might lead to packing the wheel bearings at your campsite. This section will help keep your Jeep safe and moving ahead.

NOTE—

The '86 CJ-7 is the model depicted. One upgrade is employed, the use of Warn's internal-spline wheel hubs in place of the OEM 5-bolt locking hub arrangement. As presented here, the wheel bearing adjustment is the same as the method for the OEM wheel hubs.

CAUTION—

Use care when installing bearing cups. I carefully install cups with either my hydraulic press or with a hefty brass punch and hammer. The cup must enter the hub bore perfectly straight. Cups must seat completely. When using the press, I take an old bearing cup and place its thin edge against the new cup. Applying even pressure against the old cup, I carefully press the new cup into the wheel hub bore. If you use a brass punch, follow by removing any debris. Do not scratch or damage the bearing cup! Wear safety eye protection when using the press or a punch and hammer!

7

◀ **Fig. 7-60**

These hubs and rotors for late '81-'86 CJs have a 5-bolt locking hub flange. This setup is notorious for failing under severe duty use. The earlier 6-bolt flange and locking hub work much better. I opted for Warn's internal spline hub, a heavier-duty truck design.

◀ **Fig. 7-61**

The hub removal from the rotors is easier with an air hammer. Use extreme care not to slip off the wheel studs! Wear eye protection, as these studs are very hard metal.

 Fig. 7-62

Installing new wheel studs through the rotor flange and wheel hub is best done with a hydraulic press. The studs must seat completely. I will press these studs in cross, followed by going around the bolt circle a couple of times.

 Fig. 7-63

This assemblage of parts is the wheel bearing sets for the '86 CJ. Warn's internal-spline wheel hub will work with the OEM spindle and seals. Using OEM hex nuts, the wheel bearing installation and adjustment procedure will be the same as with the original wheel hub.

 Fig. 7-64

You can drive the cup into place with these tools. I use the old bearing cup, upside down against the new bearing cup, as a driver tool. The brass punch is an alternative. In either approach, you must be certain that the new cup seats solidly and squarely. Also, remove any brass debris!

Fig. 7-65

Inner and outer cups installed, I pack clean wheel hub cavity with grease. The recess should be thoroughly coated with a thick swab of fresh grease, the same grease used to pack the bearings. Grease the cups, too.

Fig. 7-66

When the bearing is thoroughly packed with grease and installed, build a "dam" at the outer edge of the inner and outer bearings. This grease can draw into a hot bearing.

7

Fig. 7-67

I pack the inner flange and lip of the grease seal.

 Fig. 7-68

Here is my "seal driver." I use the old bearing cup as a driver tool, supplemented by a block of wood and hammer blows. Drive the seal squarely and straight! Seal's outer face fits flush with the hub.

◀ **Fig. 7-69**

Here is an inexpensive bearing packer from NAPA. Note that the bearing grease presses up through each roller. If you hand pack without a packer tool, you must squeeze grease up through each of the rollers!

CAUTION—

Always make sure the bearing is thoroughly clean and dry before repacking. Make certain there is no solvent residue left on the bearings or wheel hubs after cleaning. Most shops now use citrus-soap parts washing machines for this task. My washer heats to 180° F, and parts like bearings and hubs will flash dry after removal, completely clean and free of any solvents or grease!

WARNING—

If you air dry bearings and hubs with compressed air, do not spin the bearings! Spinning a bearing with compressed air is dangerous and could damage the bearing. Hard steel bearing rollers could fly from the cage at speed, causing severe bodily injury!

NOTE—

A packed bearing is just that---packed with grease between each of the rollers. In the field, this can be achieved by placing a glob of grease in your palm then clawing at the edge of the grease with the wide end of the bearing cage. Repeat until you see fresh grease come up through the rollers and out the narrow end of the cage. When you've gone around the bearing one full time, go around at least once more to make sure the grease fills each roller space! Saturate the bearing with grease then swab a liberal amount of grease around the outside of the bearing.

◄ **Fig. 7-70**

After packing the roller spaces, swab a liberal amount of bearing grease around the outside of the bearing. This is crucial to bearing life and safety. I use Texaco Starplex 2 type grease, a high quality lubricant designed for wheel bearing, U-joint and chassis uses.

◄ **Fig. 7-71**

Here, outer bearing is in place, a dam of grease built around its outer edge. I grease the walls of the wheel hub to protect the hub from moisture and provide easy installation of the internal-spline locking hub.

7

◄ **Fig. 7-72**

Consistent with an OEM hub installation, these OEM thrust-washers, lock washers and double nut sets will be required. I could have used Warn's four-lug nuts with interlock plate but opted to use the OEM Jeep CJ hardware instead. My strategy was an easy-to-recognize wheel bearing adjustment method. The spindle is the OEM CJ-7 type. Five-bolt locking hub flange is evident in OEM wheel hub (*bottom*).

 Fig. 7-73

4WD Hardware, Inc., was my source for new spindle nuts and lock/plate washers. OEM-type thrust washer goes into place first. This washer indexes with the notch/keyway in the spindle.

◄ **Fig. 7-74**

The inner adjuster nut is tightened against the thrust washer. Rotate the wheel hub as you tighten the nut. This will seat the bearings properly.

◄ **Fig. 7-75**

Tighten the inner nut to 50 lb-ft torque while rotating the wheel hub. Back off the nut 1/6 turn (one hex flat).

Fig. 7-76

Install a new lock/plate washer. Index the washer with the spindle's notched keyway.

Fig. 7-77

Torque the outer nut to 50 lb-ft. The factory adjustment is no lateral movement of the hub (zero endplay). Make sure the bearings rotate freely. This is a simple adjustment method, easily performed in the field. The origins of the CJ wheel bearing adjustment date to the MB/WWII Jeep models.

NOTE—

For bearing life and accuracy, I still prefer an endplay check with a dial indicator. On Warn's full-size truck style wheel hubs, I set endplay at 0.001" to assure minimal lateral movement without any risk of bearing binding. Domestic full-size trucks that use this style wheel hub generally call for at least 0.001"-0.005" endplay, checked with a dial indicator. A J-truck/Wagoneer front axle like the one seen in the 'Steering Linkage' section of this chapter (installed on the '72 CJ-5) would benefit from a bearing endplay adjustment of 0.001"-0.005". Using a dial indicator, I set endplay between 0.001" and 0.003" on full-size truck '44' axles.

Dial indicator on magnetic stand measures wheel bearing endplay. This measurement indicates how much lateral/axial movement exists at the wheel bearings. Hold hub at 3 and 9 o'clock, push straight in, and pull straight out. Measurable movement is endplay.

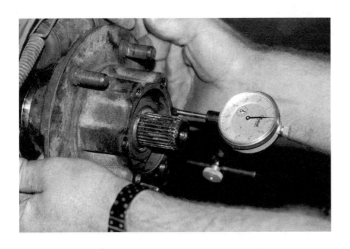

7

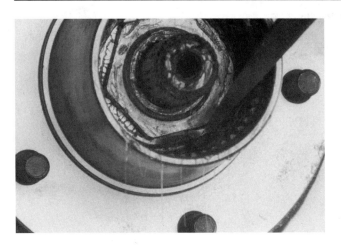

◄ Fig. 7-78

Bend the lockwasher inward against a flat. I use this pry bar end, carefully avoiding the outer wheel bearing and its cage. Make sure the tab is flat against the nut.

NOTE—

Typically, lock plate washer is bent inward against one hex nut flat. If necessary or prudent, one tab can also be bent outward against the outer nut's flat. Stay away from the bearing cage when bending lockwasher tabs!

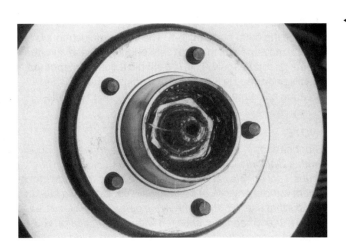

◄ Fig. 7-79

Whether a Warn wheel hub or OEM type, I pack additional wheel-bearing grease outboard of the outer wheel bearing. If the bearing's grease becomes hot, this dam of grease is available to support the bearing. It also acts as a barrier to any moisture seeping into the hub.

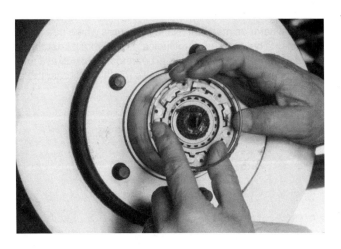

◄ Fig. 7-80

For those who use the Warn upgrade wheel hub or a full-size truck OEM axle with internal spline hubs, this is the hub installation. Slide the inner hub onto the lightly greased axle shaft splines. Hub must clear the end of the shaft and allow for installation of the snap ring.

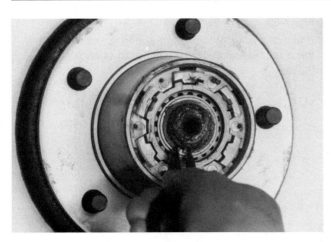

 Fig. 7-81

Snap ring retains the end of the internal spline hub. This keeps the hub in place and also sets the axle in-and-out "float." OEM CJ's 5-bolt locking hubs also use a retaining snap ring. The snap-ring fits on the axle shaft end, outboard of the hub's internal mechanism.

 Fig. 7-82

The internal spline type hub lock uses fine Allen screws with O-rings under their heads. Torque to Warn's specification, which is very light. All these screws do is hold the hub lock cover and O-ring in their place.

NOTE—

The internal splines, not the hub lock, take the axle shaft's heavy torque loads. The inner hub mechanism is held in the splined wheel hub with a large diameter lock ring. On CJs with OEM 5- and 6-bolt locking hubs, the hub lock-to-wheel flange bolts absorb all of this torque. This is why the '81-up, 5-bolt locking hubs do not hold up well.

Installing New Wheel Cylinders and Brake Shoes

Drum brake service is a part of all '72-'86 Jeep CJ maintenance and restoration. Through early 1977, all CJs had front and rear drum brakes. Subsequent models equipped with drum rear/disc front brakes still require drum brake service. Unless you convert to aftermarket 4-wheel disc brakes, you will deal with drum brake service.

Cleaning Brake Parts Safely

The cleanliness of my brake parts is the result of running the brake assemblies through a parts washing machine. When doing brake work, beware of the asbestos hazard.

OEM CJ brake shoe linings and disc pads contain hazardous asbestos. Avoid breathing dust. Do not air-blow these parts. The common commercial procedure for containing brake system asbestos is to soak and clean the drums, shoes, calipers, rotors, pads, dust shields and backing plates with an aqueous solution, using a special brake parts washer and catch basin.

If you do not have such equipment, try washing down these parts with a solution made up of water and dishwashing (grease dissolving) liquid. Catch the solution as it comes off the parts. Dispose of the solution and contaminants properly.

Protect yourself and others from brake dust exposure! Use an asbestos-rated respirator when performing brake work. Never use your shop vacuum around brake dust. The dust will pass through the vacuum's filter and contaminate the air. Dispose of materials and debris properly.

If you do a good deal of brake work, invest in a safe, aqueous solution brake parts washer or a "bioremediating" parts/brake cleaning machine! This will make brake and clutch work much safer.

 Fig. 7-83

Brake disassembly begins with spring removal. Note that this is the left rear brake assembly with self-adjusting brakes.

 Fig. 7-84

Emergency/parking brake lever attaches with a horseshoe clip. Wave washer fits beneath the clip. Lever pin is above and to right of wheel cylinder.

 Fig. 7-85

Parking brake strut fits between the lever and the forward facing shoe. Note the position of the anti-rattle spring. Retainer removal tool is seen leaning against the trailing brake shoe.

◀ **Fig. 7-86**

Removing the retainer clips, springs and shoe hold-down pins will release the shoes. Parking/E-brake lever is shown still attached to the E-brake cable. If you are merely replacing shoes, stop here.

◀ **Fig. 7-87**

Brake pipe disconnected with a flarenut wrench, you can un-bolt the wheel cylinder from the backing plate. If you plan to lightly hone the bore, you are still better off removing the cylinder. This will enable thoroughly washing and drying the cylinder before reassembly. In most instances, there will be too much pitting or corrosion to chance rebuilding the cylinder, and a new cylinder would be recommended.

> **CAUTION—**
>
> *Jeep does not describe brake cylinder honing in its service manuals. Master cylinders and wheel cylinders are now regarded as disposable if there is any sign of scratches, corrosion or scoring. Modern master cylinders, in particular, should not be honed, as manufacturers use special boring and factory finishing methods that harden the surface of the bores. Honing can cut through this hardened surface and leave these cylinders vulnerable to more rapid wear or even failure.*

7

> **WARNING—**
>
> *Cleaning brake hydraulic system parts with brake fluid or denatured alcohol is recommended. Never use mineral or petroleum-based solvents or cleaners around brake assemblies that contain rubber parts.*

◀ **Fig. 7-88**

This is a brand new Mopar replacement wheel cylinder. Original wheel cylinders showed rust, corrosive pitting and glazing. I opted for replacement with Genuine Mopar cylinders, which come complete with all internal parts and dust boots, ready to install. I use Loctite 242 on threads and torque the 5/16" stud size wheel cylinder mounting bolts to 18 lb-ft. Recheck the torque after testing the brakes.

 Fig. 7-89

This grease has been with me for a very long time. It is "brake lube," a lithium type grease designed for shoe-to-backing plate surfaces and anchor pins. *Do not use this grease on or near rubber parts or brake lining!*

◁ **Fig. 7-90**

Reducing friction, this grease is applied lightly. Note that I place it at the four shoe contact points and on the shoe anchor (near top of backing plate). Too much of this grease could seep onto the shoes and ruin the lining. Avoid use around rubber pieces.

◁ **Fig. 7-91**

I hold the retainer pin from the backside of the backing plate. Using a retainer tool, I compress the retainer and spring, turning the retainer 90° until it seats squarely with the pin seat. This is the front facing shoe with shorter lining.

 Fig. 7-92

Here, I have attached the E-brake lever to the rear (long lining) shoe. The wave washer and horseshoe clip are in place. Note that the horseshoe clip closes completely to assure that it will stay put in service. This is the left side backing plate and brake assembly.

 Fig. 7-93

Strut bar for E-brake and the wheel cylinder pushrods are in place here.

7

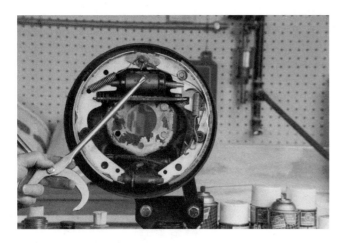

 Fig. 7-94

Put the plate over the anchor pin and install the self-adjuster lever's cable and the first (forward) shoe retractor spring. Note that self-adjuster is in place, as is the cable guide on rear shoe. Second retractor spring attaches to the rear shoe through the guide. This holds the guide in place when you hook the spring on the anchor pin.

 Fig. 7-95

Springs installed properly will not interfere with the wheel cylinder's dust boots. Note the relationship of the parts at this point.

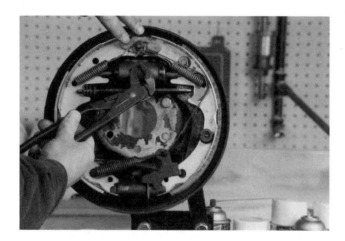

◀ **Fig. 7-96**

Now the springs are all in place. The self-adjuster mechanism is also hooked up. I squeeze the retractor spring ends to near parallel at the anchor pin. This is the parts layout.

◀ **Fig. 7-97**

The E-brake strut bar and the anti-rattle spring are in place. Check that they fit in their slots.

 Fig. 7-98

This is the self-adjuster mechanism in proper position. Note that this is the left rear brake assembly. The cable comes from the rear shoe to the lever, which then ratchets against the adjuster star wheel.

 Fig. 7-99

Here I lift the self-adjuster lever by pulling the cable. Note how this works: lever moves against the upper wheel teeth and turns the adjuster. This only happens when there is enough clearance between the shoes and drum. Backing the vehicle up and applying the brakes enables the cable to pull up on the adjuster lever. It is crucial that the adjuster wheel can turn readily. I clean and grease adjuster threads with Anti-Seize.

NOTE—

Make sure the adjuster turns in the correct direction, expanding the adjuster as each click occurs. Do not swap these parts from one side of the vehicle to the other. Test the adjuster to be certain it will work with the drum in place. Simulate the pull on the cable. In service, the adjuster will only rotate if there is excess shoe-to-drum clearance.

7

 Fig. 7-100

Here is a quick run through the right rear brake assembly. Note that the right front wheel on four-wheel drum brake systems is similar, without the emergency/parking brake mechanism.

Steering and Brake Service

◄ **Fig. 7-101**
Springs come loose first.

◄ **Fig. 7-102**
Strut bar and anti-rattle spring removed here, shoes are now accessible.

◄ **Fig. 7-103**
I use internal snap ring pliers to spread the horseshoe clip on the E-brake lever.

 Fig. 7-104

Retainer springs and pins removed, the shoes come loose. Note the direction that the self-adjuster faces.

◀ **Fig. 7-105**

After washing parts thoroughly to remove all debris and dust, I polish the wheel cylinder pushrods on my wire brush. This is a new Mopar wheel cylinder. Lube the pins with a few drops of clean brake fluid to ease installation into the wheel cylinder boots.

7

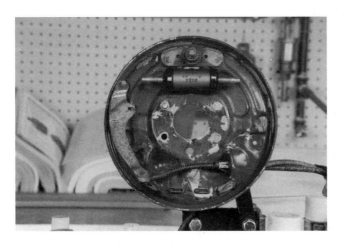

◀ **Fig. 7-106**

Parts stripped from backing plate, assembly is ready to begin. Loctite 242 on threads, I torque 5/16" stud size wheel cylinder bolts to 18 lb-ft. Recheck the torque after testing the brakes.

◀ **Fig. 7-107**

Apply brake lube to backing plate and anchor pin, as shown in Fig. 7-89. This is special white lithium grease formulated for brake shoe assembly.

◀ **Fig. 7-108**

Install horseshoe clip securely. Here, shoe is in place with pin, spring and retainer clip. This is long lining, the rear shoe on the right side of the vehicle.

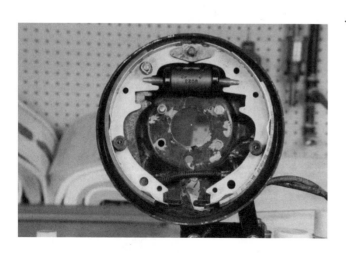

◀ **Fig. 7-109**

Lead (front) shoe on right side of vehicle is now installed.

 Fig. 7-110

Parking strut bar and self-adjuster are in place. Note anti-rattle spring in position.

◁ **Fig. 7-111**

Anchor plate and cable in place, rear shoe spring catches the cable guide. Rear spring holds the cable guide in the shoe. Note how closely the spring rests to the wheel cylinder dust boot. I do not find this acceptable.

7

◁ **Fig. 7-112**

I elected to put the lead shoe spring on the anchor first. My reason for doing this is to space the rear shoe's spring further from the wheel cylinder's dust boot.

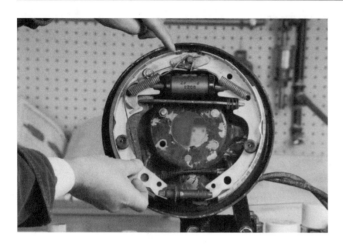

 Fig. 7-113

Now the rear shoe's spring has a reasonable gap from the wheel cylinder dust boot.

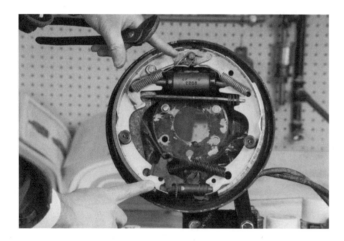

◀ **Fig. 7-114**

Retractor spring ends are now squeezed to parallel spread. The self-adjuster mechanism installed, this is a finished brake assembly for the right rear wheel of a CJ Jeep!

◀ **Fig. 7-115**

Test the self-adjuster mechanism. Make sure the screw moves readily to assure proper brake adjustment many miles down the road. Anti-Seize on clean threads will prevent freeze-up and resist moisture contamination. Wipe off excess Anti-Seize to prevent lining damage.

Installing Calipers, Brake Pads and Front Hoses

'77-up CJs have disc front brakes. Servicing calipers and pads is a routine service for these vehicles. Caliper rebuilding is much like wheel cylinder work, and again, manufacturers recommend discarding any cylinder that shows scoring, pitting or corrosive damage.

There are rebuilt and new calipers available in the market. If light polishing with crocus cloth will not clean up the bore blemishes, consider a new or rebuilt cylinder.

> **WARNING—**
>
> *Use extreme caution if you air-blow the piston from the caliper body. A stuck piston can exit with extreme force and cause severe bodily injury. Point the piston away from your body as you apply light, slow air pressure through the fluid inlet port. If blemishes/stains do not disappear with crocus cloth polishing of the bore, replace the caliper. Do not attempt to polish the caliper piston with a wire brush or any other kind of abrasive. Removing the hard outer layer will ruin a piston, leaving it loose and prone to fluid leaks and rapid wear. Use crocus to polish minor blemishes or stains in the bore or on the piston surface. Always clean and dry parts thoroughly before assembly.*

7

◀ **Fig. 7-116**

First step in removing hose is to tap the retaining clip loose. Here, I use a screwdriver and tap away from the pipe or hose.

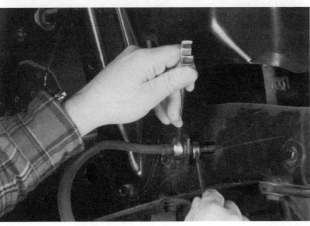

◀ **Fig. 7-117**

I use a set of flarenut wrenches to loosen the pipe flarenut from the hose.

 Fig. 7-118

Here I install a new Genuine Mopar/Jeep hose and caliper. I will do the same on the opposite wheel to assure safety and balance. Support caliper to prevent stress on hose.

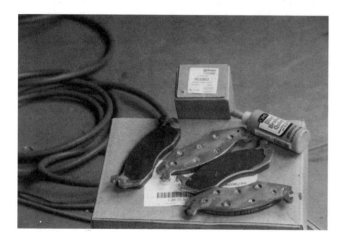

 Fig. 7-119

These brake pads are Mopar OEM replacement parts. I coat the steel backs with anti-squeal lube. This is specially made for disc brake pad work.

 Fig. 7-120

Pads go into place. I use new Mopar springs here. This is the second generation ('82-up) of AMC/Jeep CJ disc front brakes. The earlier version uses a key-and-slipper with a retainer bolt (common Ford style). Brake work here follows pad replacement fundamentals.

NOTE—

On the Ford-style '77-'81 OEM disc brakes, you will typically need to bend the shoe tabs to reduce clearance between the tabs and caliper body. Installation notes will accompany new sets of quality pads. I turn first to Mopar for assurance of quality brake parts. My next choice is the local NAPA parts source.

◀ **Fig. 7-121**

Loctite on clean threads assures secure attachment of the calipers.

◀ **Fig. 7-122**

You will tighten '82-up caliper pins of this type to 30-35 lb-ft. Recheck torque after testing the brakes. Note Warn's internal spline locking hub and anodized wheel hub. Warn heavy duty pieces are fully compatible with this otherwise stock '86 CJ-7 braking system! Rotor is stock, simply resurfaced after installation on the new Warn wheel hub. Gone is the weak 5-bolt type OEM free-wheeling/locking hub.

7

◀ **Fig. 7-123**

Springs in place, this is view of the new Genuine Mopar pieces: caliper assembly, hose, pads and hardware. This package is duplicated on the left side of the vehicle.

Master Cylinder Installation

Most high mileage Jeep CJs will need a new master cylinder. Bore finishes have changed, and the traditional rebuilding methods are no longer addressed in factory workshop manuals. According to AMC/Jeep-era OEM manuals, the '72-up Jeep CJ gets a new master cylinder if the old cylinder has any scoring, pitting, corrosion or scratches.

AMC/Jeep factory technical manuals, as far back as 1972, indicate that if light touch-up with crocus cloth does not remove a blemish, it's time for a new master cylinder! Honing a master cylinder is not recommended in OE manuals of the '72-up era.

NOTE—

This is not limited to Jeep vehicles. My research on other truck manufacturers has revealed the same kind of information. Master cylinder honing is neither mentioned nor considered as an option!

According to Jeep factory manuals, crocus cloth polishing of minor blemishes and stains is acceptable. Use of any kind of abrasive material (emery paper included) is unacceptable! So, unless the master cylinder bore looks virtually like new, you would be expected to replace the cylinder. This also applies to the wheel cylinders and disc caliper bores.

CAUTION—

If you have considered honing a cast iron cylinder, keep in mind that modern cylinders have been bored and diamond finished in a process that presses hard against the iron surface. This intentionally compresses the surface metal, and the iron behaves much like bearing steel. Of course, this improves the properties of iron, making the bore last longer, resist corrosion to a degree, and thwart scoring. However, the hardening affects only a shallow layer of metal. For this reason, it is assumed that honing will cut through this layer and expose softer material---material that would wear more quickly and surely not last as long as the original surface.

WARNING—

Never hone an aluminum cylinder! Aluminum master cylinders and other aluminum brake and clutch cylinders will not tolerate honing. Any kind of damage or evidence of wear in an aluminum cylinder will require replacement with a new cylinder.

 Fig. 7-124

A Genuine Mopar master cylinder is a quality replacement part that will assure like-new performance. This '86 CJ-7 was fifteen years old with 109,000 miles on the original master cylinder. I installed new Mopar calipers and wheel cylinders. The master cylinder and hose replacement round out the renewal of the hydraulic system---good for another 100,000 or more miles!

NOTE—

Years ago, in the era of atmospherically vented master cylinders, it was a service policy to change brake fluid every year, renewing the cylinder rubber parts at the same time. The sealed fluid systems in modern hydraulic brakes have dramatically reduced this traditional practice. The 1986 CJ-7's brake system likely had never been vacuum siphoned and refilled with clean brake fluid. Had fluid been changed periodically, the system would be even more reliable, corrosion would be inhibited, and brake fluid would be more resistant to fade.

Fig. 7-125

This is the original master cylinder, at 109,000 miles still functioning properly without leaks. One look at the brake fluid color, however, told me that this cylinder had corrosion, pitting and rubber sloughing. I opted for a new cylinder to complement the new calipers and wheel cylinders.

7

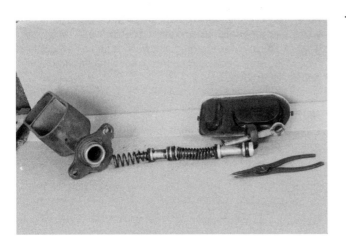

Fig. 7-126

Here is the old master cylinder disassembled. Note sequence of parts. The bore exhibited wear and corrosion, its surface pitted and scored.

 Fig. 7-127

This factory gasket seals between the master cylinder and firewall. The seal prevents moisture and engine bay fumes from entering the cab of the Jeep.

 Fig. 7-128

I could not locate an OEM master cylinder-to-firewall seal. The alternative is a gasket created with Ultra-Black RTV sealant. Note that I coat the pedal pivot hole with Lithium Grease.

NOTE—

When the master cylinder is installed with pushrod attached to the pedal pin, I will make sure that there is correct clearance between the retracted pushrod and the master cylinder piston. (See comments in 'Pedal and Brake Adjustment Tips' section earlier in this chapter.)

 Fig. 7-129

Use Loctite 242 on threads of master cylinder bolts. Pull nuts or bolts up evenly, tightening in steps, side-to-side. Torque bolts to 30 lb-ft minimum. Attach the pushrod to the pedal pin with the appropriate OEM mounting hardware. (The typical late CJ uses a nylon bushing, flat washer and a new cotter pin.) Make sure pedal and pushrod move freely, without parts interference.

NOTE—

Caps on pipes prevent debris from entering the hydraulic system during service.

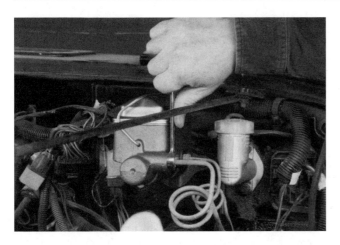

 Fig. 7-130

Carefully thread pipe nuts into the master cylinder threads. Torque brake pipe nuts to 15 lb-ft. Re-check the torque after pipes set for a while. You will now need to bleed the brake system.

Bleeding Late CJ Brakes

You can bench-bleed the master cylinder to ease the bleeding process. A pressure or vacuum bleeder is another way to quicken the bleeding effort.

There is also another consideration. If bleeding is not going well on a later model CJ, you need either a metering valve tool (Jeep #J-26869) or a helper to hold the stem of the metering valve open while you bleed the brakes. If you do not hold the metering valve open, bleeding will be virtually impossible! Remove the tool when done.

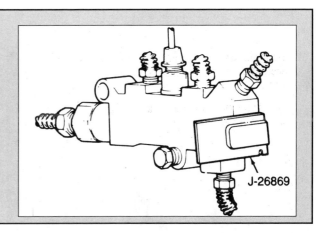

J-26869

7

Upgrading the Hydraulic System

Some users prefer a power/vacuum assist braking system. Installing power brakes offers distinct benefits, especially for trailer toting or driving in rush hour traffic. Power assist upgrades have been available to Jeep builders for forty years or more. One must be careful, however, not to "over-power" the system. This is a lightweight vehicle that may not require the same braking effort as the donor vehicle that provides the power-assist assembly!

 Fig. 7-131

A power booster can enhance the performance of your CJ's hydraulic brake system. The '72 CJ-5 boasts a Dana 44 Wagoneer front axle. This Jeep has disc brakes both front and rear. (The retrofit Isuzu/Dana 44 rear axle came with disc brakes.) The vacuum booster is a must item here. AMC-era CJs come with and without factory power assist.

If you upgrade the braking system with disc brakes, you may decide to add a power booster. The best pattern for such a retrofit is the OEM Jeep system used on later CJ models. This is a vacuum booster unit designed for a lighter weight vehicle.

◁ **Fig. 7-132**

'72 CJ-5 boasts a one-off rear axle conversion: a Dana 44 with factory disc brakes---from an Isuzu Rodeo! The axle shafts were machined for the Jeep 5-on-5-1/2-inch wheel pattern. Hydraulic lines were adapted.

NOTE—

Disc rear brakes and the Dana 44 J-truck/Wagoneer front axle with disc brakes call for a larger displacement master cylinder and a matching vacuum booster assembly. This system needs enough fluid displacement from the master cylinder to handle four disc calipers. (In the next section, see information on proportioning valves.)

Any modification to the braking system involves the need to properly proportion the front-to-rear braking effort. This can be accomplished with an OEM combination/proportioning valve or use of a manually adjusted proportioning valve. The adjustable valve is fitted on the rear braking system. A manual valve must be carefully set to assure that the rear brakes do not apply too much braking pressure.

WARNING—

Short wheelbase vehicles are prone to spinning out, especially under hard highway braking or on slick surfaces. If the rear brakes set up too quickly or too hard, the vehicle can go into a spin. Any brake upgrade should take this dynamic into account. On my '55 CJ-5, I installed an aftermarket adjustable valve that required careful adjustment and testing on secluded roads. An OEM valve from a later model Jeep, if a match for the type, size and layout of the drum or disc brakes used, could serve as an alternative.

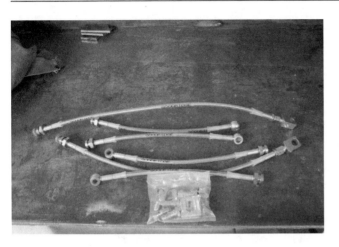

 Fig. 7-133

Hoses for the '55 CJ-5's new hydraulic system were custom built by Goodridge. The Goodridge catalog lists all pieces needed to make these stainless steel braid hoses. High performance Goodridge components exceed OEM standards. Goodridge assembled and shipped the properly sized hoses and fittings for my brake upgrades.

◀ **Fig. 7-134**

Goodridge supplied master cylinder fittings to mate with hoses. Master cylinder used in my '55 CJ-5 upgrade is OEM type for a '72-'76 CJ with four-wheel drum brakes. To use this cylinder with four-wheel disc brakes, I removed the check valves. (See earlier section in this chapter for details.)

NOTE—

Master cylinder is a tandem type. I wanted to retain the OEM through-the-floor pedals on my '55 CJ-5, which required custom fabricating a mounting bracket and linkage for the new master cylinder.

7

◀ **Fig. 7-135**

Armor guard (wire wrapped) stainless steel brake lines from Classic Tube & Performance came pre-assembled with flare nuts installed and double-flared ends. I carefully measured the entire system and ordered tubing sections in proper lengths. This high-grade tubing is easy to shape.

NOTE—

In places where hoses attach to pipes, I either used OEM brackets (right) or fabricated my own brackets (left). Pipes should follow OEM routing where possible, avoiding exposure to trail debris or moving chassis components. Visualize the vehicle in motion, with axles and suspension flexing.

Brake Hose Flex

Goodridge, a supplier of racing and high performance brake and fuel system components, recommends prudent use of brake hose. Hoses expand incrementally under pressure, and use of excessive lengths of hose can lengthen brake response time and reduce the volume of fluid available at wheel cylinders or calipers.

Note that I use hoses only at recognized flex points. As OEM Jeep engineering demonstrates, always run steel pipes along frame rails and the axle housings. This reduces the need for long lengths of hose.

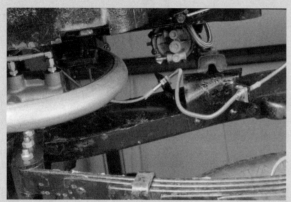

Fig. 7-136 Wherever possible, I duplicated the factory routing of steel pipes. Unlike the OEM drum brake layout, with its fixed rear brake backing plates and wheel cylinders, the rear disc brake calipers require flexible hoses between the calipers and axle housing pipes. I also used flex hoses (shown here) between the tandem master cylinder and the steel pipes at the frame rail. These hoses and fittings amply clear the engine and exhaust pipe.

NOTE—

Again, I wanted to retain the OEM through-the-floor pedals on my '55 CJ-5, which required the custom mounting bracket and placement of the new master cylinder low and next to the engine. Care was taken to see that engine and exhaust pipe movement would in no way interfere with the bracket, master cylinder, brake fittings or brake hoses. The master cylinder, brake hoses and brake fittings also have ample clearance from engine and exhaust pipe heat. Do not expose brake lines, brake cylinders, brake fittings or brake hoses to heat! On '72-up CJs, the master cylinder belongs at the firewall, in the stock location, out of harm's way. AMC/Jeep CJs have a very functional brake pedal location.

Fig. 7-137 Brake hose length from master cylinder to rear braking system is just long enough to account for any flex. I fabricated a hose bracket then MIG-welded the bracket to the frame. A hose retainer clip attaches the hose to the bracket. Stainless steel pipe runs along frame rails to the OEM hose attachment point at the frame above the rear axle.

 Fig. 7-138

I routed front axle pipes to OEM hose brackets. Note use of flexible hoses from brackets to calipers. Due to caliper "float" and movement, you must use flexible brake hoses at each caliper. Route hoses away from moving chassis parts. Consider the full range of motion that the hose will need.

 Fig. 7-139

Brake grade "T" at front axle follows OEM placement. All fittings and hardware must meet D.O.T. brake standards. Note how I bent the left pipe to clear the bump stop contact point on the axle housing. Bend coming down from the bracket relies on leaf spring to act as a shield from trail debris.

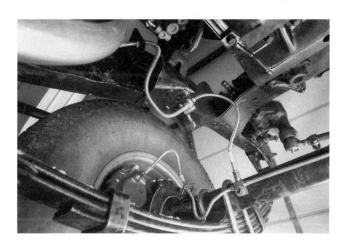

Fig. 7-140

"Factory" look is both functional and safe. Note hose positions, their length, and the angle of flex. Be certain that hoses will not rub or interfere with any other component when the chassis and suspension move!

7

Fig. 7-141

Bump stop spacer compensates for the 3-inch chassis/suspension lift that I installed on the vintage '55 CJ-5. Bump stop is functional. Like OEM design, the stop meets the section of axle housing between the spring U-bolts. Note that brake tubing and hoses will not be in the way of this movement.

 Fig. 7-142

These are tools used for bending tubing. In my experience, many bends can be done effectively with your fingers. Tighter bends require tools for establishing a radius. Armor guard does not inhibit bending. Always avoid making kinks!

Fig. 7-143

Full view of rear axle lines and hoses reveals my effort to keep brake pieces out of harm's way. Routing is similar to factory layout, relying upon proven engineering for off-highway use. Note use of brake hoses from U-bolts to calipers. Routing takes axle movement and bump stop locations into account.

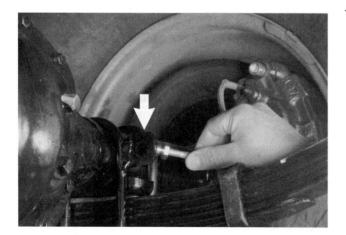

Fig. 7-144

My fabricated bracket (**ARROW**) supports line/hose connection at junction. Goodridge supplies OEM-style bracket clips. Hose ends have OEM-type grooves for clips. At caliper, the hose end fitting is a banjo type that uses Goodridge's attaching bolt and sealing washers, again following OEM design.

Fig. 7-145

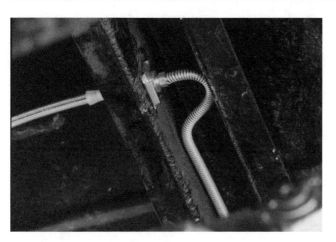

Tight bend to meet OEM mounting point for rear brake line-to-axle hose was made with a tubing bender. Unseen from this angle, the tubing clears sheet metal body edges to prevent risk of chafing. All tubing along the frame rails follows OEM routing for best protection.

> **CAUTION—**
>
> *Keep trail debris, suspension movement and jacking/hoisting locations in mind when you route hoses and brake piping. Pattern should be OEM layout or better!*

 Fig. 7-146

Always think in terms of movement and risk of chafing! Keep hoses and piping away from rubbing points and any sharp edges. When anchoring long runs of tubing along a frame rail, plastic coated metal clamps work well. Remember, your Jeep CJ is a shaking, twisting, vibrating and articulating machine!

7

Safe Brake Proportioning and Metering

When upgrading to better brakes, the short-wheelbase Jeep CJ is especially sensitive under hard braking. If the rear brakes take up at the wrong moment or apply harder than necessary, the prospect of skidding or spinning the vehicle around is very real.

NOTE—

Anyone who has driven a dune buggy or sand rail with only rear brakes (or a vehicle with just the parking brakes) will attest to how easy it is to spin a vehicle around!

The Jeep CJ's short wheelbase is no exception. If you upgrade the braking to two- or four-wheel disc brakes, pay close attention to brake front-to-rear proportioning. Here is a "glossary" of vital and essential OEM hydraulic system safety components.

Combination valve---The 1967 introduction of dual braking systems also introduced brake proportioning. As braking advanced to separate front and rear hydraulic systems, a combination valve could be placed in the circuit. Depending upon the design, this valve can serve several functions:

Metering---On disc front/drum rear brakes, the take-up time for the rear brakes is slower than the front brakes. For this reason, the metering function allows the rear brakes to receive fluid pressure slightly before the front disc calipers. The lag allows just enough time for the rear shoes to overcome spring pressure and reach the drum surfaces. (Calipers, by contrast, apply brake force almost immediately, as pads ride next to the rotors, and the caliper pistons are already in position.)

Proportioning---Typically, a disc front/drum rear brake system's proportioning valve helps balance front-to-rear braking under hard stopping conditions. Under light braking, the proportioning valve may not restrict flow. Under hard braking, however, the valve proportions the rear-to-front brake pressure for controlled, high pedal pressure stops.

Pressure differential---This function senses any significant pressure difference between the front and rear hydraulic circuits. If pressure drop occurs in one circuit, the valve will shift to the other circuit, at the same time tripping a warning light switch on the dash. One circuit can fail, and the other still functions. This is the most significant safety gain with dual braking systems, a welcome advance for rugged backcountry travel and Jeep 4WD vehicles.

When upgrading brakes, the proportioning and metering become crucial. If possible, you can pattern your brakes after an OEM engineered system for a vehicle with similar chassis dynamics and components like those found on your modified CJ.

Any brake upgrades should include the master cylinder, the pressure differential valve, metering valve and the proportioning valve from the Jeep donor vehicle. See your local recycling yard for ideas and OEM examples. Think in terms of complete, matching systems.

WARNING—

If you use later OEM components to upgrade your Jeep's brake system, gather all parts for a given year and model Jeep. Use the donor model's hydraulic components and matching valve hardware. This will assure compatible engineering.

When I built the '55 CJ-5, there was no factory example of a lightweight Jeep utility vehicle with four-wheel disc brakes. (The Wrangler TJ 'Rubicon' now offers OEM four wheel disc brakes.) I elected to use a manually adjusted proportioning valve, supplied by Classic Tube. Such valves are popular for race vehicles and other brake systems that require fine-tuning and quick adjustments in the field.

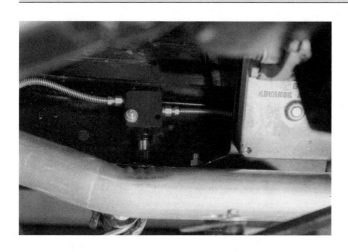

◄ **Fig. 7-147**

Manual proportioning valve attaches to frame rail, protected by channel. Accessible for adjustment purposes, the valve comes with steel brake grade fittings to accept brake tubing with flare nuts. Classic Tube was the source.

Here is some advice for installing and testing a manual proportioning valve on the rear brake system:

1) Follow the manufacturer's recommendations for installing the valve.

2) Find a secluded place to perform hard-application brake tests.

3) Follow the manufacturer's guidelines for testing the system.

4) Always start your tests with the rear brake pressure backed off to a low-pressure setting!

CAUTION—

This last point has to do with spinning the vehicle around, a common feat when rear brakes apply either too hard or harder than the front brakes!

Again, try to emulate the factory braking system for a Jeep vehicle that has approximately the same proportions, weight distribution and brake components as your upgraded Jeep CJ. Jeep engineers do their best to provide safe brakes for a particular vehicle design, GVWR and chassis dynamics. When designing your Jeep CJ's braking system, later Jeep engineering is surely a place to start!

7

Chapter 8

Electrical and Ignition System Upgrades

8

General

A spartan utility truck, the Jeep CJ offers the easiest possible access to wiring and electrical devices. You can readily perform repairs involving the wiring, charging system, starter circuit and ignition system. This experience will enhance troubleshooting skills, a valuable asset for any backcountry traveler.

All AMC/Jeep CJs have 12-volt electrical systems, the negative ground type with plastic coated copper wiring. Important electrical devices are mostly Motorcraft (Ford-type) and Delco-Remy (GM-type) components. Major components are common enough, and service parts remain readily available, many through Mopar, the rest through the aftermarket.

This chapter will familiarize builders with common trouble spots and a variety of upgrades available for the Jeep electrical system. You will find my approach pragmatic, with one goal: Every Jeep 4WD needs the most reliable electrical system possible.

Many Jeep vehicles have defective or badly compromised electrical wiring. Add-on devices are often installed improperly or in a manner that makes the rest of the system unreliable. You may have inherited someone else's idea of a nicely equipped CJ, only to find that the homespun wiring is faulty or even dangerous.

My 1955 CJ-5 was just that kind of vehicle. It was even worse in that the wiring was cloth-wrapped and of 6-volt design! The vehicle's wiring layout is similar to the '72-'75 AMC/Jeep and serves as an ideal prototype for a Jeep CJ wiring lesson.

On the '55 CJ, I chose to completely rewire the system and convert components to more modern Jeep devices. 4WD Hardware supplied a universal Jeep CJ re-wiring kit for models dating through the AMC/Jeep CJ era. The job began with stripping out the troublesome cloth-wrapped wire. I then set out to hand wire the CJ-5 from bumper to bumper.

NOTE—

The kit I chose and its requirements apply to AMC/Jeep CJs. My upgrade to a GM steering column mimics the later CJs. This installation serves all 1972-86 Jeep CJ applications. Popular accessories and improved electrical devices round out the system, and the ignition received special attention.

Whether you intend to restore your Jeep's wiring or simply repair the OEM electrics and ignition system, I offer this chapter as a guideline for dependably lighting your way down the highway---and those remote backcountry trails!

◀ Fig. 8-1

The backbone of any '72-up CJ electrical system is the alternator. For a vehicle that travels at a snail's pace off-pavement with the lights burning intensely, an alternator provides enough amperage at engine idle to meet requirements. For ample reserve power, I retrofitted this 160-amp alternator from Premier Power Welder, a high-output charging unit designed to work with an on-board welder/power supply. (See **Appendix**.)

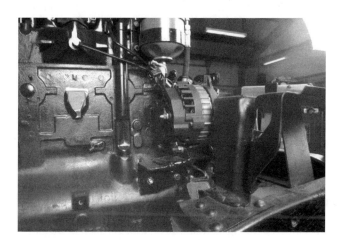

◀ Fig. 8-2

I replaced a 6-volt generator with the Premier Power Welder. If you have a transplant engine or custom charging system, you may benefit from viewing my installation. My fabricated bracket works with OEM mounting holes and layout. Here, the original generator bracket served as a pattern for the engine block portion of my mount. The engine's front support plate offers a bolt hole for the front brace.

8

◀ Fig. 8-3

Down strap braces from front of new mount to the engine front support plate. This triangle brace provides the additional strength needed. Premier provided a V-belt pulley to match the OEM F-head engine's belt size. I made the adjuster arm from an OEM generator arm and new steel. Belt was easy to find by length.

NOTE—

Premier can supply bolt-on alternators and pulleys for all AMC/Jeep CJ engines and the popular transplant engines.

Electrical and Ignition System Upgrades

Fig. 8-4

This is the Premier Power Welder. Owner of this '72 CJ-5 has used this welder on the trail, repairing equipment for four-wheelers. A frequency-type stick welder, the Premier unit does a professional job and even offers a MIG spool option. Note 110-volt AC plug for running brush-type motor power tools, electrical devices and 110-volt lights!

Fig. 8-5

I fabricated this brace to support the back end of the starter. 12-volt, high-torque starters require support. (GM and other big-block engines will break the nose end of the starter if the back end of the housing is not braced to the block.) Long bolt here is to pick up a ground strap from the negative side of the battery.

NOTE—

I ground from the battery to the engine block, to the body and the frame. Each of these grounds should be the same gauge wire as the positive battery cables. I've used '1/0' gauge in heavy-duty applications, routing all positive and ground/negative cables in 1/0 size wire with crimped ends.

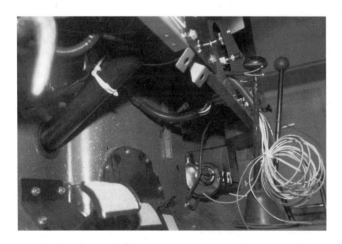

Fig. 8-6

Aftermarket wiring kits are available for the Jeep CJ chassis. Due to the age of the '55 Jeep and my plans for accessories like a winch and a high-output alternator, I opted for a "universal" kit from 4WD Hardware, Inc. This kit patterns off a GM or later AMC/Jeep CJ type electrical system. The instructions, OEM-type plug ends and circuit descriptions for wiring were easy to follow.

CAUTION—

Observe the amount of work involved with wiring a Jeep "from scratch." This is a major undertaking. With a quality wiring kit and 35 years of mechanical and automotive-electrical experience, this wiring job and the electrical device installations took the equivalent of five long days to complete (actually twice that number with my step-by photography added). You can rebuild the Jeep's powertrain in less time than it takes to hand wire and upgrade the electrics from bumper-to-bumper! There are kits that many claim are faster to assemble. In particular, builders have shared their success with the "Painless Wiring" kits, also available from 4WD Hardware and other vendors.

Fig. 8-7

On GM/AMC-style wiring, the turn indicators and other wiring routes through the turn signal switch. Kit includes a common plug jack to hook into the turn signal pigtail. Matching wires and inserting them into the plug takes time and careful consideration. The instructions detailed this step. Recall, I opted for a '70-circa GM truck steering column with OEM turn signal assembly and wiring.

Fig. 8-8

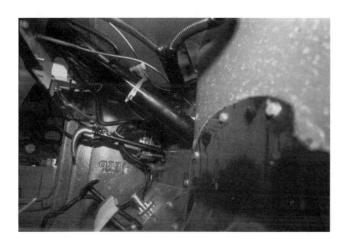

Under dash, the fuse block is GM/Jeep style. Note how I route wires, bundled neatly into convolution tubing. This tubing is modern alternative to taping wires, although tape still plays a role at junctions and splits in wire runs.

8

Fig. 8-9

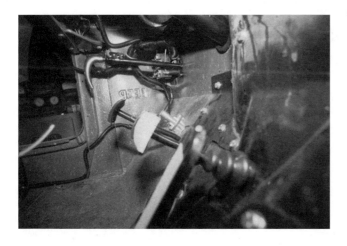

Plastic ties, tape and careful routing to insure against chafing: each plays a role in the finished appearance. Note use of plastic-coated metal clamps to secure harnesses. Universal kit is very thorough, however, you may need to buy additional clamps to suit your application.

NOTE—

Tubing headed along floorboard toward rear of tub in Fig. 8-9 includes fuel tank sender lead and all tail-lamp wiring. I patterned this harness after late CJs. Harness runs above the left fender well to avoid undercarriage hazards, then drops through rear of fender well, just above left tail-lamp.

◀ **Fig. 8-10**

Wire ends and plugs are already installed. Wires are labeled properly to help identify circuits and routing. Here, ground wire (**ARROW**) for headlamps is fixed to OEM headlamp bucket. Note use of convolution tubing to prevent wires from nicking or chafing on sharp edges.

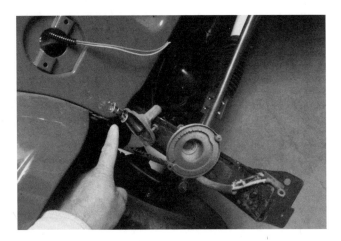

◀ **Fig. 8-11**

I reused the OEM front turn signals but opted for modern, plastic wires. Pigtails for turn signals are a common auto supply item. I spliced these wires into the new wiring harness.

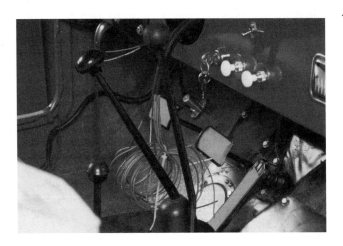

◀ **Fig. 8-12**

Bundles of wire were left in their extra long forms until I actually fit each wire to its device. This prevents premature cutting that leads to trouble. Kit came with plenty of wire, as seen here.

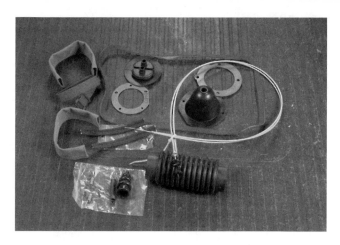

◀ **Fig. 8-13**

Beachwood Canvas Works is a wonderful source for trim and early Jeep replacement hardware. All parts seen here came from Beachwood Canvas Works. For a vintage Jeep missing hard to find trim or upholstery, Beachwood is an excellent resource.

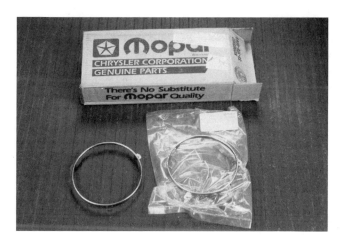

◀ **Fig. 8-14**

Ah, the timeless beauty of a Jeep CJ! Here are OEM, right out of the box Mopar/Jeep parts. Headlamp retainer rings are in the inventory. Consider your Jeep dealer a viable parts source when restoring or upgrading your CJ.

8

◀ **Fig. 8-15**

4WD Hardware supplied these rear corner reinforcement plates. For trail use and protection, this is an attractive approach.

 Fig. 8-16

I opted for more modern Jeep tail lamp assemblies, also supplied by 4WD Hardware, Inc. These taillights incorporate a backup lamp, turn signals, four-way flasher capability and parking/tail lamps. Large face meets more stringent D.O.T. requirements than the small OEM lights. Safety first!

Fig. 8-17

OEM headlamp buckets and modern wiring make a nice fit. I opted for halogen replacement sealed beams. Lights are many lumens brighter than the OEM 6- or 12-volt sealed beams—especially with the high output alternator! Note how I formed the wire junctions with plastic tape.

Fig. 8-18

Over time, tightly cinched plastic ties can cut through wire insulation. I avoid bunching wire with ties and instead run wire clusters within convolution tubing. Here, I use the tie simply to prevent wire from stripping further from the tubing. This also keeps the tube from spreading.

 Fig. 8-19

Major wire bundle to engine bay and front of vehicle feeds snugly through a rubber grommet. Once wires were routed to their devices, I formed the junctions with high quality electrical tape to assure a tight seal and proper appearance. I cut tube ends on a diagonal to aid fit-up.

 Fig. 8-20

Small items like the oil pressure sender have their own wire, too. This single wire comes down from the harness, routed in a manner that prevents exposure to rough edges or hot engine and exhaust components.

8

 Fig. 8-21

Harness along firewall clips to OEM wire harness hardware. Note use of plastic ties to secure the harness and offer an opening for the water temp sender wire (**ARROW**) to exit at the appropriate point. Convolution tubing works very well here.

 Fig. 8-22

Area near battery got very busy. Clamps, junction splices, gathering of wires for appearance and safety---each of these concerns apply here. Note that I opted for use of a Mopar/late Jeep solenoid switch to activate the starter motor with the ignition/start key switch. (This is an easy option, though some vintage Jeep owners prefer the OEM floorboard start switch.) This solenoid switch is common to '72-up CJs.

NOTE—

Using heavy-duty, battery-gauge cable, you can hard-wire an OEM early Jeep floorboard switch as an alternative starting mode. Off-pavement, some hardcore 'wheelers' like the ability to reach across the floorboard by foot rather than stretch a hand to turn the key switch. You can have it both ways, but remind the middle passenger to keep his or her feet away from the start switch! Route these high amp cables with extreme care, and use a properly rated floorboard starter switch.

 Fig. 8-23a

MSD ignition, Premier voltage regulator and upgrade battery have their wiring needs. Right fender got busy! Keep wires bundled and out of harm's way. Envision where the vibration, heat and debris might affect the system. Avoid hazards, and think of this as a "lifetime" wiring job.

 Fig. 8-23b

This '72 CJ has a Premier Power Welder, an MSD ignition box, two Optima batteries with an isolator, and an air compressor built around a York A/C compressor! Add to this a winch, off-pavement lighting, a full-speaker sound system, and a dashboard full of gauges, and the 160-amp alternator is just adequate! There are intense wiring demands with this CJ's electrical system!

NOTE—

Owner rewired bumper-to-bumper using a 'Painless Wiring' full-chassis harness kit. Comparing notes, the '72 CJ owner's approach took far less labor time than mine did. The Painless Wiring kit cost more than my Universal Wiring Kit, and both kits are available from 4WD Hardware and others.

Fig. 8-24

As simple as a CJ Jeep can be, this is still a busy wiring job. If you find the chore too demanding, consider subletting the task to an auto-electrical specialist. The '72 CJ owner and I both enjoy wiring work. Some builders do not.

Fig. 8-25

Need brake lights? Since I stayed with the OEM (through the floor) brake pedal but lost the single master cylinder's brake lamp switch with my brake upgrade, I chose this approach. The switch with lever is an OEM item for '55-'59 GM light trucks. When pedal drops, the switch lever moves, closing the circuit to the brake lamps. Simple, a switch from the same era as the '55 CJ! For your AMC-era CJ, this step is not necessary. The OEM brake pedal and brake lamp switch work well.

8

Fig. 8-26

When all lights were installed, I purchased a light switch that resembled OEM early Jeep type. Knob and switch were in catalogs at the local auto parts house. Military roots of Jeep 'Universal' CJs include use of common, often generic parts. AMC/Jeep CJs continue that theme, although you can still get OEM replacement switches from sources like your local Jeep/Mopar dealer, 4WD Hardware and retailers like NAPA.

 Fig. 8-27

Wondering what I would do with that ugly radio cutout? Here's the fix, a nice piece of diamond plate, sheared to shape, that holds two gauges. I wired gauges into the circuit with wiring provided in the kit.

 Fig. 8-28

It's always helpful to know what speed the engine is spinning. A popular Sun tachometer was one more item to wire into the harnesses, feeding wires through the convolution tubing circuits. When wiring your Jeep, plan for the accessories you intend to use.

 Fig. 8-29

Tachometer needed clamping to the steering column, and this stainless steel diesel truck exhaust clamp did the trick! Note the GM-style steering column tube with cover at base of the column tube. Within that cover are the wires that feed to the turn signal/four-way flasher switches.

 Fig. 8-30

Again, a parts house catalog turned up this nice wiper switch. Period look fits the '55 CJ, while the two electric wipers from 4WD Hardware outstrip the performance of the OEM vacuum types (even with a double-action/diaphragm fuel pump)! I opted for this switch to keep OEM appearance on instrument panel. Your '72-up CJ's OEM switches are still available in the aftermarket and through Jeep/Mopar dealers.

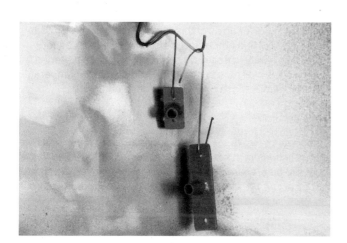

Fig. 8-31

These two brackets will bolt to windshield frame and support the new wiper motors. Bracket consists of mild steel plate and shock absorber spacers. Yes, you guessed it---I *gas welded* the tubes to the plate! Technique works well for lighter metal. OEM '72-up wiper mechanisms work well, and service parts are still available from Mopar and the aftermarket.

8

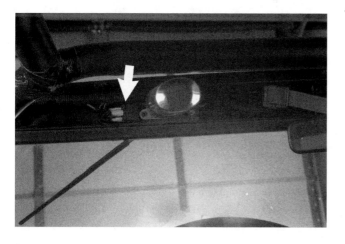

 Fig. 8-32

Electric wiper from 4WD Hardware is handy. Rather than run a cluster of wires, I used a Bosch-type relay (**ARROW**) to switch current on and off. These relays make good sense when devices require higher amperage current and the wire spans get long. Relay reduces the amount of heavier-gauge wire needed.

◀ **Fig. 8-33**

Motors and wiring in place, electric wipers work very well! Kit included wiper arms and blades, with some wire, terminals, a toggle switch and instructions. I opted to wire the devices differently, the end result being a system operated from the OEM-looking wiper switch!

◀ **Fig. 8-34**

Battery to power up all of this electrical service is from Barrett Racing. High amperage, permanently sealed battery provides safety in the event of a rollover. These batteries serve NASCAR race vehicles that require starter amperages 2-1/2 times those of an F-head Jeep engine!

NOTE—

*Nobody "plans" to roll over in a Jeep CJ, and some of us serious 'wheelers' have been lucky enough not to do so. It still pays to be prepared, and this includes the roll bar described in **Chapter 10**---plus a permanently sealed battery.*

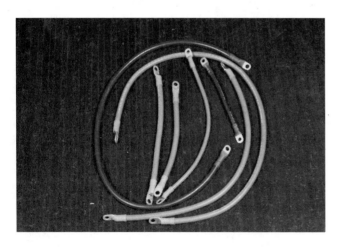

◀ **Fig. 8-35**

Barrett Racing also supplied these heavy-duty battery and high current cables. On a D.C. electrical system, *grounds and hot leads must have matching amperage capacity*. Make certain your ground (-) and positive (+) leads have the same gauge size and load carrying capacity!

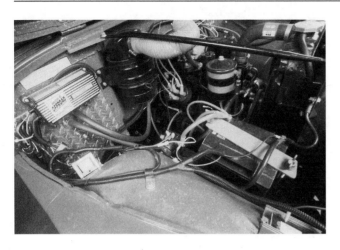

 Fig. 8-36

I fabricated the sturdy battery strap, tied down with Beachwood Canvas Works' bolts and wing nuts. Grounds go to starter support bracket (at engine block) and body. Steel body tub is easy to ground, although you need to verify continuity and ohms resistance (a sign of voltage drop) with a volt-ohmmeter.

NOTE—

I check for proper ground/resistance at every lamp housing, electrical motor and switch housing. Remember, the D.C. system takes current in full loop, from the battery positive post back to the battery negative post. This means that grounds must be able to handle as much amperage as positive leads. Grounds must have proper continuity and metal contact to maintain normal resistance. Paint, undercoating, grease and oil are not conductive contact points!

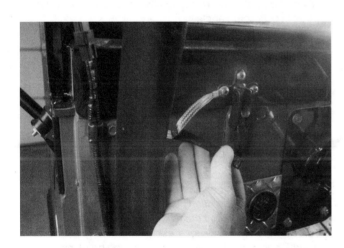

 Fig. 8-37

When I installed the wiper motors, I also installed this ground strap between the dash panel and windshield frame. The windshield mounts on hinges and rests upon a rubber insulator strip. I assured a quality ground with this strap. Tape is to protect paint. Extra length is for folding the windshield down onto the hood, which will not occur very often. (When a CJ windshield is laid down frequently, the insulator strip wears out faster.)

8

 Fig. 8-38

Here's the finished underhood look. Note use of electrical tape on tiny harnesses like the horn relay. The rest is in plastic convolution tubing, secured safely and away from hazards. This is an easy-to-troubleshoot, logical system. All primary wire circuits and devices use modern ATO-type fuses.

 Fig. 8-39

Grant steering wheel adapter provides a horn function. Speedometer and gauge cluster is an OEM replacement unit for a newer, 12-volt CJ. Style remains vintage, fit was straightforward, and this gauge/speedometer unit features turn signal arrows. Two switches to right of ignition/start switch are for original '55 circa heater and defroster. Note 12-volt power point below dash. My vintage Jeep is now road and trail ready!

Ignition System and Upgrades

Delco-Remy distributors are found in '72-'74 CJs. These durable breaker point ignitions require periodic points and condenser replacement. Breaker point gap is 0.016" for 232/258 sixes and the 304 V-8. Dwell-angle for sixes is 31-34 degrees; V-8s with window cap distributor call for 29-31 degrees of dwell/cam angle.

You can find specifications for the vacuum advance mechanism, and other Delco-Remy distributor details, in trade service manuals and the AMC shop manuals. (If you have a copy of my *Jeep Owner's Bible*, refer to the detailed breaker point and tuning information.)

NOTE—

The window-cap distributor provides a very simple means for setting points. You can usually come close to 30-degrees of dwell by firing the engine and turning the point adjusting screw inward with an Allen wrench, just to where the engine idle roughens. Back out the wrench 180 degrees. Verify with a dwell meter. I always set these distributors to 29-1/2 degrees for new points. By the time the rubbing block wears-in, dwell will be the desired 30-degrees.

> *WARNING—*
>
> *Use caution not to shock yourself while inserting the Allen wrench into the points adjusting screw! Stay away from moving engine parts like the fan!*

Most AMC-era CJs have either OEM or aftermarket electronic distributors. From '75-up, the common Ford/Motorcraft ignition has served well. Inherent to this ignition is the module failure issue, which should encourage owners to carry a spare module in the onboard spare parts box.

Genuine Mopar OEM replacement module is your best assurance of quality. If you plan to stay with the stock electronic ignition, this is my ignition module choice. The '86 CJ-7's original module was still in place and functioning at 109,000 miles. Here is our Grand Wagoneer at 134,000 miles. 360 V-8 is on its second module.

NOTE—

For extended backcountry travel, I would carry a module in your spare parts box. The Mopar module is easy to change out and will last a long time.

MSD ignition distributors are available for AMC sixes and V-8s. Other quality aftermarket distributor options exist, too. A high output ignition is desirable on an engine that holds a vehicle at the brink of rock precipices. You want hot spark to fire through the rich fuel mixes that occur at high altitude driving environments. Hot coils are also popular, available from several aftermarket sources.

I am particularly partial to MSD ignition components. If you want to upgrade and can afford the expense, these are quality components. You can also enhance the performance of the OEM ignition system, concentrating on an electronic distributor, a hot coil, and a reliable ignition module.

NOTE—

Make sure your ignition wiring is intact for proper electronic or breaker point ignition function! If you have an early Delco breaker point distributor, consider converting to an electronic ignition or at least upgrading your OEM distributor with an aftermarket electronic ignition conversion kit.

8

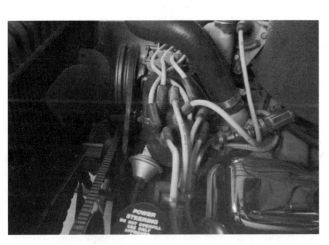

 Fig. 8-40

'72 CJ 304 V-8 originally featured a breaker point Delco distributor. Owner opted for a later AMC V-8 electronic distributor. He added an Accel coil, MSD box and high performance spark wires. This is a sensible mix of OEM and aftermarket components.

All AMC/Jeep distributors (breaker point or electronic) feature vacuum advance mechanisms. A common trouble spot when performance falls off is the vacuum advance mechanism that does not work properly. The diaphragm has failed, or the vacuum source is lost.

Vacuum loss or misrouting of the hoses can create poor performance, including lack of power (no advance) or detonation/ping caused by vacuum applied at the wrong time. A vacuum line hooked directly to the intake manifold vacuum, instead of a "ported" source just above the throttle plate, can cause full vacuum advance nearly all of the time. This is *way* too much spark advance and a cause of severe detonation---or even major engine damage!

You can confirm vacuum advance performance with a timing light. Vacuum advance, if hooked to a ported source, will not be operative at throttle idle. The vacuum advance will swing to full advance just as the throttle cracks open. By design, ported vacuum will decrease as the throttle opens further, allowing the centrifugal advance mechanism to take over. Spark advance function at higher engine speeds is solely the function of the centrifugal advance.

Even with an electronic AMC/Motorcraft ignition, you must make sure that the rotor, vacuum advance, centrifugal advance and spark wires are intact and in good shape. You will still service the spark plugs, spark wires, distributor cap and rotor at periodic intervals.

Breaker Point Ignition Fundamentals '101'

NOTE—

For the sake of those owners still interested in breaker point ignition basics, the step-by-step tuning of an early Jeep distributor serves as a good prototype. There are time-honored concerns and generic pitfalls that are readily apparent when servicing the early Jeep distributor. (See the Jeep Owner's Bible for more details on the AMC/Jeep CJ breaker point tune-up.) The distributor depicted in Fig. 8-41 to Fig. 8-60 is found in F-head 4-cylinder engines. These engines appeared in CJs as late as 1973.

It is highly likely that your Jeep engine has an electronic distributor---or that you intend to see it does. Even if your Jeep has no need for breaker points, this section could serve trail companions with older Jeep vehicles!

◀ **Fig. 8-41**

For my work on early breaker point ignitions, a set of ignition wrenches proves handy. On the bench, the condenser and points come out easily. Old Autolite point sets have one hold-down screw. The breaker arm pivot slides over a support pin on the breaker plate.

◀ **Fig. 8-42**

Primary wire comes loose with removal of nut and lock washer.

Fig. 8-43

Carefully remove inner nut, lock washer, washer and insulator.

Fig. 8-44

After cracking screws loose with a screwdriver, I use a spring-loaded removal tool to unscrew and lift out these screws. When changing points with the distributor in the engine, this tool can prevent dropping the screw into the advance mechanism.

Fig. 8-45

Carefully remove the contact stud and breaker plate. This insulating grommet is crucial to proper ignition performance. Grommet keeps stud from shorting against the distributor housing. Make certain this insulator is in good condition. Shorts like this create common ignition failures.

8

Electrical and Ignition System Upgrades

Fig. 8-46

This is another insulator that fits between the breaker plate and distributor housing. Note that certain components must be fully insulated from the housing. *The housing is an electrical ground!*

Fig. 8-47

Now you can thoroughly clean and inspect the centrifugal advance mechanism. Unit is simple: flyweights and springs. Note that this F-head distributor shaft rotates counter-clockwise. If you replace the distributor, make certain that the advance mechanism works in the same direction as the OEM unit.

Fig. 8-48

Restoration does mean painting. I carefully masked off all tags and areas that do not receive OEM paint. My paint choice was gloss black engine enamel, a high-quality type.

 Fig. 8-49

White Lithium Grease from Permatex is a good choice for this difficult to access mechanism. Dust-proof distributor design will keep dirt out. This grease dries to the touch and will stay in place for a very long time.

◄ **Fig. 8-50**

Breaker plate goes back into place. The thin insulating gasket that fits between the contact flange and housing is a critical part. (See Fig. 8-46.)

8

◄ **Fig. 8-51**

Insulating grommet is in place...

 Fig. 8-52

Install contact bolt, insulator, washer, lockwasher and nut. Secure nut snugly.

Fig. 8-53

Breaker point set can now be fitted in place. Note that grease is in the correct rubbing block location for a clock-wise rotation distributor (like the chain drive WWII MBs and the first CJ-2A L-heads). *This is incorrect, however, for a counter-clockwise rotation distributor shaft.* Grease should be on the side facing *into* the cam rotation!

Fig. 8-54

Condenser strap, breaker spring, nut and screw will slide over the slotted stand as an assembly. Leave the screw loose enough for this purpose,

 Fig. 8-55

Note relationship of parts and insulating strap of condenser. Here, point gap (0.020" for vintage Jeep Auto-Lite distributor) is checked with point rubbing block on the high point of a cam lobe. Grease has been moved to correct side of rubbing block for a *counter-clockwise rotation* distributor shaft.

NOTE—

If a dwell meter is available, confirm breaker point dwell angle. This Auto-Lite distributor calls for 42-degrees of dwell. (F-head four-cylinder engines equipped with Delco-Remy distributors call for 25-34 degrees with a 0.022" gap.) Check dwell when you have installed the distributor and started the engine.

Fig. 8-56

Ah, memories of the dual-point ignition systems and the Muscle Car Era! This scale measures breaker point spring tension. On breaker points with a slotted (adjustable) spring, setting the spring tension properly will minimize rubbing block wear and prevent point flutter or "bounce." For Auto-Lite distributor, tension should read 17-20 ounces to open the points. '72-'74 AMC/Delco-Remy 6-cylinder and V-8 distributors require 17-21 ounce pull.

8

Fig. 8-57

Felt is material for oil wick in center of the distributor shaft. I made a new wick by packing felt material into the recess. This is an early Jeep factory location for periodically oiling the distributor cam and centrifugal advance mechanism.

 Fig. 8-58

This is finished look of a reconditioned vintage distributor. Had the unit needed a shaft bushing, the drive gear and shaft would need removal. Forty years old, this distributor has no appreciable wear, much to Auto-Lite's credit.

 Fig. 8-59

A few drops of oil on the felt wick, and you can install the dust proofing cover and a new rotor on the vintage Auto-Lite distributor. The unit is ready for a distributor cap and installation in the engine.

 Fig. 8-60

Here is the restored distributor assembly, ready for installation. If there is any sign of wear, replace the O-ring on the lower housing before installing the distributor. The oil fitting (facing forward, just above clamp bracket) receives a squirt of oil during routine service and chassis lubrication.

Breaker Point Lubrication

Greasing the point set's rubbing block is easy---once you know which side of the block to grease! The grease always goes on the side of the rubbing block that faces toward the cam's direction of rotation.

As the cam rotates, it should press the grease into the block, not pull it away. If you place the grease on the wrong side, the cam can pull the grease off the block and, depending upon the layout, even sling the grease into the breaker contacts. This will cause shorting and misfiring of the ignition.

This is the correct placement of the breaker grease for a *counter-clockwise* rotation Auto-Lite distributor. (See Figs. 8-54 and 8-55.) I use quality Bosch grease for this purpose. A very light film on the cam lobes completes the job.

Static Timing the Breaker Point Engine

When the distributor is ready for installation, timing is the next step. If the oil pump is indexed properly, you will have no trouble resetting the distributor---*if you marked the distributor housing and rotor positions before removing the distributor!*

If the distributor shaft is not aligned properly, you must start from scratch. On the compression stroke for #1 cylinder, bring the timing mark to approximately 2-5 degrees BTDC.

> **NOTE—**
>
> *Turn the crankshaft in its normal direction of rotation. Bring the mark up slowly, and do not pass the mark. This will keep tension on the pull side of the timing chain to assure accurate settings.*

At this point, see where the oil pump drive slot indexes. Index the oil pump drive key properly. Install a new distributor housing base gasket or O-ring.

You can static time the breaker point distributor with an ohmmeter. With base clamp bolt loose and #1 piston at 5-

degrees B.T.D.C., rotate the housing in the direction that the distributor shaft spins. Now bring the housing in the opposite direction until breaker points just open. (Read this with the ohmmeter.) Secure the housing clamp bolt. After the engine starts, verify timing with a timing light.

When the ignition system is fully functional, you can static time the engine using an old spark plug and #1 spark plug wire. Disconnect all spark plug wires to prevent any cylinder from firing. Hook #1 wire to the old spark plug then ground the plug's housing.

With #1 piston on its firing stroke and the crankshaft timing mark indexed at 2-5 degrees BTDC, turn the ignition on, loosen the distributor base clamp bolt, and rotate the distributor housing in the direction that the shaft spins.

> **WARNING—**
>
> *Do not touch the primary (small gage) wire at any time when the ignition switch is on! (The primary wire is attached to the side of the distributor housing on early Jeep distributors.) You can receive a full condenser-load shock by touching this wire at the wrong time!*

Now, slowly rotate the housing in the opposite direction, watching the spark plug. At the point the plug fires across its gap, clamp the distributor down. This is static timing, accurate enough to start the engine and verify timing with a timing light. Once the engine starts, you can correct the timing as necessary.

> **NOTE—**
>
> *The AMC/Jeep CJs are all emission era vehicles. If your original emissions/tuning decal is still on the radiator core support, you can get the tune-up data and specifications you need without seeking a shop manual. This includes timing adjustments and even ignition data like breaker point dwell angle for the '72-'74 CJs!*

8

Jeep Ignition Performance Upgrade

There is one ignition upgrade that I have used with great success. The foundation of this system is the MSD "box," a multiple spark discharge unit. In its universal applications, this highly efficient module can be used with either breaker point or high energy, module-type ignition systems.

The enhanced spark, aided by the MSD Blaster coil, enables use of wider spark plug gaps for extended spark intervals. On an engine used at a variety of altitudes, the MSD ignition is practical. All CJ Jeep models have carburetion, and an ignition that can fire a richer fuel mix at high altitudes is one way to offset the limitations of fixed fuel metering and jets.

I was able to use the MSD 'Off-Road' ignition with the original ('55 CJ-5) Auto-Lite distributor. The MSD box uses the distributor's breaker points strictly as a "trigger" switch. There is virtually no breaker point contact wear, and if the rubbing block and distributor cam have been properly lubed, points should last a very long time!

NOTE—
This approach would also work well with the '72-'74 AMC/Jeep Delco-Remy breaker point ignitions. The points would simply be the MSD trigger.

If you want a highly efficient ignition support system that can be readily taken off line, the MSD 'Off-Road/6' box is a sensible choice. The layout is relatively easy to follow, and MSD furnishes excellent instructions, wiring diagrams and even booklets that describe the function and installation steps for various applications.

◄ **Fig. 8-61a**

MSD-6 is a proven system. "Multiple Spark Discharge" allows for wider spark plug gaps and a subsequent increase in spark duration. For an F-head four, this might sound like overkill, however, the opposite is true. A lower horsepower engine needs as much spark as it can get. Off-pavement at high altitudes, the MSD unit will help keep richer mixtures burning!

 Fig. 8-61b

On AMC-era CJ with a 304 V-8 and Motorcraft electronic distributor, the MSD box is right at home. '72 CJ will see a lot of Rubicon Trail trips, and the MSD box is ignition insurance.

 Fig. 8-62

I hard-wired my new electrical circuits for the MSD box, although the kit's design allows for easy retrofitting on OEM electrical systems. Unit is approved as a 50-State legal device for emissions purposes, as it should be! Cleaner, more thorough burning of fuel is the aim.

8

 Fig. 8-63

Ballast resistor is not used with the MSD box. My installation of the resistor enables a two-minute conversion to a standard ignition---as a backup to the MSD unit.The two wires piggy-backed on the one terminal simply split to each end of the resistor. This restores the 12-volt conventional breaker point ignition.

NOTE—

In many years of projects involving the MSD products, I have never had an MSD box failure! For the vintage CJ-5, the Auto-Lite OEM distributor simply functions like a trigger switch. The points act as a signal to the MSD box. The box interfaces with an MSD 'Blaster' coil. Secondary spark distribution relies upon the OEM rotor and distributor cap with 8.5mm 'Super Conductor' MSD spark plug wires.

 Fig. 8-64

MSD 'Super Conductor' 8.5mm spark wire cables neatly numbered to match the firing order! I assembled cable ends using the MSD 'Pro-Crimp Tool.' The tool is outstanding, providing professional results and appearance. Note that 'Blaster Coil' behind distributor mounts in OEM position at the engine block.

Fig. 8-65

Here is the complete ignition system. The contrast between these high tech components and an F-134 engine turns heads. A modest horsepower gain and, more importantly, a hot, long-duration spark, make the difference.

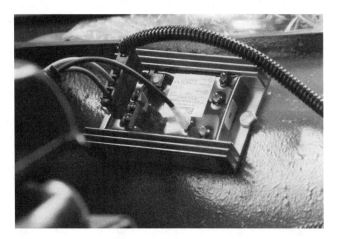

Fig. 8-66a

Like other electronic devices, the MSD/6 requires clean, reliable voltage signals. The Premier alternator and solid-state voltage regulator provide the juice. We're in the modern era and need to take advantage of this technology!

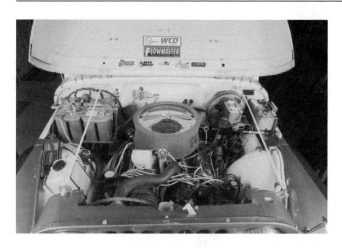

Fig. 8-66b

The AMC 304 V-8 in a CJ-5 is an ideal candidate for a high performance ignition. This '72 Jeep runs quite strongly, its original 304 very reliable and responsive. Despite transplants of virtually every popular small-block V-8 into the CJ Jeep chassis, the AMC V-8s have all the power and reliability needed. I like the AMC 360 and 401 V-8s as high performance alternatives.

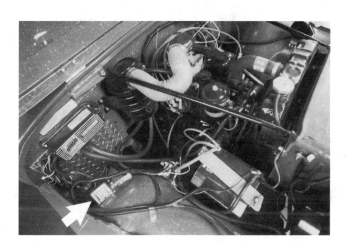

Fig. 8-67

Certain ignition-related devices, like a tachometer, must be compatible with the MSD box. The Sun unit required a special transformer-like device (standing at left of ballast resistor), available through MSD. Once I wired this device (**ARROW**) according to instructions, the tachometer worked fine.

NOTE—

MSD can furnish a list of compatible tachometers. I recommend that you read MSD literature before installing the MSD/Off-Road package.

8

OEM Wiring Diagrams

For working on your Jeep's original electrical system, a wiring diagram is helpful. Whether you intend to rewire the system or simply need a guide for repairs, these factory illustrations provide a map of the electrical system.

These illustrations were included in the **AMC/Jeep 1972 Technical Manual**. They represent an overview of '72-up Jeep CJ wiring. If you need more details on your CJ, consult a Jeep factory workshop manual or **Mitchell** manual that includes wiring diagrams for your year and model Jeep.

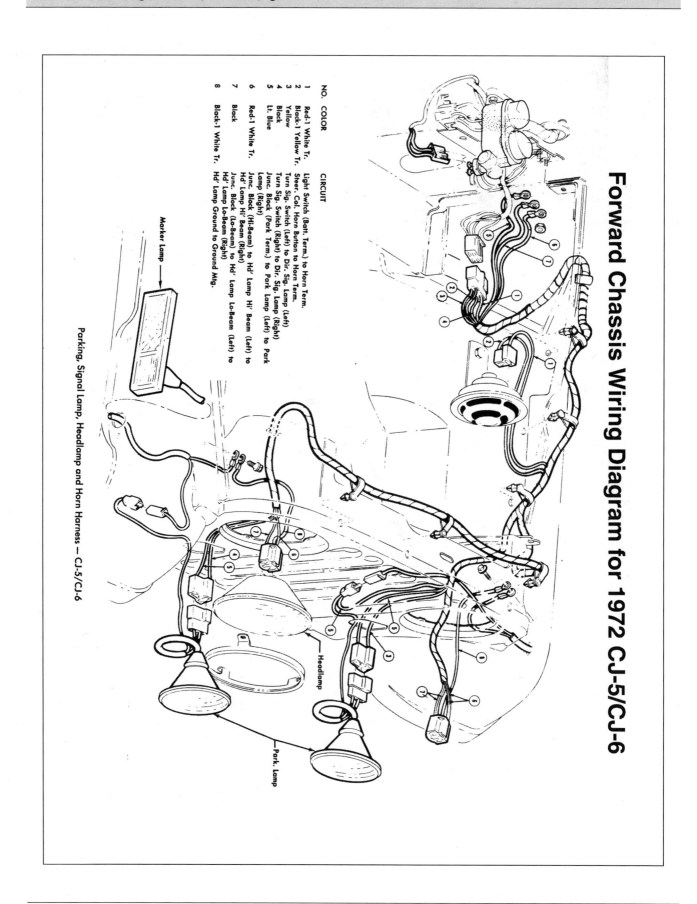

Forward Chassis Wiring Diagram for 1972 CJ-5/CJ-6

NO.	COLOR	CIRCUIT
1	Red-1 White Tr.	Light Switch (Batt. Term.) to Horn Term.
2	Black-1 Yellow Tr.	Steer. Col. Horn Button to Horn Term.
3	Yellow	Turn Sig. Switch (Left) to Dir. Sig. Lamp (Left)
4	Black	Turn Sig. Switch (Right) to Dir. Sig. Lamp (Right)
5	Lt. Blue	Junc. Block (Park Term.) to Park Lamp (Left) to Park Lamp (Right)
6	Red-1 White Tr.	Junc. Block (Hi-Beam) to Hd' Lamp Hi' Beam (Left) to Hd' Lamp Hi' Beam (Right)
7	Black	Junc. Block (Lo-Beam) to Hd' Lamp Lo-Beam (Left) to Hd' Lamp Lo-Beam (Right)
8	Black-1 White Tr.	Hd' Lamp Ground to Ground Mtg.

Marker Lamp

Headlamp

Park. Lamp

Parking, Signal Lamp, Headlamp and Horn Harness — CJ-5/CJ-6

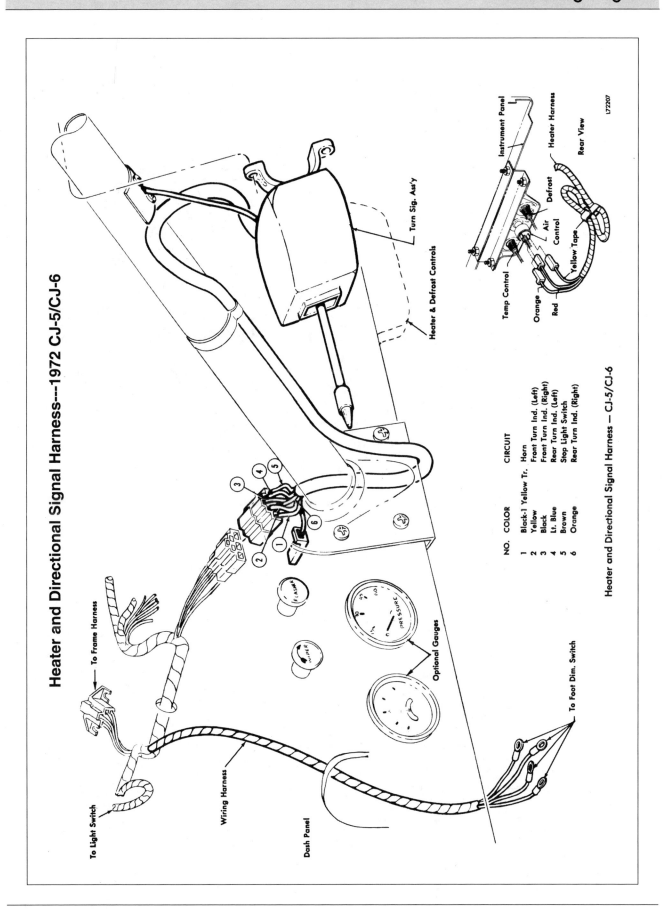

Heater and Directional Signal Harness—1972 CJ-5/CJ-6

To Frame Harness

To Light Switch

Wiring Harness

Dash Panel

To Foot Dim. Switch

Optional Gauges

PRESSURE

FLASHER

WIPER

Turn Sig. Ass'y

Heater & Defrost Controls

NO.	COLOR	CIRCUIT
1	Black-1 Yellow Tr.	Horn
2	Yellow	Front Turn Ind. (Left)
3	Black	Front Turn Ind. (Right)
4	Lt. Blue	Rear Turn Ind. (Left)
5	Brown	Stop Light Switch
6	Orange	Rear Turn Ind. (Right)

Heater and Directional Signal Harness — CJ-5/CJ-6

L72207

Instrument Panel

Heater Harness

Rear View

Defrost

Air Control

Temp Control

Orange

Red

Yellow Tape

8

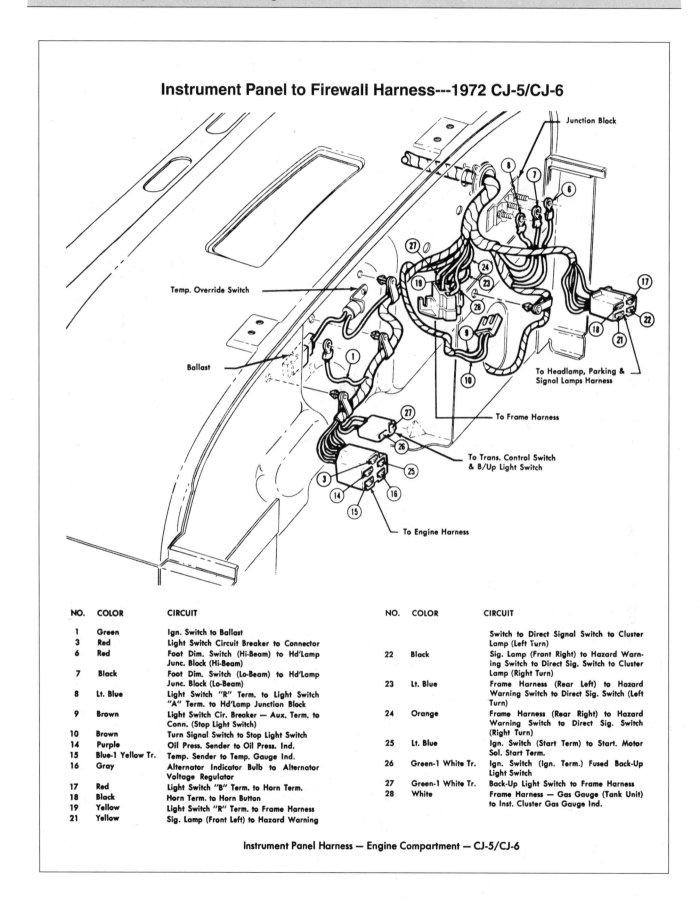

Instrument Panel to Firewall Harness---1972 CJ-5/CJ-6

Junction Block

Temp. Override Switch

Ballast

To Headlamp, Parking & Signal Lamps Harness

To Frame Harness

To Trans. Control Switch & B/Up Light Switch

To Engine Harness

NO.	COLOR	CIRCUIT
1	Green	Ign. Switch to Ballast
3	Red	Light Switch Circuit Breaker to Connector
6	Red	Foot Dim. Switch (Hi-Beam) to Hd'Lamp Junc. Block (Hi-Beam)
7	Black	Foot Dim. Switch (Lo-Beam) to Hd'Lamp Junc. Block (Lo-Beam)
8	Lt. Blue	Light Switch "R" Term. to Light Switch "A" Term. to Hd'Lamp Junction Block
9	Brown	Light Switch Cir. Breaker — Aux. Term. to Conn. (Stop Light Switch)
10	Brown	Turn Signal Switch to Stop Light Switch
14	Purple	Oil Press. Sender to Oil Press. Ind.
15	Blue-1 Yellow Tr.	Temp. Sender to Temp. Gauge Ind.
16	Gray	Alternator Indicator Bulb to Alternator Voltage Regulator
17	Red	Light Switch "B" Term. to Horn Term.
18	Black	Horn Term. to Horn Button
19	Yellow	Light Switch "R" Term. to Frame Harness
21	Yellow	Sig. Lamp (Front Left) to Hazard Warning

NO.	COLOR	CIRCUIT
		Switch to Direct Signal Switch to Cluster Lamp (Left Turn)
22	Black	Sig. Lamp (Front Right) to Hazard Warning Switch to Direct Sig. Switch to Cluster Lamp (Right Turn)
23	Lt. Blue	Frame Harness (Rear Left) to Hazard Warning Switch to Direct Sig. Switch (Left Turn)
24	Orange	Frame Harness (Rear Right) to Hazard Warning Switch to Direct Sig. Switch (Right Turn)
25	Lt. Blue	Ign. Switch (Start Term) to Start. Motor Sol. Start Term.
26	Green-1 White Tr.	Ign. Switch (Ign. Term.) Fused Back-Up Light Switch
27	Green-1 White Tr.	Back-Up Light Switch to Frame Harness
28	White	Frame Harness — Gas Gauge (Tank Unit) to Inst. Cluster Gas Gauge Ind.

Instrument Panel Harness — Engine Compartment — CJ-5/CJ-6

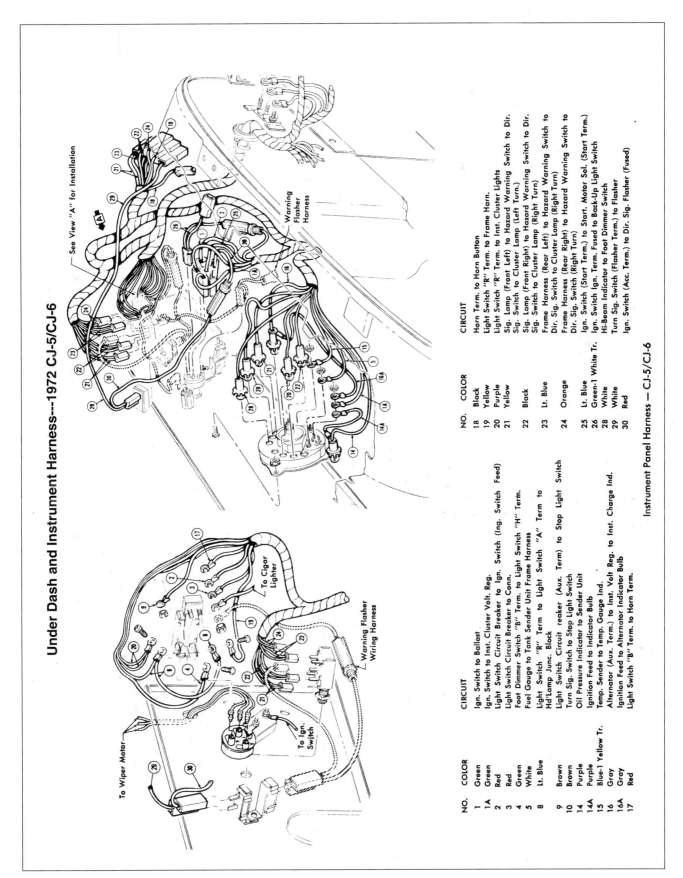

Under Dash and Instrument Harness—1972 CJ-5/CJ-6

See View "A" for Installation

Warning Flasher Harness

To Wiper Motor

Warning Flasher Wiring Harness

To Cigar Lighter

To Ign. Switch

NO.	COLOR	CIRCUIT
1	Green	Ign. Switch to Ballast.
1A	Green	Ign. Switch to Inst. Cluster Volt. Reg.
2	Red	Light Switch Circuit Breaker to Ign. Switch (Ing. Switch Feed)
3	Red	Light Switch Circuit Breaker to Conn.
4	Green	Foot Dimmer Switch "B" Term. to Light Switch "H" Term.
5	White	Fuel Gauge to Tank Sender Unit Frame Harness
8	Lt. Blue	Light Switch "R" Term to Light Switch "A" Term to Hd'lamp Junc. Block
9	Brown	Light Switch Circuit reaker (Aux. Term) to Stop Light Switch
10	Brown	Turn Sig. Switch to Stop Light Switch
14	Purple	Oil Pressure Indicator to Sender Unit
14A	Purple	Ignition Feed to Indicator Bulb
15	Blue-1 Yellow Tr.	Temp. Sender to Temp. Gauge Ind.
16	Gray	Alternator (Aux. Term.) to Inst. Volt Reg. to Inst. Charge Ind.
16A	Gray	Ignition Feed to Alternator Indicator Bulb
17	Red	Light Switch "B" Term. to Horn Term.

NO.	COLOR	CIRCUIT
18	Black	Horn Term. to Horn Button
19	Yellow	Light Switch "R" Term. to Frame Harn.
20	Purple	Light Switch "R" Term. to Inst. Cluster Lights
21	Yellow	Sig. Lamp (Front Left) to Hazard Warning Switch to Dir.
22	Black	Sig. Switch to Cluster Lamp (Left Turn.)
23	Lt. Blue	Sig. Lamp (Front Right) to Hazard Warning Switch to Dir. Sig. Switch to Cluster Lamp (Right Turn)
		Frame Harness (Rear Left) to Hazard Warning Switch to Dir. Sig. Switch to Cluster Lamp (Right Turn)
24	Orange	Frame Harness (Rear Right) to Hazard Warning Switch to Dir. Sig. Switch (Right Turn)
25	Lt. Blue	Ign. Switch (Start Term.) to Start. Motor Sol. (Start Term.)
26	Green-1 White Tr.	Ign. Switch Ign. Term. Fused to Back-Up Light Switch
28	White	Hi-Beam Indicator to Foot Dimmer Switch
29	White	Turn Sig. Switch (Flasher Term.) to Flasher
30	Red	Ign. Switch (Acc. Term.) to Dir. Sig. Flasher (Fused)

Instrument Panel Harness — CJ-5/CJ-6

8

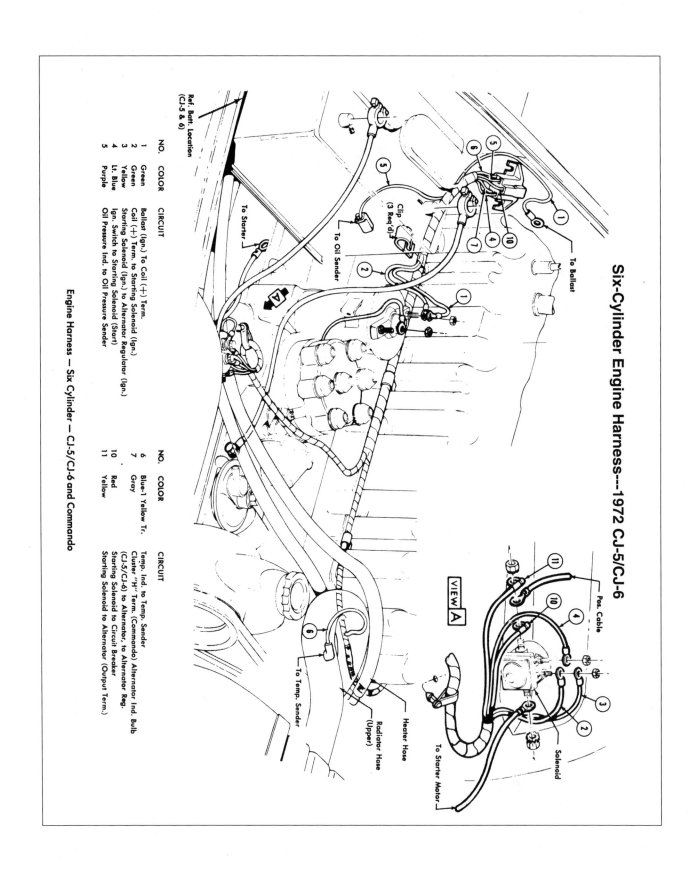

Six-Cylinder Engine Harness—1972 CJ-5/CJ-6

Ref. Batt. Location
(CJ-5 & 6)

NO.	COLOR	CIRCUIT
1	Green	Ballast (Ign.) To Coil (+) Term.
2	Green	Coil (+) Term. to Starting Solenoid (Ign.)
3	Yellow	Starting Solenoid (Ign.) to Alternator Regulator (Ign.)
4	Lt. Blue	Ign. Switch to Starting Solenoid (Start)
5	Purple	Oil Pressure Ind. to Oil Pressure Sender

NO.	COLOR	CIRCUIT
6	Blue-1 Yellow Tr.	Temp. Ind. to Temp. Sender
7	Gray	Cluster "H" Term. (Commando) Alternator Ind. Bulb (CJ-5/CJ-6) to Alternator, to Alternator Reg.
10	Red	Starting Solenoid to Circuit Breaker
11	Yellow	Starting Solenoid to Alternator (Output Term.)

Engine Harness — Six Cylinder — CJ-5/CJ-6 and Commando

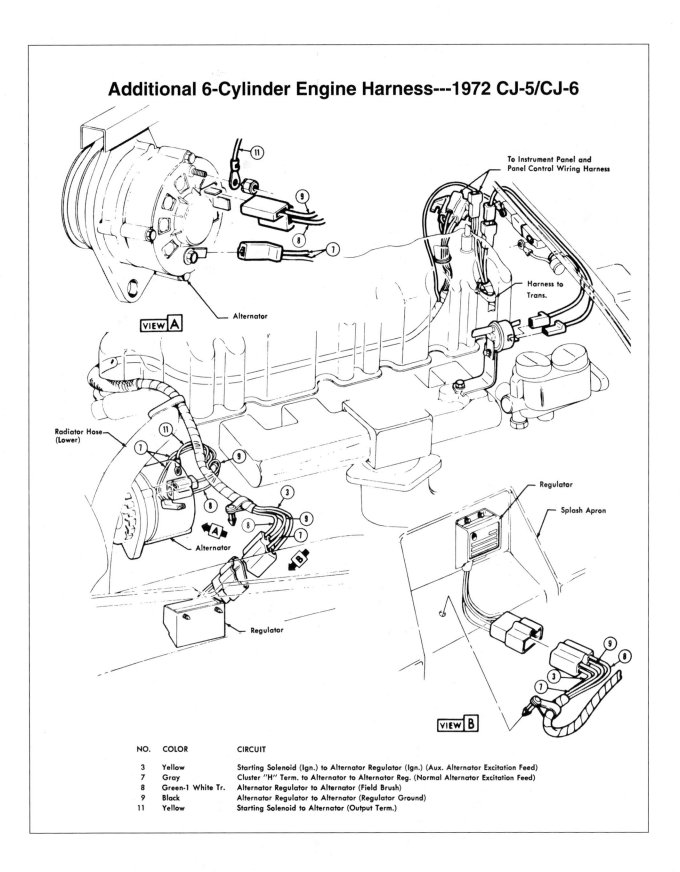

Additional 6-Cylinder Engine Harness---1972 CJ-5/CJ-6

To Instrument Panel and
Panel Control Wiring Harness

Harness to Trans.

Alternator

VIEW A

Radiator Hose
(Lower)

Alternator

Regulator

Regulator

Splash Apron

VIEW B

NO.	COLOR	CIRCUIT
3	Yellow	Starting Solenoid (Ign.) to Alternator Regulator (Ign.) (Aux. Alternator Excitation Feed)
7	Gray	Cluster "H" Term. to Alternator to Alternator Reg. (Normal Alternator Excitation Feed)
8	Green-1 White Tr.	Alternator Regulator to Alternator (Field Brush)
9	Black	Alternator Regulator to Alternator (Regulator Ground)
11	Yellow	Starting Solenoid to Alternator (Output Term.)

8

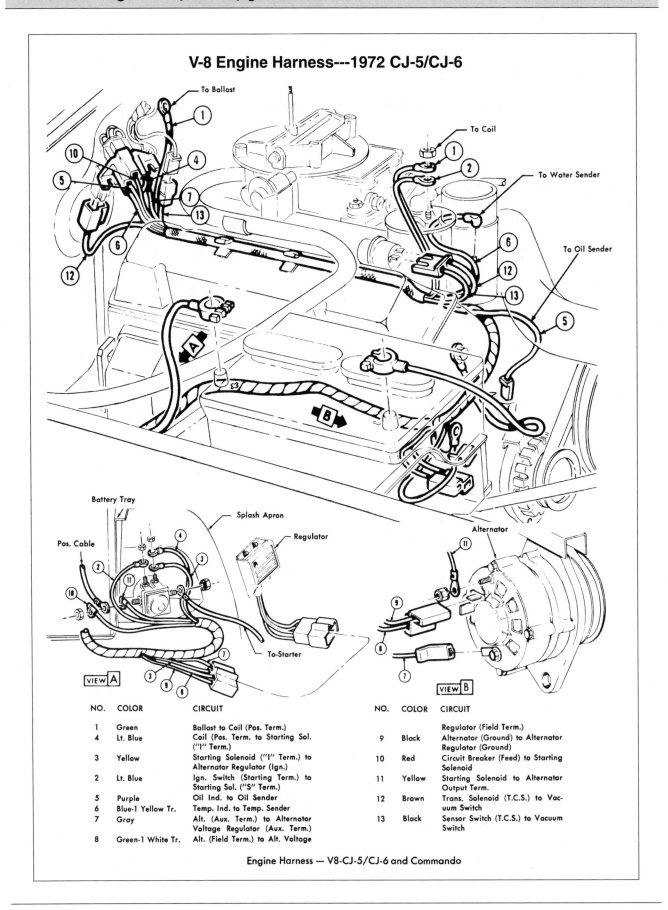

V-8 Engine Harness---1972 CJ-5/CJ-6

NO.	COLOR	CIRCUIT
1	Green	Ballast to Coil (Pos. Term.)
4	Lt. Blue	Coil (Pos. Term. to Starting Sol. ("I" Term.)
3	Yellow	Starting Solenoid ("I" Term.) to Alternator Regulator (Ign.)
2	Lt. Blue	Ign. Switch (Starting Term.) to Starting Sol. ("S" Term.)
5	Purple	Oil Ind. to Oil Sender
6	Blue-1 Yellow Tr.	Temp. Ind. to Temp. Sender
7	Gray	Alt. (Aux. Term.) to Alternator Voltage Regulator (Aux. Term.)
8	Green-1 White Tr.	Alt. (Field Term.) to Alt. Voltage Regulator (Field Term.)
9	Black	Alternator (Ground) to Alternator Regulator (Ground)
10	Red	Circuit Breaker (Feed) to Starting Solenoid
11	Yellow	Starting Solenoid to Alternator Output Term.
12	Brown	Trans. Solenoid (T.C.S.) to Vacuum Switch
13	Black	Sensor Switch (T.C.S.) to Vacuum Switch

Engine Harness — V8-CJ-5/CJ-6 and Commando

Chapter 9

Fuel and Exhaust Systems

9

General

Fuel delivery on a Jeep CJ is a simple affair. Troubleshooting and repair do not present a large challenge, and all '72-'86 engines have traditional carburetion systems. Emission controls increase from 1972 into the 1980s. These emission devices play a large part in engine tuning.

By the mid-1960s, the advent of emission controls impacted Jeep engineering. CJ engines soon included a closed crankcase, air injection and thermal air cleaner systems. By 1971, the California version of the F-head four was so overwhelmed by emissions hardware and an air pump injection system that the engine's fate was clear. AMC would drop the F-head and shift the '72-up Jeep CJs to the AMC 232 and 258 sixes and the 304 V-8.

NOTE—

*All of the AMC engines have a full complement of emission controls. For additional details on emission control systems and devices, see the **Jeep Owner's Bible**. Service and troubleshooting of the emissions system is straightforward. Emission control data is available in OEM and trade shop manuals. **Mitchell** manuals offer the most details on vacuum hose circuits and emission devices. **Motors**, **Mitchell** and **Chilton** professional series manuals are often found at public libraries.*

The fuel delivery and tuning issues of the AMC/Jeep CJs are not complicated. Aside from the mechanical fuel pump, fuel lines and hoses, the primary tuning need is carburetor rebuilding. Carburetor rebuild kits include explicit instructions and provide details for a quality overhaul.

Parts quality should be a foremost concern. There are many sources for carburetor rebuilding kits, new fuel pumps and exhaust system components. Know your sources. I have traditionally used Mopar/Jeep, Echlin/NAPA, Bendix and Delco-Rochester carburetor kits. AMC/Jeep-era fuel pumps are not rebuildable. Mopar, TRW and Carter replacement fuel pumps are the best available.

Often, either wear or cost will steer your parts choice toward new components. Jeep/Mopar OEM replacement parts remain available at this time. The aftermarket is rife with AMC/Jeep replacement parts. You will have no difficulty seeking carburetor, fuel pump or most emission control devices. Some parts will become scarcer as time goes on, in particular the emission control switches, solenoid controls and exotic carburetor feedback devices.

Fig. 9-1

The fuel delivery system begins with the fuel tank. Many Jeep fuel tanks have corrosion or contamination. The AMC-era CJ tanks are all at the rear of the vehicle, tucked up on the frame behind the axle. A skid plate protects the tank on this 1972 CJ-5. The fuel filler is at the rear of the vehicle. These CJ fuel systems are "evaporative emission" designs, sealed from the atmosphere with non-vented fuel caps.

NOTE—

4WD Hardware, Inc., and other aftermarket sources supply OEM replacement fuel tanks and larger capacity replacement tanks. When installing such a tank, make certain that you do not compromise the evaporative emissions system. Hoses and vents must follow the OEM Jeep routing to prevent gasoline from flooding the engine or risk of a dangerous fuel spill. Similarly, I recommend a new gas cap if you suspect that the cap is not sealing. The cap is very much a part of the closed vapor system. At the rear, the filler cap must seal well to prevent fuel leaks when you negotiate steep 4WD inclines!

Fig. 9-2

When fabricating fuel lines for my vintage Jeep CJ, Goodridge was my source for the fittings and fuel line. I opted for special corrosion-resistant, stainless steel braid hose. The fuel hose lining resists any type of fuel corrosion (including alcohol, ethanol and water). If you fabricate a custom fuel supply system, consider this approach. At the least, use quality steel fuel-grade piping with double-flared ends.

NOTE—

Threaded hole to left of fuel fitting is drain plug's hole. This is a convenient feature of early Jeep fuel tanks! AMC-era CJs do not offer this option. Some aftermarket fuel tanks do.

9

Fuel Pump Tips

The mechanical fuel pump is a simple unit. In troubleshooting, the aim is to determine whether the pump sucks and displaces the proper amount (volume) of fuel in a given time interval. When the pump cannot displace fuel at this rate, it needs to be replaced.

1) The specifications for fuel pump pressure and displacement will vary. Typically, AMC sixes and the 150 AMC four require 4 to 5 PSI; V-8s require 5 to 6-1/2 PSI; and the GM 151 four requires 6-1/2 to 8 PSI.

2) Before condemning the fuel pump, check all hoses from the tank to the carburetor. A leak or kink between the tank and fuel pump will not allow vacuum to draw fuel sufficiently.

3) Check the fuel filter for obstacles. Check fuel flow before and after the filter. Do not replace the fuel pump when the filter or tank-to-pump supply lines are at fault!

4) When changing the pump, loosen the bolts evenly, a small amount at a time. Apply Super 300 or equivalent sealant to each side of the fuel pump gasket, just enough to evenly coat the gasket. Apply sealant to the bolt threads.

5) Make sure the fuel pump lobe is at its lowest point when installing the pump. This relieves pressure from the pump arm. Tighten the bolts evenly, a few turns at a time. *Do not allow the pump arm to cock! This can severely damage the pump. Torque bolts to specification in steps, tightening side-to-side.*

6) Use new hoses and clamps (if old clamps show wear). Always check for leaks. Retighten or check clamps after the engine has run for a while at operating temperature.

WARNING—

Never clamp a fuel hose to a straight piece of fuel pipe! The clamp alone may not be sufficient to retain the hose under pressure! When sectioning a fuel line (as shown) to install a universal filter and rubber hoses, I take a double-flaring tool and make a semi-"bubble" flare at the cut pipe end. This is the first stage of a flaring job, when the tube end forms a hump. The hump acts as a shoulder to keep the hose from blowing off. Place the clamp(s) past the hump. This bubble flare also keeps the pipe end from cutting into the hose. (See 'EFI' installation later in this chapter for details on safe hose and fuel pipe installations.)

Carter One-Barrel Carburetors

Among the easiest carburetors to rebuild, the Carter one-barrel '596S', '636SA' and 'YF' models were used on vintage Willys and Kaiser-era Jeep CJ engines. AMC continued the use of Carter's YF carburetor on the inline six-cylinder engines of the 1970s. With simple hand tools, these 1940s technology carburetors can be a great place to sharpen your carburetor rebuilding skills.

YF single-throat carburetors can be readily removed from the engine. There are fewer moving parts in a Carter one-barrel carburetor than most other designs. Troubleshooting is straightforward.

Common adjustments consist of the float level, float drop, idle mixture screw, idle speed stop, linkages and the automatic choke. Jets are replaceable and can be changed to accommodate sustained vehicle operation at a given altitude. You will find the Carter one-barrel both predictable and reliable.

For the sake of one-barrel carburetor rebuilders, I am including a step-by-step buildup of the vintage Carter YF carburetor. The model shown is simpler and more primitive than AMC-era versions. It features a manual (hand operated) choke. Emission devices were not a part of the early Jeep's carburetor design. When you rebuild your YF Carter, a quality overhaul kit will contain detailed instructions and illustrations that apply to the carburetor on your engine.

Fig. 9-3

Carburetor cleaner remains the best method for cleaning varnish and deposits from a carburetor. This Permatex product also works well on items like distributor metal parts.

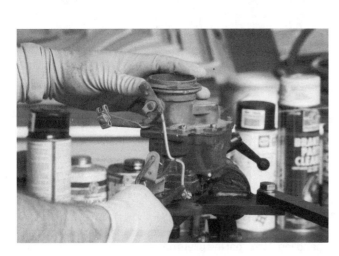

Fig. 9-4a

'YF' Carter disassembly begins with removing linkages. Use needle-nose type pliers to loosen the clips.

9

Fig. 9-4b

A power screwdriver is an excellent way to quickly disassemble a carburetor. Here, float bowl cover screws come loose.

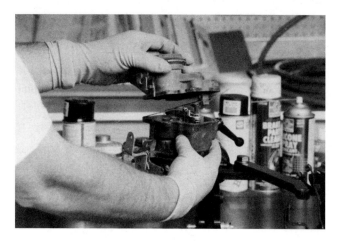

 Fig. 9-5

Lift float bowl cover loose with float attached. Lift carefully to prevent damage to the gasket and float.

Fig. 9-6

Simple enough! If you were adjusting the float, this is all the access needed.

Fig. 9-7

Check balls, needles and other sensitive parts need careful handling. Note that the pliers grips the needle away from the tapered tip.

◀ **Fig. 9-8**

Loosen the screw holding the throttle shaft arm.

◀ **Fig. 9-9**

Remove pump spring retainer clip and spring.

9

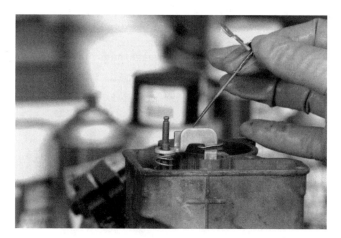

◀ **Fig. 9-10**

Remove metering rod, carefully.

Fig. 9-11
Lift out the pump link.

Fig. 9-12
Loosen screws that retain the diaphragm housing.

Fig. 9-13
Diaphragm, pump housing and related parts are now free of the carburetor body.

◀ **Fig. 9-14**

You can remove the metering rod jet for more thorough cleaning. Use extreme care. Brass jets can break or slough material when the wrong screwdriver is applied. Use a screwdriver with a blade large enough to fill the slot.

◀ **Fig. 9-15**

Once more, remove jets with the proper size screwdriver.

9

◀ **Fig. 9-16**

Float bowl area is now stripped for cleaning.

 Fig. 9-17

Throttle body screws (3) now loosened, the throttle body separates from the main (float bowl) body.

◀ **Fig. 9-18**

Cleaned thoroughly, all passageways blown clean with compressed air to remove moisture from the water/neutralizing bath, YF unit goes back together.

◀ **Fig. 9-19**

If, by chance, your Jeep runs continuously at very high altitudes, a jet change may be in order. Here, number on low-speed jet is visible and can be used as a reference for re-sizing to meet altitude requirements. There is also a sized main metering jet. (See a Carter dealer for replacement jets.)

WARNING—

If you do change jet sizing to run at high altitude, be certain to install the original jet for operating at lower elevations. If you fail to do so, there's a high risk of lean-burn troubles like detonation, upper cylinder heat extremes, and even damage to the pistons and valves.

◁ **Fig. 9-20**

You can assemble the pump link, diaphragm, springs, and even the metering rod. When doing so, be very careful installing these pieces, as the rod could easily become damaged.

◁ **Fig. 9-21**

Screw holder makes installation of diaphragm screws much easier. Once you start these screws, a conventional screwdriver can complete the task.

9

◁ **Fig. 9-22**

Note the relationship of parts from this view.

 Fig. 9-23

Side view shows pump mechanism and order of parts.

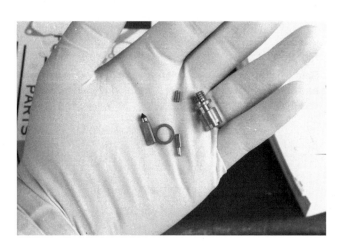

 Fig. 9-24

New needle and seat assembly comes with related pieces. This is a quality carburetor kit. I have used NAPA/Echlin products for many years. Mopar, Carter, Bendix, Rochester and other known products are also excellent. Always follow directions provided in the rebuild kit.

Rebuild Kits, Sub-Assemblies and Jet Sizing

A carburetor rebuild is no better than the parts quality and labor involved. Always seek a quality rebuilding kit. Such kits come with the kind of parts that will keep your Jeep running reliably under the most adverse driving conditions.

A quality carburetor kit will come with all of the pieces necessary to restore your carburetor. Instructions will detail the model and identification numbers for each carburetor covered by the kit.

Reusable small parts for the Carter 'YF' are easy to identify and install properly. The instruction sheet furnishes a schematic diagram of parts to assure proper assembly.

Rebuild Kits, Sub-Assemblies and Jet Sizing (continued)

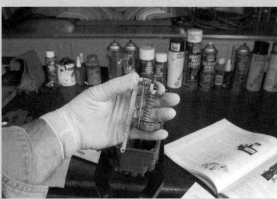

Pay close attention to layout of sub-assemblies. When in doubt, refer to the instruction sheet furnished with the rebuild kit!

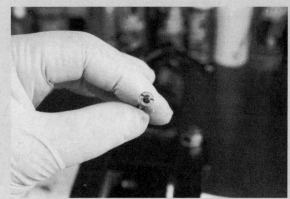

You can confirm jet sizing by the factory method of inserting a specific drill size through the jet. Here, I check the main metering rod jet with a sized drill, using the smooth shank as the test gauge. Twisting the drill's cutting end carefully through the jet will remove any varnish. *Do not remove metal, or the jet will flow too much fuel!*

◄ **Fig. 9-25**

This special tool is perfect for installing needle seats. The tool is actually designed for earlier GM six-cylinder breaker point distributor nuts. I have valued this tool for more than a quarter century, and you can see why!

9

◄ **Fig. 9-26**

Carburetor kit comes with a ruler for checking float measurements. Kits also come with instructions that reference each carburetor model and application covered. Read these instructions carefully to determine settings for your model carburetor.

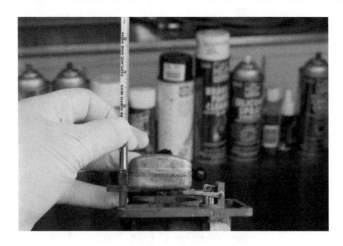

 Fig. 9-27

I use this more accurate T-rule, referencing the specifications in the instruction sheet and then confirming measurements with this rule gauge.

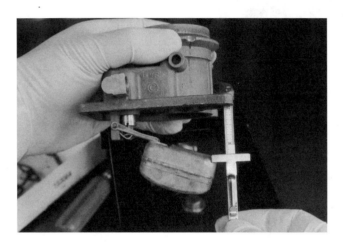

◄ **Fig. 9-28**

This measurement is float drop. Instructions indicate where to take this measurement and how to remedy out-of-specification measurements. Installing a new needle and seat generally requires some kind of adjusting. Seldom is the new assembly identical to the original settings.

◄ **Fig. 9-29**

This arm and its matching opposite arm control the float drop. Bending the arms will change the drop setting. *Always remove the float before bending these arms. Bending in place can damage the needle and seat!*

 Fig. 9-30

Float level and drop set properly, you can install the float bowl cover gasket and very carefully install the float bowl cover. Be sure not to damage the needle or float. Do not upset the float adjustment during installation.

◄ **Fig. 9-31**

Fit the throttle body and new gasket carefully to the main body (float bowl section). Make sure the pump link arm and linkage will align with the throttle shaft arm before you tighten the setscrew. A drop of Loctite 242 on these threads is good insurance.

9

◄ **Fig. 9-32**

Linkage attaches with hairpin and spring clips. Align linkage properly and make certain these clips are secure.

 Fig. 9-33

Assembled, carburetor is ready to perform many hard days of work! This is a fundamental, durable carburetor. Iron throttle body and single-barrel design provide the simple reliability that characterized the vintage Jeep 4WD vehicles.

◄ **Fig. 9-34**

Move throttle arm and observe the linkage movement. Be certain parts do not interfere with one another. The throttle shaft and arm must return readily to the closed position.

> **WARNING—**
>
> *Sticking throttle linkage could cause a serious incident on the highway or trail! Once the carburetor is installed on the engine, use appropriate throttle return springs to assure safe operation and a prompt return to idle when the throttle pedal releases.*

NOTE—
When installing your carburetor, use factory recommended throttle return spring methods. Place springs in OEM locations. Do not stress the carburetor's throttle shaft, as harmful, premature wear to the shaft and throttle body will result.

◄ **Fig. 9-35**

Last step in overhaul is preliminary adjustment of the idle mixture screw. Turn the screw gently inward until it seats, and then back out the screw the exact amount described in the rebuilding kit's instructions. Settings range from ¾-turn to 2-plus full turns.

NOTE—
If you follow the idle mixture screw adjusting specifications, the properly rebuilt carburetor should readily start the engine. Once the engine warms up, the final mixture adjustment is easy to perform.

Adjusting the 'YF' Carburetor

Adjustments for the Carter carburetor are relatively simple. When installing and adjusting a choke unit, make certain that the choke valve opens completely when the choke heats up. The throttle valve must open and close completely.

NOTE—

On older Jeep models with a hand-controlled choke, I adjust for a very small gap between the dash panel stop and the fully inward choke knob. This lets me know that the choke is fully open. On older Jeep models with a hand throttle, with the throttle knob all the way inward, I adjust for a slight gap when I pull the throttle knob outward. This lets me know that the hand throttle cable is not applying pressure to the throttle lever when the knob is all the way inward.

Accurate idle mixture adjustments can only be made with the air filter clean and installed. The engine must be completely warmed. Make certain the choke valve is fully open!

NOTE—

When adjusting the carburetor during periodic maintenance, the ignition settings (point dwell and timing) should be completed before adjusting the idle mixture. Make sure there are no vacuum leaks and that the EGR valve seats completely.

Set the curb idle speed before adjusting the carburetor's idle mixture screw. Turn the idle mixture screw in slowly until you hear the engine begin to (lean) misfire. Now, very slowly back the screw outward until the engine smoothes out.

If you are unsure how far out to turn the screw, keep going and observe the idle speed changes. Strive for the highest engine speed that remains smooth. Too far out with the mixture screw, and you will hear the engine begin to blubber from an over-rich mix. Turn the screw inward until just the point where the idle speed begins to drop. Adjust for the smoothest idle.

When mixture adjustment causes the idle speed to increase beyond specification, back the idle speed screw out to bring the idle back into compliance. Then, once again run the idle screw inward, and back the screw out to the most desirable setting.

The method described is time-honored for older engine types and simple carburetor systems. There are actually several ways to do the idle mixture adjustment:

1) The "listening to engine speed and smoothness" method I have described.

2) By using a vacuum gauge to set for maximum manifold vacuum, backing out the idle mix screw to the highest vacuum reading, then turning the screw inward to just the point that the vacuum begins to drop.

3) With a tachometer, you can back out the idle mixture screw to the highest rpm point, and then turn the screw inward just to where the idle speed begins to drop. Again, make certain that curb idle speed remains within specification.

4) For emissions test and compliance, a "lean drop" setting may be required. Find the best idle mix by the previous methods then turn the mixture screw inward until the engine speed drops as specified.

5) Using a modern emission machine, you can set the idle for optimal CO/HC readings. The caution here is that lower horsepower emission engines may not run properly at lean, modern emission levels. Tune to the HC/CO output expected, and see if this is too lean for rock crawling stability.

NOTE—

Any time idle speed increases beyond specification, readjust curb idle, and check the idle mixture setting again. When you become familiar with the proper sounds and exhaust note of your CJ's engine, you can adjust the mixture with nothing more than a screwdriver---to great results.

The two-barrel carburetors on AMC V-8s and later inline sixes are also easy to adjust. Any of the methods I describe will work. You need to make these adjustments at the *two idle mixture screws*, one at a time.

Be patient, and the result for any Jeep engine will be a quick start at the bump of the key, easy and stable tip-in of the throttle, steady low-speed pulling power, and the best gas mileage possible for your engine!

Keep the Motorcraft 2100/2150 Series Two-Barrel!

One of the most successful carburetor picks for the AMC V-8s was the use of Motorcraft's 2100 and 2150 series carburetion. These are very reliable, easily rebuilt and relatively simple designs. Ford Motor Company used the 2100 and 2150 units on many of its V-8 applications, and AMC was wise to source these carburetors as OEM equipment.

I am very familiar with these carburetors. Our family's 1987 Grand Wagoneer featured a Motorcraft carburetor on its 360 V-8. At 100,000 miles, I rebuilt the unit with a Mopar rebuild kit. The result was a remarkably stable, smooth and easy-starting engine that at 134,000 miles still functions like new.

Our Grand Wagoneer, driven daily, started in sub-freezing winter weather and scorching summer heat with equal ease. This vehicle was often mistaken for an "EFI" model, yet the Motorcraft '2150' two-barrel carburetion survived on the Grand Wagoneer through 1991, the last model year! Rock-steady idle, with or without the air conditioner on, the carburetor tipped-in flawlessly, accelerated without hesitation, and delivered consistent fuel efficiency. Highway cruise mileage for this hefty "luxury" vehicle was 14 mpg, even with the York air conditioner system sending bone-chilling air into the cabin!

So, why do so many owners opt for Holley universal replacement carburetors on CJ 304 V-8s? The Motorcraft two-barrel on a 304 V-8 is a reliable approach. If you have this carburetor and there is no appreciable throttle shaft wear, consider a rebuild kit.

Soak, clean and inspect the carburetor. Sit at the bench and carefully "blueprint" the unit. Check all of the settings and follow the instruction sheet closely. A quality kit will include detailed illustrations and all of the instructions needed. This is a basic carburetor for rebuilding.

This was the Motorcraft 2150 two-barrel on our Grand Wagoneer's 360 V-8. I rebuilt this unit at 100,000 miles, and the engine ran flawlessly at 134,000 miles. Note the altitude compensator at rear of the unit. 2100- and 2150-series carburetors are very simple and reliable for both highway and trail use.

NOTE—

The late Grand Wagoneer version has the altitude compensator, and even this emission era carburetor is easy to rebuild. Read instructions before teardown, and follow steps closely. Do not tamper with the altitude compensator if so equipped.

Engine Air Intake and Filtration

An engine must breathe, and a Jeep engine needs all the oxygen it can get when faced with the Rocky Mountain or Sierra trails! While enhancements like the MSD ignition or higher compression ratios can help, thin air is thin air! As altitude increases, manifold vacuum drops. The engine suffers progressive horsepower loss as altitude increases.

Turbocharging is one solution for overcoming rarified air. Short of this measure, the least we can do is assure an adequate, unrestricted flow of air into the intake stream.

For any Jeep used off-pavement, a well-sealed air filter assembly and ducting is a must. Paper element filters are very efficient, however, their downside is a propensity for plugging up with dust in mere minutes of travel on an alkali flat. Oil bath air cleaners, notably larger, more complex assemblies, offer service under the most adverse off-highway conditions, but these filters ended with the Kaiser Jeep era. Earlier Jeep vehicles use oil bath air cleaners.

Okay with trade-offs like oil changes and periodically cleaning the unit, I kept the oil bath air filter system on my vintage '55 CJ's F-head engine. After restoration of the oil cup assembly (depicted in an earlier chapter), the OEM air filter worked better than new.

The choice is yours. I do, however, flatly discourage the use of any open-faced, exposed element filter. Such a filter will plug up too quickly, and worse yet, when fording streams, a splash of water can pass through an open-faced filter, into the carburetor and intake manifold, and ultimately reach the upper cylinders of the engine. Such circumstances have caused engines to seize (hydro-lock) instantly and suffer broken connecting rods and pistons!

If you choose an aftermarket element like the popular K&N products, find a suitable air filter canister. Install the filter in a way that water cannot hit the snorkel or air intake opening. An OEM (stock) Jeep canister will work fine. For deeper water fording, consider a remote mounting location and an intake air duct with no restrictions or leaks. ARB makes a bona fide snorkel conversion for this kind of driving.

 Fig. 9-36

My air filter choice for the F-head was the OEM oil bath type. These serviceable filters keep nearly all dirt and dust from entering the engine. The unit mounts high, protected from water crossing hazards. Intake ducting (shown) is modern aircraft silicone rubber, an attractive, heat resistant and durable alternative. All seals and clamped points must be dust-proof, or the air filtration system will be compromised.

9

The 'BBD' Carter Two-Barrel Carburetor

No Jeep carburetor has been more criticized or maligned than the Carter BBD two-barrel. Used on 258 inline AMC sixes, this carburetor has also seen service on many other makes of vehicles. In its Jeep CJ application, the BBD carburetor has delivered good service for some and led to frustration and expensive retrofitting of aftermarket 'EFI' (electronic fuel injection) for others.

The EFI/MPI Alternative

I endorse the use of EFI/MPI systems like Mopar's exceptionally well-conceived, 50-state emission-legal kit. For the owner expecting peak horsepower output, maximum fuel efficiency and optimal performance at all altitudes, EFI is worth the cost! Many 258 Jeep CJs have undergone the Mopar conversion with highly satisfying results.

In my experience, an otherwise purely stock 258 engine can gain 50 horsepower and several miles per gallon in fuel efficiency from the Mopar MPI/EFI conversion. The clean-burning 258 with Mopar MPI/EFI easily meets 50-State emission requirements and is fully legal. Later in this chapter, I share the step-by-step installation of a Mopar EFI/MPI conversion on the '86 CJ Jeep's fresh 258 inline six.

CAUTION—

If you plan an EFI or MPI (multi-point injection) conversion, make certain that your engine is in good condition. Compression, oil sealing, valve lift and bearing clearances must be within specification. As for longevity, an EFI/MPI engine will typically outlast a carbureted engine, as air/fuel ratios are more constant and leaner overall. This prevents "fuel wash" of cylinder walls, a significant cause of engine wear (cylinder taper and ring failure in particular).

EFI conversions are not for every builder. Cost may be prohibitive. For some, there is another type of engine planned for the next phase of the Jeep's life. Regardless, some owners do not want EFI, and they also need to meet emission compliance. There are few carburetor retrofit kits that meet 50-State emissions requirements.

For those willing to rebuild the original BBD two-barrel, I have good news. I believe that if a carburetor worked well when new, it should work well after a proper rebuild. In the 1980s, I drove and tested many CJ and YJ models with the 258 six and BBD Carter carburetor. These Jeep vehicles ran just fine. Later, however, while writing technical columns for four-wheel drive magazines and Portland's *Oregonian* newspaper, I fielded many concerns about the BBD.

For the sake of this book, I singled out a totally stock '85 CJ-7 with the Carter BBD. The owner complained that the engine had not idled properly for over a year. By the time I drove the vehicle, the engine stalled each time the Jeep came to a stop or the clutch pedal was depressed! Crankcase blow-by was so excessive that the closed crankcase hoses had blown off the air cleaner canister!

I purposely did not perform any other tune-up measure beyond a carburetor overhaul. This vehicle offered nearly every driving complaint and symptom I could recall from the years of readers' letters. It was the perfect test of whether a blueprint rebuild could make a difference---and whether the BBD can be properly restored.

This section takes owners through the kind of overhaul that can restore a BBD to like-new performance. Although there are many emission control and vacuum/solenoid problems that can contribute to poor performance, this overhaul made the difference on an engine that previously would barely function, hardly made it through a warm-up cycle, stalled routinely, and delivered horribly poor fuel efficiency.

Did the carburetor rebuild work? Yes, it did. While EFI would add horsepower and high altitude improvements, this California emissions-equipped CJ now runs like a totally different Jeep. For nothing more than the cost of a quality Mopar rebuild kit, a new choke unit and several hours of labor, the overhaul paid off. You may want to try this before condemning your original equipment emissions hardware and the BBD!

 Fig. 9-37

This is the stock Carter 'BBD' equipped engine. A 1985 CJ-7 with its original engine was the prime candidate for the test! The owner complained that the engine stalled each time it came to an idle or when the clutch was depressed. Constant stalling and an off-idle flat spot were clear symptoms of trouble.

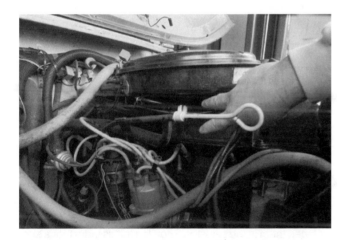

Fig. 9-38

From running rich, this engine's gummy piston rings had crankcase pressure at the danger level. These hoses, swollen badly from oil blow-by, had fallen off---a very bad sign! The hose fittings at the base of the air cleaner are inboard of the air filter. As a result, dirt easily got sucked into the engine, further stressing the rings.

9

 Fig. 9-39

Before condemning the carburetor for a bad idle and flat spot, I checked the EGR (exhaust gas re-circulation) valve. A valve stuck open could create these symptoms, and no amount of carburetor work will overcome a defective or stuck EGR valve.

 Fig. 9-40

A simple hand vacuum pump test of the EGR reveals that the diaphragm is intact and holding vacuum. The valve moves freely. With the engine running at a stable, near idle speed, I apply vacuum. The engine roughens up. This is the sign of a valve that is working: a smooth idle when closed; runs rough when the EGR is opened at an idle.

Fig. 9-41

Remove top of air cleaner. The air filter is saturated with oil. I picked a challenging engine to try a BBD carburetor rescue…Say, what's that inside the canister?

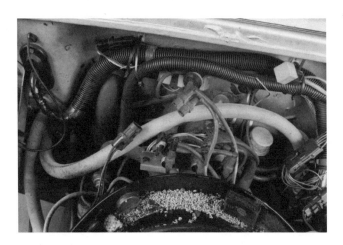

Fig. 9-42

Would you believe---field mice crawled into the canister through the air intake duct. They foraged for seeds and placed them in the canister. Effort led to this industrious supply of food! Keep track of the hoses and air filter electrical connectors. If necessary, mark these items with masking tape.

 Fig. 9-43

Note the relationship of hoses. This is the stock layout. Emission devices are busy on later CJ engines. The switch to EFI/MPI does eliminate much of this clutter. *(See Mopar MPI conversion later in this chapter.)*

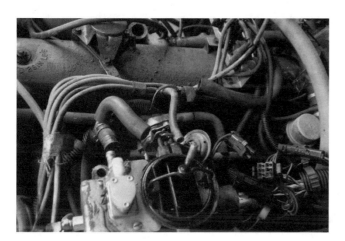

Fig. 9-44

Close-up of hoses for emissions and evaporative vapors.

Fig. 9-45

Now the vacuum hose to the "Sole-Vac" device, the wire to its solenoid, and the fuel hose at the inlet of the carburetor can come loose. Keep track of hose and wire locations. If necessary, mark hoses and wires to aid in reassembly. I like to leave these pieces in their original positions, which aids in identifying components.

9

 Fig. 9-46

Throttle rod disconnected, these hoses and wires disconnected, I loosen the mounting nuts and remove the carburetor. One nut drew out the stud. Note the relationship of these parts. I cover the intake ports to prevent any debris or hardware from falling into the engine while the carburetor is on the bench.

 Fig. 9-47

My rebuild kit of choice is a Genuine Mopar part! This kit comes with all vital pieces plus a detailed instruction sheet. There is virtually no need to consult any other manual. Mopar is my assurance that I am building this carburetor to OEM/factory standards.

NOTE—

A carburetor rebuild kit does not contain electrical devices, emissions control items, carburetor body parts, jets, metering rods, the throttle body/valve assembly or other "hard parts." The industry standard for a kit includes the needle/seat assembly, the accelerator pump assembly, checkballs, gaskets, diaphragms and other small wear items. Hard parts are available through Carter and Mopar outlets, and many emission devices have found their way into the aftermarket. Mopar and NAPA/Echlin are good sources for emission control devices and choke units.

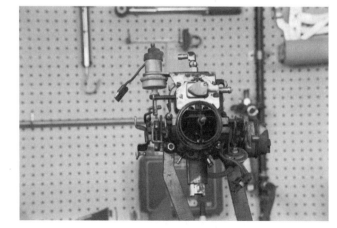

 Fig. 9-48

This is the top view of the removed carburetor assembly. Note the amount of oil that has gone down the carburetor throat. On this carburetor, the air and fuel passageways will be clogged and washed with dirt and oil. (See Fig. 9-38.) A closed crankcase must remain tightly sealed to prevent this kind of damage.

 Fig. 9-49

Choke-side view of the carburetor and lack of tension at the choke valve indicate a possible problem with the choke unit. The CJ has 140,000 miles of wear. At this point, I suspect that the electric choke element might be malfunctioning.

Fig. 9-50

Sole-Vac unit (at left with vacuum and solenoid) and Stepper Motor (right) play a crucial role in idle speed and low-speed engine performance. Considering that this engine stalled every time the throttle came back to idle after warm-up, I carefully consider the function of these two components. I will check them with electrical power (12-volts) and the vacuum hand pump.

9

Fig. 9-51

Bottom side view of the BBD shows the relationship of Sole-Vac and the stepper motor. Note the accumulation of grime. This carburetor has not been cleaned or serviced for a very long time---and you can tell it!

 Fig. 9-52

Fuel inlet view of the carburetor reveals the choke setting. Scribe the choke cover-to-housing alignment to assure resetting the choke in this position when you reassemble the carburetor.

 Fig. 9-53

Here is factory choke mark and indexing. You may need to adjust the choke for altitude or engine condition. For emissions purposes, the original setting is factory fixed on most late model carburetors. You will find that the rebuild kit and instructions address choke adjustment.

 Fig. 9-54

Disassembly begins with identifying the idle mixture screws and removing them from the carburetor body. (Soft dowel plugs are installed at the factory. You can remove the dowels for access to these screws.) If the idle was right before an overhaul, I will run these screws to the light seating position, counting the exact amount of turns to seat the needles. Make a note of the turns for quick tuning upon reassembly.

 Fig. 9-55

This choke has been serviced before. The attaching hardware is a set of sheet metal screws found in cheaper rebuilding kits. Mopar kit will upgrade the attaching method.

Choke Attachment Methods

The Mopar 'BBD' rebuilding kit has special choke cover screws. Once the choke is set to factory specification, you tighten these screws to the point that their heads twist off. Future choke service will require drilling the soft screw heads out.

Some carburetor kits come with pop rivets for the choke unit. On these carburetor applications, you set the choke to specification and install the rivets with a pop rivet gun. Future service will require drilling out the rivet heads.

The intent with either of these approaches is to meet emission compliance standards. Choke setting will impact the incoming air/fuel ratio, which in turn affects the tailpipe emission output. To make the choke more "tamper-proof," rivets or breakaway screw heads are used. Despite the extra work, such chokes are serviceable.

9

 Fig. 9-56

Vacuum choke pull-off is an important item. I will check performance with a hand vacuum pump. *Devices like this do not go into the carburetor cleaner! Carburetor cleaner would cause the diaphragm to swell up and fail.* For cosmetic purposes, I will clean the metal shell with a cleaning solvent or run such parts through my parts washing machine, which uses a hot, citrus-based aqueous solution.

NOTE—

I have learned to use disposable mechanics gloves. Years ago, mechanics soaked up solvents and VOCs in products like carburetor cleaner. I'm older and much wiser now. Today, you can enjoy this work without risking damage to your health. Wear mechanic's gloves!

 Fig. 9-57

This unique electrical device is the "wide open throttle switch." The switch feeds a signal to the engine management computer. The BBD in this application is a "feedback" carburetor. The stepper motor's tapered needles adjust the air/fuel ratio.

NOTE—

Signals that determine the BBD's stepper motor settings come from a variety of engine sensors. Included with the many other devices are the wide-open throttle switch, temperature sensor and an oxygen sensor. Feedback carburetors were the last technological stage before the changeover to factory EFI/MPI.

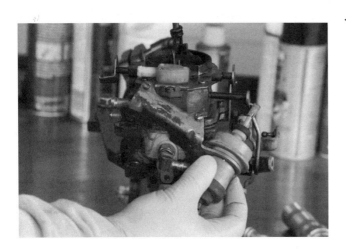

Fig. 9-58

Sole-Vac unit comes off next. Part of this device is a vacuum diaphragm. The other part is an electro-magnetic solenoid actuator. The unit ties to feedback signals and sets the throttle position for various conditions.

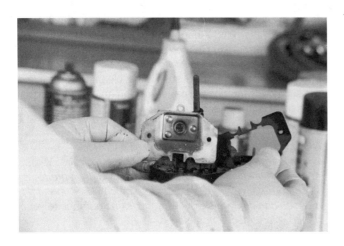

Fig. 9-59

This is the rollover check valve. It also serves as the bowl vent. The valve is a safety item. In the event of a vehicle rollover, the valve closes to prevent dangerous fuel spillage.

 Fig. 9-60

Remove the air horn screws and gently lift the air horn assembly from the main body. Note the metering rods hanging from the air horn. *Lift the air horn straight up---protect these delicate parts!*

◀ **Fig. 9-61**

Note that the gasket lifts with these parts. Hold assemblies together. Do not allow the metering rods to become bent. Do not let the weight of the air horn rest on the rods.

9

◀ **Fig. 9-62**

You can remove the inlet fitting with the needle assembly. This is a unique arrangement: The inlet fitting is the needle's seat. Note the float fulcrum retainer (hoop-shaped piece). The retainer holds the float pivot pin in place.

 Fig. 9-63

Lift the baffle out straight. Gently lift the float assembly from the main body. Try not to disturb the float adjustments. Do not bend the float arms.

Fig. 9-64

Using a pen magnet, I remove the check ball beneath the accelerator pump well.

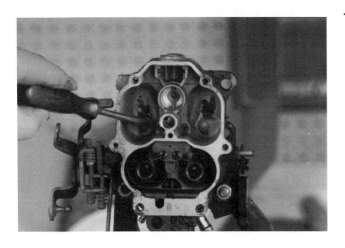

Fig. 9-65

Brass jets in base of fuel bowl are slotted. Use a screwdriver with a blade that fills the slot. This minimizes the risk of twisting the flanges of the jets as you remove them. There is one jet on each side of the bowl.

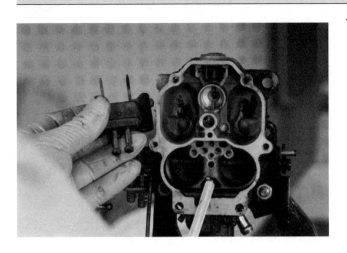

 Fig. 9-66

This is the venturi cluster assembly. Remove the two screws and keep this assembly together. Keep track of all parts.

◀ **Fig. 9-67**

Lift this check ball with a magnet. Note the diameter differences between check balls.

9

◀ **Fig. 9-68**

The stepper motor is a critical part. Expensive and very important to the function of the BBD carburetor, this closed-loop feedback device should be handled carefully. I will not dip this device in carburetor cleaner.

'MCU' and Feedback Devices

The Micro Computer Unit (MCU) is constantly reading engine functions. On BBD carbureted models that have the MCU, this microprocessor receives a host of signals from various engine-sensing devices. The MCU and closed-loop, feedback carburetor are the closest technology to EFI.

In 1991, after years of CJ and YJ 4.2L engines with BBD carburetors, Jeep switched to the 4.0L MPI/EFI powerplant.

NOTE—

The 1980s CJs depend upon the MCU and thirteen sensing devices for proper engine performance:

1) The coolant temperature switch

2) The thermal electric switch

3) 4 and 10 inch/height vacuum switches

4) An oxygen sensor

5) The Wide Open Throttle (WOT) Switch

6) A Closed Throttle Switch (only on four-cylinder models—without the BBD carburetor)

7) A knock (detonation/ping) sensor

8) The ignition distributor

9) Mixture Control Solenoid ("Stepper Motor")

10) Idle relay

11) Sole-Vac Throttle Positioner

12) Gangs of upstream and downstream solenoids

13) The PCV solenoid

Add to this the vacuum hoses and electrical wiring that support these devices. The thermal air cleaner is an emission device in itself. So is the evaporative emissions system, which ranges from the fuel tank through the vapor canister to the carburetor. Each of these devices must interface properly with all of the other devices. The sub-systems must function reliably.

◀ **Fig. 9-69**

Keep track of these stepper motor parts. Slide the rack rod outward to allow removal of the two needle valves. These metal parts can go in the parts cleaner dip.

◀ **Fig. 9-70**

Now you can separate the throttle body from the main body. Remove all screws and carefully separate these parts. Pot metal can easily scratch. *Do not pry with sharp tools or excessive force!*

 Fig. 9-71

Now the idle screws can be removed. You may need to knock out the original soft dowels first. If the carburetor's idle was factory set or the engine idled properly before carburetor removal, you need to turn these screws inward and count the turns until the screws seat lightly. Then remove the screws. Keep track of the turns for the left and right screws.

◀ **Fig. 9-72**

Loosen the screws for the two steel lock plates...

9

◀ **Fig. 9-73**

Carefully slide the accelerator pump lever (shaft) from the air horn housing.

 Fig. 9-74

Lift out the pump arm and the metering rod lifter.

Fig. 9-75

Keep track of the parts relationships.

Fig. 9-76

Disconnecting this link frees the accelerator pump shaft. The accelerator pump reaches into the air horn, and here the S-link attaches to the slot in the pump shaft. Again, keep these parts in order for a reference. A quality rebuild kit contains a new accelerator pump.

Fig. 9-77

Carefully lift the vacuum piston from its bore. This assembly includes the metering rod. Keep the assembly together at this point.

Fig. 9-78

This vent grommet is in the carburetor kit. Like other rubber parts, I remove this piece before dipping metal parts in carburetor cleaner.

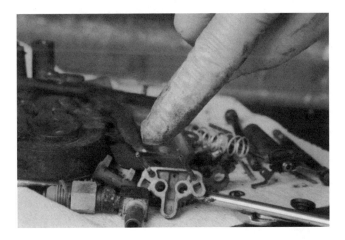

Fig. 9-79

A crucial discovery: One of the idle fuel pickup tubes is fully clogged! Recall, this is the engine that stalled every time the clutch pedal was depressed. This is a valuable find. Always look for the causes of rough running engine symptoms. I will clean this tube carefully, leaving metal intact while fully clearing the passageway.

9

 Fig. 9-80

These are parts that will not get dipped in carburetor cleaner. I will clean these pieces with a milder approach, avoiding the electrical contacts and rubber parts. An aqueous cleaner like my parts washing cabinet will serve here. Hand/brush cleaning with denatured or isopropyl alcohol will work, too. Wear gloves and eye protection!

NOTE—

Denatured and isopropyl alcohols will not damage the rubber parts. These types of alcohol are suitable for work around brake parts and rubber assemblies.

WARNING—

Denatured alcohol is highly toxic. Wear chemical-resistant gloves and safety goggles when handling denatured or isopropyl alcohol. Do not use a commercial parts washing machine around electronic devices! Pressure and moisture will damage such sensitive parts.

◄ **Fig. 9-81**

Here, I check the function of the WOT switch. A simple ohmmeter check for continuity works well. I will check all vacuum and electrical devices.

◄ **Fig. 9-82**

Vacuum choke pull-off requires testing with a hand vacuum pump. Make sure that vacuum holds. (First be certain your vacuum gauge will hold steadily by itself!) The plunger should move properly and stay in position while under vacuum.

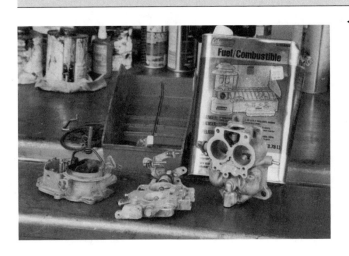

◀ **Fig. 9-83**

I keep my carburetor cleaner as clean as possible. To remove the surface grime from these parts, Coleman stove gas works well. I use a brass wire brush to remove debris. After metal parts dry, I soak them in carburetor cleaner then rinse the parts in a stream of lukewarm water.

> **WARNING—**
>
> *Stove ("white") gas is very volatile, so use extreme care and keep this process away from sparks and any heat source. Stove gas contains naphthalene, which will evaporate rapidly. I use Coleman stove gas to wipe up oil from my shop's cement floor. Stove gas will draw up the oil and leave no residue. Again, this is a highly volatile liquid and must be handled with extreme care! Dispose of used stove gas and rags properly.*

◀ **Fig. 9-84**

To dislodge any stubborn debris, I use compressed air. Do not blow toward yourself, and wear safety goggles. Passageways may contain harmful carburetor cleaner or residue.

9

◀ **Fig. 9-85**

Venturi cluster has small passageways that benefit from a compressed air blast. Dry the parts and clear all tubes and passages.

 Fig. 9-86

Remember the idle fuel pickup tubes? These require a strong blast of compressed air. Do not attempt to remove these tubes. If they need cleaning, run a strand of wire or even a fine jewelers drill through the tube. *Do not remove brass material from any jets or tubes!*

Fig. 9-87

Install a new gasket and the throttle body to the main body. With a screwdriver, tighten these screws securely and evenly. Tighten in cross. Bring the parts together without bind. Seat these screws firmly, as there is no access to them for retightening once the carburetor is on the engine. I leave these parts set for a while on the workbench then recheck each screw's tightness.

Fig. 9-88

Needles and passageways now cleaned, I install the springs and idle mixture screws. Gently screw needles to bottoming point. *(Do not over-tighten, or damage to needles will occur!)* Turn each mixture screw outward the exact number of turns noted upon disassembly. As an alternative, you can use the adjustment specification listed in the kit instructions.

 Fig. 9-89

Install the main metering jets. Again, the screwdriver blade must fill the slots. Hold the driver squarely, and tighten these jets securely. *You do not want a jet to loosen in service!* If any brass sloughs off, vacuum or air blow the debris from the carburetor body.

◀ **Fig. 9-90**

Main metering jets and metering rods are a vital part of proper fuel flow. Always use the original jets unless you know which jets will clearly improve performance without compromising engine reliability. The factory jets are usually the best overall size. On feedback carburetors, fine-tuning is accomplished with the engine computer (MCU).

9

◀ **Fig. 9-91**

Drop the check ball (**ARROW**) into its seat beneath the venturi cluster assembly. *Be sure you are using the correct check ball.* These check balls come in various diameters. They are in the rebuild kit and instructions. Make sure you install the right check ball in each location.

Fig. 9-92

Using a new gasket, install the venturi cluster. Screws must be clean, their passageways clear. Tighten evenly and secure snugly. Recheck the screws after parts set for a while.

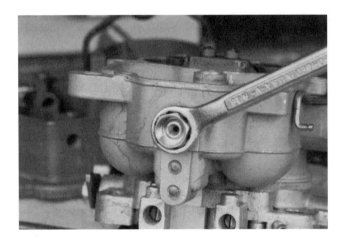

Fig. 9-93

Place the float and fulcrum pin in place. Using a new gasket, install the needle/seat fitting.

Fig. 9-94

Secure the fitting. Tighten snugly to assure a good seal and accurate float level setting.

 Fig. 9-95

Install the fulcrum retainer hoop. Install the baffle. The fulcrum retainer secures the float pin. This hoop will help with float adjustment checks, providing a means for holding the pivot/fulcrum pin in its seat while you check float height.

 Fig. 9-96

Now you can install the new accelerator pump. The spring in place beneath the air horn, press the shaft through the air horn hole (**ARROW**), and catch the shaft with the S-link and pump arm. S-link will keep the accelerator pump in place.

 Fig. 9-97

This is bottom side view of new accelerator pump and spring in place.

9

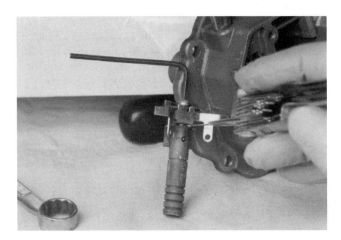

 Fig. 9-98

Check vacuum piston gap with a feeler gauge. Set gap to specification noted in the rebuild kit instructions.

Fig. 9-99

New vent grommet is placed on the lever.

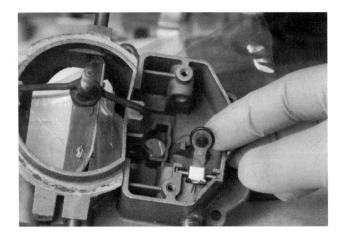

Fig. 9-100

Make certain lever moves freely. Check to be sure vent grommet seals against its seat when the spring presses the lever downward.

 Fig. 9-101

Install the accelerator pump shaft through the air horn body. Note the relationship of these parts. Lock plate screws are started but not tight. Slots in lock plate enable adjustment of the accelerator pump arm and metering rod lifter. Screws thread into the accelerator pump lever shaft.

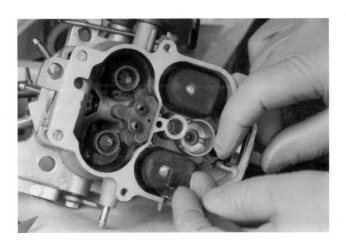

Fig. 9-102

Float height is measured with the float lever pressed very gently against the needle. *(Do not damage the needle by applying too much pressure.)* Measure to specification noted in the carburetor kit. Note that I use a metal T-gauge (**ARROW**), not the cardboard gauge that often comes with kits. If you want accuracy, use quality tools.

> **CAUTION—**
>
> *If float height needs adjustment, bend the float lever. Do not press against the needle when bending the lever. If necessary, remove the float and bend the lever/tang with a needle nosed pliers. Unlike most carburetor designs, the BBD does not require a float drop adjustment.*

9

Fig. 9-103

Once the float is set to specification, you can install a new air horn gasket and carefully fit the air horn to the main body. Before dropping the air horn into position, make sure the new check ball is beneath the accelerator pump in the main body well. Secure a couple of air horn screws lightly to keep the air horn in place at this stage.

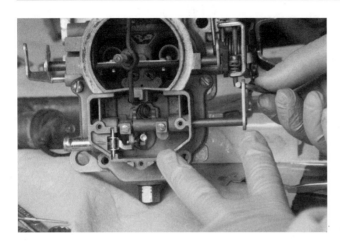

 Fig. 9-104

Hook the pump link into position. Use care here: The link must attach to correct hole in throttle linkage. A common error is hooking the link into the return spring hole.

Fig. 9-105

Remove lock plate from the metering rod lifter. Roll the lifter up far enough to allow installation of the power piston assembly and metering rods. Make sure the coil spring is inside the vacuum piston before setting the piston in its bore. *Use extreme care in making certain the metering rods drop squarely into the main jets. Do not damage these rods!*

Fig. 9-106

Metering rod lift arm is now in place above the vacuum piston and metering rod rack. You can reinstall the lock plate and screw.

◀ **Fig. 9-107**

This is the proper relationship of these parts. Note the hairspring that catches the backsides of metering rods. Power piston gap is set already. You can now make other adjustments.

◀ **Fig. 9-108**

Accelerator pump height can be adjusted now. You can set the metering rod lift height, too.

9

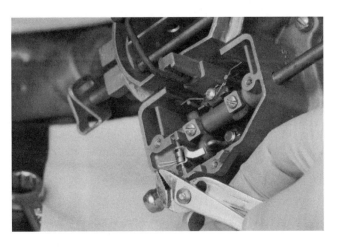

◀ **Fig. 9-109**

Vent lever is adjusted after the accelerator pump height and meter rod/power piston adjustment. I use a small channel lock pliers to bend the tab. This allows for proper movement before the vent closes and opens. Specification for your application is in the carburetor kit.

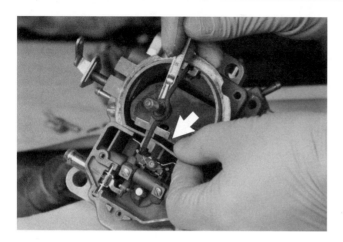

 Fig. 9-110

Choke valve specifications are given in valve-to-body gap (**ARROW**) or choke valve angle, measured with an angle gauge. I use my T-gauge to set the proper gap. Instructions for adjustments and specifications are in the rebuild kit. T-gauge measures to within 1/64th of an inch.

Fig. 9-111

Hook up choke linkage. Now I attach my vacuum pump to the pull-off diaphragm (**ARROW**) and test all adjustments related to the choke pull-off. Install the choke unit with a new gasket, and index the rich/lean marks.

Fig. 9-112

WOT switch is now in place. Check choke movement, and test the choke valve gap with the vacuum pull-off applied. Compare each of these specifications to those found in the rebuild kit instructions or a factory workshop manual.

 Fig. 9-113

Stepper motor (**ARROW**) is clean. Needles have been soaked in carburetor cleaner, rinsed in water and dried. I cleaned motor housing carefully with Coleman stove gas, avoiding the electrical connectors. *This device needed attention:* I freed up the rack rod, which was quite sticky. Install the stepper motor with a new gasket. Make certain the spring and needles are in their proper places!

NOTE—

Sticky rack rod in stepper motor and the clogged idle fuel pickup tube were two areas that created idle problems. I slid the rack in and out until it moved freely. I cleaned the idle fuel pickup tube carefully with a strand of wire and carburetor cleaner. Idle problem disappeared completely after this overhaul.

Fig. 9-114

Choke is now in place with the adjustments made. Sole-Vac is installed, and carburetor looks complete. Note position of Sole-Vac unit (**ARROW**). Air horn screws are all in place and secured snugly. Once on the engine, I recheck screws after the engine has run to warm-up.

9

Fig. 9-115.

I used Teflon tape on the fuel inlet elbow fitting. This fitting threads into the needle/seat fitting. I tighten this elbow fitting securely while holding the needle/seat fitting with a wrench.

NOTE—

When securing the elbow, do not over-tighten the needle/seat fitting. It threads into the carburetor main body, which is made of pot metal and vulnerable to thread stripping. Over-tightening the inlet needle/seat fitting will also alter the float setting on a BBD carburetor.

Fig. 9-116

You can adjust the pump height and metering rod lift with the carburetor on the engine. I am sharing this point, as you may need to make this adjustment in the backcountry. Secure the lock plate screws and confirm your adjustments. Correct power valve and accelerator pump settings have a large impact on performance.

Fig. 9-117

Make certain gasket seals properly when you put the rollover check valve/bowl vent cover back in place. Note the layout of this carburetor. A new base gasket installed, nuts torqued to specification with Loctite 242 on threads, this unit is now ready to run. All linkage is adjusted properly with new clips on the link arms.

Fig. 9-118

Hoses back in place, installation is complete. Be sure that throttle valve opens and closes freely without binding. Install the two OEM throttle return springs in their original locations.

 Fig. 9-119
Engine fully warmed with choke valve wide open, I can now set the idle mixture. Install the air cleaner assembly or tape off air cleaner vacuum lines before attempting to adjust the carburetor. Otherwise, you will experience vacuum leaks and not be able to accurately adjust the mixture. On this engine, it is easy to access the idle mixture screws with the entire air cleaner assembly in place.

NOTE—

Upon initial warm-up, I did discover that the choke was malfunctioning. Although the unit might have worked for a while, it was prudent to install a new choke cover/element. I installed the new choke cover and adjusted the unit to specification. Choke testing could have been done on the bench with a 12-volt electrical source (12 volts '+' to the choke, a '-' ground to the carburetor body). My recommendation: With the carburetor assembled, test the choke unit's function on the bench before installing the carburetor on the engine.

The result of this carburetor overhaul is a high mileage CJ-7 that now runs without stalling. Compression is adequate and uniform, so tuning was not a problem. Start-up is immediate, hot or cold. Cold start requires nothing more than stepping down on the gas pedal and releasing it (to set the choke), then cranking the engine. On warm restart, the engine fires with just a bump of the key.

Acceleration is impressive, the highway mileage has improved, and the engine is really quite frisky for its age and condition. This was well worth the cost of a carburetor kit! Even the blow-by has slowed considerably, as the air/fuel ratios returned to normal, and the cylinders are no longer fuel washing. While the Mopar MPI/EFI kit would clearly add more versatility and horsepower to a 4.2L engine, this CJ performs very well and will easily serve until engine overhaul time. At that point, perhaps an EFI/MPI conversion would be a consideration.

9

Mopar's MPI/EFI Conversion Kit for the 4.2L Inline Six

A major breakthrough for the 4.2L engine is Mopar's MPI Conversion Kit. The 258/4.2L engine has provided one of the most reliable platforms for Jeep CJ performance in history. EFI/MPI brings out the full potential of these engines.

The 258 six offers a rugged seven-main bearing inline design. This is by far the most reliable of six cylinder engines, and inline sixes are inherently smooth in balance. Ruggedness characterizes the 258, which has seen service in full-size J-trucks and even International-Harvester trucks and Scouts. The only weak link in this engine, and other carbureted sixes, is the induction system.

The BBD carburetor was a step in the right direction. With a two-barrel manifold that more evenly distributes fuel to the intake ports, the '81-'90 CJ and YJ powerplant is a better design. EFI, or more precisely, MPI/multi-port injection, fully resolves the fuel distribution issue, making the Mopar kit a major improvement for the 258 six.

NOTE—

A two-barrel manifold shows up on the 258 J-truck engines as early as 1977. Some 258 powered CJs gained this advantage as early as 1979. All 232s used a one-barrel manifold/carburetor, and the 258 had a one-barrel offering through 1978.

Mopar has offered two versions of EFI retrofits. The first design was a bolt-on kit that used some outsourced parts and some OEM Mopar pieces. The later kit, available today, takes a very practical approach.

This bolt-on kit is virtually a '94/'95 Wrangler YJ's 4.0L induction system with OEM peripheral hardware. Patterned to fit the 4.2L engine and programmed for 50-State legal emissions certification (earning a California E.O. "exemption" number), the Mopar Performance MPI Conversion Kit is packaged complete with all necessary hardware and installation instructions.

Here is 50-plus horsepower the easy way! If your engine has good oil pressure and normal compression, the kit will boost power without compromising reliability. In fact, considering the precise metering of fuel to achieve complete combustion and the lowest possible tailpipe emissions, the Mopar Performance MPI Conversion Kit should actually increase engine longevity.

Add to this the famous low-end torque inherent to the long stroke, conservative bore 4.2L engine. The 4.2L with MPI is actually a better off-pavement engine than the 4.0L six from which the MPI system has been patterned!

NOTE—

The value of the 4.2L engine's stroke is so well noted that a common high performance and racing technique is to retrofit a 4.2L crankshaft into the 4.0L engine block. This provides a long-stroke, bigger bore hybrid that delivers exceptional torque over a broader power band than either the stock 4.0L or 4.2L engine can produce.

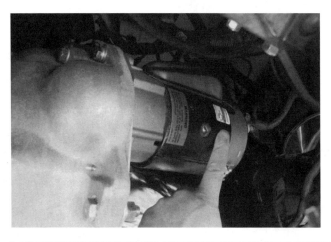

 Fig. 9-120

The Mopar Performance MPI system will increase horsepower. Starting should require less effort with the precise fuel metering and the cold-start system of EFI. As insurance, however, I installed a new Genuine Mopar rebuilt starter to assure easy cranking.

 Fig. 9-121

More horsepower means more BTUs of heat coming out of the engine. I safeguarded this installation with a new Genuine Mopar water pump, fan clutch and radiator, each available from your local Jeep dealership

◀ **Fig. 9-122**

Loctite 242 and fresh, properly graded hardware hold the fan clutch and fan in place. You want a safe, reliable cooling system. Mopar Performance insists on a 195-degree thermostat, which you will find in the kit. I stepped up to an air conditioning model OEM radiator to assure adequate margins of cooling with the higher horsepower output. Make sure your cooling system is in order before installing an MPI/EFI conversion.

9

◀ **Fig. 9-123**

A new Mopar fan/alternator belt and a rebuilt Mopar alternator round out the safeguards. Electrical system output and integrity are essential for precise computer input signals. Wiring must be in top condition, with all connections secure and reliable.

Fig. 9-124

Factory Grade 8 (six embossed marks on the bolt head) crankshaft bolt now secures the Mopar damper. There is a shorter Grade 5 OEM bolt found on 258s. Use the longer, stronger bolt with the new Mopar Performance pulley/damper.

Fig. 9-125

Here is the 50-State legal Mopar Performance EFI/MPI Conversion Kit for the 258 inline sixes! California E.O.-exempted (street legal for use in California), the kit provides a '94-'95 4.0L Jeep Wrangler parts platform. Use of OEM off-the-shelf Mopar/Jeep components means this system is easy to troubleshoot and keep working for many years to come!

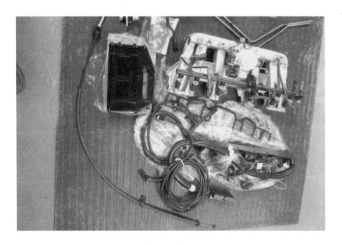

Fig. 9-126

Every wire and vacuum hose is provided. Kit is complete with all of the engine sensors and peripheral engine hardware, the fuel filter, evaporative canister, electric fuel pump, a new ignition system, and fuel injection---complete with a manifold, injectors and rails!

 Fig. 9-127

If the engine is freshly rebuilt like this Mopar factory long-block, you should fill the crankcase and prime the oil system before installing the distributor. Use a slow speed, drill-powered lubrication tool. Make certain the timing mark is aligned for #1 cylinder on its firing cycle (top of the compression stroke). Index the oil pump drive key to approximately 11 o'clock as noted in the Mopar Performance instructions…

Fig. 9-128

Note the #1 cylinder indicator on the distributor cap. Align the rotor to #1 cylinder plug wire. Now #1 piston is at top-dead-center and the rotor points to #1 spark plug wire. Make certain that the new housing base gasket is in place before installing the distributor. Do not remove the yellow indexing pin yet.

9

Fig. 9-129

With housing aligned to have rotor and plug wire in line, you can clamp the distributor down. Be aware that this distributor is strictly for sending spark to each spark plug.

> *CAUTION—*
>
> *Timing is controlled within the computer! Once you index the distributor according to the Mopar instructions and clamp the housing securely, do not tamper with the distributor housing position! Remove the yellow index pin at this point.*

 Fig. 9-130

New coil and bracket (**ARROW**) come with the Mopar kit. All wiring connectors are factory weather resistant type. This is optimal quality and sensible for a Jeep CJ's off-pavement forays.

 Fig. 9-131

Here I install the Mopar crankshaft sensor pickup. Instructions call for a gap equal to the cardboard cover on the tip of sensor. Note that I pulled the new Mopar damper/pulley into place with the original Grade 5 crankshaft bolt. I replaced this with a longer Grade 8 OEM bolt and damper washer.

NOTE—

Coat the inside edge of damper hub with Super 300 sealant to assure a leak-proof oil seal between the hub and crankshaft snout. Use Loctite Threadlocker on damper bolt threads and torque to specification noted in the kit's instructions or to OEM setting of 90 lb-ft.

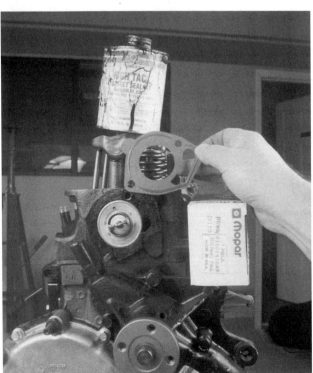

 Fig. 9-132

Here is a new thermostat and gasket, furnished with the Mopar kit. I coat both sides of gasket and bolt threads with sealant. Additional insurance is the installation of a new Mopar rebuilt water pump (not included with MPI conversion kit).

 Fig. 9-133

Thermostat housing is new part included with MPI conversion kit. Housing accepts the coolant temperature sensor, a vital signal for the engine management computer. Wiring harness has a plug for this fitting.

◀ **Fig. 9-134**

I installed a new Mopar exhaust manifold (not included in kit) with new OEM hardware and Anti-Seize on bolt threads. Gasket comes with the kit as does the new intake manifold with all OEM attachments. I coat each side of the gasket with Super 300 sealant.

9

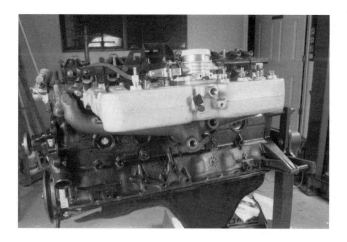

◀ **Fig. 9-135**

Manifold bolts into place of original two-barrel carburetor manifold. This is an easy fit. Torque hardware in sequence to specification.

 Fig. 9-136

Install the oxygen sensor. I put a thin film of Anti-Seize on the threads, away from the sensor tip. This will enable removal if ever necessary. Sensor is a common Jeep/Mopar part.

 Fig. 9-137

Mopar spark plug wires come with the EFI/MPI conversion kit. I added the Mopar spark plugs. This is a highly reliable factory setup, delivering the kind of performance you would expect from Jeep/Mopar Performance engineers!

 Fig. 9-138

With the Mopar rebuilt engine, I needed to install a dipstick tube assembly. Here's my quick installation tool for a new dipstick tube (not included in MPI kit). I coat the tube end's outside edge with Super 300 and use a wrench for a driver. Tapping solidly at the tube's flare lip, I drive the tube into the block without damaging the tube.

Fig. 9-139

This remanufactured Mopar 4.2L engine for the '86 CJ-7 is actually a 1987-90 version. You can tell by the cylinder head accepting the later style, leak-resistant cast valve cover. CJ versions of the 4.2L work equally well with the Mopar MPI conversion kit. System looks factory---because it is!

Fig. 9-140

Kit includes a new throttle cable. Every consideration was given to the end user. Mopar Performance realizes that the installer may be an owner/enthusiast without a professional shop full of tools. This is a well-conceived conversion kit, produced by Mopar engineers who know Jeep vehicles!

9

Fig. 9-141

If the head/clip size measures off slightly, a small flat file can bring the firewall punch-out into shape. Do not make the square any larger than necessary. *This cable end must fit snugly in place at the firewall opening.*

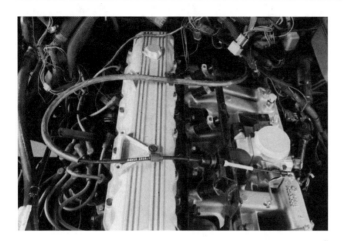

 Fig. 9-142

Cable from Mopar appears plenty long. I routed in this fashion to eat up length and maintain flowing curves. Avoid tight bends that could seize the cable or shorten its life due to excessive wear.

Cable and Hose Protection

When installing and clamping cables and hoses, make certain there is no risk of chafing damage. You can make sheaths from larger hose sizes or make certain the routing keeps hoses or cables away from rubbing surfaces.

OEM style cable comes with Mopar MPI kit. I wrapped this cable housing with a short piece of fuel/vacuum hose that has the same inside diameter as the cable's outside diameter. Clamp has insulation, too, and fits snugly over the outer protective hose. *Do not bind the cable with the clamp. Here, snug means not too tight!*

Visualize where these hoses might rub and cause wear on the plastic fuel tubing. I make certain these hoses do not rub against the plastic section of the fuel lines. These are Mopar OEM stainless steel pipes and factory clip-on hoses, very high quality components.

◁ Fig. 9-143

You're on your own with the fuel delivery lines. Mopar Performance realizes the variety of fuel tanks and lines involved with the model years for the kit. The kit supplies the fuel pump and all fuel lines attached to the engine. When addressing the '86 CJ-7, the original fuel supply system was for a California four-cylinder chassis. I began by labeling the hoses and their OEM routings.

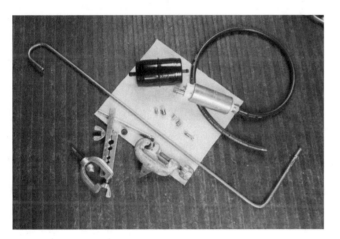

◁ Fig. 9-144

From experience, I prefer routing steel pipe when distance becomes lengthy rather than using fuel hose. Hose will deteriorate over time and expands some under pressure. My choice is steel fuel/brake grade piping. If connecting to hoses, I cut off the double-flare ends and make a half or semi-"bubble" flare with my tubing cutter and flaring tool. Mopar supplies some hose and the new OEM filter.

9

◁ Fig. 9-145

This is my half-flare bubble end (**ARROW**), constructed with my flaring tool. I cut the tubing with a tubing cutter. I then deburr the end of the tube and use my flaring tool to create this first half of a double-flare. The bubble shape will prevent the hose from blowing off under pressure. Curved drop at the end also prevents the inside of the hose from chafing against the cut tubing end. Make sure hose slides far enough up the tubing to allow clamp to seat inboard of the bubble flare.

Fig. 9-146

My curves and formed steel pipe section feeds from fuel tank supply line to the filter and pump. This is the fuel filter and pump location recommended by Mopar instructions. Near to the tank and safely above and behind the axle housing, this is a sensible place for a push-type fuel pump.

Fig. 9-147

This is a true double-flare that I am creating on an OEM fuel line. This is actually the evaporative emissions line, which is the same size as the '86 fuel line. The evaporative line ran down the left frame rail. The four-cylinder supply line ran down the right frame rail. I reversed the use of these two pipes.

NOTE—

The original evaporative line now hooks to the fuel supply line near the fuel tank. Instead of attaching to the evaporative canister, this line now serves as the fuel supply line to the intake manifold. The original fuel supply line (right side of frame) became the evaporative canister line. I attached this line to the new evaporative canister. (See my steps and illustrations.) Instead of attaching to the fuel tank, the back end of this right frame rail line now attaches to the OEM evaporative devices at the right tail section of the vehicle. Again, this layout worked for 4-cylinder '86 chassis. Determine the best routing for your CJ chassis.

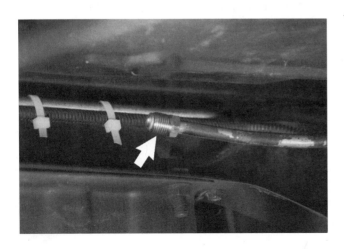

Fig. 9-148

This shortened, curved and double-flared pipe is now the fuel supply line, which will pick up pressurized fuel at the fuel pump. This pipe (**ARROW**) runs down the left frame rail. Routing provides a fairly direct link to the Mopar fuel lines at the engine. I route fuel from the factory fuel supply hose at the gas tank, to a steel pipe (see Fig. 9-146), through the fuel filter and fuel pump, to the pipe shown.

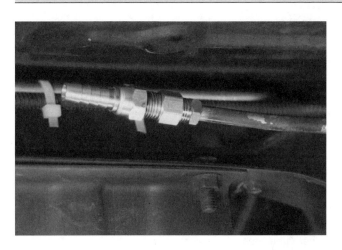

 Fig. 9-149

I install this aftermarket sourced hose nipple to the newly flared tube and flarenut. This new fitting from a NAPA store is rated for fuel injection hose applications. Note that pressures run very high in this system. This is not carburetion!

> **WARNING—**
>
> *I have upgraded every hose on the fuel supply and return lines to meet rigid high-pressure standards. Note the fuel hose for the Mopar MPI system must be of fuel injection pressure-side grade. Clamps and all other hardware and fittings must also meet high-pressure standards!*

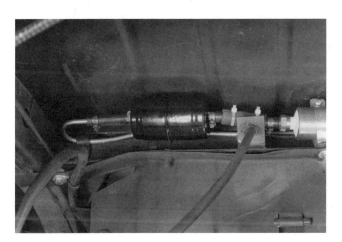

◀ **Fig. 9-150**

These clamps and hoses rate for high-pressure fuel injection. I upgraded from the bulk hose included in the Mopar MPI conversion kit. The hose shown is rated 350 PSI *working* pressure! You can find this through NAPA stores. Quality clamps shown here are from the Mopar kit. I use them on the *tank side* of the fuel pump, *not* the high-pressure side. For the high-pressure and return hoses, I outsourced high-pressure EFI clamps from the NAPA catalog.

AUTHOR'S TIP!

If you have difficulty sliding a 350 PSI rated hose over the steel tubing, lubricate the hose end with silicone spray. This serves as a lubricant that dries after the hose is in place.

9

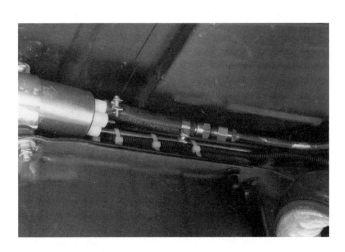

◀ **Fig. 9-151**

I sourced these EFI hose clamps from the local NAPA store. Note that hose is special high-pressure rated gasoline hose. This is expensive but worth the safety factor. You need hose that will withstand high working pressures. NAPA has a catalog with these specialty hoses.

Fuel and Exhaust Systems

◁ **Fig. 9-152**

Here is the fuel filter and pump hookup. Curved steel pipe at left comes from the OEM tank supply hose. Mopar kit supplies fuel pump and mounting clamp (**ARROW**). Hoses on tank side use Mopar clamps. Clamps and hoses on pressure side are high pressure, EFI rated items from NAPA.

NOTE—

I have plastic tied a protective hose around the fuel hose between the filter and pump. This is to protect the fuel hose from chafing against the wire-wrapped OEM brake pipe. Think in terms of movement, rubbing surfaces and vibration over time! Note that I use the shortest reasonable lengths of hose, relying upon the cost-effectiveness and safety of steel fuel-rated lines wherever practical.

◁ **Fig. 9-153**

Here you can see the factory fuel and vapor hoses: 1) larger diameter hose is OEM supply hose from the tank, 2) smaller hose to the fuel tank is the return line, and 3) the evaporative hose runs from the canister to the evaporative devices at the left rear corner of the tub.

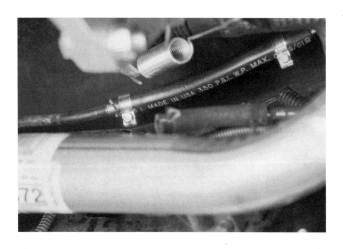

◁ **Fig. 9-154**

When I say high-pressure fuel hose, I mean high pressure! 350 PSI working pressure hose, available from NAPA and other aftermarket sources, is my choice. Expensive hose, I use this strictly at junctions and shorter length runs, relying on far less expensive brake/fuel tubing for long stretches. Note use of high quality EFI-rated clamps on this hose. Clamps were also readily available from NAPA.

CAUTION—

Be sure to bubble flare any steel pipe-to-hose connections. (See Fig. 9-145.) EFI/MPI fuel pressures run far above those of any carbureted fuel system. A hose leak presents an extreme fire hazard.

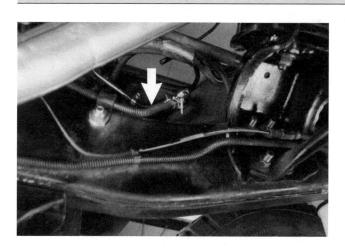

 Fig. 9-155

I used the original fuel return line (which ran down left frame rail) for the new fuel return line from the Mopar MPI system. Smaller in diameter than supply or evaporative lines, this OEM return line takes excess fuel back to the tank. Hoses (**ARROW**) are 350 PSI working pressure with high pressure EFI-rated clamps.

NOTE—

EFI systems with a rail and pressure regulator continuously return excess fuel to the fuel tank. This maintains the fuel pressure constant set by the regulator. I tested this OEM return line for flow rate, and it easily handled the return flow from the MPI system.

Fig. 9-156

This is the topside view of the fuel return line. Note the OEM pipe down below, the elbow fitting, and the hose link to the Mopar fuel line. Stainless Mopar line is very tough to bend! Although this angle does not make it clear, these fuel pipes route several inches below the steering column and joint, well out of harm's way.

9

Fig. 9-157

Here, Mopar kit's new evaporative canister (**ARROW**) fits neatly into the OEM canister bracket. (Mopar supplies a new bracket if you need to use it.) Kit is very thorough in meeting all induction, engine management and emissions needs.

NOTE—

Mopar Performance offers two versions of the MPI conversion kit. The automatic transmission kit (not needed in this '86 CJ-7 application) includes all necessary interface items for the engine and automatic transmission.

 Fig. 9-158

I chose to mount the Mopar kit's PCM (powertrain control module/engine management computer) against the fender well. Mopar instructions describe putting the computer against the firewall. I could not find a sensible location at the firewall on the '86 CJ. In mounting the computer here, I minimized the risk of exposure to water and debris. This location also provides relative ease of access.

 Fig. 9-159

Four-cylinder chassis did not have a coolant recovery tank. Mopar does not supply this radiator overflow tank as part of the kit. It is a Genuine Mopar part, however, and available from your local Jeep dealer. I mounted the tank in a convenient location for ease of access. Like the computer, you want devices out of harm's way yet still accessible.

 Fig. 9-160

Recall, I am using the original four-cylinder engine's fuel supply line at the right side of the frame as the new evaporative system pipe routing. I fabricated a pipe to run across the firewall (follow my finger), routing just above the transmission/engine opening. A hose connects from the right side pipe (much like the old fuel pump-to-frame pipe hookup). At the evaporative canister, I use a short piece of hose to connect from the new firewall tube (**ARROW**) to the canister. Note use of insulated clamps to hold the pipe in place.

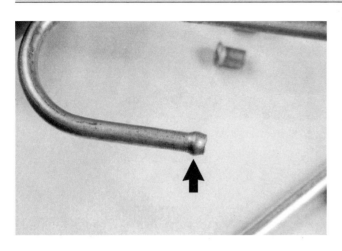

◀ **Fig. 9-161**

We're back to forming tubing properly. For the over-the-fire-wall tube, I begin with NAPA brake/fuel grade tubing. I cut off the double-flared end and remove the flarenut. I create this "bubble" (**ARROW**) with my flaring tool. This holds hose securely, allowing a place for the clamp inboard of the hump.

◀ **Fig. 9-162**

Here, I use the double-flare insert to create more of a rounded end. Note that the tool is not expensive or difficult to use. This tubing end will not nick or cut the inside of the hose. The diameter remains the same from within the tube through the flare. There is no restriction, just a safe means for connecting fuel grade hose to fuel pipe.

9

◀ **Fig. 9-163**

Mopar MPI kit includes a special speedometer-driven speed sensor (**ARROW**). This is one of the signals for the computer. The device works fine with the OEM Jeep speedometer cable drive gear mechanism. Assembly installs easily and works with the OEM speedometer cable. Make sure cable does not chafe against the body. Do not kink or make tight bends with the cable housing.

Mopar 'MPI' Installation Details

The Mopar MPI Conversion Kit for the 4.2L engine comes with useful instructions. Having installed the kit on a Mopar remanufactured 4.2L six fitted to a 1986 CJ chassis, I believe you may benefit from my experience and methods.

There are a number of variations in chassis design between the 1981-90 models. If your CJ is a candidate for this kit, you will likely discover details unique to your installation.

Some installers route hoses all the way around the front of the radiator to reach the left side of the engine. I used the OEM (four-cylinder) right side fuel line as the evaporative line, forming the line that now mounts across the firewall. I use insulated clamps to secure this pipe. Whether you use this as the fuel supply or evaporative line, the hoop over the firewall works. *When routing the pipe, avoid any moving or hot objects.*

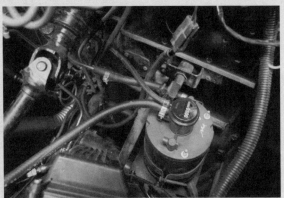

This is the evaporative canister supplied by Mopar in the kit. I now attach the evaporative return hose to the pipe over the firewall. I also tie the vacuum source line and vapor hose to the engine as described in the Mopar kit instructions.

Line for PCV system (**ARROW**) fits from intake manifold to valve cover as shown. All of these parts were included in the Mopar kit.

PCV is shown here. The MAP sensor is against the firewall. Tubes come within the kit. Note the ground wires bunched at the bolt on the valve cover. Proper grounds (**ARROW**) are very important to EFI/MPI integrity. The engine has a direct ground to the battery.

Mopar MPI kit is 50-State legal and eliminates all of these OEM parts from the engine! None of this busy hardware is used. You can see how "clean" the MPI engine appears next to a carbureted model!

Mopar 'MPI' Installation Details (continued)

Find ways to wrap the system safely around chassis and engine components. All lines, hoses and pipes widely clear the steering shaft and engine exhaust. Take vibration and powertrain movement into account when attaching parts. Allow for hose flex between the frame and body. *There is movement between each of these members! Do not make rigid attachments between these chassis, body and powertrain components.*

Factory convolution tubing is a good insulator and protection for wiring. Mopar made the tubing junctions with plastic tape. I use plastic ties to hold tubing in place and tie pairs of tubing together. Always think in terms of movement and heat when routing and protecting wires.

MAP sensor and wiring are all part of the kit. Instructions detail the routing of plastic vacuum lines and connectors. This is really a straightforward installation.

The wiring harness above the MAP sensor is convolution tubing in which I captured some unsightly stray wires. Note my plastic tape junction of the two convolution tubes. I emulate factory method.

60-pin connector in place, carefully tighten the bolt and route the convolution tube. Be very careful to keep the wiring away from sharp edges and heat. Use plastic ties to make sure the sleeve of wiring stays in place for the vehicle's lifespan. Harness goes to firewall.

Kit harness from PCM goes across the firewall to right and left sides of the engine for distribution. Injector wires fit the plastic harness sleeve next to the valve cover. Injector wires are numbered.

9

Mopar 'MPI' Installation Details (continued)

Vacuum hose and wire routings are outlined in the Mopar instructions. Note that the regulator hose goes to the intake manifold fitting. Until the hoses attach, I keep duct tape on the air and vacuum fittings to prevent dirt from entering the engine.

Oxygen sensor plug connector comes with an attachment stem. I drill a hole in the fender well and place the plug (**ARROW**) away from moving parts and heat. *Prime and paint any holes you drill in the frame or body.*

Fuel line connectors are fully snapped in place. Fuel lines have same connectors as OEM Jeep 4.0L EFI/MPI. The caliber of the Mopar Performance MPI conversion parts is tops. Although power steering will work with the kit, this CJ-7 retains its original manual steering.

Factory wiring on right side of engine and firewall is now preserved and tied together with plastic ties. Tubing conceals extra wires. I purposely did not strip or cut out wires and OEM plug connectors. This leaves the (unlikely) option that this chassis could revert to its OEM wiring system and carburetion system.

Mopar Performance provides this special 7.5 amp diode (**ARROW**) in the kit. This diode fits in the field wire circuit of the alternator. (Usually, this is the smaller brown wire.) The pink crimp-on connector faces *toward* the alternator. *Mopar emphasizes that this diode must be in place to protect the electronics of the new PCM and other devices.*

Mopar 'MPI' Installation Details (continued)

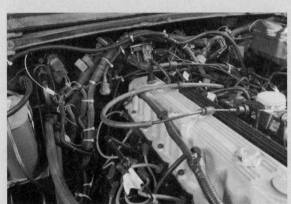

There are only four wires involved in the hookup between the OEM electrics and the new Mopar EFI/MPI harnesses! You will need a volt-ohm meter to determine which wires in the chassis system provide the appropriate voltage at the right time.

NOTE—

Make sure the ignition source wire will feed full 12-volt current with the ignition "On" and also during cranking! Otherwise, the engine will not fire!

For a battery hookup, I use a large ring eye and go to the battery cable bolt. This provides the best 12-volt current source. Actually, the battery voltage will vary with the alternator charge level and starter draw. The PCM is designed to work within these normal voltage parameters.

NOTE—

A fully charged battery reads 12.6 volts. Under normal charging, the voltage can reach 14.5 volts or higher, depending upon ambient temperature. While cranking to start, battery voltage can drop below 12 volts. This is all acceptable voltage for the PCM.

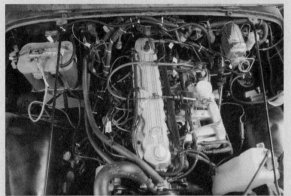

Bay-wide view of system reveals wiring and vacuum routings. The Mopar instructions clearly detail where the current should be sourced. Vacuum circuit diagrams are thorough as well. This is a relatively easy installation. An aware home mechanic could do the system in a weekend or two.

You can clean up and protect a lot of unsightly wiring with convolution tubing and plastic ties. Note that the ties secure the tubing and do not press tightly against the wires. *Pulling too tightly, plastic ties can work their way through wire insulation.*

9

Fuel and Exhaust Systems

Mopar 'MPI' Installation Details (continued)

When I attached the fuel pump wires (furnished in Mopar harnesses), I used Loctite 290 on the threads and nuts. This thread locker will wick into nuts and bolts after installation. The access was very tight, and 290 worked best. If possible, attach wires before installing the pump and fuel lines! Note use of smaller convolution tubing around these wires.

When routing the speedometer cable, make sure the bend is smooth and sweeping. Don't kink the cable or route it in a manner that will cause chafing against the body tub or wear. Allow for transmission/transfer case movement.

◀ **Fig. 9-164**

Air cleaner assembly from the Mopar kit features a K&N type filtration system. This is a low restriction air induction method. Note that I mounted the filter atop the fender, as far from water spray as possible. If you run this type of filtration, keep the element away from any water source---including fording streams and spray wands at the car wash. Air ducting must seal tightly to prevent dust contamination of the engine.

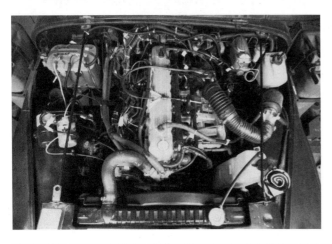

◀ **Fig. 9-165**

Mopar Performance MPI Conversion fits neatly with popular CJ accessories and upgrades. Optima battery and air compressor for ARB Air Lockers indicate this CJ's intended use. Mopar MPI is suited for every kind of driving environment, proving itself on high mountain passes, steady on the rock piles and performing all out at hill climbs---or just cruising an interstate with a light trailer in tow!

Mopar EFI/MPI Tuning and Footnotes

The MPI system makes at least 50 extra horsepower. OEM cooling system parts must be in top shape to handle this gain. I opted for a Genuine Mopar air conditioning radiator to meet BTU needs. The water pump, fan clutch and thermostat are new Mopar pieces.

The four-cylinder engine came from the factory with no coolant recovery tank. An OEM Jeep tank offers a solution. This new Mopar coolant recovery tank rounds out the system, offering an increase in capacity, less risk of oxidation in the cooling system and even an incremental increase in coolant capacity.

As a final note, the Mopar EFI/MPI is fully serviceable at any Jeep dealership. The computer (PCM) provides for tuning and troubleshooting in the same manner as a 1994/95 Wrangler 4.0L system. You simply take the vehicle to an authorized or qualified shop and approach the system as if the vehicle is a '95 Wrangler YJ. Simple!

 Fig. 9-166

OEM air duct from the radiator core support to the air cleaner is no longer used with the Mopar MPI kit. This leaves the room necessary for the new cooling system recovery tank in this position. The tank is not supplied with the kit. I installed the new Mopar tank to handle the added horsepower.

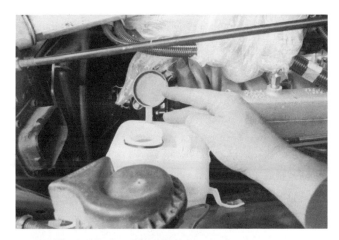

9

Fig. 9-167

I cut the overflow hose in a "V" shape. This will prevent the hose from sticking to the bottom or wall of the recovery tank. The Mopar MPI kit includes a new windshield washer tank. This recovery tank is a Genuine Mopar part but not included in the MPI conversion kit.

 Fig. 9-168

These two wires, provided within the Mopar MPI kit wiring harness, are helpful options. One is a tachometer lead for the kind of tachometer described in the kit instructions. The other wire is an engine check light lead. This wire, if run to an LED lamp on the dash, can serve as a "Check Engine" signal, indicating a possible need to have the system diagnosed for trouble. You can also use the Check Engine light to extract a stored fault code from the computer (PCM unit).

◀ **Fig. 9-169**

Installed Mopar Performance MPI Conversion Kit is an instant 50 horsepower boost for the otherwise stock 4.2L six. The induction efficiency proves that proper fuel distribution, in this case multi-point/port injection, is all that was missing from the inline six's original design. The 4.2L/258 is a reliable, efficient and powerful engine package. Tailpipe emission readings are much cleaner than the OEM carburetor and emissions hardware could ever provide!

Mopar 'MPI' Conversion: An Emissions Test

The 1986 CJ-7 that received the Mopar 'MPI' conversion was subject to California emissions testing. The fresh 4.2L rebuilt Mopar engine had less than 600 miles on it when the emissions test was run. Without any tuning other than the Mopar Performance out-of-the-box programming, the vehicle went through the 'Smog Check' inspection and tailpipe test to confirm its compliance with California's strict emission laws.

The tailpipe readings confirmed that the Mopar engineers did their job! This six-cylinder engine yielded far better tailpipe readings than the Jeep's original four-cylinder engine did when new.

Following the assembly instructions and using the supplied Mopar parts, the 4.2L inline six-cylinder engine produced these tailpipe readings the first time through the California test. *No effort was made to "tune" the engine in any way, either before or during the test.*

1) 15 mph/2348 rpm: CO_2 of 14.8%, O_2 of 0.3%, HC of 94 PPM, CO of 0.12% and NO of 1085 PPM---passed.

2) 25 mph/2200 rpm: CO_2 of 15.0%, O_2 of 0.0(!), HC of 39 PPM, CO of 0.03% and NO of 390 PPM---passed by a wide margin.

Mopar 'MPI' Conversion: An Emissions Test (continued)

These decals come with the Mopar 'MPI' Conversion Kit. They indicate the California exemption order number: CARB E.O. #D265-13. They also provide the Mopar part number for the kit: P5249610 for a manual transmission application. The computer (PCM) number is also indicated. This informs the inspector or a service technician that this specific equipment is on board and that the system is 50-State legal for use on public roads in the State of California.

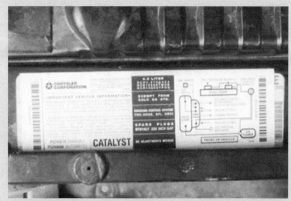

Mopar Performance includes this tuning sticker that replaces the OEM data decal. This describes the system and its components in detail, furnishing the vacuum circuit diagram, type of computer involved and a reference to the 1994 prototype emission and fuel injection system. This package is 'OBD1' compliant!

Decal included in the MPI conversion kit tells the driver that the fuel grade is "Minimum 92 Octane Premium Fuel Required." This is surely a valid recommendation for hot days at sea level or higher compression ratios created by cylinder head milling or non-dished pistons.

NOTE—

I found that at 4500 feet elevation, the 4.2L remanufactured Mopar engine would not 'ping' on 89-octane fuel. Owners' experiences vary, some claiming that their converted MPI engines will run fine on 87- or 89-octane fuel under most conditions.

Kit also contains a decal (**ARROW**) for the fuel filler housing. The recommendation is premium fuel. This is clearly a cautionary statement by Mopar Performance. Mopar wants owner satisfaction and a long engine life.

NOTE—

Jeep engineers informed me that, if needed, the spark timing can be retarded a few degrees by a Jeep dealership. (This is a computer program change, which can be done on an 'OBD1' system's PCM unit.) This would likely eliminate all but the most extreme ping (detonation) condition. In most cases of ping, either the compression ratio is too high and/or the gasoline octane rating is too low!

9

Exhaust Systems

CJ owners sometimes install high performance "side-dump" exhaust systems on their vehicles. A high output V-8 engine might encourage dual exhausts with side pipes. Still yet, some CJ owners want a throaty exhaust system that rumbles just beneath the doors and rocker panels.

Your Jeep is a short wheelbase vehicle intended for back-country travel. In slow, rock-pile driving, the fumes from an exhaust system can become annoying and highly toxic. *In my view, a side exiting exhaust system is a bad choice!*

V-type engine high performance exhaust can now be done with a Y-header pipe and single pipe/muffler approach. Larger diameter pipe and nicely flowing exhaust pipe assemblies can meet any reasonable Jeep power need.

As for vehicle occupant safety, there is no better exhaust system than a rear exit type. Any Jeep CJ should have a tailpipe(s) that exit rearward of the rear tires---in a manner that will not allow fumes to re-enter the vehicle through the doors or the rear/tailgate opening.

◄ **Fig. 9-170**

For the CJ-7 and Mopar EFI system, I needed to plug the air injection fitting in the exhaust manifold. Kit calls for use of an old tubing nut (**ARROW**) and the steel expansion plug furnished in the Mopar parts. I use Permatex Ultra Copper on nut threads and plug. For exhaust pipe flange nuts and studs, I use Never-Seize to ease service when required.

◄ **Fig. 9-171**

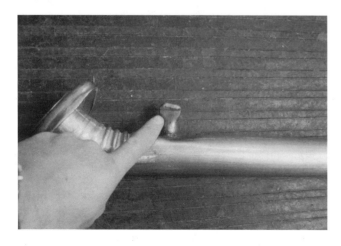

50-State legal, clean burning Mopar MPI conversion kit eliminates OEM air injection and pulse injection system. For this new Mopar 4.2L exhaust pipe, I hammered the air tube flat and carefully wire-welded the end. This must seal without risk of leakage. If you cannot do a weld like this, a muffler shop could preform this operation in minutes.

Fig. 9-172

Here, Anti-Seize works well on new exhaust manifold studs. This will enable easy installation and prevent nuts from seizing on these studs over time. Intense heat causes this kind of problem. Anti-Seize works to eliminate seizing and galling.

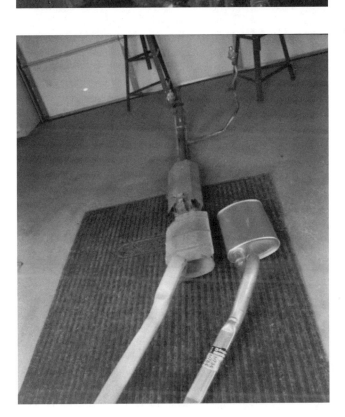

Fig. 9-173

At left is original four-cylinder exhaust. With new six-cylinder replacement engine, I confirmed that the tailpipe and muffler would work properly. Mopar MPI kit still requires a chassis with a catalytic converter.

Fig. 9-174

New Mopar muffler and catalytic converter contrast OEM four-cylinder 150 AMC Jeep parts. Some of the OEM parts are salvageable and otherwise expensive to replace. The clamps and other hardware are Genuine Mopar, proof here of quality.

9

 Fig. 9-175

Tin-ware is rusted and heat cracked. (Original owner used C-clamps to stop vibration noises for 50,000 miles!) This exhaust system is from a 109,000 mile, California emissions CJ-7 with a 150 AMC four.

◀ **Fig. 9-176**

This muffler tool and sledgehammer make quick work of rusty muffler removal. Muffler is completely worn out. Catalytic converter, however, is still in working condition.

◀ **Fig. 9-177**

I folded, hammered and welded the end of the air injection tube that goes into the catalytic converter. On the MPI installation, Mopar notes that this step must be performed. Air injection is not required with the cleaner burning conversion package!

Fig. 9-178

Here is restoration work. I welded the cracks in the tin-ware and de-scaled all of the rust from parts. High-temperature (VHT) flat black exhaust manifold paint brings back the finish on these parts.

Fig. 9-179

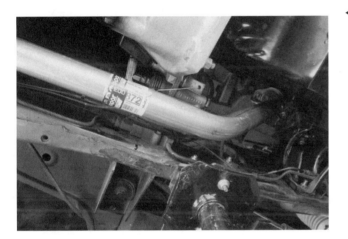

New Mopar exhaust pipe fits to the manifold. Tighten bolts evenly, but leave enough slack to permit movement as you align the other exhaust system parts.

9

Fig. 9-180

This is OEM method for securing and hanging the muffler and catalytic converter. I stay with OEM grade clamps and hangers. Generic aftermarket pieces do not have the same stamina or design as these AMC and Mopar parts.

 Fig. 9-181

Route the new tailpipe through its original location. Make sure the muffler and tailpipe clear all metal, rubber and brake parts. Allow at least several inches of clearance around the axle housing, and estimate the full travel range of the axle.

> **CAUTION—**
>
> *Note that the original tailpipe was in line with the aftermarket tubular rear bumper, creating a good deal of back pressure. New tailpipe hits nearly the same spot. The bumper is a poor design and needs to be modified for tailpipe clearance.As an alternative, you could have a muffler shop bend and re-tip this tailpipe to fit.*

◀ **Fig. 9-182**

This short, 84-inch wheelbase '72 CJ-5 features a 304 V-8 with dual exhaust. Flowmaster mufflers are popular, and owner found a way to get the tailpipes to the rear of the vehicle---where they belong. This CJ is driven on the Rubicon Trail, often with kids in the back seat, and the crawl speeds require an exhaust system that exits behind the vehicle.

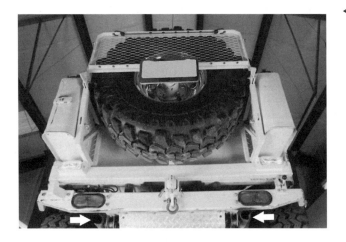

◀ **Fig. 9-183**

Note the rear exiting tailpipes (**ARROWS**). Pipes exit right below the bumper. Dual exhausts work well on V-8s, but the trend is toward large pipe, low-restriction single exhaust systems for these engines. This works well with a low-restriction muffler and catalytic converter (if required for emissions purposes).

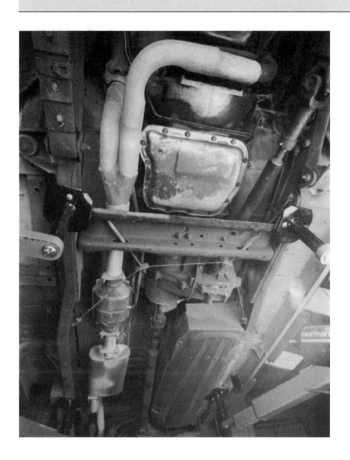

Modern muffler shops can fabricate an emission legal, high performance exhaust system. For our family's '87 Grand Wagoneer with 360 V-8, this system works very well. Rick's RV Center at El Cajon, California, performed the work, fabricating all pipe from scratch.

NOTE—

Single exhaust does not mean less performance. The Grand Wagoneer's system now has larger diameter pipe with a low-restriction turbo muffler and an emission legal, air-injected performance catalytic converter. The 'Grand' has great performance and a pleasant exhaust note. You can use a similar, 50-State legal approach with your V-8 CJ's exhaust. Take the tailpipe to the rearmost or original, factory exit point.

CAUTION—

> *Route exhaust components away from safety items and flammables! OEM layout is worth noting. Exhaust pipe should avoid brake cylinders, brake hoses and pipes, moving parts, painted surfaces, body trim and mounts, fuel lines, undercoating, plastic, and rubber parts of any kind. Keep exhaust pieces away from moving suspension, axles, drivelines and powertrain components. Keep heat away from any sensitive component, including any hoses or pipes containing fuel, brake fluid or coolant!*

9

Chapter 10

Accessories and Safety Equipment

10

General

No vehicle in the world has been more personalized than the Jeep 'Universal' and its military counterpart models. Many CJs have been fitted for hard work at agriculture, mining, construction and all-season resorts. Others, intended more for pleasure and recreation, have been detailed and fitted with a huge array of backcountry access gear.

In no way would I suggest what your Jeep CJ should be! My current '55 CJ-5 project for *Jeep CJ Rebuilder's Manual 1946-1971* and the 1981 CJ-5 I built for *OFF-ROAD Magazine*, however, feature much of the equipment that multi-purpose and family recreational users find practical. Whether that is your plan or not, any owner will benefit from the safety equipment that I cover in this chapter.

When I first drove the Rubicon Trail in August of 1967, our family's stock '64 CJ-5 had no roll bar and no seat belts. My folks had purchased the Jeep new, and in Willys/Kaiser era tradition, the options were all dealer installed. Aftermarket items included a Whitco cloth top and Cutlass "free-wheeling" (manual locking) front hubs. Jeep-supplied pieces amounted to a factory heater/defroster unit, a right-side windshield wiper setup, and a drawbar hitch that fitted nicely to the rear frame and bumper.

These add-on items totaled just under $300, a small sum by today's standards. The total purchase price of that Jeep was $2,700 for a T-98A four-speed equipped, F-head powered, go anywhere four-wheel drive machine! Oh, and that price included the rare 1/3-2/3 front seat option.

Today's TJ Wrangler buyer is just as apt to accessorize his or her Jeep as my father was with our family's '64 CJ-5. The Jeep built today, however, comes standard with a good deal of all-weather equipment and many built-in highway safety items. As you have discovered throughout this book, such modern engineering can be retrofitted to any CJ Jeep model.

More than any other work on your Jeep, accessorizing provides both a practical and creative outlet. From trail running, we discover the beneficial features that other owners have embraced. Ideas also carry over from the automotive racing community, the heavy trucking industry, and the outdoor recreational arena.

Whatever direction you choose, consider the accessories, safety items and installation methods illustrated in this chapter. In ranking priorities, safety comes first. Protecting the Jeep's undercarriage rates high if you intend to traverse the rougher backcountry trails. The rest depends upon your travel and recreational plans. Enjoy making *your* Jeep CJ the machine you always wanted!

 Fig. 10-1

Mechanical upgrades can improve the performance and handling of your Jeep. Installation of a rugged Saginaw power steering unit eases steering dramatically. AMC/Jeep CJs were available with factory power steering, easing the conversion process with OEM parts. When converting to Saginaw power steering, I always use the slower, four-turn type gear.

NOTE—

A short wheelbase vehicle is not a candidate for a 3-turn power steering gear or a small-diameter steering wheel! The high roll center and center of gravity do not lend themselves to "sprint car" steering. Saginaw gears are available in a variety of ratios. I opt for the slower speed ones for retrofitting.

Fig. 10-2

Grant steering wheel is both cosmetic and functional. Grant's marine catalog turned up this four-spoke, large diameter flat wheel that will replicate OEM "feel" of vintage and '72-'75 CJs. Horn kit/adapter mated wheel to GM truck column and upper steering shaft. *Keep thumbs out of the spokes when driving in rough, off-pavement environments!*

NOTE—

Grant makes a variety of horn/adapter kits, including Jeep CJ applications. Whether you have a stock or retrofit steering column, see the Grant catalog for listings.

10

Fig. 10-3

A common handling challenge is road and trail steering kickback. While spring anchors moved to the front end of the front springs can help offset steering wander, so does this aftermarket steering stabilizer shock, which also reduces steering kickback. Full-Traction Suspension damper directly replaces OEM item on this late CJ.

NOTE—

*See **Chapters 6** and **7** for details on chassis improvements. "Shackle reversal" kits are popular for CJs, placing the anchors at the front end of the front springs and the shackles at the rear of each spring.*

◀ **Fig. 10-4**

Backbone of this '72 CJ's electrical system is a 160-amp output Premier Power Welder alternator. Alternator powers Premier Power Welder and high output electrics. Above the alternator is a York air conditioning compressor converted to an air compressor for use in the field. This provides a high-output compressor capable of tire inflation and running certain air tools.

◀ **Fig. 10-5**

This is the electrical arsenal for ultimate backcountry travel. '72 CJ has been fitted with two Optima batteries with an isolator/switch between them, an air compressor, an on-board Premier Welder and a full complement of backcountry lighting and sound equipment!

◀ **Fig. 10-6**

Fuel lines and connections are a safety item. Vintage Jeep's OEM use of a rigid steel pipe from flexing body to frame is not as safe as a stainless steel braided hose. Here, Goodridge elbow is highest quality racing industry component.

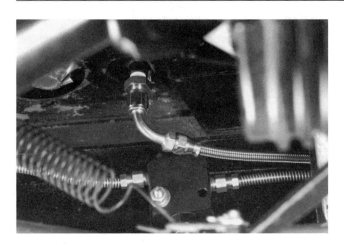

Fig. 10-7

Vintage Jeep hose attaches to elbow at fuel tank. Flexibility of braided fuel line addresses any movement between the tank (tub-mounted) and frame. Hose also provides the necessary flex needed between the frame rail and fuel pump. Use plastic coated steel clamps to attach hose securely to the frame rail. '72-up CJs have OEM fuel tank mounted to the frame, a better method.

NOTE—

On fuel supply connections between the frame and body or frame and engine, you must use fuel-grade flexible lines or hose. All '72-up AMC/Jeep CJs use fuel-grade hose from the tank to the fuel pipes, the pipes to the fuel pump, and the return pipe to the frame and tank. Evaporative systems use steel pipe and fuel-grade lines.

Fig. 10-8

This six-point roll bar kit from Kentrol is a must item! Six-point mounting means that the body tub ties directly to the frame. In the event of a dangerous rollover, this cage keeps the body attached to the frame. (This may not be the case with factory and tub-only roll bars.) Cage comes with hoops pre-welded.

NOTE—

As the front hoop is patterned after the later Jeep CJ tubs, I widened the front hoop for floor fitment to my '55 CJ. This would not be necessary for a 1972-'75 CJ. Overhead fore-and-aft tubular braces weld between the two hoops.

> *CAUTION—*
>
> *This high-quality Kentrol kit requires welding. If you do not have the skills for all-position welding, have a certified welder run the beads. I used my MIG welder and 0.035" wire.*

10

Fig. 10-9

Finished cage received coating of spray can bed liner material. Clean metal surface provides good adhesion, and the mottled finish is both durable and easily touched up. *Always use a respirator when working with these kinds of chemicals.*

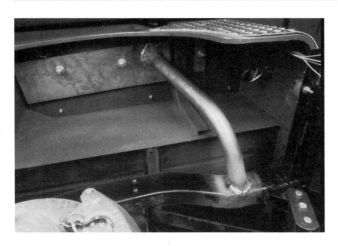

 Fig. 10-10

Tube section welds directly to the frame. Here, I located the rear tub plate just below and parallel to the angle base of the rear double-hoop. This is the left rear fender well view.

Fig. 10-11

Right rear fender well mount is welded into position. Bent tube can be welded to flat plate before you weld the down tube to the frame. Wire feed MIG welder is good method for all-position, tube-to-frame welds. Kentrol furnishes all of the steel plate and tubing needed to complete this installation.

Fig. 10-12

Goodyear rubber belting material is placed between top of the plate and the base of the body tub. Belting is thick enough to allow body tub-to-frame flexing, which occurs to some degree. Without belting, the sandwich (clamshell) mounting method would not allow tub movement between the rear hoop base and the frame bracing. Body flex would be impossible.

CAUTION—

Preventing the body from moving and flexing would stress the sheet metal and cause fatigue or fracturing of the fender deck sheet metal. Knowing that the Jeep CJ frame flexes considerably, especially off-pavement in the rocks, engineers intentionally isolated the body from the frame. Body-to-frame mounting cushions reduce the transfer of road shock and minimize the tub unit's flex. This helps prevent body stress and cracking.

 Fig. 10-13

Front hoop base plates fit flush to the floorboard. Holes drilled through floor require careful application of primer/sealer. (This is a common point for sheet metal rust on many Jeep CJs.) I re-drilled plate holes to accept next larger size Grade 5 bolts and self-locking, aircraft-type nuts.

 Fig. 10-14

Kentrol kit includes a bottom plate to match the front hoop base. Universal Jeep CJ kit, patterned for AMC-era models, comes with weld-on frame brackets that support these front plates. Due to the OEM body mount location and frame design of my early model CJ-5, tying the front hoop to the frame was not possible. This kit works best with AMC-era CJs.

NOTE—

For full benefit and safety of six-point mounting, the front hoop base should tie to the frame like the rear hoop does. Kentrol recommends front hoop-to-frame tie-down method, using belting between the lower/frame mount and the body (to enable flex). The '72-up CJs have space for the brackets to tie the front hoop into the frame as Kentrol intended.

10

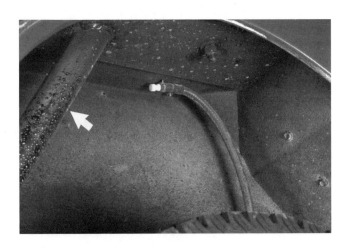

 Fig. 10-15

Down tubes (**ARROW**) and brace plates require coverage with bed liner material or undercoating. Read instructions to determine whether primer is necessary. Rust is a major issue, especially in the Midwest. Make certain all welds are watertight to prevent rust formation within the tubing.

 Fig. 10-16

When fully installed, all underside plates and tubing require careful coverage with bed liner spray or undercoating to prevent rust formation! If you use paint, prime with a rust-inhibiting primer unless otherwise specified.

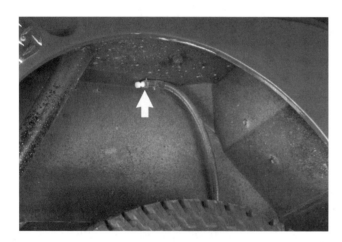

 Fig. 10-17

The check valve (**ARROW**) for the rear axle vent on my vintage CJ is high in the fender. I move these vents high in the chassis or body to prevent water from entering the axle during stream fording. Note that valve is free to open and shut as designed. If you install a retrofit axle or expect to ford streams, take these vents into account.

NOTE—

These valves are replacement types for later CJs, available from your Jeep dealer or sources like 4WD Hardware. Bulk automotive hose is fuel and oil resistant.

 Fig. 10-18

This is a custom rear axle vent that I built for the '55 CJ's '44' unit. Brass fittings and hose from the local auto parts store complete the vent modification. Be certain that the hose will not interfere with any moving part of the chassis. For insurance, I use Teflon paste on fitting threads.

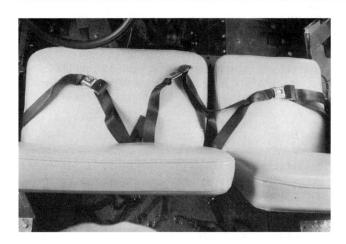

◀ **Fig. 10-19**

Seat belts are crucial to safety. '55 CJ-5 came from the factory without belts. These lap belt kits from 4WD Hardware include mounting hardware. This kind of belt will also serve aftermarket rear seat installations. For additional safety, consider full seatbelt/harnesses.

> **CAUTION—**
> *Always anchor seatbelts to the floor with large, thick washers on the bottom side. This will spread load over a wider area and reduce risk of strained belts pulling loose from the floor. For a full review of seatbelt needs and installation tips, see the **Jeep Owner's Bible**.*

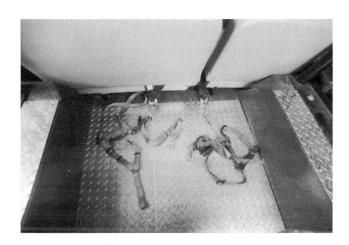

◀ **Fig. 10-20**

Don't forget the dogs! We use chest harnesses that safely support our dogs' weight in the event of a rollover. These eye anchors are high-grade, special mounting bolts from Filler, an aftermarket seatbelt manufacturer. Straps with safety clasps come from a horse tack supplier. Beneath the floor, I use thick, large diameter washers or steel plates to distribute the load over a broader area.

> **NOTE—**
> *In the event of a rollover, the dogs would suspend within the protection of the roll bar. Envision such a prospect when designing harnesses for your dogs. (Nobody wants a rollover, and I prefer that you never experience one!) These harnesses also serve as a good means for keeping the dog(s) within the body tub. Top down, our dogs get a great view and fresh air---without the risk of falling out! Their four-wheeling chest harnesses prevent neck stress and support weight over a longer body span. We have a Golden Retriever and a Chocolate Lab. They enjoy four-wheelin' in the backcountry!*

10

◀ **Fig. 10-21**

The spare tire rack for the '55 CJ-5 was sourced through 4WD Hardware and has a substantial rear frame mount. This mount fits AMC-era CJs as well. To support weight, the kit includes a pair of angle plates that can either bolt or weld to the frame/bumper junction. This provides reinforcement and support for the added weight. I chose to plug ("buttonhole") weld the plates to the frame members, using my MIG wire-welder. This metal now needs a coating of frame paint.

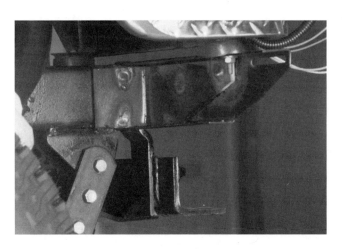

Accessories and Safety Equipment

 Fig. 10-22

Spare tire mount is well engineered. The support plate for a swinging rack section bolts to the reinforced rear bumper. When swung outward, the rack carries the tire neatly out of the way, providing easy access to the tailgate. Racks like this have a rating for wheel/tire weight and diameter.

NOTE—

There are a variety of ways to mount a spare tire rack to the vehicle. Jeep used a body (sheet metal) mount that worked fairly well with lightweight tire/wheel assemblies. For the mildly oversized tires that I use on the CJ-5, the rack pictured here offers an adequate load rating. A rack mounted to sheet metal could not support such weight. (See Fig. 9-183 for ideas on one builder's homemade tote rack that serves as a tire carrier and spare can carrier.)

 Fig. 10-23

Tires of choice for this vehicle are Goodyear Wrangler AT/S types. This is an LT265R75-16 size, load range 'D.' I used 235R85-16s on my '81 CJ-5 depicted in the *Jeep Owner's Bible*. Goodyear was a Jeep OEM supplier throughout the CJ era. Attractive and functional American Racing type 'AR-23' 7"x16" alloy wheels make an ideal fit for quality and safety. Tires stand at approximately 31-1/4" diameter.

Wheel and Tire Choice

The AR-23 wheels *(shown here)* offer more than looks. These rims rate a 2500-pound load capacity per wheel, more than twice the capacity needed for a CJ Jeep at GVWR! If you prefer steel wheels, American Racing offers a range of alloy and steel types. The AR-23 has a maximum tire diameter limit of 33-inches.

CJ models in stock form will not tolerate wide, tall tires. The steering angle is restricted, and body clearance is an issue. My experience has shown that even a 31" tire is often too much for a stock vehicle.

NOTE—

For CJs like my '55 and the '81 CJ-5, I needed at least a 2-inch lift to run the LT265R75-16 or LT235R85-16 tires. With the lift, these relatively narrower tires did not require steering stop/angle changes on either vehicle.

On a late CJ with 8-inch rims at stock height or a very mild lift, 31"x10.50"x15" tires will usually work without the need to adjust steering turn angles from OEM settings. (Caster angle settings also impact the steering angles and turning radius. Check caster angle.) This means I maintained a tighter turning radius, which is desirable for off-pavement driving.

Choose your tire/wheel combination wisely and conservatively! On an AMC/Jeep CJ, 7"x16" rims (maximum 265R75-16 or 235R85-16 tires) or 8"x15" rims (for a maximum of 31"x10.5"x15" tires) may require a modest suspension/spring lift kit (1- to 2-inch lift range). Trial fit any tire, checking clearance over the full range of suspension travel and sweep of the steering angles.

Remember, many vintage Jeep CJs have scaled rough trails with their original 6.00X16 or 7.00X15 size tires on stock width rims! Be sure you need big tires and wider rims before investing here. The package generally includes quality wheels and hardware, premium tires and a well-engineered suspension lift kit. (See my ***Jeep Owner's Bible*** for in-depth details.)

For my driving needs, the maximum size tires I would run on a '72-up CJ would be a 32"x11.50"/15" (on 8-inch rims) or 33"x12.50"/15" (on 10-inch rims). Either of these tire sizes will require a suspension lift, likely 2- to 3-inches for the 32" tires and 3- to 4-inches for the 33" tires. I recommend use of a dropped pitman arm to offset bump steer and maintain a near-stock draglink angle.

 Fig. 10-24

Contemporary spare tire rack and Bestop's stylish and functional 'Super Top' fit nicely together. This top converts into a variety of configurations for all-season outings. I have used Bestop products for many years and find them very versatile and durable! They are popular on '72-up CJ models. Bestop is now manufacturing a spare tire rack *(not shown here)* for the later CJs.

10

 Fig. 10-25

Rear window area is large and provides dramatically better visibility than the early soft tops. On the highway or trail, visibility is vital to safety. If rolled up, the window can easily drop down and zip shut when that thundershower comes.

 Fig. 10-26

Rear quarter sections removed, bracing is evident. Bestop has engineered this top for quick changes. Printed instructions and a video help ease installation. I take my time with cloth top installations; this installation still took less than a half-day to complete. Any holes drilled require primer/sealer.

Fig. 10-27

Doors are two-piece type with weather-resistant rubber outer seals and a Velcro strip between the upper and lower sections. Note the sturdy latch and ability to secure the lower door without the top piece attached. Roll bar provides the occupant protection necessary for cloth doors.

Fig. 10-28

Upper door section installed, the convertible top is now a full top. Sealing is very good on this Bestop 'Super Top.' Super Top engineering first appeared on the Wrangler YJ as an OEM item. Bestop met rigid Jeep corporate standards to qualify as the OEM supplier.

◄ **Fig. 10-29**

The door open with window zipped down, quality is evident. Hefty door latch mechanisms, a rugged frame, and durable canvas material have become Bestop trademarks. You can convert this top to a half-dozen configurations---in minutes.

◄ **Fig. 10-30**

Hood latches from 4WD Hardware add a chrome dress-up item with function.

◄ **Fig. 10-31**

Chrome hood hinges replace OEM strap hinges. 4WD Hardware kit comes with hardware and fits nicely.

10

Accessories and Safety Equipment

'Bestop' Seat Installation Tips

Original equipment CJ seats receive a real beating. Weather and off-road driving take their toll. The seat frames and upholstery can break down over time, and many Jeep owners find themselves replacing the seats---and often the seat frames.

On the '86 CJ-7, the OEM seats revealed an even more insidious concern: The seat frame nuts and surrounding metal had corroded and rusted to the point that merely loosening the adjuster rail hardware caused the frames to break apart! This was a clear hazard that AMC/Jeep CJ owners should consider. Inspect your seat frames carefully!

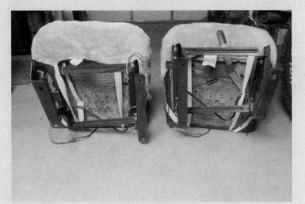

Seats set in proper relationship. Seat at right is driver's seat with the sliding rails and rail release lever.

Seat removal is simple enough. Loosen the four floor bolts that hold the seat frame to the tub.

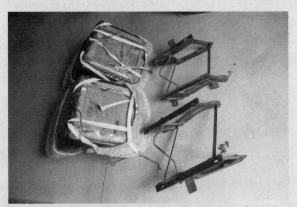

Bolts and nuts removed, seats readily separate from the seat frames. Unless you know a German car or Euro mechanic who lends out tools, you will need to invest in an E-socket set to remove the rail bolts on some CJ models (like the '86 CJ-7).

Left/driver's seat comes out as easily. The left seat, however, has a pair of sliding rails. Make a note which seat frame fits left side. Release latch is on left side of left seat, right side of right seat.

Here was a surprise. California vehicle had no rust anywhere on the body. Attempting to simply loosen the rail bolts, I discovered that the seat frame nuts readily broke loose from the frame! Note the E-socket on my ratchet.

'Bestop' Seat Installation Tips (continued)

Rust had the seat frame so thin that two nut sections were already cracked through---the other two broke with little effort.

Bestop hardware was hex-bolt, and the OEM bolts were E-head. I preferred the grading on the OEM bolts. I recommend replacing seat bolts with new OEM grade bolts.

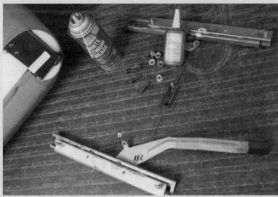

Grease the rails with lithium "white" grease. Normally, if the rails are in good shape, you can install them on the new seats at this point.

Oh, boy! Here is another weakness to watch for: Seat rails had cracked around the square-punched bolt holes. There are aftermarket rails and frame brackets available. If your seat frames or rails show defects, I recommend that you consider replacing them with new parts.

I decided to attempt a repair on the OEM rails. Wire-brushing first to determine metal type, I gas-welded the cracks using mild steel rod and penetrating the metal deeply enough to meet welds from the opposite side.

I made the welds in a manner that would reinforce the adjacent metal.

10

'Bestop' Seat Installation Tips (continued)

Some primer/sealer, and this part is strong enough for service. Gas welding minimizes heat concentration and lessens risk of embrittling adjacent metal. I allow metal to air cool.

Light dressing with a file on the mounting surface makes welded area flush for use of OEM spacer/washer. Opposite side can afford the metal buildup, as the round OEM bolt heads fit snugly in the rail's square holes, clearing the reinforcement welds. Primer/seal any bare metal.

New Bestop seats are durable and adjustable. Upholstery will hold up well. These TrailMax "Sport" high-back recliner seats will adjust/recline securely.

This full-vinyl seat pair features elasticized mesh pouch for storage at the seat backs. Seats come with detailed instructions and hardware.

Use Loctite 242 on nut or bolt threads. If lockwashers are in the kit, use them. Here, I torque the hardware to specification.

'Bestop' Seat Installation Tips (continued)

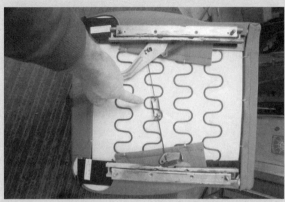

The release latch needs adjustment. After the rails are firmly in place, you can adjust the release latch. Make absolutely certain that the catches release completely and seat completely. Time/adjust the release so that the latches release at each side uniformly and catch uniformly. *Each side must lock readily.* Lube sliding rail and lock mechanisms with lithium grease.

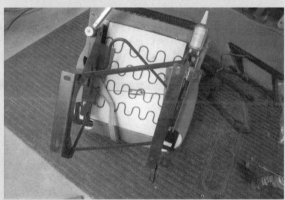

Loctite and a torque wrench assure proper seating of nuts. I tighten graded 5/16" or 8mm studs and nuts to 18 lb-ft, pulling up torque gradually and in steps. OEM grade hardware will take this torque. Re-check the torque after parts settle.

I went to the local auto supply and stepped up the grading on the metric hex bolts and shake-proof lockwashers. I use Loctite as well. My aim is to safely secure these seats in a manner that will not allow the hardware to fail or loosen over time. Seat installations must follow safety guidelines.

Threadlocker is a must item. Note the improved grading on the bolts, washers and lockwashers. I sourced these through the local auto supply.

Align floor bracket with the carpet impressions, and bolt the seats to the floor. I use Loctite on these OEM seat bracket-to-floor bolts and set torque to 45 lb-ft. Re-check the torque after parts settle. Carpet can make torque settings awkward.

10

'Bestop' Seat Installation Tips (continued)

Push back the vinyl upholstery before attempting to install the knob ratchet mechanism. Note how seat folds forward with OEM seat bracket. This is a well-engineered design and fit. For years, I have used Bestop products on Jeep projects.

Use Loctite on threads and tighten the ratchet bolt securely. The plastic handle/knob will snap into place securely. OEM seat belts will work with these seats.

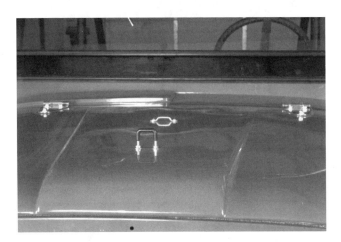

◄ **Fig. 10-32**

The new hood rest for windshield and the tie-down for windshield strap add appearance and function. These pieces came with trim kit from 4WD Hardware.

NOTE—

A chrome front bumper is also available from 4WD Hardware. I secure the front bumper with Grade 8 fasteners.

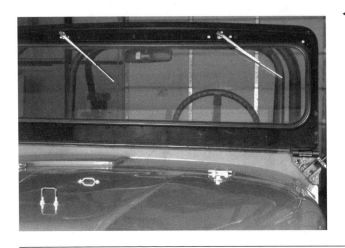

◄ **Fig. 10-33**

4WD Hardware was source for the windshield seal, glue-on rear view mirror and wiper assemblies (used on vintage Jeep models). Glass is lightly tinted safety type, cut at a local auto glass shop. Shop fitted the seal and new glass. Flat Jeep CJ windshield glass has always been easy to find or make.

◀ **Fig. 10-34**

To mount mirrors, I removed, drilled and carefully tapped threads into the vintage OEM windshield hinges. This enabled installation of these contemporary side-view mirrors available from 4WD Hardware.Kit is for AMC-era CJs.

◀ **Fig. 10-35**

Rectangular mirror heads fit on new mirror arms. Assembly fits later Jeep mirror arms. A quaint, vintage OEM round mirror designed for the driver's side only is museum and parade vehicle material. If you intend to drive in modern traffic and along rough trails, use modern mirrors on your CJ!

10

◀ **Fig. 10-36**

Matching right side mirror has distinct arm shape. You may prefer aftermarket metal arm clamps for firmer mirror settings. Brass and steel arm bushings are available. The upgrade is practical if you want steady mirror settings on those rough trails.

 Fig. 10-37

Attractive underhood appearance is a Jeep must. The large CJ hood rests back against the windshield, revealing the entire engine bay. Owner of this 1972 CJ-5 spent time building a fully functional and highly attractive, truly trail worthy Jeep. From the shovel and heavy-duty Warn winch to the rear tote rack, this vehicle is what serious trail-runners want. All your work comes together when you lift the hood!

ARB Air System

Off-road users gravitate toward the use of locking axle differentials, and the ARB Air Locker system has been popular. The ARB air supply system can double as an air source for tire inflation and other chores.

NOTE—

In some cases, users install larger air compressors to supply air for a variety of uses, including an air supply for the ARB Air Lockers. In Fig. 10-4, the York compressor air supply system could easily supply air for air locking differentials and any other chores. If you use such a system, make certain the air pressure to the ARB lockers is regulated to ARB guidelines!

Many users rely on ARB Air Lockers, and builders can benefit from knowing proven ways to install the air supply system. I have been very successful in having ARB Air Lockers that do not lose air or leak down. In the axle build chapter, you will find details on how to build an ARB locking axle. Here, I address the air system.

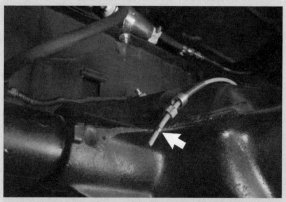

When installing the plastic hose, be aware of the ferrule fitting (**ARROW**) size. The U.S.-size tubing inside the axle does not use the same size ferrule as the metric plastic air lines. Make sure the protective coil sleeve is on the tubing.

Silicone spray eases installation of the plastic tubing into the bulkhead fitting. Make sure tubing seats completely before securing the brass compression fitting. Use a flarenut wrench. Make certain the nut is tight enough to make a good seal.

This is the ARB Air Locker kit to service a pair of front and rear locking axles. The air compressor and micro-switches form the core of the system.

10

Accessories and Safety Equipment

ARB Air System (continued)

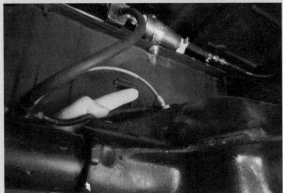

Nut secured, slide the protective coil over the fitting. This coil sleeve protects the tubing from kinking in service. Make sure coil seats on the nut.

Allow plenty of slack for full range of axle movement. CJ is on my hoist, so axle is suspended. I route the tubing to a wire-wrapped fuel line located on the frame and begin securing plastic tubing with plastic ties.

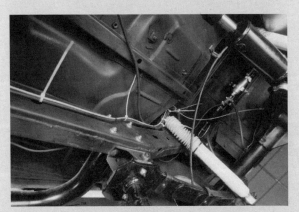

Continue tying the tubing out of harm's way. I follow the pipe along this frame rail, using ties at uniform points. This is factory fuel pipe with protective spring wire wrapped around tubing.

CAUTION—

Plastic ties can cut into steel tubing or even chafe sheet metal! Do not over-tighten plastic ties, and make every effort to tie onto items that will not become damaged over time. Be aware that plastic ties can cut into wire insulation.

I often use convolution tubing to insulate areas where I install the plastic ties. Note that I clip off excess tie material 1/8"-1/4" from the tie's clasp. ARB wire harness goes through floor hole (**ARROW**). A few steps from now, you will see how I insulate this hole…

At front axle, I install the plastic tube and coil protector. Again, axle is suspended, and I route tubing to allow for full range of axle movement. Estimate where the tubing will go as the axle moves. Allow for adequate clearance. Note how I insulate the tubing as it passes through the clamp on the frame.

ARB Air System (continued)

I locate the air compressor and drill holes to receive the compressor and its backup plate. As with the Bestop seat mounting hardware, I choose to upgrade from the bolts supplied, stepping up to Grade 5 or 8 (U.S.) bolts, lockwashers and nuts to secure the air pump assembly. Bracket holes (**ARROW**) required slight reaming for larger bolts.

I mount the sturdy ARB switch panel beneath the dash, well within reach of the driver. Note the orientation: the left switch is compressor on/off; middle switch is for the rear (more frequently used) air locker. The front air locker switch is at right.

This is how I insulated the ARB wiring harness coming through the floorboard hole. This is a factory hole, and I use a split piece of vacuum hose to serve as an insulator hoop. The automotive wiring clip on the floor holds the harness in place. Note my use of convolution tubing to keep clip from gnawing at the harness' tape wrap.

NOTE—

I formed a 360-degree loop with the harness below the floorboard to allow ample freedom for body and frame movement. Harness wiring runs to the compressor atop the right front fender bucket.

Wire comes from floorboard to the ARB switches. This is a top quality, preformed harness. Illuminated switches are of very good quality, too. Wiring and switches came with the kit. ARB can supply the switch panel as an accessory.

Here is the compressor, all hoses and wiring installed. Make sure hoses and wires are routed out of harm's way and secured properly. Periodically, test the system for leaks with soapy water in a spray bottle. With compressor pumping until the reservoir is full, spray around the air lines and fittings. Look for bubbles, and repair any leaks.

10

What's Next?

For many owners, a Jeep CJ is a work in progress. Back-country runners and competition Jeep builders can always find room for improvements and upgrades.

For my '55 CJ, the current plans include enhancing the seating capacity. I will install a Bestop rear tumble-and-fold seat. This universal seat, grey in color to match the CJ-5's front seats, will be carefully anchored to the floorboard, using large, thick bottom-side washers---much like the seatbelt fasteners. Rear passengers will have seat belts, too!

As with all of my project vehicles, a Warn winch is in the works. My unit of choice for this vehicle is the classic '8274' upright design. In contemporary, rugged form, this is now the Model 8274-50.

The 8274-50 is more than enough pulling power for any Jeep, and I will mount the unit on a sturdy, custom platform built from several pieces of a Warn winch mount kit. My fabrication will involve side plates that clear the Saginaw steering gear unit. ***Jeep CJ Rebuilder's Manual: 1946-1971*** is now complete, and I will do that winch installation in preparation for this fall's hunting and fly fishing season.

Beyond that, I did abandon the blasphemous notions, like the installation of a smaller V-8 powerplant coupled to an automatic transmission for Mrs. Ludel's convenience. Instead, I have built a 3.8L Buick V-6 in the Kaiser-era tradition. Using Advance Adapters' components, I am mating an NV 3550 5-speed to the Model 18 transfer case. The V-6 requires a custom radiator assembly to accommodate the higher output engine. Of course, the new 160 horsepower engine begs the installation of a Saginaw power steering gear at some point.

Is all this necessary? Not really. In low-range, four-wheel drive, with a four-speed's compound low first gear and 5.38:1 axle gearsets, even my vintage '55 CJ-5 easily climbed the steepest tractable surfaces---with its trusty F-head four-cylinder engine!

Now, for high altitude trail running, there could be room for a retrofit EFI system to replace the fixed-jet, two-barrel carburetor on the V-6 engine. Perhaps a Mopar throttle body injection 'EFI' system from an '80s 3.9L V-6 Dodge Dakota powerplant would work.

As you can see, there are plenty of options for personalizing a Jeep CJ. For the highway user, engine size and passing power might be important, perhaps demanding a V-8 engine swap or the 4.2L Mopar Performance MPI Conversion Kit for the original inline six.

By contrast, the trail runner content to trailer a vintage CJ to 4WD trailheads might be perfectly content with even less changes than I performed on the '55 CJ-5. My '81 CJ-5 (featured in the *Jeep Owner's Bible*) and the '55 CJ-5 each follow a long tradition of sensible trail and street improvements. The '86 CJ-7 featured within this book transformed into the ultimate trail runner and multipurpose Jeep vehicle.

For my tastes, I purposely retain the appearance items that characterize a Jeep. Like the majority of Jeep CJ builders, I make modifications and upgrades to suit my driving environments and perceived performance needs.

Drive the trails and roads that help *you* decide what your Jeep needs. Learn what your Jeep can do before you seek to change or accessorize it. When you make the decision to upgrade or enhance your Jeep, follow proven and safe approaches. Above all, remember, the real fun lies just over that next hill!

10

Appendix

A

Bearing Fundamentals

 Nothing can ruin a day of four-wheeling more quickly than a failed bearing! Your Jeep's axles, steering and powertrain rely on sound, well-lubricated bearings.

Fortunately, bearing trouble usually offers some forewarning, so total bearing failures are frequently avoidable. Premature bearing failures most often reflect improper maintenance, poor fit-up, or overloading. The rigid standards set for new bearings make out-of-the-box defects unlikely.

NOTE—

Emphasize the word "quality" when ordering bearings. Stay with known manufacturers like Timken, BCA, and SKF. Do not waste money on unknown brands of bearings. If in doubt, you can always depend upon Mopar OEM replacement bearings from your Jeep dealer.

Understanding the design and intended use of automotive bearings can help assure better bearing life. Each bearing application on your Jeep CJ has been carefully engineered. Before making modifications to the chassis or powertrain, consider the OEM's intentions.

Engine or 'Sliding' Bearings

The majority of engine bearings are sliding types, technically known as "circular cylindrical radial sleeve bearings." A sliding bearing relies on a film of oil to prevent shaft-to-bearing friction. Automotive engines use sliding bearings to support the crankshaft, rods, piston pins and camshaft. Thrust type sliding bearings also control the axial movement or "end play" of shafts.

Preventing wear to these bearings depends on an ongoing supply of oil under pressure. Oil and coolant temperatures must stay within normal levels for the bearings to function safely and not break down or scuff against their shafts.

Oil cleanliness is an absolute necessity, as sliding bearing "embeddability" (the ability to absorb and hold contaminants safely away from the shaft) is slim. Typical insert-type engine bearings have a steel back, aluminum section, electroplated copper bond and lead-tin surface coat. The lead-tin coat cannot withstand dry friction or overloading. Dry operation will quickly ruin an engine bearing.

The best protection for engine bearings is quality lubrication, ample oil pressure and proper filtration. On AMC/Jeep inline sixes and V-8 engine designs, a full-flow oil filtration system with regular oil and filter changes will provide the best protection.

NOTE—
Especially on a 4WD Jeep used off-pavement, you must
keep dust from entering the intake system. Service the air
cleaner whenever necessary. Each 2,500-3,000 miles is a
good time for oil filter changes, far more frequently in severe
dust conditions.

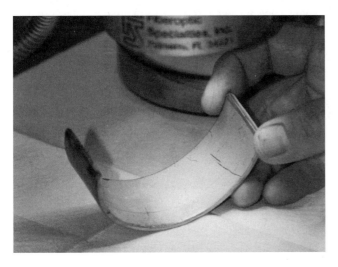

 Familiar automotive crankshaft insert bearing is a sliding design. Such bearings depend totally on adequate lubrication
and oil film strength for their survival. Note scratches caused
by minute contaminants running through lubrication system.

When assembling an engine, take care that each sliding
bearing has proper clearance. Clean the bearing saddles
thoroughly before installing bearing shells. Use Plastigage
to confirm bearing clearances wherever possible.

NOTE—
Proper bearing clearance allows oil to flow between the
crankshaft and the bearings. Oil keeps bearings from con-
tacting the crankshaft journals. Excess clearance reduces
oil pressure. Tight clearances can cause bearing scuff.
Proper bearing and journal sizing, confirmed with Plasti-
gage, assures the correct oil film and proper oil pressure.
Quality oil, with adequate film strength, will maintain bearing
clearance.

Anti-Friction Bearings

The Jeep geartrain and chassis also have their share of
bearings. Although bronze and even nylon bushings and
thrust washers serve in some transmission, steering system
and chassis applications, more heavily loaded and high-
speed parts require anti-friction type bearings.

Automotive anti-friction bearings have a wide range of designs and uses. The broad classifications are roller and ball
type, although these groups break into a variety of sub-
classes and applications.

Roller bearings fall into two categories: tapered roller type
and ball bearings. We usually find ball bearings in areas that
require both radial and lateral (end play) control of movement. A good example is the caged ball type rear wheel
bearing found on some semi-floating axles or the typical
generator/alternator shaft bearings.

A caged ball bearing, pressed onto the axle shaft just inboard of the brake backing plate location, supports the vehicle weight and also controls axle endplay or thrust loads.
The balls ride in curved rails that counter the lateral as well
as radial movement.

A

Caged ball-type bearing assemblies also serve transmission systems by controlling both end movement and radial runout of a shaft. A ball type bearing can serve in areas requiring a designated degree of preloading and/or a zero-endplay setting. (The Saginaw steering gear's worm shaft ball bearings are one example.)

Typically, caged ball bearings lube from oil immersion, oil spray, serviceable/packed grease or grease that is "permanently sealed" with molded plastic seals. (Permanently sealed means zero maintenance for the life of the bearing.) Since the typical ball bearing runs under heavy loads at close tolerances, these bearings require a constant supply of lubricant.

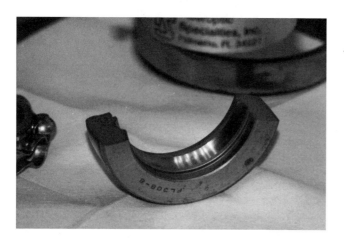

◄ Severe shock broke this ball bearing race. Hardness of quality bearing steel failed under tremendous force. This damage, called "brinelling," shows as impact imprinting on the ball race and fracture.

◄ Heat melted the metal from the interior of this ball bearing! Imagine the temperature necessary to cause such damage. Movement of bearing prevented ball from welding to race.

◄ Caged ball bearing is common to automotive transmissions. Shown is a king-size version used on a Caterpillar application. Basic design applies, as this bearing handles both radial and thrust loads.

◀ Movement of inner race illustrates wear in this caged ball bearing. Play between races and balls allows inner race to cock sideways.

Roller-type bearings come in a variety of designs. Tapered, flat and barrel shaped rollers fit a number of special uses. On the automotive chassis, the tapered roller bearing is common to front wheel and full-floating rear wheel assemblies. Tapered roller bearings also show up in transmissions, differentials and other gear assemblies.

◀ Popular tapered roller anti-friction bearing design serves a multitude of applications. Tapered shape of rollers and a cone race can counter radial and thrust loading. This bearing failed in service, breaking the cage.

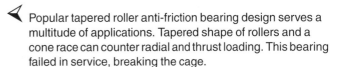

◀ Broken cage allowed bearings to shift and bind. Note roller damage and signs of severe scoring. This kind of failure would produce noise and possible seizure of parts.

Jeep CJ mechanics are familiar with tapered roller wheel bearings, as they require periodic maintenance. With the hollow spindle running through the wheel hub center, the wheel hub assembly has a smaller grease cavity.

For the full-floating type Jeep 4WD front wheel hubs, there is a need to seal both ends of the hub from atmospheric contaminants. This makes an oil bath system impractical. (An oil bath within a sealed hub would mean substantial heat in a confined area, lack of ventilation, sealing issues, the need for finite bearing clearances and a host of other problems.) The use of wheel bearing grease and periodic repacking is a sensible alternative to an oil bath.

A

Wheel bearing grease cannot stand up indefinitely, though. Contamination and heat cause the grease to break down. Periodically, you must thoroughly clean, dry, inspect and re-pack these bearings with fresh lubricant/grease. Any wear signs mean time to replace the bearing cup and cone as an assembly.

Causes of Bearing Failure

Bearings should last a long time. Bearings fail prematurely for several reasons. The broad-heading cause of bearing failure is fatigue. Fatigue can directly relate to abuse, misuse or overloading.

OEM engineers give due consideration to bearing design and applications. Sometimes, however, a bearing's failure results from unanticipated loading or misuse. Heavy application of torque, such as a hybrid engine swap for more horsepower, is one way to stress parts. *Example: The AMC/Jeep CJ's Warner T-4 four-speed transmission works fine with engines in the 100-120 horsepower range---yet the T-4 breaks readily when subjected to a V-8's 250-300 horse-power!*

NOTE—

Oversize tires and wheels also add to the problem, especially with taller axle gearing such as 3.54:1. Another weak area is the smaller pinion gear tooth-count on the 4.56:1 and lower (numerically higher) ratio axles. Added loads placed on the geartrain can waste a T-4 or T-5 (Jeep light duty version) transmission, burn up the smaller diameter clutch assembly, or break gears in a lighter front axle like the Dana 30 unit.

The use of wider wheels and tires, with more offset on the wheel rims, places an extra load on the front and rear wheel bearings. Manufacturers design hubs, axle shafts and bearing assemblies to withstand a particular wheel offset. Modifying the offset can alter the load placed upon bearings, bringing about premature bearing failure.

With regard to oversized tire use, Jeep CJs have been more tolerant than many other vehicles. Reasonable spacing between inner and outer wheel bearings, decent bearing sizing, and a light overall vehicle weight have enabled owners to use mildly wider, more negatively offset wheels---without dire results. (See the **Jeep Owner's Bible** for further wheel and tire details.)

Another cause of bearing failure is contamination. A worn hub seal, or parking your 4WD Jeep in a flowing stream, can allow moisture to enter the hub. Wheel bearings and differential assemblies fail when lubrication breaks down or becomes water contaminated. Manufacturers recommend cleaning and repacking bearings whenever you submerge a 4x4 in a stream or have reason to suspect water contamination.

If your Jeep has chassis modifications, gear ratio changes or aftermarket wheels with excess offset, shorten the period between lubrication intervals. Clean, inspect and repack your wheel bearings using a top quality "high temp" grease. (I prefer Texaco's 'Starplex 2' grease as noted in the service sections of this book.) Always adjust the bearings properly.

Bearing Clearances and Adjustments

Permanently sealed rear axle bearings and one-piece (unit-type) caged ball bearing assemblies require no adjustment. Proper installation on the shaft and correct fit-up into the housing bore are the only concerns. Common Jeep two-piece tapered roller bearings, which include a bearing "cup" and the "cone" or race, require careful adjustment or correct shimming.

Bearing adjustment is critical for safety and minimizing wear. An improperly adjusted front wheel bearing set or rear axle bearing can cause bearing failure---or even the loss of a wheel assembly! Guidelines for proper bearing installation and adjustment are available within the service chapters of this book or a Jeep official workshop manual.

Tapered roller bearing adjustment varies between applications. Some bearings require running clearance or measurable endplay. In high torque and heavy load applications, even "zero clearance" may be too loose under load. For this reason, differential carrier and pinion bearings require a *preload* to maintain gear alignment as the carrier runs under load.

The differential pinion shaft and carrier bearings require a specified rolling resistance. Pinion preload is measured with a torque wrench on the nut end of the shaft. Carrier preload is set with a specific thickness of shim material. On Jeep axles, added shims actually spread the differential housing to preload the differential carrier bearings.

NOTE—
*In **Chapter 5**, I provide specific details on how to adjust the differential bearings.*

Tapered roller bearings used in front wheel hubs have a free running clearance. Timken, the widely respected manufacturer of tapered roller bearings, notes a 0.003"-0.005" endplay setting for smaller size wheel bearings and 0.007"-0.010" for larger bearings.

A

The general adjusting procedure for a tapered roller wheel bearing set begins with seating the bearings in their cups. Torque the spindle nut to the recommended specification while rotating the wheel hub. Once you have fully seated the bearings, back the nut off as recommended. In Jeep CJ applications, you will then install the lock plate washer and outer nut. Torque the outer nut to specification, and check for correct bearing adjustment.

An overly tight adjustment causes excess heat buildup, which quickly fries the bearings. Over-tightening also encourages "roller skidding," which can flatten rollers and quickly destroy the bearings.

Reciprocally, loosely adjusted bearings allow too much axial movement/endplay or sideplay. Looseness creates uneven loading of the rollers and also permits bearings to pound destructively against their races.

These straight roller bearings show obvious damage from skidding along the race. Damage such as this results from overloading, poor lubrication or excess preloading.

Wear at cone back face rib can result from an overly tight bearing adjustment or poor lubrication. Over-tightening will also cause excess heat buildup and loss of effective lubrication, as grease cannot establish a film between rollers and the race surfaces.

◁ This is "fretting corrosion," not rust. Fretting or "friction oxidation" results from slight oscillating motion between a shaft or spindle and the inner cone surface. We see this when spindle and bearing surfaces have a rough fit-up.

Service Precautions and Details

Bearing failure can result from incorrect service. The most common problems are poor cleaning and drying methods.

After thoroughly cleaning the bearings in a suitable solvent, remove all solvent. Final air-drying or careful drying with compressed air is acceptable, *but never spin a bearing with compressed air. The bearing could explode violently or become scored from such stress.*

NOTE—
Always install new grease seals, your cheapest insurance against contamination.

Repack the bearings thoroughly, working grease between the rollers from the bearing's large end. Swab a liberal amount of grease on the surface of each roller bearing and inside the clean and thoroughly dry hub housing.

Take care not to over-pack wheel hub cavities. Too much grease can lead to grease leaks, seal failure and churning of lubricant. Place enough fresh grease within the hub casting recesses to reach the inner edge of the bearing cups. Here, you can create a grease dam to keep hot, thinning grease from leaking out of the bearings.

Building an ample grease dam at the inside and outside of each bearing is important. After final bearing adjustment, create a grease dam outside the outer wheel bearing.

NOTE—
Some manufacturers require adjusting wheel bearings with a dial indicator. This method assures proper endplay (axial or lateral movement of the hub along the spindle). You may need a magnetic or gooseneck stand to support your dial indicator.

A

Once you learn to properly clean, repack and adjust your wheel bearings, the service becomes a routine part of your Jeep's maintenance. Correct lubrication and adjustment procedures assure long bearing life and a safe vehicle.

Resources

Axle, Transfer Case and Transmission Service

M.I.T.
1112 Pioneer Way
El Cajon, California 92020
619-579-7727
(Geartrain, axle, transmission rebuilding; custom gearbox and axle retrofits; shortened transfer case output kits)

Holbrook Specialties/4 Wheel Drive Center
115 E. Arlington
Gladstone, Oregon 97027
503-655-4747
(Geartrain, axle and transmission rebuilding)

Warn Industries
12900 S.E. Capps Road
Clackamas, OR 97015-8903
503-722-3019
(Full-floating rear axle conversion kits, disc brake conversion kits and wheel hubs)

Drive Line Service of San Diego
1090 W. Morena Blvd.
San Diego, CA 92110
619-275-0150
(Custom driveshafts and specialty driveline products)

Moser Engineering---Axle Shafts
(One-piece replacement axle shafts for AMC Model 20 rear axles---See your local Moser Engineering dealer or 4WD Hardware, Inc.)

Manual Clutch and Engine/Transmission Conversion Kits

Advance Adapters
P.O. Box 247
Paso Robles, CA 93447
805-238-7000
(Transmission/transfer case adapters; Atlas II transfer case, Saturn overdrive and Orbitor drop box; source for NV 3550, NV4500 and other transmissions)

Midway/Centerforce Clutches
2266 Crosswind Drive
Prescott, AZ 86301
520-771-8422
(Performance replacement and retrofit manual clutch assemblies; billet steel flywheels)

Electrical

Wrangler NW Power Products
4444 S.E. 27th Avenue
Portland, OR 97202
503-235-1038
(High output alternators and battery management systems; quality electrical components)

Premier Power Welder/Pull-Pal
P.O. Box 639
Carbondale, CO 81623
970-963-8875
(High output alternators and on-board welder/electrical power sources)

Centech Wiring
7 Colonial Drive
Perkiomenville, PA 18074
610-287-5730
(Replacement wiring kits; rebuilt steering columns and power steering gears)

Painless Wiring
9505 Santa Paula
Ft. Worth, TX 76116
817-244-6898
(Chassis wiring harnesses patterned after OEM design; multiplex chassis wiring harnesses)

Harnesses Unlimited
Box 435
Wayne, PA 19087
610-688-3998
(Reproduction wiring harnesses for authentic restoration of early Jeep trucks)

4WD Hardware, Inc.
44488 State Route 14
Columbiana, OH 44408
800-333-5535 (to order)
(Wiring harnesses, electric wipers and accessories)

Barrett Engineering, Inc.
7636 Miramar Road
San Diego, CA 92126
858-693-9000
(Racemate high performance batteries and high amperage leads)

Auto Diesel Electric, Inc.
410 E. 6th Street
Reno, NV 89512
775-329-0707
(Starter and generator rebuilding)

Quadratec
www.quadratec.com
800-745-5337
(full line of service and restoration parts for Jeep CJs)

Engine

Clifford Performance Products
32840-B Wolf Stove Road
Temecula, CA 92592
909-303-2333
(Specializes in high performance components for in-line sixes and four-cylinder engines)

K&N Engineering
P.O. Box 1329
Riverside, CA 92502
909-684-9762
(Performance air and oil filtration products; A/F meters)

Mopar Performance/Jeep Accessories
See your Jeep dealer or Mopar Performance supplier.
("Factory engineered" performance components for AMC- and Mopar-design Jeep engines; a full line of high quality utility items, sound systems and appearance enhancements for later model Jeep vehicles)

MSD/Autotronic Controls Corp.
1490 Henry Brennan Drive
El Paso, TX 79936
915-857-5200
(Ignition performance products; emission legal ignition systems; A/F meters)

Competition Cams
3406 Democrat Road
Memphis, TN 38118
901-795-2400
('High Energy' grind camshafts for rock-crawling, off-pavement use)

Speed-Pro Performance/Sealed Power
A Division of Federal Mogul: See your local dealer.
(OEM and high performance engine components)

4WD Hardware, Inc.
44488 State Route 14
Columbiana, OH 44408
800-333-5535
(Performance and OE replacement components)

Engine Parts and Machine
Mike Patterson, Proprietor/Master Machinist
9 Mason Road
Yerington, Nevada
775-463-5528
(Engine restoration, automotive machining and engine parts)

Exterior Trim, Tops, Light Bars, Roll Cages and Seat Harnesses

Beachwood Canvas Works
P.O. Box 137H
Island Heights, NJ 08732
732-929-3168
(Restoration canvas, trim items, upholstery and drivetrain pieces for the vintage models)

Bell Auto Racing
Route 136 East
Rantoul, IL 61866
217-893-9300
(Harnesses/safety equipment and helmets)

BesTop
2100 W. Midway Blvd.
Broomfield, CO 80020
303-465-1755
(Jeep tops, front and rear seats, tire carrier/racks)

Crown Automotive Sales Co.
Fax: 617-826-4097 or contact nearest dealer.
(1941-up Jeep replacement parts)

Filler Products
9017 San Fernando Rd.
Sun Valley, CA 91352
818-768-7770
(Racing safety equipment)

Kentrol
550 W. Pine Lake Road
North Lima, OH 44452
216-549-2235
(Stainless steel trim/body panels, front and rear roll bar assemblies as depicted in Chapter 10)
Schroth

(See your local performance parts outlet)
(Safety harnesses/rally belts)

TRW
(See your local performance parts outlet)
(Safety harnesses/equipment)

4WD Hardware, Inc.
44488 State Route 14
Columbiana, OH 44408
800-333-5535 (to order)

Quadratec
www.quadratec.com
800-745-5337

Free-Wheeling Front Hubs, Electric Winches

Warn Industries
12900 S.E. Capps Road
Clackamas, OR 97015-8903
503-722-3019
(Winches/supplier to Mopar/Jeep Accessories; full-floating axle conversion kits and wheel hubs; free-wheeling hubs; fender flares and accessories)

Ramsey Winch Company
1600 N. Garnett Road
Tulsa, OK 74116
918-438-2760
(Winches and winch accessories; supplier to Mopar/Jeep Accessories)

Superwinch
Winch Drive
Putnam, CT 06260
203-928-7787
(Winches and winch accessories; free-wheeling hubs)

HUB-A-LERT
4x4 Specialty Products
P.O. Box 813
Highland, CA 92346
(LED monitor for detecting front axle engagement)

Manuals and Books

Four-wheel drive enthusiast magazines provide performance tips and review aftermarket Jeep accessories. A healthy aftermarket exists for Jeep performance parts and accessories.

Catalogs from Mopar/Jeep Accessories (available through your Jeep dealer) provide a standard for well-engineered accessories and upgrades. Advance Adapters (engine and transmission conversion parts for Jeep 4wd vehicles) can provide useful reference guides for Jeep geartrain components and modifications. Similarly, catalogs from 4WD Hardware, Dick Cepek, 4-Wheel Parts Wholesalers, Leon Rosser Jeep, Quadratec and other outlets serve as valuable information sources.

Book Sources:

Brian's 4WD Parts & Literature
260 Tyler Street
East Haven, CT 06512
203-469-4940
(Willys, Kaiser, AMC and Chrysler era books)

Classic Motorbooks
Osceola, WI 54020-0001
Fax: 294-4448/www.motorbooks.com
(Jeep-related books and workshop manuals)

Military Vehicles
12-H4 Indian Head
Morristown, NJ 07960
(Bi-monthly magazine covering military MB/GPW, MC/M38, MD/M38A1 and derivative models, M151 and civilian CJs)

Quadratec
www.quadratec.com
800-745-5337

Advance Adapters
P.O. Box 247
Paso Robles, CA 93447
805-238-7000
(Catalogs and books)

4WD Hardware, Inc.
44488 State Route 14
Columbiana, OH 44408
800-333-5535 (to order)

Mopar/Jeep
(see your local Jeep dealer)

Walter Miller
6710 Brooklawn Parkway
Syracuse, NY 13211
315-432-8282/www.autolit.com
(This large auto literature source likely covers each Jeep model ever built)

Maps And Travel Guides

A variety of map sources and atlas guides serve Jeep travelers. U.S. Forest Service and B.L.M. topographical maps remain my primary choices.

Specialty map sources include a series by Sidekick, which produces a range of maps on popular Western U.S. and Baja California four-wheel drive trails. A Sidekick Map details each region, including highlights of local sites, the area's history, minesites, ghost towns, directions from major highways, access costs, camping facilities and public agency offices in the area. Sidekick map/pamphlets are printed on high quality paper stock and include color pictures.

Sidekick
12188 Central Avenue, Suite 352
Chino, CA 91710
909-628-7227

Parts: Rare, OEM and Restoration

4WD Hardware, Inc.
P.O. Box 57
44488 State Rte. 14
Columbiana, OH 44408
330-482-4924
(Serves Jeep owners with popular accessories, performance parts and quality replacement parts; rugged fiberglass replacement bodies, trim, utility items and enhancements; knows what satisfies a loyal following of Jeep owners)

Asssi-Willys Jeep Parts
P.O. Box 4189
Yuma, AZ 85366
Fax: 520-343-1200
(Focus is Willys era: parts source for CJs plus military MB, M38 and M38A1 Jeep models; literature/shop manuals)

Quadratec.com
www.quadratec.com
800-745-5337
(Full range of service parts, accessories and geartrain components for '55 - up CJ models)

Archer Brothers
19745 Meekland Ave.
Hayward, CA 94541
415-537-9587
(A Bay Area institution for many decades, the supplier of surplus and replacement Jeep parts)

Capitol Jeepers Supply
3130 Fulton Ave.
Sacramento, CA 95821
916-481-2326
(Complete parts line for '41-up Jeep vehicles)

AJ's Four-Wheel Drive Center
RD-3, Box 284A
Jersey Shore, PA 17740
717-398-7520
(Specializes in body pieces and other Jeep items)

Border Parts
3875 Bancroft Drive
Spring Valley, CA 92077
619-461-0171
(Need a right side hand wiper for a Burma MB Jeep? Jon Compton likely has a box full of them. Stores of military surplus and civilian geartrain, axle and engine pieces)

J.C. Whitney
P.O. Box 3000
La Salle, IL 61301
312-431-6102
(Valued mail-order source for body panels, fuel tanks, axle, engine, chassis, cooling system and tune-up parts)

MEPCO
7250 So. 620 West
Midvale, UT 84047
801-561-3299
(Parts source for Jeep components, replacement parts and accessories)

Brian Chuchua Jeep
777 W. Orangethorpe Ave.
Placentia, CA 92670
714-879-5337
(A longstanding Jeep dealer and enthusiast/rally competitor, Brian has promoted Jeep since the Kaiser era)

A

Dick Cepek, Inc.
17000 Kingsview Ave.
Carson, CA 90746
310-217-1805
(Dick Cepek, an avid Jeep 4WD enthusiast and family rec-
reationalist, served as mentor for many of us....Tom Cepek
has expanded the Cepek tradition with a huge inventory of
Jeep accessories, geartrain parts, tops and specialty tires)

Don-A-Vee Jeep/Eagle/Motorsports
17308 So. Bellflower Blvd.
Bellflower, CA 90706
213-867-7256
(A Jeep dealership totally committed to the Jeep lifestyle.
Supplier of genuine Mopar/Jeep Accessories and Mopar
Performance components)

Walck's Four Wheel Drive
700 Cedar Street
Bowmanstown, PA 18030
610-852-3110
(Full line of Jeep new and used parts for all years of Jeep
trucks. Manuals, literature and military pieces, including
tires)

The Jeepster Man
238 Ramtown-Greenville Road
Howell, NJ 07731
732-458-3966
(Source for Jeepster as well as Willys/Kaiser era CJ, truck
and wagon body panels, trim and hard parts. Restorers will
find repair and restoration body pieces, books, manuals
and parts guides)

Red River Parts and Equipment
I-30 West, Exit 206 N.
P.O. Box 817
New Boston, TX, 75570
903-547-2226
(A vast store of military surplus parts including Jeep
geartrain, axle and body components)

REWECO Truck Parts Co.
711 E. Rosecrans Ave.
Los Angeles, CA 90059
310-217-1800
(Geartrain, military Jeep parts, steel bodies and more)

Leon Rosser Jeep/Eagle
1724 1st Avenue North
Bessemer, AL 35020
205-424-1640
(Leon Rosser staunchly serves the Jeep community. A catalog full of Mopar/Jeep Accessories, Mopar Performance
products and aftermarket specialty items distinguishes the
Leon Rosser Jeep dealership. A huge OEM parts inventory meets Jeep owner needs. Leon Rosser also supports
four-wheel drive activities and recreation.)

Sarafan Auto Supply, Inc.
23 N. Madison Ave.
Spring Valley, NY 10977
914-356-1080
(Vintage Jeep parts, military models included; canvas
products)

Shell Valley Fiberglass
Route 1, Box 69
Platte Center, NE 68653
402-246-2355
(Durable replacement panels and full bodies for those salt-
eaten and beaten Jeep CJs and Wranglers!)

Specialty Parts Four Wheelin'
1617 Old Country Road, #8
Belmont, CA 94002-3931
415-592-2130
(Source for military surplus and civilian Jeep replacement
parts)

Surplus City Parts
11796 Sheldon Street
Sun Valley, CA 91352
818-767-3666
(Source for military and civilian Jeep vehicle parts)

JP off road
PO Box 14651
Spokane, WA 99214-0651
509-893-1488 www.jpoffroad.com
(Aluminum replacement body/tubs for CJs, including cus-
tom built tubs for racing and speciality uses)

Restoration and Specialty Tools

Eastwood Company Tools
Box 296
Malvern, PA 19355
1-800-345-1178
(Niche tools for the restorer or home mechanic; unique products for those wanting original appearance or show quality results)

Easco/K.D. Tools
(Contact Eastwood Company or your local tool supplier)

Mark Williams Enterprises
765 South Pierce Avenue
Louisville, CO 80027
303-665-6901
(Precision ring-and-pinion gear setup tools; the 'Bench Mule' fixture)

Suspension/Chassis

Rancho Suspension (USA)
P.O. Box 5429
Long Beach, CA 90805
562-630-0700
(Complete suspension packages for Jeep trucks; steering stabilizer shocks, RS5000 and RS9000 shock absorbers and springs kits)

Full-Traction Suspension
6600-B McDivitt Drive
Bakersfield, CA 93313
805-398-9585
(Chassis/frame spring bracket upgrades and shackle reversal kits; steering linkage systems; axle trusses; suspension lift kits)

Skyjacker
212 Stevenson Street
West Monroe, LA 71294
318-388-0816
(Suspension/lift kits, shock absorbers, springs; dropped pitman arms)

Superlift
211 Horn Lane
West Monroe, LA 71292
318-322-3458
(Complete suspension/lift kits, traction bars; dropped pitman arms)

Dick Cepek, Inc.
17000 Kingsview Ave.
Carson, CA 90746
310-217-1805
(Full suspension kits, shocks and more)

Trail Master
420 Jay Street
Coldwater, MN 49036
517-278-4011
(Complete suspension kits, springs, shock absorbers; dropped pitman arms)

National Spring
1402 N. Magnolia Ave.
El Cajon, CA 92020
619-441-1901
(Bonafide spring manufacturer; need springs made or duplicated, National Spring can do it; suspension kits)

Heckethorn Off Road/Rough Country
P.O. Box 526
Dyersburg, TN 38024
901-285-9000
(Shocks/steering stabilizers; Rough Country Suspension Systems)

Advance Adapters
P.O. Box 247
Paso Robles, CA 93447
805-238-7000
(Steering linkage kits and Saginaw gear mounting brackets for upgrades)

Flaming River Industries
17851 Englewood Drive
Cleveland, OH 44130-3489
440-826-4488
(Custom Saginaw manual steering gears; steering columns for retrofit manual and power steering)

Energy Suspension Systems
1131 Via Callejon
San Clemente, CA 92673
714-361-3935
(Urethane bushings)

American Racing Wheels
(See your local dealer or on-line at: americanracing.com)

A

Classic Tube
A Division of Classic & Performance Specialties
80 Rotech Drive
Lancaster, N.Y. 14086
716-759-1800
(Custom stainless steel and armor guard brake tubing, sized to fit; manual brake proportioning valves; brake upgrade kits)

All Drum and Rotor Warehouse
7922 S.W. Nimbus Ave., Bldg. 8
Beaverton, Oregon 97008
503-641-9070
('Sure Stop' fitted calipers and brake hardware)

Trailside Toolbox and Spare Parts Kit

Properly maintained, your Jeep may never break in the back country. Yet for long and remote trips, like the spur roads from the Alaska Highway or the remote reaches of Baja California, a full set of tools and spare parts provide the likelihood that you can keep going and remain safe.

Store your tools and spare parts securely. Take into account the worst case scenario, the possibility that your Jeep could break in desolate country. There, you would need ready access to your winching accessories kit or tools!

WARNING—
Be certain that your tools have been neatly boxed and strapped down firmly to avoid severe physical injury or even death in the event of a vehicle roll-over. Loose tools, jacks or cargo become lethal objects during an accident or roll-over situation.

On-board Tools for Remote Trailside Fixes

1) A complete socket set

2.) A full set of common hand tools

3) Oil filter wrench

4) Compact volt-ohmmeter

5) Induction ammeter and starter current meter

6) Flare nut wrench set

7) Plumber's small chain wrench

8) Snap ring plier set

9) Front wheel bearing spindle nut wrench

10) Sizable pry bar

11) Vacuum gauge

12) Compact timing light

13) Wire repair kit and crimping pliers

14) Tubing flare tool and repair fittings

15) Grease gun with chassis lube

16) Enough tools to break down and repair a tubeless tire

17) Air compressor

18) High output alternator and on-board welder; welder's face shield, protective welding gloves and assorted, dry welding rod (stored in a waterproof container)

19) Jacks for tire repairs and transmission/axle work

20) Minimum 8000-pound capacity (single line pull) winch in top working condition with a complete winch accessories kit; dual battery system with isolator/manager

21) "Pull-Pal" winch cable anchor

22) "Hi-Lift" jack with cast iron foot

23) Multi-purpose Max Tool Kit

24) Assortment of *properly graded* hardware

25) A copy of this book to assist with troubleshooting and unit overhaul procedures for your Jeep

26) An installed CB radio plus a spare CB radio backup

27) A quality first aid kit: I recommend taking American Red Cross or equivalent 'First Aid' and 'CPR' classes.

28) Fire extinguisher(s), approved and within expiration period (*Caution: Securely mount fire extinguishers to prevent unplanned dislodging or discharge!*)

29) GPS and cellular telephone—and knowledge of areas where phone reception will be available.

NOTE—
In serving at search-and-rescue, I found a cellular phone to be much more effective for emergencies than a CB radio. A cell phone can serve as your link to prompt medical and law enforcement services. A CB radio has limited range and function in mountainous country.

WARNING—
When choosing hardware for field backup use, select fasteners of the appropriate grade and type. Do not use lower-grade, "general purpose" hardware on safety items! Match hardware to OEM grading. Follow tightening/torque guidelines in your workshop manual(s). Use proper tightening procedures. Note torque and whether threads should be dry or lubricated. Use liquid thread-locking compound where recommended.

Spare Parts for the Long Trail

1) Fuses, light bulbs and at least one headlamp, wrapped securely to prevent damage

2) 25-foot rolls of 10-, 12-, 14- and 16-gauge automotive wire; for high amp charge system, carry extra 4-gauge wire

3) Two rolls (minimum) of electrical tape

4) Solderless crimp connectors and terminals

5) Roll of duct tape

6) Package of radiator and gas tank repair putty

7) Proper fuel hose and spare clamps for carbureted engines; high pressure (steel braid or OEM replacement) fuel hose with attached, pressure-rated fittings for EFI/MPI systems; high-pressure EFI/MPI fuel hose and high pressure clamps

8) Spare drive belt(s)

9) Upper and lower radiator hoses and spare clamps

10) Thermostat and housing gasket

11) Tubes of silicone gasket sealant

12) Tube of metal mender (Permatex's LocWeld or equivalent)

13) Exhaust system patch kit

14) Liquid thread locking compound

15) Teflon tape

16) Clean, sealed brake fluid

17) A fuel pump with pump mounting gasket or fuel tank gasket (for in-tank pump)

18) Roll of mechanic's wire or "baling" wire!

19) Spare tire valve stems

20) Patch kit for repairing tubeless (radial or bias ply) tires

21) Spare axle and driveline universal joints

22) Front wheel grease seals (full-floating axles)

23) At least one oil filter and enough oil for a crankcase refill (plastic bottles wrapped and stored properly)

24) An oversized, self-tapping oil pan drain plug with gasket

25) Two squeeze bottle quarts (minimum) of gear lubricant

26) Clean tub of wheel bearing grease

27) Clean shop rags or towels

28) Fuel filter(s)

29) Air cleaner element

30) Spare fuel and potable water (minimum 5 gallons of each), secured safely with a vehicle roll-over in mind!

31) Ignition distributor cap, rotor, points or module; EFI relays

32) Ignition spark plug wire set; extra coil lead

33) Carburetor float and air horn gasket

33) Water pump and mounting gasket

34) Bucket/pan for draining and saving fluids

NOTE—
Always carry a quality first aid kit, safety flares and dry matches. Stow a waterproof ground cloth, shelter materials and rope for setting up an emergency habitat or weather-proof "garage." Freeze dried or canned rations and a portable stove will provide a means for survival in the event that your Jeep becomes stranded.

New or Rebuilt Engine Break-in Procedure

There is little information available on the proper break-in of a new or freshly rebuilt engine. Your Jeep engine's performance and longevity depend upon correct break-in. The following procedures are those recommended by Sealed Power Corporation, a major supplier of parts to the engine remanufacturing industry.

CAUTION—
These run-in schedules are "good basic procedures" to follow for engine break-in. They are recommended as a practical guide for engine rebuilders who are not advised of specific factory run-in schedules.

Engine Run-in Procedure (engine in vehicle)

A) Before starting engine, make preliminary adjustments to the carburetor (diesel injection system— where applicable) tappets and ignition timing

B) Install new oil and air filters

C) Priming of the engine lubrication system before starting is definitely recommended

NOTE—
A common cause of scuffing and seizure, when an engine is started for the first time, is effected by a "dry start." This can happen in a short length of time before the oil, under pressure, is delivered to bearings and other vital parts. Priming the oil system can be accomplished with a pressure tank or pre-lubricator attached to the system or mechanically driving the pump to supply the necessary oil throughout all oil passages.

A

D) Clean crankcase ventilation components—breathers, road draft tubes or positive crankcase ventilation system.

E) Check coolant and crankcase oil levels

Initial Starting (before run-in schedule)

A) Start engine and establish throttle setting at a fast idle (1000 to 1500 RPM) and watch oil pressure gauge. If oil pressure is not observed immediately, shut engine down and check back on assembly of oil pump and lubricating system.

When engine running is resumed, continue at the fast idle until coolant reaches normal operating temperature.

B) Stop engine and recheck oil and water levels.

C) Retorque cylinder head(s), following engine manufacturer's recommendations.

D) Make necessary adjustments to carburetor (or injectors), ignition timing, tappets, fan belt tightness, etc.

E) Check for oil and coolant leaks, making corrections where necessary.

Run-in Schedule

For Passenger Car Engines

Begin the break-in schedule by making a test run. Accelerate to 30 miles per hour and then immediately to 50 miles per hour and decelerate to 30 miles per hour. Repeat this cycle for approximately 30 to 50 miles avoiding any periods of slow idling except for minor adjustments.

For Buses, Light, Medium and Heavy Duty Trucks

Set engine at a fast idle. Put vehicle under a moderate load and accelerate to 50 miles per hour with alternate deceleration. Continue this intermittent cycling under this load for at least 50 miles. Additional time is desirable.

NOTE—

Many Jeep conversion engines have passenger car origins. Early Jeep engines were bona-fide light truck designs.

Harmful Practices

A) Avoid lugging under any load condition. Lugging exists when the vehicle does not "readily respond" as the accelerator is depressed. The engine speed being too low, does not allow the engine to develop sufficient horsepower to pull the load. (Keep rpm up.)

B) Avoid long periods of idling. Excessive idling will drop engine temperature and can result in incomplete burning of fuel. Unburned fuel washes lubricating oil off cylinder walls and results in diluted crankcase oil and restricted (poor) lubrication to all moving parts. The relatively dry cylinder walls depend upon oil throw-off to lubricate them, and a speed above a slow idle is necessary for this. Long idling periods produce glazing of cylinder walls, detrimental to ring and cylinder wall seating.

C) Avoid stopping engine too quickly. When an engine has completed the test run-in schedule or at any time it becomes heavily worked, it is a good policy to disengage the load from the engine and decelerate gradually. Allow it to idle a few minutes before turning the ignition to the "off" position.

The few minutes of idling will allow the engine to cool gradually and promote a desirable dissipation of heat from any localized area of concentrated temperature. Such good practice avoids the rapid cooling that can cause valve and seat warpage, block distortion, etc.

Engine Run-in procedure
(engine on dynamometer)

NOTE—
Follow necessary "preliminary" procedures outlined
for engine in vehicle.

Gasoline Engines: Light Truck and Passenger Car*

Stage of test	Complete test cycle of dynamometer break-in						
	1st	2nd	3rd	4th	5th	6th	7th
RPM	800—1200	1500	2000	2500	3000	3000	800
Manifold vacuum in inches of mercury	No load	15 in.	10 in.	10 in.	6 in.	Full load	No load
Time limit	Warm-up 10 min.	10 min.	15 min.	15 min.	15 min.	5 min.	3 min.

*Dynamometer break-in is a loaded condition (manifold vacuum readings indicate degree of load). To simulate these loads, drive your Jeep on various grades. Match manifold vacuum noted for each rpm range.

Hardware Grading and Torque Charts

Selecting safe, correct hardware is a vital part of Jeep truck repairs. New fastener technology and liquid thread locker also affect torque settings. When you follow torque guidelines, clean the fasteners thoroughly and note whether the tightening torque is for dry or lubricated threads.

Lubricating the threads will dramatically alter torque requirements. Liquid thread locker creates drag. You must increase torque settings, using the manufacturer's recommendation, to overcome this drag.

In Jeep factory repair manuals, individual Torque Charts appear at the end of many Repair Groups. At right, a Jeep Standard Torque Specifications and Bolt Identification Chart provides maximum torque settings for bolts not listed in the repair sections of this book.

Jeep notes that the torque specifications given in the chart reflect the use of clean and dry threads. Jeep recommends reducing the torque by 10 percent when the threads are lubricated with engine oil.

NOTE—
Consider thread material when applying torque. Often, an aluminum casting will require less torque than an iron or forged steel piece. Refer to shop manual for recommended torque settings.

Bolt Torque

Bolt size	Grade 5		Grade 8	
	Nm	ft-lb (in-lb)	Nm	ft-lb (in-lb)
1/4-20	11	(95)	14	(125)
1/4-28	11	(95)	17	(150)
5/16-18	23	(200)	31	(270)
5/16-24	27	20	34	25
3/8-16	41	30	54	40
3/8-24	48	35	61	45
7/16-14	68	50	88	65
7/16-20	75	55	95	70
1/2-13	102	75	136	100
1/2-20	115	85	149	110
9/16-12	142	105	183	135
9/16-18	156	115	203	150
5/8-11	203	150	264	195
5/8-18	217	160	285	210
3/4-16	237	175	305	225

A

Inch		Metric	
5/16 – 18		M8 X 1.25	
Thread major diameter in inches	Number of threads per inch	Thread major diameter in millimeters	Distance between threads in millimeters

Grade Identification

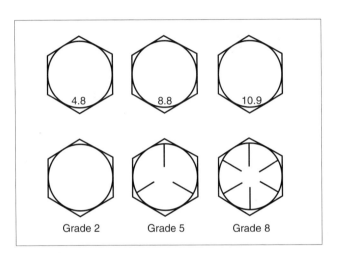

Grade 2   Grade 5   Grade 8

Metric and SAE thread notations differ slightly. On metric bolts (top), identification class numbers correspond to bolt strength. Increasing numbers represent increasing strength. Common metric fastener strength property classes are 9.8 and 12.9 with the class identification embossed on the head of each bolt. Some metric nuts will be marked with single digit strength identification numbers on the nut face.

On SAE classified bolts (bottom), markings on top of bolt head indicate grade. Common classes range from Grade 2 to 8 with embossed line identification. Increasing number of marks represents increasing grade, and number of marks is always 2 fewer than strength classification. For example: Grade 8 bolt will exhibit 6 embossed lines on the bolt head.

Suggested Assembly Torques in Foot-Pounds (Inch-Pounds)								
	Property Class 8.8		Property Class 9.8		Property Class 10.9		Property Class 12.9	
DIA	Dry threads	Lubricated threads	Dry threads	Lubricated threads	Dry threads	Lubricated threads	Dry threads	Lubricated threads
M4	(27.5)	(17)	(30)	(18)	(38.5)	(24)	(53)	(32.5)
M5	(56.5)	(33.5)	(61)	(37)	(78)	(47)	(107)	(65)
M6	(95)	(57.5)	(103)	(61)	(132)	(79)	(180)	(109)
M8	19	12	21	13	27	16	37	22
M10	39	23	42	25	53	32	73	44
M12	67	40	73	44	92	55	127	76
M14	107	64	116	69	148	89	203	122
M16	167	100	181	108	230	138	316	190
M20	325	195	352	211	449	269	617	370
M24	562	337	609	366	775	465	1066	640
M30	1117	670	1210	726	1540	924	2188	1271

Metric hardware has found its way into some late model Jeep vehicles. Note one hardware manufacturer's maximum recommended torque settings for metric cap screws. By comparing torque limits and load capacities with U.S. graded bolts, you can determine the approximate strength of metric hardware.

About the Author

An avid fly fisherman, hunter, canoeist, dirt motorcyclist and four-wheeler, Moses Ludel took his first driver's license exam in the family CJ-5. Two years later, at age eighteen, he drove the Rubicon Trail by the back route, entering from the Miller Lake access and tracking the largely unmarked route across the Sierra Mountains to Placerville, California.

Moses worked as a master truck mechanic and heavy equipment operator before earning a Bachelor of Science (Pre-Law/Sociology) degree with honors from the University of Oregon. In 1982, he began teaching adult education courses in Automotive and Diesel Mechanics at the San Diego Job Corps while simultaneously pursuing an automotive writing and photojournalism career with an emphasis on performance and four-wheel drive vehicles.

A body of work now exceeding 2,500 illustrated technical features, stories and columns, plus five lengthy *Owner's Bible* books for Bentley Publishers, distinguishes Moses' publishing career. Magazine freelance credits include *Off-Road, Four-Wheeler, 4WD SUV, 4x4 Magazine Japan, Trailer Life, Motorhome, Popular Hot Rodding, Chevy Truck, Jp Magazine,* and many others. While living in the Northwest, Moses wrote the 'Drive Time' technical column for the *Portland Oregonian*, the region's largest metropolitan newspaper. For a dozen years, he served as technical editor and columnist for *Off-Road Magazine*. Moses shot the cover photo for the premier issue of *Jp Magazine* and wrote the *Jp* 'Q&A' tech column for several years before his return to the vocational education field.

Past media board member for the national TREAD Lightly! program, Moses has served on that organization's Environmental Relations Committee. As four-wheel drive expert and author of the *Jeep Owner's Bible*, Moses Ludel has consulted to 4WD truck/SUV manufacturers, including Jeep, General Motors and Mercedes-Benz. Moses conducts Mopar technical workshops at the annual Camp Jeep events, sharing nearly four decades of Jeep four-wheel drive experience with owners and enthusiasts.

Acknowledgements

Inspiration for the ***Jeep CJ Rebuilder's Manual,*** began in 1964, when my parents, Leonard and Ruth Ludel, bought a new CJ-5. That F-head powered Jeep soon transported us through the desolate alkaline valleys of northern Nevada, following corrugated, sagebrush-lined dirt roads that led to ghost towns like Belmont, Manhattan and Pine Grove. Fascinated by that colorful mining history, coming of age with backcountry four-wheel drive adventures and High Sierra winter travel, I built an unwavering bond with Jeep 4WD vehicles.

As a truck fleet mechanic, I plunged headlong into the sea of information and technical nuances of four-wheel drive systems. The 'sixties and 'seventies were years when "old school" mechanics and automotive master machinists shared their wealth of knowledge generously, and to such professionals, I am surely indebted.

My attention to detail stems from exposure to automotive parts systems, machine shop practices and the high performance and racing industries. Later, as a four-wheel drive photojournalist, I expanded my circle of professional colleagues and friends to include performance specialists and Jeep community notables like Jon Compton, Tom Reider, Warren Guidry, Lloyd Novak, Jeff and Karen Sugg, Jack Clifford, Trent Alford, Scott Salmon, Tom Telford, Keith Buckley, Jim Marski, Bill Vicencio, John and Mike Partridge, Gene Humrich, Rick Dailey, Steve and Randy Kramer and the highly supportive staff at Mopar/Jeep Accessories and Mopar Performance.

As an educator and director of vocational training over four charter high school campuses, I owe much to my students. They have taught me to convey critical, highly technical information in an accessible manner. Teaching secondary and post-secondary (trade school) level automotive courses to at-risk male adolescents has proven invaluable. There is no better ground school than winning over a classroom full of tough, skeptical learners!

I thank Michael Bentley, President of Bentley Publishers, for supporting my book concepts and providing the staff and resources necessary to produce these large and detailed works. Editor Peter Nason, assigned to the ***Jeep CJ Rebuilder's Manuals,*** with no prior exposure to my work, earned respect the hard way. He enthusiastically juggled my largest pictorial and editorial packages to date, honoring my vision and expectations for the work. 'Dauntless,' a Jeep engine trademark from the Kaiser/Jeep Corporation era, best characterizes Peter Nason's willingness to assemble these weighty blocks of material. Many thanks, Peter!

As a foremost consideration, I thank my wife, Donna, and our youngest son, Jacob, for their incredible patience and understanding. I shot the first photo for these two books in June of 1996. Jacob had just finished his first year of high school. As these works go to press, Jacob enters his fifth and final year of Civil/Structural Engineering studies at the University of Nevada, Reno. These two manuals represent seven years of commitment, the last four while juggling a full-time role as an education administrator. My 3,600 studio-level photos, the painstaking disassembly, rebuilding and reassembly of two CJ Jeep vehicles, and years of spare time spent drafting the text had a substantial impact on family life.

Despite these demands, Donna and Jacob remain fully supportive of the importance I have placed upon these two works. Our home is whole and happy, and Jacob has joined his older siblings as a third generation Jeep 4WD enthusiast, equally at home behind the wheel of our vintage '55 CJ-5, Donna's Liberty, an AMC-era CJ or a new TJ Wrangler 'Rubicon' model!

Selected Books and Repair Information From Bentley Publishers

Other Books by Moses Ludel

Jeep CJ Rebuilder's Manual: 1946–1971
Moses Ludel ISBN 0-8376-1037-0

Jeep Owner's Bible™, Third Edition
Moses Ludel ISBN 0-8376-1117-2

Chevrolet & GMC Light Truck Owner's Bible™ *Moses Ludel*
ISBN 0-8376-0157-6

Ford F-Series Pickup Owner's Bible™
Moses Ludel ISBN 0-8376-0152-5

Toyota Truck & Land Cruiser Owner's Bible™ *Moses Ludel* ISBN 0-8376-0159-2

Harley-Davidson Evolution V-Twin Owner's Bible™ *Moses Ludel*
ISBN 0-8376-0146-0

Driving

Alex Zanardi: My Sweetest Victory
Alex Zanardi with Ginaluca Gasparini
ISBN 0-8376-1249-7

The Unfair Advantage *Mark Donohue*
ISBN 0-8376-0073-1(hc); 0-8376-0069-3(pb)

Going Faster! Mastering the Art of Race Driving *The Skip Barber Racing School*
ISBN 0-8376-0227-0

A French Kiss With Death: Steve McQueen and the Making of *Le Mans*
Michael Keyser ISBN 0-8376-0234-3

Sports Car and Competition Driving
Paul Frère with foreword by *Phil Hill*
ISBN 0-8376-0202-5

The Technique of Motor Racing
Piero Taruffi ISBN 0-8376-0228-9

Engineering/Reference

Supercharged! Design, Testing, and Installation of Supercharger Systems
Corky Bell ISBN 0-8376-0168-1

Maximum Boost: Designing, Testing, and Installing Turbocharger Systems
Corky Bell ISBN 0-8376-0160-6

Bosch Fuel Injection and Engine Management *Charles O. Probst, SAE*
ISBN 0-8376-0300-5

Race Car Aerodynamics *Joseph Katz*
ISBN 0-8376-0142-8

Road & Track Illustrated Automotive Dictionary *John Dinkel*
ISBN 0-8376-0143-6

Scientific Design of Exhaust and Intake Systems *Phillip H. Smith and John C. Morrison* ISBN 0-8376-0309-9

Audi

Audi A4 Service Manual: 1996–2001, 1.8L turbo, 2.8L, including Avant and quattro
Bentley Publishers ISBN 0-8376-0371-4

Audi A4 1996–2001, S4 2000–2002: Official Factory Repair Manual on CD-ROM *Audi of America*
ISBN 0-8376-1072-9

Audi A6 Sedan 1998–2004, Avant, including allroad quattro, S6 Avant, RS6: Official Factory Repair Manual on CD-ROM *Audi of America*
ISBN 0-8376-1076-1

BMW

BMW 3 Series Enthusiast's Companion™
Jeremy Walton ISBN 0-8376-0220-3

BMW 6 Series Enthusiast's Companion™
Jeremy Walton ISBN 0-8376-0193-2

BMW 3 Series (E46) Service Manual: 1999–2001, 323i, 325i, 325xi, 328i, 330i, 330xi Sedan, Coupe, Convertible, Sport Wagon *Bentley Publishers*
ISBN 0-8376-0320-X

BMW 3 Series (E36) Service Manual: 1992–1998, 318i/is/iC, 323is/iC, 325i/is/iC, 328i/is/iC, M3 *Bentley Publishers*
ISBN 0-8376-0326-9

BMW 5 Series Service Manual: 1997–2002 525i, 528i, 530i, 540i, Sedan, Sport Wagon *Bentley Publishers*
ISBN 0-8376-0317-X

Chevrolet

Corvette Illustrated Encyclopedia
Tom Benford ISBN 0-8376-0928-3

Zora Arkus-Duntov: The Legend Behind Corvette *Jerry Burton*
ISBN 0-8376-0858-9

Corvette from the Inside: The 50-Year Development History *Dave McLellan*
ISBN 0-8376-0859-7

Corvette by the Numbers: The Essential Corvette Parts Reference 1955–1982
Alan Colvin ISBN 0-8376-0288-2

Chevrolet by the Numbers: The Essential Chevrolet Parts Reference 1965–1969
Alan Colvin ISBN 0-8376-0956-9

Corvette Fuel Injection & Electronic Engine Management: 1982–2001
Charles O. Probst, SAE ISBN 0-8376-0861-9

Corvette 427: Practical Restoration of a '67 Roadster *Don Sherman*
ISBN 0-8376-0218-1

Ford

The Official Ford Mustang 5.0 Technical Reference & Performance Handbook: 1979–1993
Al Kirschenbaum ISBN 0-8376-0210-6

Ford Fuel Injection and Electronic Engine Control: 1988–1993
Charles O. Probst, SAE
ISBN 0-8376-0301-3

MINI Cooper

MINI Cooper Service Manual: 2002–2004, including MINI Cooper, MINI Cooper S
Bentley Publishers 0-8376-1068-0

Mercedes-Benz

Mercedes-Benz E-Class Owner's Bible™ 1986–1995 *Bentley Publishers*
ISBN 0-8376-0230-0

Porsche

Porsche: Excellence Was Expected
Karl Ludvigsen ISBN 0-8376-0235-1

Porsche 911 (964) Enthusiast's Companion: Carrera 2, Carrera 4 and Turbo, 1989–1994
Adrian Streather ISBN 0-8376-0293-9

Porsche 911 Carrera Service Manual: 1984–1989 *Bentley Publishers*
ISBN 0-8376-0291-2

Porsche 911 SC Coupe, Targa, and Cabriolet Service Manual: 1978–1983
Bentley Publishers ISBN 0-8376-0290-4

Volkswagen

Volkswagen Sport Tuning for Street and Competition *Per Schroeder*
ISBN 0-8376-0161-4

New Beetle Service Manual: 1998–2002 1.8L turbo, 1.9L TDI diesel, 2.0L gasoline
Bentley Publishers ISBN 0-8376-0376-5

Golf, GTI, Jetta 1999–2004, Jetta Wagon 2001–2004: Official Factory Repair Manual on CD-ROM *Volkswagen of America*
ISBN 0-8376-1081-8

Jetta, Golf, GTI, Cabrio Service Manual: 1999–2003, 1.8L turbo, 1.9L TDI diesel, 2.0L gasoline, 2.8L VR6
Bentley Publishers ISBN 0-8376-0323-4

Passat Service Manual: 1998–2004, 1.8L turbo, 2.8L V6, 4.0L W8, including wagon and 4motion *Bentley Publishers*
ISBN 0-8376-0369-X

Passat 1998–2004: Official Factory Repair Manual on CD-ROM
Volkswagen of America ISBN 0-8376-1084-2

Super Beetle, Beetle and Karmann Ghia Official Service Manual: Type 1, 1970–1979 *Volkswagen of America*
ISBN 0-8376-0096-0